WRITING FOR YOUR LIFE

Writing for your Life

edited by
Sybil Steinberg

with an introduction by
John F. Baker

PUSHCART

Library of Congress Catalogue Card Number: 92-060884
ISBN 0-916366-75-8 (hardbound)
     0-916366-78-2 (paperback)

For information address Pushcart Press
PO Box 380, Wainscott, NY 11975

distributed by W. W. Norton & Co., New York, N.Y.

cover design by Mary Kornblum; Hudson Studio

This book was produced for the publisher by Ray Freiman & Company.

INTRODUCTION

W E AT *Publishers Weekly* have been interviewing writers for 30 years—because we thought our readers would be interested in what they had to say about the writing life, and because without writers there is, after all, no publishing.

I used to do a lot of the interviews myself at one period, before I got too busy running the magazine to spend the time, and always enjoyed those encounters about as much as anything I ever did. Because although writers can be cranky people, with each other, and even with those nearest and dearest to them, they're always at their best when talking about their work, even with a perfect stranger. They love to think back to how they began, to the thrill of their first publication, about how their themes and interests have developed over the years. They take on a glow and become positively endearing. I think I can probably go most of the way in adapting Will Rogers: "I never met a writer I didn't like—at least while talking about his or her work." And although writers are not much known for going out of their way to help each other in life, on the printed page it can be different. There they enjoy giving advice, describing how they work, giving tips on how they first found agents and publishers.

So on the pages that follow you'll find 92 interviews with contemporary writers, most of them American, most of them still in mid-career, most of them written within the last five years or so—almost certainly the largest number of such interviews ever gathered into one book. What will you learn from them? How and why they started out as writers, achieved publication, made career changes and choices along the way, coped with success, or sometimes lack of it, and fitted the writing life into the rest of their life. We try to meet them in their natural habitat, so you can visualize the writer at work, whether in city apartment or rural hideaway or even suburban bedroom. They talk about their writing methods—a source of unending fascination to other writers or would-be writers—their own favorite authors, their influences, and what they hope to accomplish in their lives.

It's a great deal to cram into pieces that average no more than 2000 words or so, but I think that the ones in these pages mostly cover all that ground, and sometimes more. We selected these, from several times as many, on the basis of a variety of factors: the interest of the writers involved (and they cover a wide range, from poets to novelists to true-crime reporters to philosophers and historians); the fact that most of them are still active, and therefore involved in developing careers; and the extent to which we think the interviewers have succeeded in bringing their subjects alive. It's worth noting, by the way, that many of our subjects have never been interviewed before, or elsewhere, so you're getting a series of particularly privileged glimpses.

This seems like a suitable point at which to pay tribute to the editor of this volume, and of most of the Interviews herein: Sybil Steinberg. It is she who makes the choices each week, from a bewildering range of clamoring authors, agents and publishers, who shapes the pieces firmly to their necessary pace and length, and who chooses what interviewers can best encapsulate the life and work of their subjects. Without her, the feature, and therefore the book, would not exist.

We hope you find reading the words and thoughts of these writers as useful, and suggestive, to you as it has been for thousands of our readers over the years. It might even inspire you to start writing yourself, or to persevere if you've been discouraged. That's what all these people did, at one time or another—and look where it got them!

John F. Baker
Editorial Director, Publishers Weekly

CONTENTS

EDITOR'S NOTE

IF AN AUTHOR'S work must speak for itself, why are readers universally fascinated by what writers say about their lives and their craft? It may be perennial human curiosity about how creativity is inspired and flourishes. It may be the desire to know how much of an author's own life has been transmuted into fiction, or has influenced the choice of a biographical subject or nonfiction topic. Or perhaps it is merely the need to learn how one goes about getting published or achieving an audience. Whatever the reason, the interviews that appear in *Publishers Weekly* each week are one of the most popular sections of the magazine. As I culled and collected them for this volume, some distinguishing features became apparent.

Determination is the linking thread when writers talk about their craft: the obstinate, passionate need to tell a story that possesses them, to convey a moral judgment, or to reflect on a wrenching experience or a transcendent view of existence. How they cope with the mundane details of the process—dealing with agents, publishers and editors—elicits ire and praise, resentment and gratitude. Luck and grit seem to be the dominant variables that make one writer's lot blessed and another's beset by publishing woes.

Choosing these particular interviews from almost a decade's accumulation was pleasurable and painful at the same time. In some ways, making the selections resembled my weekly dilemma of trying to pick the best interview subject from a multitude of equally qualified, interesting and timely candidates. In the end, three criteria governed my choices: a writer's importance as a literary figure, or his or her high stature among those with bestseller appeal; the interviewer's cogent prose style or talent for eliciting provocative quotes; and in some cases, the fact that the interview with *PW* was among the last the subject granted before his or her death, and thus became a significant record of a distinguished career. In every case, my desire was to preserve illuminating conversations with writers who have influenced 20th-century literature. For that reason, I believe these interviews will continue to be an enduring resource.

Sybil S. Steinberg, Interviews Editor, Publishers Weekly

WRITING FOR YOUR LIFE

DIANE ACKERMAN

DRIVING AWAY FROM a small airport terminal in upstate New York on a brilliant late summer day, Diane Ackerman points to a hangar with the words "East Hills Flying Club" painted on the side. "That's where I learned to fly," she says. In her carefully modulated voice, pleasure and pride are tinged with regret. "I've had to give it up for a while," she explains. "I haven't had the time to fly regularly. It's dangerous to be a sometime pilot."

Yet the activities that have kept her from the pilot's seat are hardly risk-free, being principally the expeditions described in her book *The Moon By Whalelight* (Random House), a project that took her across the treacherous waters of South America's Drake Passage to penguin rookeries in the Antarctic, and swimming with whales in a bay off the Argentine coast.

Subtitled *And Other Adventures Among Bats, Penguins, Crocodilians and Whales*, the volume expands upon articles written originally for the *New Yorker*. For each of her four ventures, Ackerman undertook a hands-on, out-in-the-field study, accompanied by an expert on each of the aforenamed species. The explorations of creature and habitat, which she calls "thrilling and nourishing journeys," are described with the same powerful mix of sensuality and science that propelled her 1990 book *A Natural History of the Senses* (Random House/Vintage) onto the *New York Times* bestseller list.

Ackerman's prose, described by critics as voluptuous and invigorating, is fiercely sensual, full of color and sound, aroma and

15

texture—the ammonia-rich air of a guano-filled bat cave, huge floating icebergs of "palest blue and mint-green." The information packed into her essays is delivered in immediately felt images and instantaneously understood metaphor, which explains the echo location of bats as "vocal Braille"; likens alligators, mating on the perpendicular, to Swiss Army knives; or describes a downy baby king penguin as having the frayed look of an "old weathered tennis ball."

Now she leads the way along a path in the woods behind her suburban house to a red caboose hidden, trackless and stranded, in the middle of thickly growing young trees—an unlikely annex that, she explains, came with the house. Inside the fully outfitted interior, sitting on a cushioned bench, she tucks up her feet and talks about her work. "I began as a nature poet. But the terrain of prose has always fascinated me. Mine is a miscellaneous muse."

She is dressed in silk pants and shirt of electric blue, her hair a wild black nimbus of curls around her delicately molded face, eyes black beneath widely arcing eyebrows. Sunlight and shadow playing through the trees in the window above her, wearing brilliant lipstick and, on her wrist, a purple watchband, she could be one of her own subjects—an exotic tropical bird.

Whether writing prose or poetry, Ackerman's perspective is more than likely to take a scientific bent. Her degrees include an M.F.A. in creative writing and a master's and a Ph.D. in English—all from Cornell—but her doctoral dissertation was an interdisciplinary study of the metaphysical mind in science and in art.

"It's hard for me to keep science out of my writing," Ackerman says. "A critic once said that airfoils, quasars, corpuscles aren't the proper form of art. But to agree ignores much of life's fascination and variety. Writing, which is my form of celebration and prayer, is also my way of inquiry.

"I have always been interested in how we perceive the world, in how we collect information. But as I tried quietly to teach myself, I found that everything I read was dry and ignored the texture and feel of life. *A Natural History of the Senses* was the result of three years of intense effort."

Ackerman's first book, *The Planets: A Cosmic Pastorale*, published by William Morrow in 1976—before the Voyager flights, she points out—is a series of poems structured upon the main bodies in our solar system and ranging in reference and scope

16

from ancient myth and the origins of astrology to 20th-century space exploration. Her next, two years later, was another volume of poetry, *The Wife of Light*, also from Morrow. There the poems are more personal but still draw upon—and delineate—the elements of the natural world: the moon, a fish, menstruation, the value of *pi*.

Twilight of Tenderfoot (Morrow, 1980) was her first published book of prose. In it, Ackerman recounts her year spent on a cattle ranch in the West where she had intended to research a book on the aesthetics of the horse. Instead her attention was seized by the life of the cowboys and the lure of the landscape. The next prose work followed her third volume of poems (*Lady Faustus*, Morrow, 1983). *On Extended Wings*, published in 1985 by Atheneum (Scribners paperback), chronicles the adventures—often misadventures—of learning to fly. "I didn't want to be a passenger in my own life," she says, explicating the draw of flying, an exhilarating but clearly hard-won skill.

Diminutive and attentively groomed, gracious and mannerly, Ackerman speaks with an authority that makes plausible the otherwise unlikely image of her straddling an alligator or reaching out to touch the whale swimming next to her, which she describes as "big as a reclining building" with a flipper as "large as a freight elevator." One senses an impulse toward understanding that is experienced as urgently as an appetite.

"I'm driven by a nomadic curiosity," Ackerman observes. "For as little as six months or as long as some years, I'll be obsessed with the ocean, with bats, with space. My feeling of ignorance is often so overwhelming that I find myself in a state of rapture about a discipline or a field and rapidly coming down with a book.

"I try to give myself passionately to the subject with as much affectionate curiosity as I can muster. The information, the facts themselves, fuel my work but are really secondary to my rage to learn about the human condition."

In this vein, she relates that her pursuit of whales began with her interest in the evolution of the human mind, leading her back to whale expert Roger Payne, whose work she had first come across in the mid-'70s when he lectured at Cornell on the songs of humpbacked whales. In arranging her study of these aquatic mammals for her book, she signed on with Payne both to observe and to help in the projects he was involved with, a journey that

17

took her from the island of Maui in Hawaii to a laboratory in Massachusetts to a wind-swept observation station on the rugged Patagonian coast of Argentina. Ackerman's practice in all of her animal studies is to encounter the species under the aegis of an expert who can answer her myriad questions and, usually, keep her out of danger as she interacts with unfamiliar creatures.

Pre-expedition research ("I read everything I can—science, folklore, novels, whatever") includes extensive correspondence and travel arrangement. "Much of the excitement and fun of learning about these creatures and landscapes comes in setting up the trip. It becomes a kind of romance."

On site, Ackerman's research switches into a different mode—the poet comes to the fore and her notes become, if less scientific, more personal and sense-oriented. "I will fill a notebook with sensory notes when I'm working, so that when the trip is over and I'm back home writing, I can immediately recapture what a given moment felt like—the odor of a bat cave, the feeling in my calves climbing a glacier."

The West Texas desert and penguin rookeries of the Antarctic's South Georgia islands are far removed from Waukegan, Ill., the suburb of Chicago that in the 1950s of Ackerman's childhood was nearly rural, full of open, undeveloped spaces. "I was always writing—neighborhood newspapers, musicals, limericks," she recalls. But little else in her conventional upbringing—her father ran a McDonald's; her only brother studied accountancy—seems related to the shape of her adult life. Except, of course, that she has settled in this rural-like town in a ranch-style house, which she and British novelist and short-story writer Paul West have shared for many of the 20 years they've been together.

In the yards, interspersed among yew and a redolent apple tree, raised flower beds sport phlox, cosmos, salvia and coleus; inside is topsy-turvy from a kitchen renovation in full swing. Pots and pans are piled on living room furniture, though a fresh arrangement of flowers graces a table before patio doors that open onto the unprepossessing pool in the backyard. Reminders of her travels and interests share space with walls of books—including hers and West's in various editions and translations—establishing clear claim on this place as home. Ackerman has made the hooked rugs that decorate the walls, their designs depicting, variously, the amino acid leucine, brain cells of infants, a neuron "in

18

the act of imagining." Another rug, made by her mother, who is "a seasoned world traveler," features meandering patterns and is called "Wherever the Road Leads You."

In her study down the hall, a Macintosh computer occupies center stage amid photos and mementos of her subjects. A leathery patch of gray skin shed by the whale she swam next to in Patagonia is preserved between two pieces of glass. On a corkboard are pinned the jackets of her books. The most recent three are from Random House, part of a five-book contract negotiated by agent Anne Sibbald at Janklow-Nesbit.

Her fourth book—its manuscript due soon to Sam Vaughan, her editor at Random—is a kind of companion piece to *Whalelight* that will include essays about seals, the lion-maned tamarin of the Amazonian jungle ("a habitat that's like a chapter from the Garden of Eden") and the short-tailed albatross, and will be called *The Rarest of the Rare*. Ackerman is unqualified in her respect and admiration for Vaughan, whom she describes as a true gentleman. Ackerman says the next work will be a natural history book but beyond that she is determinedly, perhaps superstitiously, mum.

Outstanding among the jackets is the elegant *The Jaguar of Sweet Laughter: New and Selected Poems* (Random House, 1991), featuring a lush jungle painting by Henri Rousseau reproduced on a background of purple, her favorite color.

Some of the new poems offer an intensified version of her expedition experiences. Others are home-based, addressed to the deer that frequent her backyard or to hummingbirds; another describes unpicked ripe strawberries that "dangle like miniature organs/—hearts, lungs, testes."

"When I was a freshman in college in Boston, I used to walk around with a volume of Wallace Stevens's poetry in one back pocket and Dylan Thomas in the other. I wanted my poetry to combine the rigorous sensuality of one with the voluptuousness of mind of the other," Ackerman recalls.

This observation reinforced the moment when, departing the caboose and reentering the yard, we sidestep a scattered pile of flower petals—blue delphinium, bright yellow coreopsis, the deep pink and soft peach of roses. "That's from this morning," she explains. "Every day I cut some flowers and sit out here to arrange them for the house. It's a ritual."

But the petals, like colorful crumbs, suggest as much an early, delicate repast. It's not an implausible image for this writer who declares, "I'm interested in having as full-bodied a response to life as possible."

DULCY BRAINARD

ISABEL ALLENDE

WHEN ISABEL ALLENDE's first novel, *The House of the Spirits*, was published in Europe in 1982, it quickly became a bestseller. Her extraordinary chronicle interweaves a family saga with the history of her native Chile, its merging of the supernatural and the real drawing consistent comparison to Gabriel García Márquez's *One Hundred Years of Solitude*. Allende's novel is a tale of the human conditions and passions that lead to historical change and displacement. She has honest claim to her material—niece of assassinated President Salvador Allende, she now lives in exile in Venezuela.

Allende, a petite woman in her early 40s, is warm and lively, with a generous smile. She speaks with *PW* in her fluent English in the offices of her publisher, Alfred A. Knopf. She tells us she was born into the upper middle class, to a diplomat father. But her parents divorced when she was small and Allende never saw her father, growing up instead in the house of her maternal grandparents.

"I had a very lonely life when I was a child," she recalls, "but very interesting—only adults around me, very extravagant people, a very extravagant family, really." Although *The House of the Spirits* isn't autobiographical, it is nevertheless based on the house and the family in which Allende was raised. Two of the book's central characters—the passionate, violent, landowner-politician Esteban Trueba and his compassionate, clairvoyant wife Clara—were inspired by her grandparents. Her grandfather, she explains, was indeed "a conservative, a patriarch, a very violent person, but he was adorable in many ways, and I loved him dearly. And I had a grandmother who was a very sweet, gay, incredible woman. She liked spiritualism and astrology and tarot. In that time, all those things were not allowed by the church, so there was always something hidden and mysterious at home. I participated many times with my grandmother in her spirit sessions. She was always telling me stories, and I had an uncle who had the passion of books, so the house was full of them, and I had permission to read anything. I remember that I was eight when I read Shakespeare and 10 when I read the Marquis de Sade."

Allende's mother remarried, again to a diplomat, and so as a young teenager Allende lived in Bolivia, the Middle East and Europe, returning to Chile at 15 from a Lebanon caught in civil war. Shortly thereafter, she met a young man whom she eventually married, retaining her maiden name. About her romance, she says, "Nothing very original about that. We are still married—that's the only part that's original," she laughs. They have two children, a daughter, now 21, and a son, 18.

Allende left school at 16 and became a secretary in the Food and Agricultural Organization at the United Nations in Chile. Soon she was working with journalists and eventually became one herself, with her own program on television, time spent in Europe on a scholarship, then working on an important radical women's magazine in Chile. She worked in movie newsreels, wrote some plays and short stories for children. "I led a very interesting life, and I was very happy," she says.

"And then in 1973, the military coup changed everything, and I felt as many Chileans did, that my life had been cut into pieces, and that I had to start over again."

For Allende, the coup and the assassination of the president had particularly personal ramifications. She explains that her relationship with Salvador Allende had been through her father's side of the family: "After my mother divorced, she never saw my father again, and all contact with him was eliminated. We never knew anything about my father, and we asked—nobody would answer. But Salvador Allende—at that time he was a politician, but he wasn't the president—was very close to my mother. He helped her very much in many ways. We would see him on Sundays, go out on picnics, visit him sometimes in his house. He had three daughters, more or less my age, and my mother was close to his wife. And we went on being close together until he died. Of course, when he was the president, we wouldn't see each other so often, because he was very busy. The last time I saw him, it was three days before he died.

"I think I divided my life before that day and after that day. In that moment, I realized that everything was possible—that violence was a dimension that was always around you.

"We didn't leave immediately. The day of the coup, after Allende was killed, the Mexican embassy had a plane to take the family out to exile in Mexico. But my husband and I decided to stay, because we thought that a military coup in Chile was just an historical accident. It was impossible that the militarists would stay in power, because we had such a long democratic tradition in Chile—150 years of democracy. We had absolutely no experience in dictatorship, no experience in repression. We knew nothing. I had never heard the word torture applied to an actual situation; I always thought torture was something that happened in medieval times, in the Inquisition, but I never thought it could happen nowadays in our country. We were badly informed. We stayed in Chile for some months, but after a while, we understood that it was impossible to go on helping people and that we were in danger."

Allende and her husband spread a map of the world on a table to see where they could go. They needed a country where they could speak the language and where they could work, she as a journalist, he as an engineer. And they wanted a democracy.

"So that's how we went to Venezuela," Allende continues. "We knew nothing about Venezuela. We had no friends. We had a tourist visa. We had no money, and we arrived there with our two children, feeling paralyzed as people in exile feel at the beginning. But after a while, we began to feel better, because Venezuela is a very warm country. People are very kind. It's a real democracy—one of the most solid democracies in Latin America, and that was very important for us. And we made friends. We started living again."

How does Allende feel about the United States in the wake of revelations of CIA involvement in her uncle's assassination? "One thing is the United States government, and another very different thing is the United States people," she replies. "I think the United States government has a terribly stupid foreign policy towards Latin America, which is causing now all this mess in

Central America, which protected, in a way, the dictatorships in South America, like Pinochet [in Chile], like the ones in Argentina and Brazil and Uruguay. When we left Chile in 1973, half of the population in Latin America was living under dictatorships, all of them supported by the States.

"But I like the people in this country. You believe in your way of life, you believe in God, you believe in honesty, you believe in justice. When you face injustice, violence, war, corruption, you feel terribly disappointed, like children who finally discover that fairy tales are not true. We [in Latin America] live in violence, we live in corruption, we live in misery, and that's why, for us, it's not disappointing. It's wonderful to see that there is a country in the world who believes in that."

Allende's very Latin American novel had an unusual but understandable genesis. "I was never planning to write a book," Allende says. "When I left Chile, I didn't dare tell my grandfather. I used to visit him every day. I went the day before and wanted to tell him that I was leaving, but I couldn't. I couldn't find the words. I think he knew all the time. We kissed and hugged for the last time, and I left him sitting in his armchair with his beautiful hair and his blue eyes"—an image Allende would eventually evoke in her book.

"And then we started living our new lives in Venezuela, and it was very difficult for me to be in touch with my grandfather—he didn't like to write, and he *hated* the telephone. Years passed, and in 1981, the beginning of the year, I received a phone call from Chile, saying that he had decided to die. He was very tired, he was nearly a hundred years old, and he had stopped eating and drinking. I knew he would die in a few days, maybe in a few hours.

"And I sat down to write a letter to him, because when my grandmother died, my grandfather said that death does not exist, that really you die when people forget you, but if you can remember people, they never die. He decided to remember my grandmother always, to have her always present at home, and he would speak with her, and she would always be a spirit, a presence, in the house. That's why the book is called *The House of the Spirits*, because the spirit of my grandmother and all the lovely people that we wanted to be kept alive were there, always present in our hearts. I wanted to tell my grandfather that I was never going to forget him, he would never die, just as my grand-

mother had never died. I wanted to tell him I remember everything we have spoken about all these years. And I started writing
a letter, telling him the same things he had told me when I was a
child.

"He died. He never received the letter. But I wrote and wrote,
and stories of other people, other spirits, came to the book, and I
went on writing during a whole year, this very long letter to my
grandfather, just to keep him alive, to keep his memory alive.
That's why at the beginning of the book Alba, one of the characters, writes to keep alive the memory of her past and to survive
her own terror. That's how I felt. I wanted to survive the terrible
experience of exile, and I wanted to keep alive the memory of the
past—the house that I lost, the people that are dead, those that
disappeared, the friends that were scattered all around the
world."

Allende wrote instinctively at the beginning, revised extensively at the end. Her husband encouraged her to publish the
book, but she encountered difficulty in Latin America. "Nobody
wanted to read the book because they said it was too long. I was
a new author, nobody knew me. They would not read a manuscript with more than 300 pages, and this one had 500. The fact
that I was a woman also was something against me; there's great
prejudice in Latin America with the work of women."

At about that time, Allende, reading a novel by José Donoso, a
Chilean author, came across a character who was a literary agent.
She didn't know such agents existed. But she inquired and was
told that the best agent for Latin Americans and Spanish-
speaking authors was Carmen Balcells in Barcelona. Allende says,
"So I mailed the manuscript to Barcelona to this woman I had
never met, with a letter saying I had written this, and I wanted
someone to read it." Six months later, the book was published in
Spain by Plaza & Janés. It became an immediate success.

About the current boom here in Latin American literature,
Allende says, "I think that finally Latin America has found a
voice. When our authors stopped copying, or trying to accept,
foreign influences—European especially—and we turned ourselves toward our reality, we started speaking for ourselves. We
know in Latin America so much about Europe, so much about
the United States. All your books are translated, and we read
them; all your films are translated, and we see them. That cultural

penetration affects us so much. We know so much about you, and you know so little about us. It's very important that we begin saying who we are, speaking for ourselves, so that you will know us better."

Allende explains the magical realism that is so often present in Latin American writing. "In Latin America, we value dreams, passions, obsessions, emotions, and all that which is very important to our lives has a place in literature—our sense of family, our sense of religion, of superstition, too. That's magical realism—the emotions that everybody has plus our reality. Our reality is different from yours. We are a continent with such a terrible history, with all that violence, with that incredible geography, with this mixture of people—Indians, Africans, immigrants from all over the world. This mixture makes a very complex, a very rich reality. Fantastic things happen every day in Latin America—it's not that we make them up. Every morning I read the newspaper, and I cut out all the news that I find so incredible, so fantastic, that I would never be able to invent it, and when I put it in books, people say, 'Well, but you have an incredible imagination.' "

Since *The House of the Spirits*, Allende has completed another book, *De Amor y de Sombra*. That novel is based on the true story of the discovery of 15 bodies in an abandoned mine, victims of political persecution. "Politics are always present in our life in Latin America," Allende affirms. "It's impossible to ignore that."

Will Allende ever return to Chile? "I left my country because I could not stand the dictatorship. But I am sure that we will have democracy in Chile very soon, and then I will go back.

"For one torturer, you have a thousand people who are willing to risk their lives to help someone. We say in Spanish, *Los buenos van a ganar*, 'The good people are going to win.' "

AMANDA SMITH

26

JEAN AUEL

JEAN AUEL, THE nonstop neophyte author of the fast-selling
Earth's Children fictional saga—*The Valley of Horses*, *The Clan
of the Cave Bear* and, *The Mammoth Hunters*—began her writing career after reaching 40, having engaged in several others,
including housewifery and the raising of five children, in Portland, Ore. Auel, a plump, cheerful woman with blue eyes and
blonde hair, had, with her husband Ray, also earned a college
degree by attending night classes for 12 years.

In 1977, with the children growing up and the studies completed, she was just about to raise her sights and go into the
banking profession when one night at bedtime, an inspiration
came to write a story. Suddenly alive, unbidden, in her head,
was a tale concerning a young woman in some undetermined prehistoric era who, having attained a higher level of mental and
physical development, was shunned by the other members of her
society. To this day Auel has no inkling of how the idea arose, but
she was determined to write it down. At first she thought she
would simply be passing the time until she found the right job. "I
didn't know I had just found it," she says now. But it is characteristic of Auel that she did not wait until morning to begin writing.

She did not get very far into the story before running into a
snag: "It was great fun, but I didn't know what I was writing
about. I didn't know whether these people had the use of fire or
not, or what part of the world they were living in." With typical
directness, she went to the *Encyclopaedia Britannica* and next
morning to the Portland library. "I just started digging through

the anthropology and archaeology texts," she recalls. "Within a short period I had taken out about 50 books. I had no background for this. All I had to start with was a story—and I thought it was going to be a short story!"

Auel remembers her state of mind at the time. "I was looking for something to do. I had had five kids before I was 25, and then I started going to college when I was 28. By the time I was 40 I had a master's degree in business administration, three daughters in college and two boys in high school. I had been spending practically every minute of my life raising my family, working [as a computer programmer and credit manager] and going to school, and now suddenly I had my degree. My kids were grown up. I had quit my job with the idea of getting to a higher level, so I was in this free-floating state. . . . "

The research for the story took her "into a world I did not know existed. As I read about prehistoric people, the story kept growing in my mind, and before long I knew I had a novel. So I simply tried to tell the whole story to myself on the typewriter. For six months I did nothing else. I was literally obsessed. I worked at it 16 hours a day, seven days a week—you could not have dragged me away. I ended up with a rough draft for a novel in six parts."

On rereading her work, however, Auel discovered "it was just awful!" Hardly deterred, she returned to the library and checked out books on how to write. "Every writer goes through a period when you play it safe," she says. "You don't tell anyone you're writing—in case you fail at it. But there has to come a point when you say to yourself, 'I'm serious, I'm going to give this every bit of effort I have.' That time finally came for me, even though I still thought that writing was a way to fill time until a wonderful job came along. During this period I replied to an ad for a credit analyst in the Portland branch of a large California bank. After an interview, they called to offer me, not the job I'd applied for, but a position as manager of the bank's credit department. I negotiated a higher salary than their original offer and then found myself saying: 'Wait a minute, I must tell you I'm considering an alternative—one with a much higher risk factor.' I said I needed a week to consider it.

"My husband and I went hiking in the Columbia Gorge, and I kept thinking that this was the kind of job I had wanted. I knew

Ray wanted me to take it; we had three kids in college. But I was halfway through this first big chunk of material in my story, and the thought of giving up and not finishing it brought tears to my eyes. I had to make a choice." Her husband said he would be supportive whatever her decision. When she called the bank to decline the position, they offered "anything anybody else is paying—just tell us how much you want."

Auel frequently gives herself warnings and advice, and at this point she told herself: "Okay, if you are going to give up *this* for writing, you had better be serious about the writing!" She also vowed that she would persevere until she got published, no matter how long it took. Then, of course, she turned to the Portland library for help and pored through books on how to go about it.

The book she found most helpful was *Techniques of Fiction Writing* by Leon Surmelian. "I bet I've read it three times," she says. "I knew that to make my story believable I would have to get in some depth of description. Anyway, I hate a book that just says, 'They went out and got food and ate it.' How did they get it? Where did they get it? How did they cook it? I want to know."

She also determined, from Surmelian, how to find her writer's viewpoint. "I came out with the 'omniscient author.' I had to be able to think for each of my characters, but I also had to be able to step back into the author's voice to give description and information the characters could not provide. Sometimes I get into a tone that is like nonfiction." She likes this tone, she admits in a pleased, conspiratorial whisper, "because people believe it!"

Auels' original story holds the germ for the whole of the six novels she is embarked on. After completing her research and starting a rewrite, she was only halfway through the first of the six sections of the story when she had written 100,000 words, and the realization the whole thing would take a million and a half words before it was finished brought the project to a brief halt. "That was the point where I realized I didn't have one book—I had six books," she recalls. "Now when people ask me how I know I have six books to write, I tell them it is because all six of them are contained in that rough draft. That is the outline for the entire Earth's Children series."

She devised a separate story for each of the six novels, which are nevertheless all linked. "I am striving hard to write them as individual books," she declares. "I want each book to be complete;

29

I don't believe in leaving loose ends." The woman Ayla is the central figure in all the books and serves to unify the series, and other characters reappear as well. "I want you to care enough about those characters that you want to go on to the next book."

Auel has not only read a good deal about the Neanderthal people, but also has learned at first hand some of their ways of living. She knows how they might have survived in winter in a snow cave, because she went with a group to Mt. Hood and spent the night in one. She learned how to trap animals, to build a fire—without matches—from sticks found by digging down through 20 feet of snow. She enrolled in classes in wild plant and wild food identification, learned flint knapping at a wilderness area field station, took part in an aboriginal life skills course in which she made her own buckskin clothing.

She has come to have a deep love and respect for the characters in her books and is a champion of their human, caring qualities. "I wanted to make it clear that we are talking about people no different from ourselves," she says. "I tried to show that these young brothers [Jondalar and Thonolan] are thoroughly modern in their emotional responses, their intelligence, their psychological reactions. Anything we allow ourselves, we have to allow them."

From a book on an archaeological excavation in Iran titled *Shanidar*, by Ralph R. Solecki, Auel read of the discovery of the skeleton of an old man in the Shanidar caves. His arm had been amputated; he was lame and blind. "The question is," Auel says, "who took care of him when he was a crippled boy? Who took care of an old man who obviously could not hunt mammoths? I began to get this sense of *why* they took care of him." Auel believes that the weak and wounded were protected in prehistoric society. "Suddenly I was seeing a real humanity in these people, and that became my obsession—what I really wanted to tell."

In Auel's first novel, her heroine Ayla takes care of an old man with a crippled arm. "When I read about him in *Shanidar*, I said, 'There's my man! He really existed!'" She is convinced that "these ancient ancestors of ours were very human. We call them *homo sapiens*—they are not a different species. This idea that we were savages is wrong! We cannot try to prove that we are violent by nature and therefore warlike. We are by nature cooperative, compassionate."

The verisimilitude in her writing of the details of everyday life among ancient peoples has won Auel admiration from the scientific community. She found herself treated as a celebrity at a symposium on prehistoric people at the Museum of Natural History in New York not long ago, and she lectured a group of specialists at the Smithsonian Institution in Washington on the subject, "The Novelist's View of Paleoanthropology." She explains, "I told them that I start from a base of *their* work, but I can extrapolate on a human level." When she read about the discovery of ancient musical instruments made of mammoth bones, she wanted details for use in her new book; to get the information, she made a five-week research trip to Kiev, where the objects are displayed. Finding that the only book on the subject was published in Russian, she commissioned an English translation. From the excavations of a Czech archaeologist, Auel has determined the exact floor plans of dwellings of people 25 millennia in the past.

Scientists disagree on how much speech prehistoric people had developed, but Auel sees them as talkative and uses a modern idiom. She explains, "In fiction you can't cite one expert who says these prehistoric people could talk and another authority who says they couldn't; here they all either talk or they don't, and whatever you do you are going to upset some part of the academic community. Because there may have been some limit to their articulation, I decided to limit the names of characters to certain letters, with all the male names starting and ending in a consonant, and all the female names starting and ending in a vowel."

When Auel had rewritten enough of *The Clan of the Cave Bear* to show a publisher, she went about finding one in her usual straightforward way by reading every issue of *PW* and such books as *Maybe You Should Write a Book* and *How to Get Happily Published*. After query letters and sample chapters got no response, Auel met literary agent Jean Naggar, who spoke to a Portland writers' group. Naggar suggested she write a letter describing the project. "I wrote her the best sales letter I could manage—it must have taken me two weeks. I had no writing background; I had no background in anthropology or archeology. But I tried, in one page, to get her interested in my book. And it did!"

Not only did Naggar agree to represent Auel; she decided, in a rare move, to put up for auction this first novel by an unknown writer. There were offers from two publishers, both with an advance of $130,000. Auel recalls Naggar told her to sit down before relaying this news on the phone. "We decided to go with Crown," Auel says, "and I am very pleased. They treat people like individuals, and they know how to get behind a book." That first novel went through eight printings and stayed on bestseller lists for more than a year; Bantam's 3,473,000 paperback printing did almost as well; there is a movie in the works. The second volume's sales were comparable; the third, *The Mammoth Hunters*, greeted the world with a hardcover print order of one million plus and hit the national bestseller charts at #1 in its first week on sale.

The Auels now live in a bright new multi-level modern seaside mansion with many windows and decks overlooking the Pacific surf. Ray Auel has quit his job as a computer-plant executive to become his wife's business manager. Jean Auel likes to say, "We raised five kids in a one-bathroom house, and now we've got no kids in a five-bathroom house." It is here within the sound of the sea that Auel has her writing studio in a top-story room. She writes from right after dinner, at about eight, straight through the night to five or six in the morning.

"I like the night for working," she says. "It's the way my daily cycle goes." She tries to put in 10 hours a day, but cannot predict how many pages she may write. "I may have Ayla out hunting ermine, and she had better really know how you hunt this animal. So I may have to read five books to find out everything I can about weasels and ermines before I can go on. I work seven days a week, straight through." Explaining her unflagging enthusiasm, Auel says: "I was over 40 before I learned what I wanted to do when I grew up!"

ROY BONGARTZ

PAUL AUSTER

PAUL AUSTER BRAVES the sunny afternoon cold in jeans, a sweater and an open leather jacket as he and *PW* walk briskly to his studio. This is his writing quarters, a block or so from the Park Slope apartment in Brooklyn where he lives with his wife Siri Hustvedt, a writer and translator, and small children Daniel and Sophie. In person, the brooding, smokey-eyed Auster of the photographs materializes into a younger, handsome version of himself, not at all gaunt and unsmiling.

On the way, we chat about the international success of his books, translated so far into 15 languages, among them French, German, Spanish and Danish. "The New York Trilogy [*City of Glass; Ghosts; The Locked Room*, published by Sun & Moon, reprinted by Viking Penguin] has been very big stuff in Europe," Auster tells *PW*. "And in England, Faber & Faber did a remarkable job; it was on the bestseller list, which was—crazy! Things have gone very well there." He adds, "I'm not disappointed with the way my books are doing in America. I know there are people out there who really care about them." Indeed, his novel, *Moon Palace*, out from Viking is being touted as his breakthrough book here.

In Auster's spartan studio there are bookshelves, a desk, business-like chairs and a manual typewriter, though he prefers to write in longhand. "Having started as a poet, really, I've always been very attached to my fountain pens. I like the feel of the pen scraping along the paper. There's a tactile immediacy to it." *Disappearances* (Overlook, 1988), one of his collections, prints poems culled from literary magazines where they first appeared. "For years I only wrote poetry—it just took me over."

Auster has a BA and an MA in English and Comparative Literature from Columbia University. Although the influence of American writers like Poe, Hawthorne and Melville is evident in his fiction, his primary field was Renaissance literature. He was in the middle of a Ph.D program when he realized he "just didn't want to do it."

His anthology of translated French poets (Random House) dates from a Paris sojourn in his early 20s, after a stint as a seaman on an oil tanker: "The pay was very good, and I saved everything, and that's what got me over there." In Paris, Auster published a poetry magazine, *Living Hand*, with his first wife, translator Lydia Davis. "When the money finally ran out, I did all kinds of things. I translated art books. I worked as a tutor. Like Fanshawe in *The Locked Room*, I was a telephone operator. For quite a while I worked for a movie producer."

Born in 1947 in Newark, N.J., Auster grew up in suburban South Orange and Maplewood. He documents this period in a memoir, *The Invention of Solitude* (Sun & Moon Press, 1982; Penguin, 1988). The book's first part probes his feelings for his father, who died abruptly "in the best of health, not even old." Auster acknowledges that a father/son theme "seems to pop up in many of the things I write. My relationship with my father was an unresolved and difficult one, and probably for that reason I keep writing about fathers and sons."

But he qualifies this. "The more I write, the more it seems to me that an idea becomes powerful almost to the extent that I don't understand it. When I start writing a book, it's because I feel forced into a corner. I'm haunted by certain images or ideas or a kind of story, and I *have* to do it. When I was younger I would analyze my motives much more carefully. As I get older I don't do that anymore. I just let it happen."

Though he started his writing career as a poet, translator and essayist, he says, "My dream was always to write novels. Absolutely. From the beginning. Writing novels gives you the opportunity to explore all these sides of yourself—more than anything else I can think of."

In Auster's case, these explorations have produced elegant, highly original fiction. Influences on his work range from Giordano Bruno, Montaigne and Pascal to Wittgenstein and Merleau-Ponty, Edmond Jabès and Beckett. Of the moderns, he values DeLillo and Coetzee. As a stylist, Auster is meticulous and highly wrought; even the workaday worlds he creates border on the eerie, the fantastic, the déjà vu. While he dislikes having his works categorized ("any writer who's any good is going to be unique"), Auster acknowledges himself as a postmodernist, "because there's a certain reflexiveness about the activity of writing in the books."

Moon Palace contains, besides its father/son quests, an "Uncle Victor," a dreamy clarinetist who bequeaths books and money to the young protagonist, Marco Stanley Fogg. The name evokes Marco Polo and the American journalist who tracked down Dr. Livingstone, as well as Phileas Fogg of *Around the World in 80 Days*. The immigrant Fogelmans having been trimmed to "Fogg" on Ellis Island, Marco's uncle nicknames him Phileas. "I do have an uncle who is very important to me," but who in no way resembles the character in the novel, Auster says. He is Allen Mandelbaum, the noted poet and translator of Dante and of modern Italian poetry. "He was the first reader of my poems when I was a teenager. He was very hard on me, very strict, very good."

Auster views *Moon Palace* as "a novel of growing up, the story of someone coming to grips with his life, someone standing on the threshold of adulthood. In order finally to grow up you have to have been in love and lost that love. This is almost a requirement of being human. You have to have experienced death, in some way. Marco does go through all these things. And I think he's a much stronger, healthier person by the end than he is at the beginning."

The novel's imagery isn't only lunar and sublunar. It forms a network that is highly personal to Auster, and plugs into American painting and history. In one effective scene, Marco goes to the Brooklyn Museum to see a painting entitled *Moonlight* by 19th-century artist Ralph Blakelock. He stands hypnotized before its shimmering light, which seems to drain his energy. "Blakelock is a fascinating person to me," says Auster, who wrote a story on the painter for *Artnews*.

In using the moon as a subtext, Auster had several things in mind. "It all has to do with America, the idea that Columbus set out on a voyage to discover the East, a new passage to India, or Cathay. I like to think of America as China. That's Number One.

Number Two would be the westward movement in the United States, which is also part of the book. And Number Three would be outer space. Going to the moon is the third era of exploration and discovery, and so the moon is an extension of America in some sense, yes, as the new frontier. I just keep shuffling these ideas around."

"Also," Auster sighs explosively, "there was a lot of intellectual material that I really made a great effort to expunge." Auster's cuts are self-imposed. "I always work that way, and when I finally hand in a book, that's it. And no one has ever tampered with anything."

The idea for *Moon Palace* began long ago. "It took 15 years of thinking through that story. I've never kept a notebook; it's all in my head—sometimes the stories go kicking around in my head for years." So too with his other novels, including the recent *In The Country of Last Things*, about life in a crumbling, strangely futuristic city. He started that book in 1970, and it gradually "changed and grew and evolved. I didn't write it every day. I'd pick it up, put it down, get disgusted and discouraged. But finally I went back to it and wrote the first 30 pages and showed it to Siri. She's my real critic, she's the only one I really trust. I said 'It's terrible, isn't it?' And she said, 'Oh no, this is great, this is the book you have to write for me.' That's why it's dedicated to her.

"She pushed me on. I was troubled by the idea of writing in the voice of a woman. It's not that I didn't want to do it, but it somehow seemed wrong to try to do that. But every time I tried just to do the book, it was the woman who spoke."

Auster remarks that his daily output is "very slow, it's anguishing. I seem to be afflicted with this disease, which is that words come very slowly to me. I don't have ready access to language. There's always a gap. I feel as though I'm falling into a void every time I try to fish up the next sentence. I *know* there are other writers who can sit down and just blast it out. I've never been able to do that. I prefer to inch along. I have a much better grip on what I'm doing. I feel satisfied if I can get one page out of the day. It's a page that is pretty good but that will need a real careful going-over later."

Inspiration comes to Auster "when I'm alone. I never see or hear something and say 'Aha, I'm going to work this into my book.' Sometimes, years later, some little thing I might have read in the newspaper, some little incident I might have witnessed, does work its way in, but it has to go deep into the unconscious, I think, before it can be cooked enough to be used. The body as an oven!"

Getting a publisher for *City of Glass* wasn't easy. "Everybody turned it down. All in all there were 17 rejections. Many of the bigger commercial houses in New York were hesitant. They didn't understand the book, they were confused by it. Probably they thought they wouldn't sell any copies at all. A few publishers wanted to take it if I agreed to make changes, but I didn't want to do that." He says he thought that he was "just going to keep on writing books that no one would ever publish, let alone read."

Then his poetry connections led Auster to Sun & Moon Press in California. Douglas Messerli wanted to publish *City of Glass* immediately. "I told him there were going to be two more, it's going to be a trilogy. He said, 'Fine, I accept the other two, sight unseen.' Messerli has a passion for literature. He's very committed to his own tastes and he's willing to follow his own instincts. He thought they were good, and that was it." Though it was nominated for an Edgar Award by Mystery Writers of America, *City of Glass* was not intended to be read as a mystery. "It's simply a novel that uses genre conventions."

An AP reporter who interviewed Auster recommended a friend of hers, Carol Mann, as an agent. "I had written a detective novel under another name—I can't say what it is, no, that's a secret. I gave it to her and she got it published in about two minutes. But she said, 'Listen, forget this detective stuff, I'd really like to be your agent.' We've been together ever since, devoted to each other. She's been very faithful and very solid for me. She's never given up."

Auster experimented with playwriting, and in 1977 had a play produced in a private performance for The Artists' Theater in New York. Of his several other plays, one became the basis of *Ghosts*. But he never found playwriting congenial to his goals as a writer. "I wanted just narrative, telling the story. There are definite narratives in all the books. I'm very interested in telling stories, because I think as human beings we crave stories. I think we absolutely depend on them for our survival."

Auster's favorite novel is "the one I'm writing. I'm into something new, and I'm very excited because it scares the living daylights out of me, the whole story. And the new book is very much a story, without a lot of peripheral material creeping in. Every time I come to work on it, I'm scared. I think maybe that's a good sign."

MARCELLE THIÉBAUX

RUSSELL BANKS

AT HOME TO *PW* on a snowy Saturday morning, Russell Banks welcomes us to his apartment high over Riverside Drive. Bright with spiky plants, fish tanks, a solid wall of books and some exotic bric-a-brac, the room has a comfortable ambience. The eclectic surroundings represent "the coming together of two lives," that of Banks and his third wife, Kathy, to whom he has been married three years. Banks at 45 looks like a genial, handsome satyr; he has a grizzled beard and cropped hair, a ruddy face. A man of middle height, he's a little paunchy. He smiles readily, and, quick to savor the incongruous, he laughs a good deal, revealing the engagingly spacy front teeth that he has bestowed on a number of his favored fictional characters.

The first copy of *Continental Drift,* just out from Harper & Row, has arrived the day before. Early reviews have been enthusiastic. James Atlas in the February *Atlantic* called *Continental Drift* a "profound and gripping narrative . . . a great American novel" and "the most convincing portrait I know of contemporary America."

The book tells the story of Bob Dubois and his family, stuck in a run-down New Hampshire mill town. At the other end of the hemisphere, in Haiti, lives Vanise Dorsinville with her infant. Vanise and Dubois, both seeking a better life, will converge tragically in a squalid region of Florida. Their hopes betray them, as do the people they trust. Vanise hands her money over to the sailor who runs illegal aliens from the Caribbean to Florida; Dubois lets his future be manipulated by his older brother

Eddie, and by his flaky best friend, over-the-hill hippie and drug runner Avery Boone.

Banks, who likes geographical and geological metaphors, anticipated the notion of continental drift—people wandering over the earth's surface while the earth itself moves and ages—in his novel *Hamilton Stark*. There, "glaciers and glaciation, melting and refreezing," represent Stark, "a frozen man."

The drawings at the chapter heads of *Continental Drift*, *voudon* symbols called "*vevers*," were researched and executed by Banks. He also built the Cornell box that forms the book jacket's collage of the novel's elements: maps, a ganja (marijuana) leaf, a skeleton, a Renaissance Virgin and Child. The Nativity theme signals the touching mother/infant relationships, and indeed the novel opens with Dubois shopping disconsolately for Christmas toys at Sears.

Weighing the book in hands that are squarish, stubby, competent-looking, Banks tells of his emergence as a writer. "Writing isn't one of those things, in a literate culture, like music or painting, where the gift is obvious at a young age. My obvious gift as a young boy was in painting. I could draw well; I had the gift genetically. I didn't know whether I had any particular writing talent at all. I set out to be a painter in my late teens and gradually discovered that I was writing, as one discovers one is breathing—and so you feel you must be alive! The discovery, the definition, came after the activity."

The realization came in his early 20s. Having left Colgate College after "eight horrible weeks" (he felt isolated, "a poor kid" among "the sons of the captains of American industry"), Banks embarked on his own continental drift. He traveled to Mexico and the Yucatán; some of his experiences appear in stories in *Searching for Survivors*.

He also went to Florida. "I was headed for Cuba to join Castro. It seemed like a noble thing to do," Banks tells us. He breaks off. "I was just up at the Columbia library rereading old news accounts to see how he was portrayed in the late '50s. First of all he was called *Dr.* Castro. He was very, very handsome, but also the photographs made him look so glamorous, so attractive, so sexy— and politically he was absolutely pure! In the late '50s we had very few political heroes, us young folks, us kids." He wryly grins. "And here came the first of the romantic political heroes, and along with him came Che Guevara. I means, *this is wonderful. These* are wonderful *guys!"* He gives the words amused, ironic emphasis. "We could project romantic, altruistic, idealistic, political feelings onto these people. I was running off to try to make it real."

The book that Banks is writing now, provisionally called *Success Stories,* centers on just such a young man who goes to join Castro, whom he sees as a Robin Hood. "I only got so far as St. Petersburg, Florida, when I ran out of money," Banks continues. "I was hitching; I didn't need much, but I couldn't hitch any further. Then I'm moving furniture in a hotel and trying to survive, and pretty soon I forget about Castro." For a time Banks stayed in a trailer in Islamorada Key. In *Continental Drift* he brilliantly anatomizes the dingy side of an American trailer lifestyle, when the uprooted Dubois family occupies a cramped, rusting house trailer in Florida. (A collection of outstanding stories, *Trailerpark,* is set in New Hampshire.)

Living in Florida in the '60s, Banks pumped gas, wrote stories and fished. At 22 he had already married, had a child and been divorced. These were "terrible years," he recalls. "I thought I was in agony. I seemed disconnected from myself and the rest of the world. I was writing, and absorbing an awful lot of information, I guess, but my memories of myself in that period are those of a person who had very little self-knowledge and a great deal of conflicted feelings. I was doing something that seemed a self-destructive kind of compulsion. Wanting to be a writer seemed to be a terrible waste of a life to my family and to me."

If Banks was able to forget about Castro in those early years, he continued to feel drawn to the Caribbean, which he so earthily recreates in *Continental Drift* and *The Book of Jamaica.* "I went down to Jamaica just by accident," Banks recalls. "I had been to the Caribbean, like most Americans who can swing it, a week here, a week there in the wintertime. I was always fascinated by the Caribbean—maybe like most New Englanders. It's where the sun shines. You know how Englishmen and Scandinavians love the sun and are fascinated by the Mediterranean—the longing for the 'other.' " In the 1970s, when Banks had been teaching for a number of years at Emerson College and the University of New Hampshire, he had a chance to rent a house in Jamaica. "I became deeply attracted to the culture, the people, and fell in love with the place." Awarded a Guggenheim Fellowship to write a book, he took his family and stayed a year and a half.

While on the island, Banks spent a lot of time "up in the back country with the Maroons," a people descended from Ashanti warriors who had rebelled against the British. Besides making friends—and one can imagine Banks, affable and sensitive as he is, doing this with ease—he read about Caribbean life. "Like most fiction writers, I'm really a library rat, and look for excuses to research something."

Banks' knowledge of the French-Canadian Dubois family in *Continental Drift* comes firsthand. Born in Newton, Mass., he grew up in Barnstead, N.H., a small town. "My family is very Yankee. We were at the bottom of the Yankee ladder, and we had nobody else to look down on except the French-Canadians, and so we *did*." He laughs energetically. "They were the next level down in the socio-economic scale. All our prejudices and attitudes came out of *that*." His family was "disintegrated by divorce and economics and moving, scrambling for a living. My father was a plumber, my grandfather was a plumber. I was a plumber for a long time, off and on, from about 1959 to 1964. I was an AFL-CIO card-carrying member, Concord, New Hampshire, Local."

His parents divorced when Banks was 12. "My mother went to work as a bookkeeper, and she had four children to raise. It was a hard life," he recalls. The youngest boy was killed in a train accident; he had hopped a freight, and the train was caught in a mudslide in Santa Barbara.

As the oldest sibling, Banks stresses the importance for him and for *Continental Drift* of the "power relationship" between the older and younger brothers, Eddie and Bob Dubois. "Power" is a word that crops up frequently as we talk, a word that Banks associates in his writing with complex feelings of guilt and betrayal between brothers, blacks and whites, men and women. Of the brother nearest him in age he remarks, "When my brother reads this book, I think he'll understand. He's going to see a lot of me in Eddie."

Kathy Banks has tiptoed in to pour more coffee into our blue mugs. She snuggles down in the teal-blue Victorian sofa "to eavesdrop" and to add that her husband's family had been Tories who had run off to Canada in 1776, then returned to New England in 1930 because of the Depression. Kathy is an editor at Harper & Row, but it turns out that this has nothing to do with the publication of Banks's latest book. "We came in separate doors," he laughs.

Banks has had a variety of publishers, from alternative to commercial presses, and ran his own press for seven years. When he went back to complete his degree at the University of North Carolina, he and friends founded a literary magazine called *Lillabulero*. "It was a great focus for our chaotic energies and ambitions. We thought of ourselves as young Turks. Before long, the magazine turned out, to our surprise, to have a following that wasn't just Chapel Hill." The enterprise taught Banks what was going on in contemporary writing and helped him to channel his own efforts from poetry to prose as a means of accommodating his range of interests in history, politics and social structures.

He also experiments with various literary modes to embrace these interests. In a recent novel, *The Relation of My Imprisonment,* an odd, quasi-allegorical work that he speaks of with clear affection, Banks assumes the style and persona of a 17th-century divine like Cotton Mather. He frames *Continental Drift* with an Invocation and Envoi, enabling him as author to step out of his work. He calls on the *loa*, the Haitian *voudon* spirit of the dead that speaks through the mouth of the living, to help tell the story.

"I'm really interested in re-inventing the narrator," Banks remarks. "It's a convention that went out the window in the 20th century. I want to feel I have my arm around a shoulder of this reader and I'm explaining, narrating, telling a wonderful story to this person that I've stopped, like the wedding guest in Coleridge's *The Ancient Mariner.* I'm like the ancient mariner stopping the wedding guest in his rush to tell this wonder to him. And I want to have that sense of intimacy, a face-to-face, arm-around-the-shoulder contact."

Banks maintains a four-day teaching stint, conducting writing workshops at Sarah Lawrence and Princeton, a schedule that affords him only "broken time" for writing. During the school year he works on short stories or revises the longer fiction he has roughed out during summer and Christmas vacations, when he can draft "the arc and orbit of a book." He likes living in New York, which he feels has come at the right time in his life. He still thinks of himself, however, "as existing in some other place and visiting here," which is probably why his deepest source of subject matter continues to be his past.

As a writer, he feels his experiences need time to be absorbed and assimilated. The present "may take a little while to settle in and find its niche and place in the cluttered closet—one's past— there where all the shoes and things are around in the back, all the stuff that turns up in your fiction, the flora and fauna." He makes the point with a reaching gesture as he grins. "But eventually it finds a place, and then it's there when you reach down in the dark."

MARCELLE THIÉBAUX

RICHARD BAUSCH

Like bob and Ray, Richard Bausch and George Garrett collaborate effortlessly. It's late June, and both writers are teaching at the Wesleyan University Writers Conference in Middletown, Conn. Officially the afternoon session on the short story is Garrett's, but he is sharing the time with Bausch, an old friend and fellow Virginian, whose second collection of stories, *The Fireman's Wife*, is just out from Simon & Schuster's Linden Press.

Forty or so writing students line the dim paneled lounge called Butterfield A, blinds closed against the heat, to listen to these old hands and firm friends discuss short story techniques. Garrett wears modified fatigues, Bausch a turquoise shirt, cotton trousers, sandals and a wide-brimmed panama hat. Sitting unceremoniously at a conference table, they talk about methods to establish authenticity and to get distance from autobiographical material. Mostly, however, they tell stories.

They tell stories to illustrate ideas, to make points, to entertain. They tell stories, one suspects, because they cannot help themselves. Before this class is over, they will have spun tales about serial killers and clowns, about themselves and about other writers—Tim O'Brien, James Joyce, Hilma Wolitzer, Henry Taylor, Kelly Cherry and Saul Bellow. Embellished with expansive gestures, in varied voices and accents, the stories are told for varied purpose and effect; they are told continually, instinctively and for the simple joy of it.

Later, Bausch stretches out on grass shaded by venerable wide-branched maple trees. Drinking seltzer and eating from a box of cookies brought by his 17-year-old son, Wes, who has joined his father and "Uncle George" for the week-long conference, Bausch continues to talk about stories.

"For me they're a form of profound recreation. Writing short stories satisfies me in a way that no other activity does. Novels are forms of profound commitment and obsession. There are so many waves, so many ebbings and flowings in them that I feel better to have finished writing a novel, whereas every stage of a story is fun to me. I began as a short story writer; I wrote novels because I couldn't sell my stories. I'm still a pretty good novelist but my first love is the short story."

Selling his stories isn't a problem lately. Seven of the nine in *The Fireman's Wife* have recently appeared, or are about to, in national magazines: two each in the *New Yorker* and *Atlantic Monthly*, another in *Esquire*. Bausch has had two PEN/Faulkner nominations and garnered two National Magazine Awards for short fiction. Two of *The Fireman's Wife* stories will be in *Best American Short Stories of 1990*, selected by Richard Ford, edited by Shannon Ravenel, out from Houghton Mifflin. "The only other writer with two stories," he says, delighting in the association, "is Alice Munro."

Bausch grew up in Virginia in the rural suburbs of Washington, D.C. Writing wasn't his first ambition, though he was preoccupied with reading. He tells a story of getting lost in a book one winter morning and rushing late to high school to find, when he took off his jacket, that he'd forgotten to put on a shirt.

He was initially determined to be a rock musician. Both he and Wes have brought guitars to Connecticut and later, playing together, they debate the merits of acoustic vs. electric guitars, of brands and models, of songwriters, chords and styles. Bausch sings a little; Wes picks and strums, sometimes following his father, sometimes leading—he's good, and he's clearly in love with making music.

"I was really moved by Bob Dylan," Bausch recollects, bowing to the early draw of words. "When you listen to those tapes you can hear the astonishment in the audience at a line like 'The ghost Electricity howls in the bones of her face.' I wanted to write songs like his.

"Then I was going to be a poet. When I was a teenager I'd read that John F. Kennedy liked poetry, so I started to read it myself. I like to tell people that later I found out how much money poets don't make, but really I finally found it wasn't so energizing for me, and that I didn't have the talent for it."

After high school, a couple of years working and a stint in the Air Force teaching survival skills, Bausch, at age 25, enrolled at Virginia's George Mason University. By the end of four years there, his interest in writing had solidified enough for him to study for a master's degree at the University of Iowa Writers' Workshop, where he went with his wife and baby. This was 1974 and his class included Jane Smiley, Mark Jarman, Allan Gurganus, Douglas Unger, Richard Wiley, Robert Chivka, Joanne Meschery, Chase Twichell and Barbara Grossman, now a senior editor and publisher at Scribners. "We were one hell of a group and we had a great time. Even so, I was unhappy. I was terrified—Karen and I had a new baby and I was convinced I'd made a terrible mistake, that I wasn't a writer."

He tells another story. After Iowa, unable to sell his work and needing to support his family, seeing no future for himself as a writer, he agreed to take a job with the U.S. Census Bureau. But the prospect was tearing him up inside. He recalls that Karen sat with him at the kitchen table, listing all the positive reasons for him to take the job. Then she pointed out the powerful, overriding negative: he would hate it. He turned down the position, and shortly thereafter got an offer to fill in for an instructor at George Mason. Two years—"of controlled desperation"—teaching full-time at Northern Virginia Community College followed before he returned to George Mason, where he's now a full professor of creative writing.

While peddling his work at that time, he acquired both his agent and a Gordon Lish anecdote. "I sent Gordon some stories at *Esquire*. He didn't take them but liked them well enough to send one to Harriet Wasserman. The story had, he said, the elements of the gesture of a novel, and Harriet was crackerjack at placing first novels. She's been my agent for 15 years, representing me for seven before she ever saw a penny. I still owe Gordon for her."

Bausch's first novel, *Real Presence*, published by Dial in 1981, was followed the next year by *Take Me Back* and a few years later by *The Last Good Time*, brought out by Dial/Doubleday. *Spirits*, his first collection of stories, issued by Linden in 1987, was widely reviewed and praised, as was his next book, the novel *Mr. Field's Daughter,* in 1989.

The Fireman's Wife, Bausch feels, may be his breakout work. "With the magazine appearances and the awards, I have a feeling this is the main chance. I don't hunger for great overwhelming success and am pretty happy with things the way they are. But like any writer, I'd like my books to have the chance to be read. I don't have to have bestsellers, but I'd like my books to be in print and not have this feeling that there's some huge ghost coming along behind me sweeping it all away as fast as I can produce it."

Bausch's stories illuminate the questions beating at the heart of ordinary lives. His characters, as recognizable, imperfect and lovable as one's brothers and sisters, are observed in their small-town worlds with an avidity of interest and affection that brings to mind the stories of Anne Tyler, Peter Taylor and Flannery O'Connor. The people in Bausch's stories are responding to shifts in their deepest expectations. Frequently the quake is major, such as the loss of love and the death that propel the title story in *The Fireman's Wife* and its follow-up tale, "Consolation"; often, the change is subtle but no less shattering, as in "Design," with its young priest whose anxious uncertainty is refracted in the terminal illness of the elderly, untroubled minister of the neighboring church. Bausch's people have flaws and bad habits—they drink, turn blind eyes, do drugs—but their resilience, dignity and effortful survival suggest possibilities of redemption.

Despite his range—he writes of the internally disaffected, of women, the elderly, the faltering middle-aged and disappointed young adults—some character types seem to crop up frequently. Round-faced, thick-bodied, ungainly men leave their bedrooms on sleepless nights and wander their houses puzzling over private sorrows and predicaments. Bausch, fair-skinned with reddish beard and thinning hair, while neither thick or clumsy, could be one of them having the same observant, unconvinced air. Talking about the dilemmas his characters face in keeping faith with themselves or with those whom they have loved, he observes, "I can say not only as writer, but as a person that I don't know anything more important than trying to figure out the right thing to do. Everything else pales in front of that question: how does one live fully without living selfishly?"

Wes bobs in and out of the conversation, bringing phone messages, grabbing cookies, leaning on his upended skateboard to listen. He and his father are remarkably comfortable with each other. Bausch, whose five children include a year-old daughter, came from a large family himself. His twin brother, Robert, is also a writer. ("Are you the Emily Dickinson Bausch?" demanded a student in Butterfield A. "No, that's my brother," Bausch answered with a smile.)

Bausch's stories map the family landscape: his characters contend with parents and siblings, spouses and children. His favorite story in *The Fireman's Wife*, "The Brace," is narrated by a young married woman whose quiet, satisfying family life is periodically disrupted by visits from her father, a notorious film director. "There's a crucial moment when she looks at her son, feeling all the complications of loving somebody, and knows a time will come when they'll stand before each other and nothing will be any good—it'll be the same as it is between her and her father. She wonders if the idea of maintaining any love is absurd and, at the end, reveals something of herself that she both knows and doesn't know to be revealing. There's such a bravery about her."

His teaching has a family quality, too. The snapshots he displays, taken at his home in the countryside 30 miles from D.C., feature his students as well as his wife and children. "I see a lot of my students outside of class, they often come to the house. Teaching is like a salon for me, it's like a group of friends. The only bad part is when they graduate and go off."

Other writers, many in the Washington area, provide another supportive community. He offers a story about a dinner with Alan Cheuse, also at George Mason, and Mary Lee Settle; he talks about Susan Richards Shreve, who, he says, does everything she can to advance his career, and about Jane Smiley—"We sometimes ride horses together and tend to argue a lot, but in a good way." He talks about Fred Chappell and Stephen Goodwin, with a story about Goodwin and Peter Taylor reading Chekhov on a Key West beach; mentions Henry Taylor, who lives in Virginia, and Garrett, of course, godfather to one of the Bausch children.

No less important are the admired writers whose work he refers to and quotes frequently throughout the afternoon: Tolstoy, Chekhov, Chaucer; line after line of poetry, from Berryman,

James Wright, James Dickey, even, to the tune of "The Yellow Rose of Texas," a sprinkling of Dickinson. His passion for poetry is surely tied to his delight in music, but his primary allegiance is unequivocal. "I published some poems, but really it's fiction. I'm just not interested in writing anything but stories, long and short, for as long as I have to do that."

DULCY BRAINARD

ANN BEATTIE

LEANED AGAINST A window in Ann Beattie's kitchen is a family portrait of President Lyndon Johnson, his wife Lady Bird and their daughters Luci Baines and Lynda Bird, an official photograph taken (it is obvious from the clothing and hairstyles) during the White House years. Why is it there? In the late 1950s Lady Bird was Ann Beattie's dancing teacher at the Wesley Methodist Church in Washington, D.C.

Beattie, now 38, lives in Charlottesville, Va., little more than two hours from where she grew up in D.C., and she writes short stories and novels that have been variously criticized and praised for including such extraneous or telling details as the above. When we meet, her fourth collection of stories, *Where You'll Find Me*, has just been published by Simon & Schuster.

"My writing is full of things seen, not heard," Beattie says. "I get more material staring out at the world, not overhearing things." She is a "specific" writer. "I focus on detail, but that's not what my work is *about*."

Beattie is fascinated by "reflective people in a mess," she says, offering her own partial and generalized view of her work. "What catches my attention are situations that are ironic. Look what everyone takes for granted. Look at how that makes everything ironic. The subtext, the detail, the telling gestures that reveal it," mesmerize her. Her characters, and she understands them, "are not forthcoming. When they say something 'emphatically,' I believe they believe it emphatically." Writers, the author says,

51

"don't trust surfaces because they're so used to making things. . . . Writers are deciphering."

Seeking meaning in fiction seems, to Beattie, somehow beyond the point. Fiction describes, fiction depicts; it is its own world. "Writing communicates a lot. But not answers to direct questions. I just want to make [a story] satisfying in and of itself," Beattie says. "I don't want to explain it to someone. Writing is not a corrective activity. . . . You either get it or you don't," she adds, not coy or evasive. "It resonates or not."

After all, the writer "only knows the world he knows," Beattie points out. "And he has any number of attitudes—critics fixate on the *details*, trying to dismiss them; readers fix an author thematically—but he doesn't have one attitude. There are fluctuations and complexities in fiction."

Beattie says that "ambiguity is what I want in writing," her own and others. "I don't read fiction for answers. I like writers who imply questions. Complexity is really consoling. . . . Put life out as a puzzle and acknowledge it as a puzzle."

Beattie began writing "seriously" when she was in graduate school at the University of Connecticut, in the early '70s. Her first stories were accepted for publication by the *Atlantic* and the *New Yorker* within " about 10 days of each other" in 1972 or 1973. After the *New Yorker* took two or three more stories, she signed a first-read agreement with the magazine, under which they have first refusal of any story she writes for publication. And the *New Yorker* does reject her often, she says; ironically, her income for the stories they do run has also been diminishing, since the magazine pays by the word and her stories, by design, have become briefer. There is rarely any correlation between what she expects will be accepted and what is.

But sending stories to the *New Yorker* has at least one advantage for Beattie, who often can't come up with titles and submits them untitled. Roger Angell, her editor at the magazine, titles stories he rejects. "Letters come back to Lynn [Nesbit, Beattie's agent] saying, 'We are returning X . . . ,' and the title is almost always perfect."

Beattie is seized by "the dramatic moment that radiates in a story. Remembered moments, something happening, and remembering or anticipating at the same time. Hopefully, always, the moment means more than the moment." She "types fast . . .

if a story is going to work. It's a wonderful way to get out of control." If she doesn't come up with a rough draft "fairly quickly, if I'm not two or three pages into it fast," Beattie throws it away. There will be no undiscovered Beattie manuscripts— Beattie also throws away completed stories if she can't come up with a last line, because if "a zinger" doesn't come naturally, she feels she either didn't have a story of she hasn't gotten to the story she wanted to tell. Her short narratives are much revised, though, and "take a long time" to sharpen, Beattie says. She sometimes will leave a story for as long as a month before she can understand it enough to revise it.

In assembling her tales for publication in a book, she is selective. "Tonally it's nice to pick up a book with coherence," she believes. *Where You'll Find Me* contains about two-thirds of her work since *The Burning House* and three unpublished stories that fit in with the "sensibility of the collection."

In novels, though, "you have to deal with chronological time," which Beattie says she finds difficult to do. In *Love Always*, her most recent novel, "I didn't want to tell a story chronologically." Beattie wrote that novel in pieces, and when all the chapters were finished she spread them on her living room floor and reassembled them "like pieces in a puzzle." She was "foiled by having to fix it technically, to go back and revise the chronology." Novels are "episodic," and though they, too, tell "stories" and "have many moments. . . . People are always waiting for a distillation, an answer," which Beattie avoids stating. "This whole syndrome of looking for truth," as she calls it, confuses her.

So writing another novel is not something Beattie is thinking about right away—she has written three, *Chilly Scenes of Winter*, *Falling in Place* and *Love Always*—and she prefers to write stories. "The forms are radically different. Who can say why my proclivity is for one or the other? It's like being in a store where there are all these beautiful things you can touch. Of course, it's perfectly nice if you don't *want* to touch something. Choosing a form somehow demonstrates a tactile relation with the world. . . .

"The writer knows what he wants to write about. You wonder about private things and figure out how to present aspects of what you are thinking about," Beattie says. "You find very easily what part of you is the actor you're positing" for each emotion or each scene. "You're the basis," she adds, quickly qualifying that

53

"that doesn't make it autobiographical. . . . But you don't want to pretend you're a machine. . . .

"You make educated guesses," Beattie says about characters. "The writer's subconscious makes a distinction" between self and them. "You put a character out there and you're in their power. You're in trouble if they're in yours," Beattie feels.

Beattie does not "lead a very structured life. If you don't allow time to write, how do you know you will?" she asks. She no longer teaches (although she did for eight years), and now, thanks to a lucrative contract with S & S (rumored to be around $500,000 for a collection of stories and a novel), she does not have to, though teaching was not really a drain on her. She writes better at night, she says, "and it didn't matter whether I was teaching during the day or, now, vacuuming, or running errands." But "I have a lot of freedom," Beattie admits.

"This is the life I've chosen. But I've paid a price, I've given up a lot," she says, referring vaguely to marriage, children, *other* lives she might have had. Beattie was married once, is divorced, and she lives with someone in Charlottesville, but for a self-described "specific" writer she is not forthcoming about her personal life. Even the spare biographies on the back flaps of her books have been "incorrect by the time the book gets published," somehow "foiled" by chronology, as Beattie says she is in her novels.

"I have a lot of leisure," she says, although that is not at all the word she wants to describe what she's doing when she does not seem to be doing anything. "It's not an ideal life, necessarily, but I'm not sorry I figured this life out for myself. I have a lot of worries, crazy hectic things. People say writing is a lonely life, but that's not what occurs to me.

"I truly have so much free time that it's hard to explain how other things psychologically pollute that." Beattie pauses. Even a week on a beach, "something that's leisure for someone else. . . . I can spend a week of my life fairly bored or depressed, thinking, 'What a life!' I can float around (although I don't know any writers who work nine to five), but I find out about the world by observing."

Beattie is "always storing things up," she says, although she doesn't "save things" for her writing. "The process of transformation is what amazes me."

She compares herself to a photographer: "Writing is not a 'hands-on' skill," she says. "It's all in your head. Private. There

54

isn't anything you can do if you feel helpless. I imagine that at least as a photographer you can strap a camera around your neck, go out and *get* into it. Maybe I'm wrong. But I can't go out and find a story. And I can't just sit at a typewriter tapping keys. It would be the best thing in the world if that worked." Painters, she suspects, may face her problem. She has been working for the past year on an essay about Alex Katz for a book of his work Abrams is publishing.

"I've been girl journalist, going around with a tape recorder, interviewing people about Alex Katz, being analytic, trying to tell the truth about his paintings." This is her first nonfiction project. "In fiction," Beattie says, the goal is a little bit different: "You just have to be right," she says.

"The subtle ironies of [Katz's] work" attract her. "He does a lot of diptychs and triptychs. They're essentially narrative paintings. Our work is different, obviously, but as a story writer I'm drawn to how he implies things visually that we do tonally. I write about what I see. We [both] start with a visual image." Beattie says that Katz "has been simplified by people who haven't caught his tone."

Wearing shorts, her very tanned legs swinging over the arm of a beige leather chair in her sun-drenched, domed-ceiling living room, she combs a barrette through her medium-long blond hair, drawing the separated strands up into the air and letting them fall back down to her shoulders. She could be talking about herself.

WILLIAM GOLDSTEIN

WILLIAM BOYD

W HAT A GOOD time it is for William Boyd. When we meet
him, his most recent novel, *The New Confessions*, which delin-
eates in autobiographical form the adventures and misadventures
of John James Todd, 20th-century filmmaker and Rousseau-like
character, is just out from Morrow, and the side-splittingly funny
film of his previous novel, *Stars and Bars*, for which he wrote the
screenplay, has recently been released with a brilliant central
performance by Daniel Day-Lewis as the hapless Englishman
lurching through the American South.

Boyd is a handsome, amiable and soft-spoken man whose first
novel, *A Good Man in Africa*, about another bumbling Englishman, was an extraordinary debut. His next, *An Ice-Cream War*,
dealt with the First World War in East Africa. *School Ties*—an
essay and two television scripts—reflects his preoccupation with
the English public school system. In addition to his collection of
short stories, *On the Yankee Station*, Boyd has done a TV adaptation of Evelyn Waugh's *Scoop* as well as a screenplay for Mario
Vargas Llosa's *Aunt Julia and the Scriptwriter*.

Boyd lives in London in a wonderfully pleasant house with his
wife, Susan, formerly the publicity director at William Heinemann. The author tells us that he rarely admits English journalists to his home: "They all want to write about the wallpaper," he
laughs. Such is Boyd's stature in England and elsewhere, and
such too the English curiosity about the private lives of writers,
that when Boyd and his wife recently bought a new home, the

real estate agent, unbeknownst to him, distributed a press release about the purchase.

If this is a small chuckle in the human comedy, perhaps that is fitting, because the human comedy is what Boyd writes about. He was born to Scottish parents in 1952 in what is now Ghana, where his father was a doctor. Boyd lived in Ghana for the first 10 years of his life, "a typical colonial background." At the age of nine, he was sent back to Scotland to private boarding school, where one of his schoolmates was Prince Charles; there he put in nine years, spending holidays in Africa. "Even though I'm a Scot," he says, "I always thought of myself as being a white West African."

After school, Boyd lived in France for a year, doing a course in French studies at the University of Nice. "I felt as much at home there as I did anywhere. It was good to get out of Britain and the hothouse society of a boarding school. I have a bit of an obsession about what we call public schools but are in fact private schools, especially single-sex private schools. The effects of that education are an appalling snobbism of the most crude and unreflecting type and a terrible sexism because you've been living in a society where there is only one sex and the female sex is outside in the other world. The two filmscripts I wrote that appeared in *School Ties—Good and Bad at Games* and *Dutch Girls*—explored this. Given that 75% of our writers have been to these schools, it's curious that our literature hasn't produced any classic, true and realistic novels. They're all about plucky young chaps scoring the winning goal in the final match of the term or about homosexuals turning into spies, which is equally nonsensical."

Boyd did return to Scotland to do a degree in English literature and philosophy at Glasgow University, followed by an M.A. He went on to Oxford, where he taught for three years, and began writing; he completed his first two novels and his short story collection there. "Then I decided that this double life I was leading was not the right one, so gave up my academic career, which wasn't a great wrench—I was paid such a tiny amount of money. My wife was offered a job in London, so we uprooted and went. As I had just given up my lectureship, I am deeply grateful to William Heinemann." Boyd smiles; his wife's employment there underwrote his career for several years, even though he is published in England by Hamish Hamilton.

57

Oxford wasn't Boyd's cup of tea. "It's a nice place to live, but it is a small, rather inward-looking provincial town, whatever its reputation and whatever mythology surrounds it. Having dinner at High Table in an Oxford college, which is reputed to be one of the great intellectual treats of all time, is for me a nightmare, because it's very, very boring. A lifetime of that seemed to be a terrible sentence."

Boyd says that the first time he remembers being affected by literature "was actually Scott Fitzgerald's Basil Duke Lee stories, which I remember at the age of 13 or 14 thinking absolutely fantastic. I chart an awareness of literature working from that moment. The writers that had an influence on me are people like W. H. Auden and Seamus Heaney, not necessarily any practicing contemporary novelist. Coleridge says poetry is the best words in the best order. When you read excellent poetry, you see how precise language can be; you see words being used with great respect. I think that's a very healthy influence on a novelist.

"The things that happen in my books are things that never happen to me. I've led a rather banal life in a way, nothing out of the ordinary. There are other novelists who actually need something to have happened to them in order to write about it, or even worse, who engineer crises of traumas in their life to provide themselves with raw material. I'm completely the opposite—I don't draw on my own life at all except for the big emotions that everybody has had. It's not so much the details, but the quality of your imagination that makes the reader think, yes, this sounds plausible.

"I almost know how a book's going to end before I start. In some cases, I have the good last paragraph before I start on page one. Iris Murdoch writes that way. She says the real pleasure is in the invention, a process that takes place without putting pen to paper. That can take a year: to invent the characters, find jobs for them, flesh it all out. But it means that I then write the book faster than somebody who is inventing as he goes along."

Boyd has drawn from time to time on historical figures. The original idea for *The New Confessions* came when he was doing his Ph.D. thesis at Oxford, writing on the intellectual background to romanticism. "I was reading a lot of Rousseau, because I thought Wordsworth had ripped off Rousseau, to quite a large extent, unacknowledged. I read *The Confessions*—that must have been about 1978—and I was bowled over. Reading up the background is usually incredibly dull, tedious stuff, so when you come across a book like *The Confessions*, it's a wonderful moment. It is an extraordinary document, very candid, very explicit; for something that was written in the middle of the 18th century, it's quite astonishing and modern. He's completely neurotic, vain—a kind of late-20th-century feel about him. And I started thinking: what would a 20th-century Rousseau be like?

"I was also engaged by the autobiographical form and its potential for intimacy and vividness, so I started thinking of writing a novel set in the 20th century. Some time later I thought, being a film director is a wonderful career for this kind of downgraded Rousseau figure. You have a lot of power, but you're subject to terrible pressures, and your vanity can be indulged but also your paranoia and your fear and loathing. Those two ideas then meshed, and the thing gradually took off. But the starting point was this egomaniacal figure, loosely originating from the historical Jean-Jacques Rousseau, but borrowing from a lot of other famous egomaniacs like Boswell and Emile Ganz and Alfred Hitchcock, and his character grew, and he ceases to resemble any of the prototypes and becomes his own man. You do get a sense, at the end of the book, that you have almost read a real life. I wanted Todd's life to have that kind of up and down, meandering bits, dead ends, doubling backs, that sort of grainy texture of a real life."

War figures in *The New Confessions*, and we note that this is one of Boyd's recurring concerns. "It's a metaphor for the human condition. I think that life is a chaotic mess. We see that mess writ large in a war zone. The role chance and luck plays in your life *anyway* is magnified 2000 times the minute you step into a war zone. A war setting gives me a perfect opportunity to show how lucky or unlucky we are. In many ways, *The New Confessions* is a book about luck. When you look back at your life, you realize how these so-called momentous events are really just a sum of accidents. At the end of the book, we see that the universe is a haphazard, random place, and our lives are part of that random pattern.

"I take war as a metaphor," Boyd goes on. "You can't get anywhere more random than the battlefield. I realized that fact intuitively, unconsciously, guilelessly when I was 16 or 17, looking at a country in the middle of a terrible civil war. You'd be stopped at a roadblock by federal troops, ordered out of your car, searched. These guys had been drinking beer all day and they were wearing basketball shoes and camouflage jackets with pajama trousers; it was a ragtag and bobtail army. You suddenly thought that the things that could prevent things from getting out of hand are terribly weak. Anarchy was loosed on the streets. And you suddenly realized how that kind of anarchic fortune, good or bad, is in many ways the natural state of the universe. You weave a really uncertain path through it. All my fiction is about luck and destiny, so-called, and how you cope with it, how you come to terms with it.

"At the back of your mind, there's always some point of view that you inevitably put across, and as I look back over what I've written, I can see that there's a fairly consistent ironic, absurd view of the world. It's to do with comic tradition in the sense that things are crazy and totally unpredictable and nobody knows what's going to happen, so what sort of attitude do you have in the face of this kind of indifferent and random universe? I think that the comic absurd is the only way to cope with it, because if things don't make any sense, then sensible interpretations are some sort of smokescreen. In my heroes' case it's usually to do with recognizing that the universe is utterly indifferent to the fate of individuals. Once you realize that, all sorts of choices and dilemmas don't come any easier, but there's some sort of perverse logic there working."

Boyd thinks of his central characters as heroes. "In the modern or the post-modern sense, deeply flawed. But that's much more interesting. They're not innocents and they're not rogues; that's why I like to think of them as plausible characters. They may be a bit inept and bumbling, but then we all are. Woody Allen's great thing: 'You can't control life, but you can control art.' I think you shouldn't control art to the extent where it looks like life can be controlled. All the absurdities and incongruities, unfairnesses, injustices in life should be there in art. It's terribly tempting to punish the guilty and reward the virtuous. That's dangerous, because life isn't like that."

AMANDA SMITH

T. CORAGHESSAN BOYLE

Like many of his contemporaries, T. Coraghessan Boyle waits for the "big book," the novel that will convert a smallish but enthusiastic following into a broad national audience. One day, he hopes, people will not respond to his admittedly difficult name with a quizzical look, a moment of hesitation. The publication of *World's End*, his historical novel dealing with several generations of settlers in the Hudson River Valley, may hasten that day. At least Boyle thinks so, as do his editors at Viking.

The novel comes out of Boyle's early years spent in New York's Westchester County. *PW* finds him in California, however, where he has been living while teaching creative writing at USC. In the backyard of his home in the San Fernando Valley, we sit beneath a warm, sunny sky, the sound of a power mower echoing down the street.

Boyle, whose stories and novels cover a wide range of personal interests, has maintained that he writes from imagination rather than from experience. Yet *World's End* touches some responsive chords from his past. A tip-off comes in the dedication: "In memory of my own lost father."

"The major theme of the book is Walter's search for his father," comments Boyle, stretching his long jeans-and-sneakers-clad limbs across a wooden picnic table. "Walter is not always a likable character—he's got some elements of the antihero—but I think the reader sympathizes with him, wants him to straighten out his life, find his way." Boyle admits that the young Walter of the first few chapters embodies many personal qualities from his own youth, when as a self-described "punk kid" he grew up in the rebellious '60s. During the time he was "in opposition to just about everything," he never came to understand his father, whose life he describes as "rough." "He was raised in an orphanage, later fought in the Second World War, an experience that changed him, made him morose and silent. Life had beaten him down in a way that I couldn't understand, and I was probably too young to care. Later, in my early 20s, when I was able to appreciate him, he was dead. [The elder Boyle was a victim of alcoholism at age 54.] *World's End* was a way of redeeming some of the things from my past; it was an attempt to get some of it back, or at least to explore it, to think about it."

The novel incorporates a more distant past too: it is rich in the history of the Hudson Valley and skillfully conveys the region's social and cultural climate. The 17th century forms one of the story lines, especially the relations between tenant farmers and wealthy patroons. The other focuses on the 20th century, on events that had their source in the settlement known as Mohegan Colony. Founded during the 1920s by radicals and anarchists, the colony aroused the rancor of the valley's conservative element during the Cold War period. That conflict came to a head in 1949, when the leftists attempted to stage a series of summer concerts featuring the noted black singer and civil rights activist Paul Robeson. The response of the ultraconservative mob, violent and bloody, figures pivotally in *World's End*, making it perhaps the most political of Boyle's works thus far.

"The 1949 riot has always fascinated me," Boyle says. "It's been a blot on the morality of the valley, yet as I portray it in the book, the politics are somewhat ambiguous, just as they are in real life. When I started to write the book, I was gung ho to expose the redneck point of view, but when I talked to people in the area, I realized that it wasn't as simple as that. There was provocation: it served the Communist cause better to have blacks and women beaten and bloodied than it did to have a peaceful concert. On the other hand, the local people were blindly intolerant."

The structure of *World's End* gave Boyle even more problems than its politics. "My first two novels came from fixed stories," he comments. "*Budding Prospects* was the fictional account of a Northern Californian pot plantation that had been started by two friends of mine, and *Water Music,* the story of Mungo Park's adventures in Africa, which, even though it contained several stories moving concurrently, had a clear beginning and end. In *World's End,* I wanted to see if I could immerse myself in the subject and have a story work organically out of my reading in the history of the valley. So it was much more difficult to get it going and to keep it going."

World's End alternates between the story of the 17th-century Dutch and Indian families, told in a linear fashion, and the account of their descendants, set in the late 1960s but involving long flashbacks to the '20s and '30s. (A helpful list of characters and their time frames prefaces the book.) "I worked on it as it reads, from start to finish, and it just about tore the lining right out of my brain," Boyle laughs. "But in looking back, it was a happy experiment; I think it came together. One of the most interesting things about the writing talent is that it contains some magical power of synthesis—I don't know where it comes from. But you can take disparate elements—a theme, a character—and set them in action and somehow, if you're a good writer, you tap some unconscious level of the mind that enables it to come together. I wondered if this would work over the course of a novel as big and complex as *World's End,* and it did, although it just about killed me."

Clearly, the novel demonstrates the qualities that reviewers have praised in Boyle's other books: the humor—black as it often is; the richness of language—Boyle often nudges the reader toward a dictionary; the rhythm of his sentences—he reads aloud to his wife in an effort to find "the beat, the music of the words"; and certainly the sense of time and place—Boyle likes to mine history for ideas and characters.

"As a kid I had no notion of the history and tradition of the Hudson River Valley," Boyle admits. "Then eight or nine years ago I began to reread Washington Irving and to absorb the legends and myths surrounding the area. The whole experience brewed up some pretty potent material. In 1983 I spent four months there, working mainly at the Peekskill library and going to all the historic sites and homes."

All the place names in the book are authentic except for Peterskill, a name Boyle invented for Peekskill. "My editor, Amanda

Vaill, asked me why I did that; I told her that it was my way of letting the reader know that this is fiction. It's important that the reader understands that.

"You see, historical novelists have a bad name," Boyle continues, the words coming unhesitatingly in his direct, assured manner. "Many of them have no sense of story; they might as well be writing a historical account. That's not my approach. In *Water Music* and *World's End*, as well as in my short stories that are historically based, I like to use history as part of the myth that informs what we are now, rather than reproducing factually what might have happened. I do the research and I think I know the history, but what I want to end up with is a story that uses the history, the characters and the place as elements in a satisfactory, artistic whole. Gore Vidal and other writers like to stick close to the facts; I'm more concerned with how the facts become fictional in the memories of people."

The "facts" of the 1960s, and that decade's political attitudes and sense of history were for Boyle at that time filtered through a restive and somewhat lawless nature, one more concerned with the immediate sensations of drugs and rock 'n' roll than with anything cerebral. Saxophone in hand, Boyle sought respectability for his musical bent by enrolling at SUNY Potsdam. By his junior year he had discovered that he had neither the discipline nor the talent to perform at a top level. He drifted into a class in creative writing and wrote a play in the absurdist mode that won the acclaim of his instructor and classmates. After graduation Boyle taught English in a delinquent-ridden high school in Peekskill. He also slipped back into "a bad scene," as he describes it—a drug culture lethal enough to cause the deaths of several of his friends. Boyle had continued with his writing—he'd had a short story published in the *North American Review*—and it was that story that opened up an academic door for him, to the Iowa Writer's Workshop.

"The sole criterion for admittance to the workshop is the work itself; they didn't look at my grades, which were so bad I couldn't have gotten into graduate school," Boyle says. While enrolled in the workshop, however, he began to accumulate credits that would eventually admit him to the University of Iowa's Ph.D program. Having completed his doctorate, he came to California to accept the teaching position at USC, where the publication of four books in seven years has earned him tenure. The "wild and woolly days," as he calls them, behind him, Boyle—with his wife Karen and their children Kerrie, Milo and Spencer—has settled into a quieter routine. He writes each morning from nine until one and teaches classes two afternoons a week.

For the past year he has been writing short stories, reverting to a cycle that has worked well for him, the short fiction coming as a relief from the exhausting work of a novel. "Many novelists don't feel comfortable writing short stories, but I began as a story writer and I'm committed to them."

Boyle spent the summer in Ireland, working rather than resting. "It rained constantly; I wrote stories as I've never written them before." The best of those tales will find their way into what will be Boyle's third collection, after *Descent of Man* and *Greasy Lake*.

Boyle is devoting his attention now to what he sees as his breakthrough book. He didn't write it with that larger public in mind; the difference, he feels, lies in Viking's handling of the book. And that brings up some old resentments. "With my last two books, I felt that Viking wasn't behind me and I had to fight them. All publishers program how a book is going to do based on how much they paid for it. They make marketing decisions separate from the editorial. With the good reviews I've gotten, plus the strong cult following I've had, that [discrepancy] rather upset me. But we've worked it out since then. They gave me what I want and that makes me happy. See, that's what compromise is all about—getting what you want," Boyle laughs.

Some of the questions he'll have to parry on tour will no doubt have to do with his given name. "I think I'll change it to T. C. Boyle, so I won't have to deal with that," he comments, only half seriously. "In the beginning I used it to attract attention."

In any event, *World's End* carries his full middle name, and after the tours are over and people have had a chance to read and evaluate the book, he hopes that "T. Coraghessan Boyle" will be something more than an attention-getter. If his expectations come to pass, it will be eagerly recognized by the reading public.

WILLIAM BRISICK

ANITA BROOKNER

Anita brookner's first four novels charted, exquisitely and elegantly, the lives of "unclaimed" women and the social and personal ramifications of the solitary life. Her novel *Family and Friends* marks a departure for her and arguably surpasses even its predecessor, *Hotel du Lac,* which won England's most prestigious literary award, the Booker Prize, and was a bestseller here. Worked on a larger canvas, *Family and Friends* chronicles the lives of an "unbending matriarch" and her four children, of European descent but living in England. Like its antecedents, this novel examines seriously and wittily the tension between inner passions and outer conduct. As always, the surface of the writing is beautifully clear and transparent, its knowledge of human behavior profound.

Brookner is as elegant and precise as her novels. Attractive and articulate, she greets us warmly in her New York hotel room and orders tea to sip while we talk. Brookner was born and raised in London of Polish parents. "My mother was born in England, my father in Poland, so in a sense I'm an immigrant's child. I'm a sort of Jewish exile, but I have this straightforward English public school upbringing, and the two sides war with each other for supremacy from time to time."

Brookner studied history at Kings College, London, then took a Ph.D. in art history at London's Courtauld Institute of Art, where she now teaches. Her specialty is the period from 1750 to 1848, which includes neoclassicism and the romantic movement—"of very great interest to me, because it's to do with modes of

66

behavior as much as ways of seeing things." She has published books on the artists Greuze, David and Watteau.

Why did she turn to writing novels? "It was most undramatic," Brookner says. "I had a long summer vacation in which nothing seemed to be happening, and I could have got very sorry for myself and miserable, but it seemed such a waste of time to do that, and I'd always got a lot of nourishment from fiction. I wondered— it just occurred to me to see whether I could do it. I didn't think I could. I just wrote a page, the first page, and nobody seemed to think it was wrong. An angel with a flaming sword didn't appear and say, 'You shouldn't be doing this.' So I wrote another page, and another, and at the end of the summer, I had a story. That's all I wanted to do—tell a story." The book was accepted by Liz Calder at Jonathan Cape, and came out as *A Start in Life* in England and as *The Debut* in America.

Brookner wrote mostly in her apartment. "When I got tired of sitting in my flat, I walked to my office. I just carried on, and it was fine—a lot of interruptions, people came in, people went out, there were cups of coffee, and it was a most agreeable way to spend the summer." That was in 1980. Happily for her growing number of readers, Brookner has done the same each summer since.

Brookner's ties to literature have been central to her life. "I got so much information from fiction about human behavior and oddness of character and varieties of motive—things I could never have picked up from my friends or my parents or my family because on the whole, in society, people dissimulate, are really quite dishonest about what they're doing. People are also fairly dishonest about their failures, I think. But in fiction, it all comes through.

"Fiction is the great repository of the moral sense. The wicked get punished. I was brought up on the works of Dickens, which my father fed me from the age of seven. So I grew up with a terrific sense of justice. But I didn't find it in the world—I only found it in fiction. I found it in Dickens, and in Henry James, and I'm quite content to claim these two great men as my mentors."

Behavior is indeed one of Brookner's primary concerns. "It's form and style and standards of behavior that are going to save us all. Once we abandon any kind of obligation to behave well or to present ourselves in a good light, then I think it's the jungle."

Brookner writes, too, about the inner landscapes of women. "I know about women," she says. "I know about their inner lives. I hate the way that certain women get ahead. I'm interested in the reasons for failure. It looks very small the way I write it, but it can concern everybody—everybody is, I should think, beset by worries about how to live their lives properly and yet how to achieve some satisfaction out of them. It's the conflict between the moral sense and the desire to win."

We protest that Brookner's books aren't at all small. She replies, "I think they just set out to tell a little story, set a little moral puzzle, and they really don't aim at anything more than that. If they have reverberations, I'm delighted because a certain amount of thought has gone into them. I'd like some to come out. But they don't aim very high. I couldn't. I would be pretentious if I thought I was doing anything more important than writing love stories. They still need writing. I'm not apologetic."

Is love, indeed her subject, as some reviewers have suggested? "I think that, and something more," Brookner agrees. "How to achieve love, how to be worthy of love, how to conduct love. These are serious matters. It is a messy business. The rules are really crude. The rules are: Who dares, wins. This is bad news for people who don't dare and who see others win. That's the central problem, I think. I think it's the matter nobody gets completely right.

"There are two kinds of love," she goes on. "There's the one impossible love that really takes up all your dreams and all your longings and all your imaginings, and that rarely resolves itself into anything practical. The love you settle for may be simply a form of friendship in which there's no fear, no dread, no anxiety, and you're very wise if you do settle for that, except that the true romantic never can. Romantic love is a terrible thing. It can make you commit follies. It is a form of madness, I think, and the people who are never visited by it are extraordinarily lucky. I don't think it's got anything to be said in its favor. Except it does sweep you up to a very exalted level of feeling. That may be valuable in itself. But it's also very punishing. I think it's more creative than the other kind. It *enables* you in an extraordinary way. It gives you powers that you didn't know you had, because it's being at an extreme pitch of something or other. You discover yourself."

Another of the themes that run through Brookner's work is the humiliations that lie in wait for the unclaimed woman. "This is a painful subject which it doesn't do to discuss," she says, "because—in England—if you talk about it, it is assumed that (a) you are humiliated, and (b) you are unclaimed. And tremendous shame still attaches to these two conditions. I suppose I was brought up among the sort of self-important woman who had a husband as one has an alibi, and if you don't have that sort of alibi, you're quite at a loss in the company of women. There is a stigma attached to being unmarried, still. In certain very traditional quarters, like my family, yes, it's a stigma. And you're a failure if you haven't brought if off. But I think that mentality, underneath a very urbane surface, still obtains."

Asked how her novels differ from the less literary romances which sell so well, she replies, "The interesting thing is that women still want to read these romances. I think they read them for consolation. They want to know that it can work out in the end, and it can come out right. My books differ in the sense that they're more realistic—things *don't* work out. They're more fragmented. There is no safe conclusion. They've been called very depressing. But anyone who has had unhappy experiences won't find them depressing. It's very unrealistic to find them depressing. Life is depressing if you're frightened of it. The thing is not to be too frightened.

"In England, they say, 'Why do you write such depressing books? You poor thing, if that's all you've got to write about.' [The English] are a high-spirited and ungracious people. Foreigners always saw them like that in the 19th century. They haven't changed. And I speak as a semi-outsider."

Brookner says emphatically she doesn't feel like an Englishwoman. "I feel more at home in Paris. I lived there for three years. I blended in there. It's got a large expatriate community. The French don't ask you what your background is all the time. They seem content to take you at face value. The English want to know immediately—antecedents, money, the lot. They want to place you in classes.

"I have thought about leaving England, but I am a recluse. It doesn't really matter where I live, because I'm indoors most of the time, I like solitary street walks in cities—yes, I love that. I doubt if I shall ever transplant. I might move to the country—that's all I'll do."

Asked the often-posed question of whether or not her novels are autobiographical, Brookner replies, "It sounds disingenuous to say this, but when I've written a novel, it's gone, it's left me, it's somebody else's. I never reread them. I can't remember the names of the characters. It's largely a sort of unconscious process. Having said that, I must admit that if it's an unconscious process, then a lot of me must be in them. Yes—aspirations, longings, desires. Sadnesses, too. I don't think I give hostages to fortune in admitting that much.

"I think I'm only writing for one person. If I get a secret reader somewhere, I feel rewarded. I don't think in terms of numbers. Certain women have taken fright at reading about despair and have hastened to dissociate themselves. That makes *me* despair, frankly. The dishonesty involved in that is really too shattering for me to contemplate. It has not said much for women. My women friends have been quite cruel in some instances. I'm thinking of specific instances, obviously, but on the whole, men have been much more open and welcoming. They're not frightened, you see. They needn't identify. [They feel] quite safe, and quite touched.

"Women are not automatically good to women. There's a great pecking order there which is sort of undisclosed. And they don't want to be left behind in the race."

Brookner has, of course, won England's biggest book race. Asked how winning the Booker affected her, she gives an unexpected answer: "It's made me awfully sleepy, to tell you the truth. I've had to write a lot of letters and give a lot of interviews and carry on with my daily work as well. I seem to have been slightly knocked out by it, but it's been great fun. And a wonderful surprise. More or less undeserved, I think, but that's the nicest kind. Many people thought [J. G.] Ballard's *Empire of the Sun* should have won. And, being British, went on saying this 'til about last week. It's a very good book.

"The interesting thing about this year's Booker Prize—and I can speak about this quite dispassionately—is that in recent years the prize has gone to a very masculine type of novel. And there seems to have been a slight reaction against that tradition. I say 'a slight reaction' advisedly, because it is felt, I think, subliminally, that the big money should be on the male yarn and should stay there. But I think there's room for another kind of novel."

Where did Brookner's new novel come from? "It was an accident," Brookner tells us. "Somebody showed me a wedding photograph in which my grandmother was standing rather regally. I didn't know who the other people were. But it was such a potent image that I took off from there, literally from the photograph. I wrote the story of my family, my mother, her sisters, her brothers. Of course, I made it up as I went along. But it helped having known them.

"What was liberating about it was the amount of affection that came through, because I had been constantly at odds with my very high-spirited family to whom I appeared sort of lazy and quiet and disappointing—nose in a book and not getting anywhere. They became characters in their own right, which it wasn't possible to see them as when I was connected with them, when they were alive. They made too many demands of me for me to see them clearly. But writing about them in this way does seem to have resolved anything left lying around. When I was writing it, I would walk into a room and almost see my mother there. They were very present; they were ghosts. I rarely think of them now."

Brookner wrote her novel in only three months, an amazingly short period for so refined a work. "I couldn't get it down fast enough," she says. "I only work half the day. It's really tiring, writing a novel. It requires an enormous amount of energy. It's like writing examination papers every day until you've finished."

For Brookner, the first draft is essentially the only draft. "It's just lucky that it comes out that way," she says modestly, but the truth is that *all* her novels have "come out that way." She says she is "entirely dependent on nudges from the unconscious, or little incidents. I never decide to write a book. It somehow happens. I don't know how the thing is going to end." She is hard into another book this summer, yet she worries each time. "I hope I can do it again. If it didn't happen again, I should feel absolutely incapacitated."

AMANDA SMITH

71

FREDERICK BUSCH

FREDERICK BUSCH WRITES fiction in a barn built for sheep in the small upstate New York town of Sherburne. Visible in the distance is Cooperstown, with the Baseball Hall of Fame he loves. A few hundred yards from his study is the renovated farmhouse he shares with his wife, Judy, and their two sons; the kitchen is toasty from a wood-burning stove. It's clear, crisp and cold outside on the late January day on which we speak with Busch, a man of moderate height and immodest heft, about his novel *Invisible Mending,*

At the age of 42, Fred Busch, with five previously published novels and three collections of stories, has an enviable reputation for the sensitivity he brings to his characters, a striking ability to assume a wide range of fictional personas, and elegant prose. *Invisible Mending*, which shares the virtues of its predecessors, also charts what is for Busch hitherto unexplored territory: his Jewishness. As it begins, Zimmer, a Jew separated from his non-Jewish wife and their young son, hears the voice of an old girlfriend, Rhona Glinsky, calling to him on a Manhattan street. He flashes back on their relationship—especially their relentless pursuit of a supposed Nazi war criminal.

Why this subject now? we ask Busch. "I don't know," he admits. "I was not raised in any particularly Jewish way, though I had the awareness I was Jewish. It was hard to grow up in the '40s and '50s and '60s and *not* know you were a Jew; periodically, people might beat you up to remind you. I guess when people hit their 40s they think about things they've not thought about

72

before. I think it was the overwhelming mass of books and movies about the Holocaust—one should legitimately never tire of them, and I don't mean to say I was tired of them, I was *burdened* by them. I felt there was a worship of death going on in the culture and that there was an intellectual interest and a sort of worshipful zeal in talking about dead Jews in ways that disturbed me. I wanted to see people getting on with being Jewish without worshiping death, even though they as Jews had been enslaved by death, thanks to the Nazis.

"I wrote the book in hopes that I could puzzle a way through to seeing love become stronger than history. Now that is a horrible contest for a Jew; a Jew is supposed to worship history, including the history of the murdering of the six million. So maybe I'm treacherous in this. I don't mean to be—I mean the book very respectfully, and I don't mean to tell people how to think, I don't even mean to tell *me* how to think, and I don't know what to think. But I suppose I was hoping for something as sappy and direct as the healing powers of love that would enable us to, if not defeat history, at least come to terms with it."

Busch has been writing fiction for 20 years, after giving up poetry for short stories. ("A little star poet in college," he realized he was "a bad poet because I didn't know where to end the lines on the right hand side, and found that if I didn't end the lines on purpose but just let them end arbitrarily and kept on talking, I had stories.") After graduating from Muhlenberg College, he was a Woodrow Wilson fellow at Columbia, ostensibly studying 17th-century English poetry. Most of the time, however, he cut classes, spent his fellowship money on beer and paperback books—the works of Malamud, Saroyan, Vance Bourjaily and the English author Frank Tuohy—and wrote stories. When his funds ran out and Columbia refused him more without his commitment toward a Ph.D., he left.

He married Judy, whom he had met at Muhlenberg, and the two lived in Greenwich Village and worked at a variety of jobs which included, for Busch, doing market research, writing for uninspired magazines and teaching English at Baruch College. At night, he sat in the bathroom of their one-room apartment, his typewriter on the toilet seat, himself on the edge of the bathtub, and wrote. During that period, he "got fired a good deal," because he was "cranky and selfish, confident all the while that it was a matter of minutes before people recognized that Ernest Hemingway was working on 42nd Street in this office building in his new incarnation as me. So I always felt I was too good for what I was doing, which is a terrible way to be."

Impressed by Colgate on a 1966 visit to his brother, an undergraduate there, he thought college teaching would be an improvement over the work at hand; he's been at Colgate ever since. Early on, he began to publish stories in *Transatlantic Review*, *Quarterly Review of Literature* and *New American Review*. His first novel, written at the age of 22, "was a very bad thing," and it went unpublished, as did his second. The title of that work, *Coldly by the Hand*, came from a poem by Robert Nye, who lived in London and to whom he'd written for permission. The two men became friends long distance, and when Busch sent Nye his third novel, *I Wanted a Year Without Fall*, Nye showed it to his publisher, Marion Boyars, who liked it. Boyars published *Breathing Trouble*, a book of short stories, in 1974, the year that New Directions in the U.S. published his novel *Manual Labor*. Two years later came his second American publication, *Domestic Particulars*, a cycle of stories about a single family.

The Mutual Friend, Busch's next novel, was a result of his teaching. In London with a group of Colgate students for a semester's off-campus study, he was searching for a subject when a friend suggested Dickens. Busch, no Dickens fan then, resisted, but he read him again, with growing excitement, and thought, "The man's a genius." Then he read a biography of Dickens and wondered, "How could anyone have lived with this man? So I thought I would try to answer that question." He started to write a play about Dickens, but "within a page it turned into a novel."

New Directions' James Laughlin wanted to publish *The Mutual Friend*, but told Busch that if he could get more money from "an uptown publisher," he was to take it "with his blessing." Harper & Row's Fran McCullough offered five times the advance Laughlin did, and Busch switched publishers. When Harper & Row pronounced his next book, *Hardwater Country*, "unsuitable," he went to Knopf. Then, for reasons he doesn't go into, he moved again, to Farrar, Straus, for the next two novels: *Rounds* (1979) and *Take This Man* (1981), before finally settling (he hopes) with David R. Godine, whose "witty and incredibly hardworking"

74

publicity director, David Allender, had been trying to recruit him for several years.

Busch acknowledges a major debt to Bill Goodman, his editor at Godine, for the book's present state. "Rhona Glinsky is bewitching and infuriating and funny, and she interests me. Bill agreed with me that she was wonderful, but he thought that Zimmer's wife, Lillian, was a little pallid, couldn't compete with Rhona, and if the book was to work, she would have to compete with Rhona, and that was hard to do. He talked me round into adding many, many pages about Lillian, until—I think it was his intention to make me find out who she really was that she could take a man away from a Rhona Glinsky, and I did—I found out she's wonderful. It was a wonderful tug-of-war, I think, that he led me to see."

Indeed, redemption by love is not absent from Busch's earlier books, in particular, *Take This Man*. "Boy, that was a hard book to write! It ended up with the burial by a boy and his mother of her husband and his father, and it killed me to write the end. I was horribly shaken by it. But I felt that that was a novel about a couple who had been together over so many years, driven together by circumstances and staying together because of what had begun as romantic love and ended finally as profound commitment and respect."

It's not unusual for Busch to find himself moved by his own characters, but this doesn't happen while he's creating them. "When I write, I'm the coldest-hearted bastard in the world. I make children sick, I ruin men's lives, I bully women, and I do it with an absolutely cold heart. When I write it, I don't believe it, I'm living it. I'm an actor speaking his lines except I'm also writing his lines, and I'm thinking . . . I don't know what I'm thinking. I don't think when I write, I just write. But I suspect what I'm trying to do is be as cunning as possible. Then, when I'm revising it, it shatters me, it breaks me. Then I cry."

Often Busch doesn't want to let go of his characters. *Manual Labor*, he says, "started out as a long story, and six months after I had written it I realized I had kept thinking about the characters and would have to find out what became of them. So I wrote the rest of it to find out; it grew 200 pages." Still not content, he wrote *Rounds* to follow the fortunes of some of them, and his latest novel, *Sometimes I Live in the Country,* as yet unpublished, in response to the woman Lizzie Dean, in *Rounds.*

Very recently, impressed by a TV production of *King Lear,* with its twin subjects of family life and government, Busch has found himself "attracted to the idea of attempting a novel about the larger world of public events and the smaller, common world of daily living." What's on his mind is a book dealing with, and set during, the Korean War. Already into the research, he's "even had wild thoughts" of visiting Korea. But he adds, "I hope I don't follow through—I'd much rather go to Paris!"

Writing short stories has helped him as a novelist, Busch feels, and he invokes Hemingway, who wrote short stories as a young man while working up the energy to write a novel, just as one does short sprints before running longer distances. "If you have real talent—which means that you are enough in love with the world to describe it and respond to it—then the most crucial element in your life is energy. I believe that writing is manual labor"—he points to the depression made by his thumb on the space bar of his typewriter—"but also takes psychological energy." In addition, "short stories have to be the most precise in language and form, and if you learn your lessons from them well, you can write novels with a certain justness and delicacy and aptness of language."

Before beginning to write, Busch does careful research. For *The Mutual Friend* he returned to London for a week to study a site important to Dickens. A central character in *Rounds* is Eli Silver, a pediatrician, who is based on a real-life doctor friend. To prepare for this book, Busch went on actual hospital rounds and joined Silver's prototype is his office practice for many weeks. In addition, he studied *Nelson's Pediatrics Handbook, Gray's Anatomy* and a wealth of pharmaceutical literature. He also watches and listens to workmen and tradesmen of all kinds. "I always hang around when these men come and work," says Busch. "First of all, there's so much I don't know and need to know. Also, they're smart and they do stuff that matters. I really admire that. I'm not being romantic—they do things with their hands that produce useful results and make your life happier."

Fred Busch is pleased when he can, in his writing, "expunge Busch. I get very tired of his prose, I roll around in it all the time." For this reason he's fond of the Dickens book, and even more so of *Sometimes I Live in the Country,* about a 13-year-old boy. "I've cut myself out of the book totally, and I've totally served that boy, and I'm very proud of myself."

That people remark on the harmony between the voice of a character and the time and place in which he or she belongs is to Busch somewhat remarkable, and, despite his gratitude for appreciation, worrisome. "That's our job, isn't it? My mission is to satisfy this insane need to write. But what I hope the books do, once I have satisfied my own itches and cravings, is tell wonderful stories about people who matter to readers, stories that have significance and that are useful and fun. I don't know what there is to write about if you can't write about women and children. I happen to love a number of women and children, and so I write about them perhaps with a lot of enthusiasm. But that's what you're supposed to do."

Fatherhood, says Busch, which "has profoundly, radically, permanently changed me, I hope for the better," has been important both for his subject matter—these same women and children—and for the way in which he looks at the world. "Obviously, I'm so impressed with it, I keep on writing about it. I love being a father, I love the boys I'm father to. When you have children, you are offering the world a hostage, as Hemingway said. You're so much more vulnerable to the world as a parent, just as when you become married you're that much more vulnerable. And you become more aware of it, you listen to it, you can't ignore it. As a writer, you have to pay homage to it, you write about the dirt and the earth and the stones and the water, and you have to get it right—it's more than you. That's what happens! Less and less of yourself matters, because there's more and more of *it* and them."

MIRIAM BERKLEY

JOSEPH CAMPBELL

JOSEPH CAMPBELL STARTS talking about myth even before we exit the elevator en route to his room at the Clift Hotel in San Francisco. He has just returned from the coastal town of Mendocino, three hours to the north, where he participated in an annual retreat organized by the poet Robert Bly. Campbell is brimming with enthusiasm—he walks right by his suite on the first attempt, too busy describing his recent experience to remember which corridor is which. "You know that white Masonic hall in town? With that freemason symbol, the Time and the Virgin statues on the top? The town is wonderful, and that building—marvelous!"

"Marvelous" is a word one hears frequently while listening to Campbell, this year's recipient of the National Art Club's Medal of Honor and considered by many to be the world's foremost authority on mythology. So many things seem to excite Campbell and influence his writing—art, literature, history, archaeology, linguistics, psychology, philosophy—that it's hard to keep up with him. At 81, but looking at least 15 years younger, Campbell can't stop celebrating new experiences and, yes, marveling at how they so frequently seem to have a mythic dimension. Even the necktie reflects the man and his beliefs; the pattern is undeniably Celtic, interlocking circles and snaking, connecting lines.

"Robert Bly put on such a show in this wonderful redwood forest," Campbell says. "These devotees sang choral music in four parts—I was enchanted—and as a farewell, a magician did a whole lot of tricks while reciting a poem of Goethe's. They asked me up to help. The magician puts a thing in my hand, I open it up and there are two things, I open it up again and there are three! It was marvelous! The magic of things happening that shouldn't happen—I had a ball. The mysticism—that's basic, that's what primitive people are hearing, that's what one wants to hear. That's what you *do* hear if you'll open your ears, in the woods."

Primitive cultures are very much on Campbell's mind as he begins to talk about the second volume in his ambitious—and celebrated—*Historical Atlas of World Mythology*. The atlas has evolved into six volumes to be released over perhaps 10 years. Van der Marck published the series' first book, *The Way of the Animal Powers*, in 1983, and the second volume, *The Way of the Seeded Earth*, is nearing completion. Volumes three and four will deal with the early high civilizations up to 500 B.C., and the last two will take myth into the present.

"In *The Way of the Animal Powers*," Campbell says, "people are killing animals all the time; that's where the base of the culture rests. This second book is about women's magic—birth and nourishment. The myth shifts from the male-oriented to the gestation-oriented, and the image is of the plant world—out of death and rot comes life. The basic myth is of an earthly paradise, like the Garden of Eden, when there is no distinction between male and female, between men and animals, and no movement in time. Then a killing takes place, the bodies are planted, and out of that come the food plants. So begetting and death come together. You see in some ritual sacrifices the repetition of that original mythological act, you go back to the beginning and get a renewal of energy. And it's the same thing, really, in the Roman Catholic sacrifice of the mass."

These ideas about the development of myth are now new discoveries by Campbell, who has been fascinated by mythology ever since he saw Buffalo Bill's Indian show in Madison Square Garden as a child. He studied literature and languages as a graduate student at Columbia, but two years on scholarship in Europe showed him that America had a very limited point of view. He returned to the U.S. in 1929 (with a smuggled copy of *Ulysses* in hand) two weeks before the Wall Street crash. With no money and no job, he dropped out of Columbia and society and spent five years in Woodstock, N.Y., "reading, reading, reading, reading. I began to see that Joyce, and Mann, and Spengler, and Jung are all talking about the same thing, and then I traced those sources back. Those years were terrific. I was out in the woods—thrown out, you might say, by the collapse of society—and I found my own path."

Campbell, who now lives in Hawaii, suggested similarly independent routes to his students at Sarah Lawrence College after landing a teaching position at the experimental school in the 1930s. And the wording of his advice, as might be expected, is memorable: "Follow your bliss, I told them. Go with the thing that really talks to you." Campbell taught literature there for 38 years, always with an emphasis on mythology. "Thomas Mann and James Joyce helped me build my life and see the relevance of mythology to everyday life," he says. And his interest in Joyce led to his first book: he coauthored *A Skeleton Key to Finnegans Wake*, published in 1944. Five years later came the book for which Campbell is best known, *The Hero with a Thousand Faces*.

Campbell has written or edited more than a dozen books on myth, including the four-volume Masks of God series, and has ideas, he says, for more than a dozen more. One of them is already written, a "talk book" that Van der Marck will publish this fall. Titled *The Inner Reaches of Outer Space: Metaphor as Myth and as Religion*, it delves into the nature of mythic values. Metaphors either connote or denote, Campbell says, and mankind has, unfortunately, lost much of its ability to read metaphors properly—for their connotations.

"What myths are dealing with are the powers of the psyche that are in you," he says. "If you read myth in terms of denotation rather than connotation, you get stuck with the image and lose the message. It's a little like going to a restaurant and eating the menu instead of the food." Campbell paraphrases a statement by his late friend Heinrich Zimmer: "The best things cannot be told, and the second best are misunderstood"—because the second best are metaphors for the best, and are read—actually, misread—literally.

The loss of the connotative reading, he says, "occurs with the Bible, though I'm not hitting that point too hard. This accent on historicity is quite specific to Judaism and its descendants, Christianity and Islam, taking these things so literally." Reading myths for connotation allows for symbolism, Campbell says—his arms flying and hands crashing to make his point—which has a personal relevance for the individual listener and reader. Reading for connotation remains alive primarily in the gnostic traditions of Judaism and Christianity, he says, "with the god being inside instead of out there—and that's blasphemy in the mainstream of these religions. The notion that God is a fact . . . he *can't* be a fact, he's a metaphor!"

Without the metaphorical dimension to myth, Campbell says, "you lose the radiance. The clergy today, instead of talking about the radiance of the symbols, are telling you whether to vote for atom bombs. And the artists are doing the same thing—the whole mythic dimension is wiped out, it's short-circuited into ethics." And ethics, he says, "is exactly what cuts you short"—making rules for other people to follow, rather than letting them find their own paths. "It's a very different thing in Buddhism, where the third temptation of the Buddha was social duty. With Buddhism, the consciousness is in everyone: the Buddha becomes an example because he realized his consciousness."

Campbell believes that myth, properly handled within societies, "is not to control nature, but to put society in accord with nature." He points to the civil war in Beirut: " 'The three great religions of the world,' Judaism, Christianity and Islam, and they can't even live in the same town. And they're the same religion, just in three different inflections, and they can't even read their own metaphors! One group calls God Yahweh, another God the Father, another Allah, and so we go to war! I think the world's insane—at least the people who are running the world."

The problem today, Campbell argues, is that most of our myths are out of date. "Myths do not export very well, either through time or through space," he says. "They grow up in a certain environment, and now these circles have collided and fallen apart. A myth has to work the way a picture works: either you say, 'Aha!' or somebody has to explain it to you. And if it has to be explained to you, it's not working." What the world needs, he says, is "a modern, planetary myth, not one of this group or that group." In Joyce, Campbell says, "You've got the modern mythographer; he's affirmative of man even where he stinks—and he does, by God."

The modern myth, Campbell says, "has to do with machines, air shots, the size of the universe, it's got to deal with what we're living with." That's one reason Campbell found himself enamoured of George Lucas's *Star Wars*, which Lucas says was inspired by Campbell's *The Hero with a Thousand Faces*. "*Star Wars* deals with the essential problem," Campbell says: "Is the machine going to control humanity, or is the machine going to serve humanity? Darth Vader is a man taken over by a machine, he becomes a machine, and the state itself is a machine. There is no humanity in the state. What runs the world is economics and politics, and they have nothing to do with the spiritual life. So we are left with this void. It's the job of the artist to create these new myths. Myths come from the artists."

And that is one reason Campbell became so enthusiastic about doing a well-illustrated book on myth. "Myth is expression, not just reading," he says. But there are logistical problems. "The reader has to see the picture and say, 'Aha!', so the reference has got to be right there, the picture and text need to be on the same page. I just can't tell you what agony it is getting the illustrations into the book, though I love working with them." *Animal Powers* went through four designers, Campbell says, and he is not looking forward to the design process with *Seeded Earth*—which was actually ready four years ago when the designer died unexpectedly. Campbell subsequently had to rework the book, he says, because "You leave this stuff around and it blooms, like those Japanese knots of paper you drop in tea that open up into flowers."

Campbell's many projects may seem ambitious for an octogenarian, but he is not daunted in the least. He recently bought a computer to write on, even though he has never learned to type, and is frequently jetting hither and yon to give lectures and seminars, or perhaps to accompany his wife of 47 years, choreographer Jean Erdman, on one of her professional trips. "When you're my age," Campbell says, "death is no problem. . . . It's the experience of death that I regard as the beginning of mythic thinking—the actual seeing of someone dead who was alive and talking to you yesterday—dead, cold, beginning to rot. Where did the life go? That's the beginning of myth."

For his own self, Campbell volunteers, "I feel a little like Woody Allen when he said, 'I'm not afraid to die—I just don't want to be there when it happens.' But that's not the death problem, that's the *dying* problem. The mystical problem is what you identify yourself with—your consciousness, or your body, which is a vehicle of consciousness. There comes a time, and I think it comes naturally in people as they reach later ages, of shifting the identification from the vehicle to the consciousness. You begin to see the body as a frail vehicle, you think of all it's missing. Once you've got that idea, you can drop off the vehicle; the consciousness isn't worried." And neither is Campbell himself, who seems prepared to go on forever.

CHRIS GOODRICH

RAYMOND CARVER

DURING RAYMOND CARVER'S 25-year writing career, he's been alternately honored and maligned for the careful, sparely written, usually bleak stories about working class life with which he first came to national attention. Many of those stories were published in two books, *Will You Please Be Quiet, Please* (McGraw-Hill, 1976) and *What We Talk About When We Talk About Love* (Knopf, 1981). In recent years, however, Carver's fiction has been swerving in new directions as the writer has added some glimmerings of hope to his steely-eyed examinations of contemporary angst, as in the stories of *Cathedral*. Since 1982, Carver has also returned to his first love, poetry. He's published two well-received collections of poems, *Where Water Comes Together with Other Water* and *Ultramarine*.

With *Where I'm Calling From: New and Selected Stories*, issued by Atlantic Monthly Press, most of what Carver hopes are his "most durable" stories from the first three collections are gathered under one cover. Five newer, previously uncollected tales close out the book. The stories are selected, rather than collected, so he could leave out "some of the stories, which I just don't like and would never write again," Carver explains.

When *PW* visits Carver in his Port Angeles, Wash., living room, the writer seems alert yet relaxed. He's a bulky man who moves slowly and carefully, and the eyes behind his tinted glasses are serious, a little shy, but immensely kind. His breathing is somewhat labored, the legacy of an operation for cancer last October that took two-thirds of one lung, but he speaks clearly and is rarely at a loss for words. Occasionally he folds his hands in front of his mouth while considering a question—particularly if the question touches on how the treatment he's undergoing for a new tumor is affecting his life and writing—but he doesn't hedge his answers. Spending half of each week in Seattle for radiation therapy has greatly disrupted his life, Carver admits, but, "God willing, when all this mess is over with, I'll have my mornings clear and be able to get back into the swing of things. Things are sort of up in the air right now. It's hard to get focused in this interregnum."

The first hardcover copies of *Where I'm Calling From* are expected from Atlantic Monthly Press any minute, but the books don't arrive, much to Carver's disappointment. Late in the day, when Gary Fisketjon, the Press's editorial director, calls to get his author's reaction to the books, Carver is able to air his feelings in a friendly yet definite manner. "He and I go back a long way," Carver says of Fisketjon. Fisketjon describes himself as a Carver fan since the mid-1970s, who while "working up the food chain" to a top editorial position at Random House was instrumental in arranging for the allied paperback house, Vintage Books, to reprint *What We Talk About, Cathedral* and *Fires,* a collection of Carver essays, poems and stories first issued by Capra Press. Random House also published Carver's two recent poetry collections in hardcover. When Fisketjon moved to Atlantic Monthly in 1986, Carver followed him.

Carver was born in Clatskanie, Ore., 49 years ago and grew up in nearby Yakima, Wash. His father was an alcoholic sawmill worker, and his mother worked off and on as a waitress and a clerk. Carver married, had two children and began to hold a series of low-paying jobs before he was 20 years old.

He started writing poetry and fiction at 17 or 18, and "I got serious about it in my very early 20s," he says, although he ever made a conscious decision to become a writer. The decision "was sort of made for me. I liked to read, and I simply wanted to make my own stories," he says, Eventually he attended Chico State College in California, where he studied fiction with John Gardner, the late novelist, essayist and teacher, before going on to earn a degree at Humboldt State College. He won a Stegner fellowship to Stanford to study fiction, and later attended the Iowa Writers Workshop for one year.

Poverty cut short his stay at Iowa. But soon Carver began publishing his stories and poems in both small magazines and larger publications such as *Esquire*. He began teaching writing at universities around the country, and finally became a literature and creative writing professor at Syracuse University.

"I never figured I'd make a living writing short stories," Carver says. "How far in this world are you going to get writing short stories? I never had stars in my eyes, I never had the big-score mentality." He was "very startled" when he became well-known, Carver says, and fame "never ceases to amaze me. And that's not false modesty, either. I'm pleased and happy with the way things have turned out. But I was surprised."

One big surprise came in 1983, when Carver was given a Mildred and Harold Strauss Living Award by the American Academy and Institute of Arts and Letters, which gave him $35,000 a year for five years. With the Strauss fellowship, Carver said good-bye to his Syracuse teaching job and moved to Port Angeles, where his current mate and fellow writer Tess Gallagher has deep roots. While on the fellowship, Carver wrote many poems, some essays and a few new stories. He edited *Best American Short Stories 1986* (Houghton Mifflin) and he co-edited *American Short Story Masterpieces* (Delacorte, 1987) with Tom Jenks.

Recently the Strauss fellowship ended, and Carver has been asked back by Syracuse, but "with any luck I won't have to teach," he says. "The books have been translated into a lot of languages, so there is income that comes in from Japan and Holland and England and other places. I'm also counting on income from the books I'm going to write. I recently signed a three-book contract with Atlantic Monthly Press for a book of poems, a book of stories, and the third book will be either a novel or a memoir. Maybe I'll write the memoir. Tell all," he says, laughing quietly.

"I've never made a commitment like this before now. I've been offered contracts before for books of stories or novels, but when I wasn't writing stories and had no intentions of writing a novel, I shied away from signing a contract or taking money. Now I want to become more organized, and I can see my way clear," Carver says. "I know I'm going to continue to write. It gives me a good feeling, it gives me a sense of security, that I kind of know what I'll be doing the next few years."

Much of the new poetry book is already written, Carver says, and "I can feel the stirring now of wanting to write stories, but I'm going to finish the poems first. Poems seem like a great blessing, a mystery to me; I can't account for where they come from. When I'm writing poems, I don't know if I'll ever write a short story again, I feel incapable of it, because the poetry is so much with me." His agent of the last seven years, Amanda Urban of International Creative Management, "won't say much, but she'd much prefer I'd be writing fiction. But she knows it keeps me happy to write poetry," says Carver, who adds that Urban is "aces, she's the best. She's well-respected, and she's a straight-shooter, and I like her a lot personally."

Carver's poetry often draws on the real events of his life, on memories of his father, on fishing and hunting trips, and on his relationships with Gallagher, his two children and others. He says that "I'm much more vulnerable in the poems than in the stories, I can be much more intimate in the poems than in the stories." Yet, as fond as he is of writing verse, if he had to choose between writing in one genre or the other, "it would be hard, but I guess I would come down on the side of the stories," Carver says. "I just don't think I could give up the fiction."

Carver's stories also draw on his life, but while real incidents or people may spark the tales, much more is invented than in the poetry. For instance, in one of the newer tales, "Boxes," a man tries to balance his own needs, those of a mother who's losing touch with reality and those of a new lover. The mother character, Carver says, is "not really my mother, but there are certain characteristics I guess the character shares with my mother. I'm not writing autobiography, but there are certain reference points, real lines and real ropes that are going out from the story to the real world."

While many of Carver's earlier stories drew on his memories of his impoverished boyhood and difficult early adult life and first marriage, "that doesn't happen so much any more," he says. "Most of these stories now, they're taking place right now. The stories are changing. They've experienced a real sea change, for which I'm grateful." One of the new stories, "Errand," is an imaginative re-creation of events that took place around the death of Chekhov, one of Carver's literary idols.

Carver's decade-long relationship with Gallagher, a well-known poet, fiction writer and essayist, has influenced some of the changes in his fiction, Carver says. Gallagher's example also helped him return to poetry and begin writing essays. The relationship has made Carver happier. "It's healthy, it's a good thing, I can't imagine living with somebody who's not a writer," he says. "You share a set of common goals and assumptions, you understand each other's need for privacy and solitude." Carver and Gallagher read and critique all of each other's work. Gallagher is a "very tough" critic, Carver says. "She cuts me no slack at all, and that's the best way." Gallagher has her own house, a few minutes away from Carver's, so the writers can separate for work and get together for company.

While he initially settled in Port Angeles (where Gallagher was born) because his partner is happiest there, Carver says he's become fond of the town. Yet, he adds, because Port Angeles is out of the mainstream, "if I didn't have the writing, I couldn't live here. I'm just not hung up on a pretty place to live, the mountains and water. I'd be gone in a flash if I didn't have any writing." Several times a year he does leave Port Angeles, to spend time in New York or travel overseas.

Often called a "minimalist" writer in the past, Carver has never been fond of that term, which he says "seems to be going away. I think there's enough different kinds of stories so I won't be hammered with that hammer again. I've been hammered by the right-wing critics because they say I'm 'putting America in a bad light. Foreigners are getting a false impression of America.' But how can you say that about a story like 'Boxes'? There's nothing political about that story, [the protagonist] losing his mother to madness. Or a story like 'Errand.' Chekhov said you don't have to solve a problem in a story, you just have to present a problem accurately."

If a label is going to be put on him, Carver adds, he'd prefer that of writer. "I can't think of anything else I'd rather be called than a writer, unless it's a poet. Short-story writer, poet, occasional essayist."

PENELOPE MOFFET

SANDRA CISNEROS

Taped to her word processor is a prayer card to San Judas, a gift from a Mexico City cabdriver. Her two indispensable literary sources are mail-order catalogues and the San Antonio (Tex.) phone book. She lights candles and reads the *Popul Vuh* before sitting down to write long into the night, becoming so immersed in her characters that she dreams their dialogue: once she awoke momentarily convinced she was Inés, bride of the Mexican revolutionary Emiliano Zapata.

Such identification with her characters and her culture is altogether natural for Sandra Cisneros, a writer who has always found her literary voice in the real voices of her people, her immediate family and the extended *famiulis* of Latino society.

"I'm trying to write the stories that haven't been written. I feel like a cartographer; I'm determined to fill a literary void," Cisneros says. With the Random House publication of her new collection of stories, *Woman Hollering Creek*, and the simultaneous reissuing of her earlier collection of short fiction, *The House on Mango Street*, in a Vintage edition, Cisneros finds herself in a position to chart those barrio ditches and borderland arroyos that have not appeared on most copies of the American literary map but which, nonetheless, also flow into the "mainstream."

The 36-year-old daughter of a Mexican father and a Chicana mother, Cisneros is well aware of the additional pressure to succeed with this pair of books that represent the opportunity for a wider readership, not only for herself but for scores of other Latina and Latino writers right behind the door that she is cracking open.

"One of the most frightening pressures I faced as I wrote this book was the fear that I would blow it," Cisneros says, sweeping a lock of her closely cropped black hair from her forehead as she sips a midmorning cup of coffee. "I kept asking myself, What have I taken on here? That's why I was so obsessed with getting everybody's stories out. I didn't have the luxury of doing my own."

Coupled with that "responsibility to do a collective good job," is Cisneros's anxiety about how her work will be perceived by the general reading public. Universal as her themes are, Cisneros knows her characters live in an America very different from that of her potential readers. From her friend Lucy, "who smells like corn," to Salvador, whose essence resides "inside that wrinkled shirt, inside the throat that must clear itself and apologize each time it speaks," Cisneros's literary landscape teems with characters who live, love and laugh in the flowing cadences of the Spanish language.

Yet, unlike her character Salvador, Cisneros offers no apologies when she speaks. Energetic and abounding with *gusto*—only the Spanish word will do to describe her engaging humor—Cisneros relishes the opportunity to startle the jaded reader and poetically unravel stereotypes, especially those that relate to Latinas.

"I'm the mouse who puts a thorn in the lion's paw," she says, with an arch smile reminiscent of the red-lipped *sonrisa* on the cover of *My Wicked Wicked Ways* (The Woman Press, 1987), a collection of poetry celebrating the "bad girl" with her "lopsided symmetry of sin/and virtue."

"An unlucky fate is mine/to be born woman in a family of men," Cisneros writes in one of her "wicked" poems, yet it is that very "fate" that laid the groundwork for the literary career of this writer, whose name derives from the Spanish word for "swan."

Born in Chicago in 1954, Cisneros grew up in a family of six brothers and a father, or "seven fathers," as she puts it. She recalls spending much of her early childhood moving from place to place. Because her paternal grandmother was so attached to her favorite son, the Cisneros family returned to Mexico City "like the tides."

"The moving back and forth, the new schools, were very upsetting to me as a child. They caused me to be very introverted and shy. I do not remember making friends easily, and I was terribly self-conscious due to the cruelty of the nuns, who were majestic at making one feel little. Because we moved so much, and always in neighborhoods that appeared like France after World War II—empty lots and burned-out buildings—I retreated inside myself."

It was that "retreat" that transformed Cisneros into an observer, a role she feels she still plays today. "When I'm washing sheets at the laundromat, people still see me as just a girl. I take advantage of that idea. The little voice I used to hate I now see as an asset. It helps me get past the guards."

Among the first "guards" that Cisneros sneaked past were the literary sentinels at the University of Iowa's Writer's Workshop, which she attended in the late '70s. Her "breakthrough" occurred during a seminar discussion of archetypal memories in Bachelard's *Poetics of Space*. As her classmates spoke about the house of the imagination, the attics, stairways and cellars of childhood, Cisneros felt foreign and out of place.

"Everyone seemed to have some communal knowledge which I did not have—and then I realized that the metaphor of *house* was totally wrong for me. Suddenly I was homeless. There were no attics and cellars and crannies. I had no such house in my memories. As a child I had read of such things in books, and my family had promised such a house, but the best they could do was offer the miserable bungalow I was embarrassed with all my life. This caused me to question myself, to become defensive. What did I, Sandra Cisneros, know? What *could* I know? My classmates were from the best schools in the country. They had been bred as fine hothouse flowers. I was a yellow weed among the city's cracks.

"It was not until this moment when I separated myself, when I considered myself truly distinct, that my writing acquired a voice. I knew I was a Mexican woman, but I didn't think it had anything to do with why I felt so much imbalance in my life, whereas it had everything to do with it! My race, my gender, my class! That's when I decided I would write about something my classmates couldn't write about."

Thus it was that *The House on Mango Street* was born and Cisneros discovered what she terms her "first love," a fascination with speech and voices. Writing in the voice of the adolescent Esperanza, Cisneros created a series of interlocking stories, alternately classified as a novel and as a collection of prose poems because of the vivid and poignant nature of the language. Since its first publication in 1984 by Arte Público Press, *Mango Street* has sold some 30,000 copies. The book is used in classes from junior high school through graduate school in subjects ranging from Chicano studies to psychology to culture, ideas and values at Stanford University, where it has been adopted as part of the "new curriculum."

Mango Street was also the catalyst that drew Cisneros to her literary agent or, to be more accurate, that led Susan Bergholz to Cisneros. Bergholz was so moved after reading the book that she did something she had never done before: she set out to track down the writer. "It was a delightful chase," Bergholz recalls, in spite of the fact that it took some three to four years to accomplish.

Ironically, even while Bergholz was enlisting the aid of Richard Bray of Guild Books to contact Cisneros, the writer was going through what she calls the worst year of her life, 1987. She had spent the previous year in Texas through the auspices of a Dobie-Paisano fellowship. Though the experience had convinced her to make Texas her permanent home, the writer found herself unable to make a living once the fellowship expired.

While her boyfriend waited tables, Cisneros handed out fliers in local supermarkets and laundromats, trying to scrape together enough students to teach a private writing workshop. At last, she was forced to leave her newly adopted home, her confidence shaken and her outlook on life darkened.

The depression she sank into followed her to California, where she accepted a guest lectureship at California State University in Chico. "I thought I couldn't teach. I found myself becoming suicidal. Richard Bray had told me Susan was looking for me, but I was drowning, beyond help. I had the number for months, but I didn't call. It was frightening because it was such a calm depression."

An NEA fellowship in fiction revitalized Cisneros and helped her get on her feet again, both financially and spiritually. Finally calling that Manhattan phone number stuffed in her pocket, Cisneros sent Bergholz a small group of new stories. With only 39 pages in hand, Bergholz sold *Woman Hollering Creek* to Joni Evans and Erroll McDonald at Random House/Vintage; Julie Grau became the book's enthusiastic editor.

Then, of course, the real work began for Cisneros, whose previous output had been about one story every six months. "There's nothing like a deadline to teach you discipline, especially when you've already spent your advance. *Gusto* helps," Cisneros says, explaining that fear motivated her to put in eight-to-12-hour days. Though exhausting, the experience was genuinely empowering.

"Before, I'd be scratching my *nalgas*, waiting for inspiration. Now I know I can work this hard. I know I did the best I could."

That's not to say Cisneros believes she's done the best work of her career. "I'm looking forward to the books I'll write when I'm 60," she observes. She's also looking forward to the contributions other Latina and Latino writers will be making in the future. "There's a lot of good writing in the mainstream press that has nothing to say. Chicano writers have a lot to say. The influence of our two languages is profound. The Spanish language is going to contribute something very rich to American literature."

Meanwhile, this self-described "migrant professor" plans to contribute her personal and literary search for the "home in the heart," as Elenita the Witch Woman describes it in *Mango Street*. As "nobody's mother and nobody's wife," Cisneros most resembles Inés Alfaro, the powerful central character in "Eyes of Zapata," the story Cisneros considers her finest achievement.

Small, but "bigger" than the general himself, Inés is the woman warrior, the *Soldadera* who understands what the men will never comprehend, that "the wars begin here, in our hearts and in our beds." She is the *bruja*, the *nagual* who flies through the night, the fierce and tender lover who risks all, the eater of black things that make her hard and strong.

She is, in short, a symbol of the Latina herself, the Mexican woman whose story is at last being told, a story of life and blood and grief and "all the flower colors of joy." It is a story at once intimate and universal, guaranteed to shove a bittersweet thorn into the paws of literary lions everywhere.

JIM SAGEL

TOM CLANCY

Tom clancy and *PW* rendezvous at 1340 hours, roughly 40°
43' N, 74° 01' W, approximately 30 feet above sea level and mere
steps from the first booth in Costello's, a smoky, traditional restaurant and bar favored by many Manhattan journalists.

Clancy's trip to New York City from his permanent bivouac in
rural Maryland has been agonizingly slow, limited to technologi-
cally primitive vehicles—several combustion-engine, rear-wheel-
drive automobiles and one unarmored, electric-powered *civilian*
train with effective cruising speeds barely over 100 miles per hour.

Clancy is hungry (Amtrak was late), and while waiting for his
corned beef sandwich, he eagerly sips a 12-fl. oz. soft drink
cooled to about 50° F. He seems slightly ill at ease, perhaps because he is far from the disciplined, orderly military world that is
at the heart of his two works of fiction: *The Hunt for Red October,* his wildly successful first novel about the defection of a Soviet submarine crew, and *Red Storm Rising* (Putnam), an epic
work about a World War III fought with up-to-date non-nuclear
weapons on land, air and sea.

"More than anything else, I'm a technology freak," he explains.
"And the best stuff is in the military."

The fascination with high-tech gadgets began at an early age.
"I read about the space program before there was one," the 39-
year-old author says, smiling. He also dove into Samuel Eliot
Morison's many works of naval history and sea exploration. In recent years he has culled most of his knowledge of equipment and
tactics from *Armed Forces Weekly, Jane's Defence Weekly* and

various Naval Institute Press publications. (Poor eyesight kept him from serving in the military; it's one of his few regrets.) And ever since high school, he states, "I've wanted to write a novel." As an English major at Loyola University, he adds: "I wanted to see my name on a book."

These various interests and goals converged in *The Hunt for Red October*, much of which Clancy wrote during "downtime" at his family's insurance agency. (He still works there one day a week, noting, however, that "it's hard to get worked up over a homeowner's policy nowadays.") He submitted the manuscript to an editor at Naval Institute Press (affiliated with the Naval Academy), who had handled a short article by Clancy about the MX missile. Wanting simply "a professional's opinion" of the work-in-progress, Clancy had tremendous luck: Naval Institute Press had recently decided to try publishing fiction, and *The Hunt for Red October* became the press's first such work.

The submarine thriller has sold over 300,000 copies in hard-cover and two million in a Berkley paperback, leading to a three-book, $3 million hard/soft deal with Putnam and Berkley. Asked if he was surprised by the book's reception, Clancy says, "I was thunderstruck, dumbfounded, bowled over, amazed. But I wasn't surprised."

The novel proved particularly popular with men in the military, from submariners to Pentagon analysts to the Commander-in-Chief himself, who pronounced *The Hunt for Red October* "the perfect yarn." In fact, President Reagan liked the book so much that he invited Clancy (and his wife) to the Oval Office for a private meeting. Commenting on the visit, Clancy grows quiet and says solemnly, "It was a neat experience." After a pause, he returns to his usual staccato delivery: "I've met a lot of people, and all have reinforced Clancy's Law of Society—that important people don't act that way."

He prizes the entrée to his heroes in the military as well. Indeed, as he considers the changes in his life in the past two years, Clancy says, "The nicest part of it all is meeting the people in the service. The guys in uniform are like cops and firemen. They're basic, solid people, and they're in the business of risking their lives for people they don't know."

His new soldier and sailor friends have taken him under their wing and let him drive an M-1 tank and fire its gun, travel for a week at a time on American submarines (he had never been aboard a sub before *The Hunt for Red October*) and tour British Royal Navy vessels (where he met Prince Andrew). "People who fight wars are the smartest people I know. The smartest person I ever met is a submariner." He pauses and shakes his head, adding, "They're also the happiest people I know. Sometimes it's disgusting how happy they are. They all look forward to going to work because there's always a challenge."

Clancy quickly notes that the job of leading the troops is not fun and games. "One of the things I tried to bring out in *Red Storm Rising* is the pressure and responsibility of a commander. He must accomplish his mission and keep his men alive. If he screws up and kills himself, so what? If he screws up and kills 50 men. . . . " His voice trails off. Then he goes on: "It's a lot of responsibility for 20-year-old men."

Does Clancy borrow from the classic military strategists, such as von Clausewitz? He laughs dismissively. "Clausewitz is like reading Nietzsche. No, like Hegel." He notes that Viscount Montgomery, the British World War II hero of El Alamein, "couldn't finish Clausewitz, and he went on to make field marshal."

Discussing his idea of military warfare, he says, "Tactics are merely applied logic. Military operations are simple in theory, different in actuality." Then he quotes Frederick the Great, the masterful leader of Prussian armies, who said that no battle plan survives first contact with the enemy. Clancy calls this "the aphorism of military life."

Returning to the subject of the challenges faced by today's fighting men using high-tech war equipment, Clancy says, "Playing the piano is child's play compared to learning to fly a plane. It takes a year to learn what all those buttons in the cockpit are for." Moreover, while on land "you can at least see the opponent, at sea all you see is a blank ocean. Warfare is a lot more abstract in the water."

In a preface to *Red Storm Rising*, Clancy notes that he and coauthor Larry Bond (a naval analyst and professional war gamer) "took lots of information from a variety of sources and synthesized it. We tried to come up with a logical overview of where such a war would go." For example, in the novel Iceland assumes a key role in the Atlantic. After a Soviet invasion of the island, bombers are able to attack Allied convoys resupplying Europe. Clancy comments: "No one has acknowledged that Russian airplanes are a bigger threat to convoys than subs." He states that "feedback from guys in the know says we portrayed it right."

Clancy scoffs at the idea that he has carried military analysis further than the professionals in Arlington and Langley, Va. "I've spoken with lots of military types, but I'm not the guru of the Pentagon," he says. "They won't tell me sensitive information. If they did, I wouldn't use it. I leave it to the *Washington Post* to publish government secrets. The information I use is available; it's a matter of putting it together and making sense of it."

How has success changed Tom Clancy? "Having money allows me to pursue my hobby," he says. His enhanced income has also enabled him to buy a new house—"although we were going to do that. My four kids will go to college. I bought a Mercedes. And I bought a Rolex." He waves a shiny wrist over the table. "The rest of the money goes to my financial guy," he continues. "I sign stuff, but I don't know what's going on."

In a more serious tone, he says, "Success could ruin my life. For one, I don't want to get into an ego trip." He illustrates the issue by discussing his overflowing mailbox. "It's getting to the point where I need a secretary. But I have a working-class thing about that. Having a secretary would make me feel like I'd taken an importance pill, and the deadliest disease known to man is feeling important." He shrugs, then adds, "The choice is not answering the mail."

Clancy states that he's determined to remain the "nerd" he's always been. "After all," he adds with enthusiasm, "I'm in it for the fun. Writing is so much damned fun. I play God. I feel like a kid at Christmas. I make people do what I want, and I change things as I go along."

Asked about his personal tastes, he says he reads "everyone," particularly writers of science fiction and espionage and action-adventure. Two of his favorites are Fredrick Forsyth ("the best thriller writer") and British author Gerald Seymour ("I can't understand why he doesn't sell well here"). Among his literary friends and acquaintances he counts Jack Higgins and Clive Cussler.

"One of the great things about the writing fraternity is that we're not in real competition," he says. "And we all suffer from the same thing—the matter of you and the blank videoscreen."

It would seem, however, Clancy's disks are rarely empty. Already, he is working on his third novel, titled *Patriot Games*, which stars Jack Ryan, the Navy intelligence analyst who was a key character in *The Hunt for Red October*. The thriller following *Patriot Games* will also feature Ryan. And another book derived from *The Hunt for Red October*, tentatively titled *The Cardinal of the Kremlin*, is planned.

Asked for more information about *Patriot Games*, Clancy answers as though he is discussing official-eyes-only material. "It's about terrorism, and it takes place before *The Hunt for Red October*," he says quickly. "That's all I can say about it."

But he will talk more about one of his themes, his love of country. "I wish I had served in the armed forces," he says, again mentioning his bad eyes. "I don't relish the idea of being shot at, but America has been decent to all of us. Too many people think they can take without giving back. It's not right."

He praises, too, what he calls "America's fundamental vitality. This is a magic place," he states, adding that his British service friends who are posted to the U.S. say they'll "miss the enthusiasm and optimism when they get rotated back." Lest anyone be misled by his relatively sympathetic depiction of some Soviet commanders in his two novels, Clancy comments, "The people over there aren't different. People around the world are the same." He shakes his head. "But the political system is different, very different."

In moments lunch is over, and Clancy gets ready to stop by his publishers' offices before catching a late-afternoon train back to Maryland. He is cordial, but seems eager to get on his way. One senses that all in all he'd rather be aboard a sub or shooting more tank guns or puzzling over the meaning of intelligence intercepts—or at least at home writing about them.

JOHN MUTTER

ROBERT COLES

In 1960 ROBERT Coles was a young Air Force doctor stationed in Mississippi. Trained in pediatrics and child psychiatry, he was finishing his psychoanalytic education, reading Walker Percy and, as a New Englander raised in the tradition of liberal intellectualism, trying to understand the culture of the South.

"Had I not been right there," he writes in the introduction to *The Spiritual Life of Children*, the eighth and final volume of his Pulitzer Prize–winning study of children begun 30 years ago, "driving by the mobs that heckled six-year-old Ruby Bridges, a black first-grader, as she tried to attend the Frantz School, I might have pursued a different life."

Child psychiatrist, teacher at Harvard, author of more than 50 books, Coles remains best known for his investigations of children's lives and the books that witness "the attention children give to a world which at times doesn't give them credit for such attention."

The first volume in the Children of Crisis series, *A Study of Courage and Fear,* comprises extended (often over years) conversations with children and their families, black and white, who were directly involved in the desegregation process. The following, similarly structured books, containing interviews with other groups of children coping with the limitations and demands of their sociological backgrounds, are: *Migrants, Sharecroppers, Mountaineers; The South Goes North; Eskimos, Chicanos, Indians;* and *The Privileged Ones. The Spiritual Life of Children,* out from Houghton Mifflin, continues in the direction Coles headed with *The Moral Life of Children* and the *Political Life of Children* (both published in 1986).

"This is a circle, a journey," Coles says, settling into a comfortable chair in the room where he writes at the back of his sprawling yellow clapboard home in Concord, Mass. He is wiry and narrow-shouldered, with a focused, amiable presence and a raspy voice that readily erupts in a short barks of laughter. Outside wide windows, beyond the books piled on deep sills, the early morning light intensifies the mottled bark of old apple trees, the red barn, the just-turning colors of the leaves in the woods beyond.

"The five Children of Crisis volumes look at children as they are connected to historical and regional events. Then I started to become—as George Eliot said, although she used the word with some sarcasm—more *theoretical*, and shifted to children as they are defined by their moral, political and spiritual lives."

Asked what he believes he's produced in these studies, Coles pushes at his rolled-up sleeves, runs fingers through metal-gray hair and deliberates at length before answering. "I think I've spent these 30 years trying to show the importance of the kinds of observations that Freud, and especially Anna Freud and Erik Erikson, have made about the nature of childhood. I have learned that childhood is connected not only to the drama of the family but with race and class and nationality, with religious and spiritual life, with neighborhood, regional life and ethnic life, and with events that take place historically, such as racial struggle. In other words, that childhood is the mirror of the world in all of its complexity and ought not be regarded as a phenomenon occurring within one particular home setting."

While he says that he "maintains a loyalty to the psychoanalytic paradigm" in his approach, Coles's studies go against the grain of many works published by his peers in his deliberate avoidance of elaborate formulations and what he calls "overwrought generalizations." In his books, the children are their own witnesses. They describe their experiences; thoughts and expectations to Coles, who, quoting extensively, presents the speakers, their settings and ideas, and, most markedly in *The Spiritual Life of Children*, his own responses, to the reader.

"In Europe this is called phenomenological inquiry; it is a legitimate, well-respected tradition. In America, we have these absolutely dreary sociological categorizations that impose on life's complexities the most naïve kinds of structures and templates—it makes me want to yawn or vomit.

"I tell you, if I hadn't found this way of working, I might have left the whole world of psychiatry and been an English teacher, which is what I started out thinking I'd be, or in public health. It was tough. For three or four years I couldn't get grants for what I proposed to do."

Obtaining funding for this latest book was hardest of all. Writing to 15 foundations of his interest in exploring the religious experiences of children, he was turned down very quickly by all but the Ford and Lilly Foundations. "Even the Ford Foundation called it 'a further exploration of the moral life of children.' Only the Lilly Foundation was able to put it in writing: 'Spiritual and religious lives of children,' " he says.

Yet no one was more aware of the thorny, often personal difficulties and hands-off response raised by the topic than Coles himself. "We have been taught to be secular in our liberal upper-class educated culture." To some, religious belief equals neurosis, he suggests: "something for the ignorant, the masses. For someone of my background to take this seriously, to find these children who are not crazy or kooky but are leading ordinary lives and let them testify to their faith is a step, believe me."

Raised by a religious mother who took him and his brother to the Episcopalian church every Sunday and a father who waited for his family outside in the car, Coles came to this book fully aware of his own secular leanings. He admits that "at times I couldn't stand some of the sentiment and sweetness and unqualified faith that I heard from some of the kids. I badly needed the skepticism of those agnostic and atheist kids who were ready to throw cold water on the others and keep some tension going. I think that's a part of religion anyway, part of Jesus's life and the Hebrew Prophets': that struggle with doubt and misgivings and betrayal."

It's a struggle he admits to readily: "It's the story of my life, this back and forthness between faith and doubt." He touches a copy of *The Diary of a Country Priest*, one of the few volumes he keeps on his desk. "I mean, if even that priest couldn't resolve it, how could I?" He underlines the question with an eloquent shrug.

A picture of that book's author, Georges Bernanos, is hung with two dozen or so other photos on the wall behind him. The gallery includes writers James Agee, Walker Percy and Flannery O'Connor, photographers Walker Evans and Alex Harris, psychoanalysts Erik Erikson and Sigmund and Anna Freud; interspersed among them are anonymous figures of ordinary people.

Nodding toward the wall, Coles observes, "These are the people who taught me to do this work. I could have wrapped up some of my stuff as 'discoveries' or 'formulations.' The books would probably have sold better as people rushed to get answers. And I would have felt like a first-class imposter. I have to live with myself and"—he points to the pictures—"with them. They would laugh me out of the room."

The continuing reality of those figures—"my jury"—has been another life-shaping force. Profoundly influenced as an undergraduate by William Carlos Williams, he acknowledges similar debts to Dorothy Day and his time with her in the Catholic Worker movement; and to Erikson, with whom he taught at Harvard and whom he credits with encouraging him to write directly about his early encounters with children.

No less influential are the writers—he often mentions Tolstoy, George Eliot—whose works have taught him not just how to work, but how to live. "My heroes, after all, are novelists."

Not surprisingly, he's written biographies of many of those represented on the wall, including Erikson, Percy (to whom *Spiritual Life* is dedicated), Williams, Day, Simone Weil and Anna Freud, the latter due out next year. ("This will be the end of my biographies too, by the way. It's a series of circles I've completed.") He's tried his hand at children's stories too, written when his three sons—two now in medical school, one in premed—were young; written two books of poems; plus the Women in Crisis volumes with his wife, Jane; and commentary to accompany photographic studies, such as *The Last and First Eskimos*. Collections of essays focus on aspects of psychiatry, e.g., *The Mind's Fate*, or on literary topics, as in *That Red Wheelbarrow* and last year's *The Call of Stories*, in which he testifies to the centrality of fiction in his life and the lives of his Harvard students, many enrolled in his literature courses at the medical, law and business schools.

A more recent hero is Raymond Carver. He's teaching a seminar at Harvard now on Carver's fiction and the paintings of Edward Hopper, focusing on themes of isolation and alienation and the way writers and painters evoke them.

The new volume has precipitated his first book tour, which, arranged for December and January to fit around his teaching schedule and his family's vacations, will take him across the country. "For years Walker Percy, whose daughter has a bookstore in Louisiana, told me that booksellers are my intermediaries, and I owe it to them to visit their stores. I'm going to some of the places where I've worked and used the bookstores. I think this is important."

An agentless writer, Coles has been with the same editor since he began publishing. Poet and writer Peter Davison was an editor at Atlantic Monthly Press when Coles's first published article, "A Young Psychiatrist Looks at His Profession," appeared in 1959 in a special supplement to the *Atlantic Monthly* magazine. A few years later, Davison went to Atlanta and met Coles, who had begun his research with children involved in desegregation. Atlantic Monthly then gave Coles a grant from funds supplied to promising new writers, and in 1967 published the first Children of Crisis book. In the mid-'80s, when Atlantic Monthly moved to New York, Davison elected to stay in Boston, bringing Coles with him to Houghton Mifflin.

With a laugh, Coles makes it clear that *The Spiritual Life of Children* is "*my* final volume—I have not exhausted the topic. If I were to do another project like this it would be five or six years working with kids, and I just decided no. Maybe it's a mid-life or old-age crisis, but this is very demanding work, to go from home to home, school to school, neighborhood to neighborhood, church to church. I'm blessed so far with good health but I'm not sure I could sustain the effort."

Instead, the 61-year-old Coles has leapfrogged to the other end of life. "I'm interested in the elderly who manage to make a go of it, living with resiliency and independence no matter how old and sick and troubled. I've begun having some conversations with elderly people around Boston and in the South," he says.

The modest appraisal implied in "having some conversations" is typical of Coles's assessment of his work. Calling his 30 years' effort "a kind of documentary child psychiatry" and "a series of photos, a series of stories," he describes himself, with some ironic discomfort, as a "novelist manqué. That's about the best definition there may be for me. I pick up what I think are illuminating and suggestive experiences that the children have and then share with me, which then become my experiences, which I then offer as a writer. Then you take that and it becomes part of *your* life and it helps you think and feel and see and know. I'm hoping to do as the children do, to suggest and hint and illuminate—these are the words—rather than hand down paradigms and laws.

"I don't have the novelist's gifts, but I have that set of mind—not the sociologist's—and the novelist's sensibility: to show, not to tell."

DULCY BRAINARD

PAT CONROY

Pᴀᴛ ᴄᴏɴʀᴏʏ's ʙɪɢ, two-story brick house on Peachtree Circle in Atlanta is empty when we arrive on a steamy summer morning. A couple of forlorn chairs stand in the middle of the parlor. A scattering of pencils, paper clips and empty envelopes lie about on the bare floor. The Conroys—Pat, his wife Lenore and four of their six children—are moving to Rome (Italy, not Georgia) in a few days, and the household has been dismantled.

But Conroy seems less dismayed than most people by moving day. That could be because of his mobile childhood; his father, a Marine fighter pilot whom Conroy used as the model for *The Great Santini*, was transferred to a new base every year. Or it might be because Conroy laughs so much. Easygoing and jovial at 40, he throws his head back and guffaws over a wisecrack or a funny story. He laughs even harder when the joke is on him. Or maybe his equanimity comes from knowing that his suitcase-sized novel *The Prince of Tides* is finished after six years of toil.

In no time at all, Conroy is regaling us with the story of how he became a writer. It was over 15 years ago in Beaufort, S.C., where his family finally put down roots when he was in high school. He had completed a manuscript called *The Boo*—"one of the worst-written books in the English language," Conroy swears. This vanity press debut was a homespun portrait of his friend Colonel Thomas Courvoisie (nicknamed "The Boo"—short for caribou), an assistant commandant in charge of discipline at the Citadel, Conroy's military alma mater in Charleston.

"I can't tell you how naïve I was," Conroy deadpans in the thickest Southern accent since Billy Carter's. "I went to Willie Shepherd, at the People's Bank of Beaufort, I said, 'Willie, I've written this book about the Citadel and I'd like to borrow some money to get it published.' He said, 'Sure, Bubba, how much you need?' I said, 'Fifteen hundred dollars.' So I thought I had discovered the secret of getting your books published. I said to myself, 'This is easier than I thought. I think I'll be a writer.' "

A couple of years later, Conroy had a new manuscript, but it wasn't one Willie Shepherd could finance. This one was *The Water Is Wide*, Conroy's touching, often rollicking account of the year he spent teaching underprivileged black children on Daufuskie Island, off the South Carolina coast. Too unconventional a teacher to please the creaky educational establishment, Conroy was fired and "began writing the book about an hour later."

When it was finished, someone told Conroy he needed an agent. He had never heard of such—Willie Shepherd certainly hadn't mentioned that—but someone located the name of Julian Bach, and Conroy phoned the formidable New York literary agent on a typical high-pressure day. "He was as rude as any son-of-a-bitch could possibly be on the telephone," Conroy laughs. "He would hardly listen to me without interrupting. But he heard 'black children on an island' and he snapped, 'Just send me your manuscript. I'm so tired of people like you who call me every day. I don't know why I'm talking to you. Send it up and I'll read it when I get time.' "

Even in his benighted state, Conroy knew the manuscript should be typed. But he couldn't do it. "My father wouldn't let me take a typing course in high school. He thought it was sissy. No decision of an ignorant father has ever cost a son so much money in one lifetime." Friends in Beaufort came to his aid. He gave them a chapter each; they typed all weekend and delivered the manuscript on Sunday night. "But," Conroy groans, "I had forgotten to tell them to use the same kind of paper, so there was onionskin, yellow foolscap, long sheets, short ones, some with lines—well, we put together this unbelievable looking thing and shipped it off to Julian. He read it, thinking it was the most adorable hayseed thing he'd ever seen—and he sold it.

"He called me up and said, 'Pat, Houghton Mifflin, one of the oldest publishing companies, wants to publish your book. Here's the really good part: $7500.' I said, 'Julian, I don't think Willie Shepherd down at People's Bank is going to lend me $7500.' Julian, stunned on the other end of the wire, said, 'Pat, you realize *they* pay *you* the money.' He will never let me forget it; no matter what I do, I can't convince him I'm anything but a hick. That's how I thought publishing was done."

Conroy changed from naïve to worldly overnight. Shortly after Bach accepted him as a client, the brash young writer started to wonder if he was being taken for a ride. So he wrote a no-nonsense letter: "Dear Mr. Bach, Who are you? I've never heard of you. You're an agent? What exactly do you do? Have you ever done this kind of work before?"

A long letter arrived in Conroy's mailbox a few days later. His then-wife Barbara opened it, and when Conroy came home she said, "You poor, dumb son-of-a-bitch; he just mauled you." Conroy recalls sheepishly that Bach had detailed the history of his agency and had also provided a client list. The estate of Charles Dickens was at the top. "It included John Fowles, Ted White; I felt utterly humiliated." Despite their screwball beginning, author and agent have stayed together. "We get along terrifically well," Conroy says earnestly.

He has also stayed at Houghton Mifflin. "Moving around so much as a kid damaged my soul, so now I don't want to leave a good situation. My only complaint is that I've had a different editor for every book. Nan Talese edited *The Prince of Tides*. Shannon Ravenel—she's from Charleston—did *The Water Is Wide*. Then there was Anne Barrett, who retired as soon as she finished editing *The Great Santini*. When I learned that Jonathan Galassi was to edit *The Lords of Discipline*, I asked Houghton Mifflin, 'Why are you giving me an Italian kid from Harvard when I'm a Southern guy; how did you match us up?' They explained it very well, and he did a great job. But then he went to Random House. I stay still, but editors go flying out of my life.

"I asked Nan recently if I have the reputation of being hard to work with, and she surprised my by saying yes. Everybody assumes that since my editors leave after doing one of my books, I must be a monster. But I like the fresh viewpoint an editor brings to my writing. I tell them beforehand, 'Anything that would cause people to laugh at me, or tease me in New York

City, please get rid of it.' The only thing I pray for is that I'm not made fun of."

Within his own family, it's not the derision as much as rebuke that Conroy dreads. On his mother's side, they are Scotch-Irish Southerners; on his father's, Chicago Irish. Writing to please such diverse interests would test any author, and Conroy hasn't always won their approval. After reading *The Great Santini*, his Chicago relatives were livid. According to Conroy, "My grandmother and grandfather told me they never wanted to see me or my children again. But the wounds have sort of healed now, because Dad loved the movie made from the book. He still sends out Christmas cards signed, 'The Great Santini.' "

The Bible Belt branch of the family recoils from the sex scenes and the "immodest" language in his novels. After *The Lords of Discipline* was published, Conroy's Aunt Helen telephoned him and said, "Pat, I hope someday you'll write a book a Christian can read." "How far did you get?" her nephew asked. "Page four, and I declare, I've never been so embarrassed."

Hollywood felt just the opposite. Beginning with *The Water Is Wide* (filmed as *Conrack*), moviemakers have snapped up the rights to each new Conroy book. *The Prince of Tides* is no exception. The only difference this time is that Conroy himself wrote the screenplay. "I kept noticing in the screenplays of my movies how much of my dialogue they used. I also noticed that the screenwriter was getting paid more money than I was. Before I started writing the script, I said to the producer, Andy Karsh, 'I don't want to be a pain in the *be*hind [Conroy accents the first syllable], the way other novelists are. Tell me what you want from this novel and I'll write it for you.' "

Asked why his books make such entertaining movies, Conroy says, "I always figure it's because I'm incredibly shallow. I write a straight story line, and I guess that's what they need. The dialogue also seems to be serviceable in a Hollywood way. But most important, I do the thing that Southerners do naturally—I tell stories. I always try to make sure there's a good story going on in my books."

Conroy still has the good-natured charm and ingenuous idealism of the down-home boy who wrote books about his experiences and just happened to sell them in New York and

Hollywood. In every book he fills up at least a page with acknowledgments and gratitude for the help he was given. In *The Boo* he thanked 30 people; in the new book 33, including the lawyer who got him out of jail in 1980. We ask why he was in jail; he seems such an unlikely offender. "My wife's ex-husband threw a drink in my face at a party. I chased him and turned him upside-down in some bushes. He filed assault-and-battery charges, and I went to jail. The case was dismissed, but he sued me for $75,000. My lawyer was terrific through all of that; I also thank the judge who let me off. I feel bad that I couldn't thank my next-door neighbors on both sides, but the list was already ridiculously long."

Although he has written about 50 pages of his next novel, he doesn't really know what it's about. "I've got some general ideas; you know, Southern stories you collect all your life. And I might work in some recent Atlanta stories." In the meantime, he is pulling together a collection of nonfiction pieces, including an essay about the six months he lived in Paris while finishing *The Lords of Discipline*, and another one on coming back to Atlanta after living in Rome. Conroy's nonfiction writing has often been at the behest of friends needing help. "A friend of mine was in danger of being fired from *Atlanta* magazine, so I wrote an article for him. He got fired anyway, then he went on to another magazine. Soon he needed me again, so I kept writing stuff, trying to help. Eventually I ended up with enough material for a book."

Conroy takes us on a driving tour of his part of Atlanta, pointing out the gleaming new hotels and office buildings nudging out the graceful old Southern houses. We eat lunch in a restaurant that specializes in Dixie cooking: cornpone, pot likker, hush puppies, collard greens and blackeyed peas. Then it's time for us to head for the airport.

As the plane taxis on the runway, we are perusing the copy of *The Boo* that Conroy autographed for us. The woman in the next seat peers at the book. Then she says, "That's a charming story, isn't it?" We express surprise that she has read it. "Oh yes, all three of my sons attended the Citadel, so I'm naturally very fond of Mr. Conroy's book. Has he written anything else?" We assure her that he has written several others, and that his new novel has all the makings of a bestseller. "I guess then he must be making a good living from writing books." We nod, and inform the lady that Mr. Conroy's success has enabled him to live in both Atlanta and Rome. "Oh, I think Rome is one of the nicest towns in Georgia. He must be doing well!"

SAM STAGGS

K. C. CONSTANTINE

"Are you k. c.?" we're about to ask the middle-aged man, the spitting image of Mario Balzic, standing in the lobby of Pittsburgh's William Penn Hotel, the place fixed for our assignation. Balzic, the down-to-earth police chief of Rocksburgh, Pa., a mining town on the skids, is the hero of K. C. Constantine's six superlative mysteries. The first of these were published a decade ago by Saturday Review Press. Critics liked them, the public ignored them and the books went out of print. Constantine stopped writing. Then mystery critic Robin Winks discovered an old Constantine novel in a secondhand book shop and brought it to the attention of editor Bill Goodman at David R. Godine. Godine inaugurated its detective series with a new Mario Balzic novel, *The Man Who Liked Slow Tomatoes*, issued simultaneously with a single-volume reprint of two earlier ones. Now, there's *Always a Body to Trade* and a Penguin paperback of *Slow Tomatoes*.

Meanwhile, we've got the wrong man—not surprising, considering that the pseudonymous author keeps his identity a closely guarded secret. There are not photographs of him. He's only given one interview before, long ago. His contract with Godine forbids the house ever to reveal his name. Most of his friends and relatives know nothing of his literary life. We can't come to his hometown, but must agree to nearby Pittsburgh and the anonymity of a hotel. We can't get in touch with him directly, either—it's always "We'll call you." His letters are rerouted through his publisher to camouflage their point of origin. Not even his editor has set eyes on him. But now we do, as the real K. C. Constantine steps forward, flanked by his wife.

We find him less forbidding than reputation has him. Dressed in corduroy pants, wool blazer and cap, he's short and stocky. Broad, pleasant Slavic face. He wears his 48 years amazingly well. He speaks slowly, quietly at first—his voice grows louder as he relaxes and the glasses of red wine succeed each other—his words reasoned, enthusiastic, profane (in this and in his recreational use of wine he's like Mario Balzic). And he's honest, a man who believes strongly about things and says what he believes: writing and crime in America are two subjects about which he's passionate. He's frank about everything except the facts of his life: his name, address, profession. He's not, however, a famous author writing mysteries on the side; he's neither a cop nor a criminal. He's been a laborer, U.S. Marine, ballplayer, and is proud of his blue-collar past. He loves golf.

Why all the cloak-and-dagger stuff—a publicity ploy? Not so. Constantine's reasons for maintaining anonymity are both personal and professional. When he played minor league baseball he was surrounded by admirers, women among them. He found "it got old in a real hurry. I want to mind my own business and don't want to be bugged."

If there's such a strong feeling of reality in his books, it's because they're taken from life: "Man, I love being in public places and staring off into space, pretending I'm zoned out—which doesn't take very great pretension—and just eavesdropping."

When people know you're a writer, "They want to tell you a great story, and it always starts out with, 'I know this guy who. . . .' They're talking about themselves." He experienced this when he lived in Iowa City. He attended the Iowa Writers' Workshop, a terrifying place where they played "critical karate." Turned down by the program ("My academic record was *so* bad," he says, laughing), he got in when his wife, without asking him, wrote to the workshop: "You can't do this to this guy. I don't know what he'll do." He was accepted.

Constantine took only one course at Iowa, all he could afford. "This guy told me I had a lot of work to do. Talent was one thing—talent ain't enough. What he said was, 'Yeah, you can write, but being able to write a sentence, being able to write a paragraph—they may be great and everybody says, hey, that's a great sentence—but a great sentence isn't a great story.' " This helped: "It told me I could do it."

Born during the Depression, K. C. Constantine grew up in a town like Rocksburgh—small, ethnically varied, heavily immigrant—on the Pittsburgh periphery. A sickly child, he had a lot of time on his hands and spent it with books: "Books were my friends. To this day, I know Robert E. Lee Pruitt of *From Here to Eternity* better than I know my brother." He read before he started school. He loved the Beatrix Potter stories, Mark Twain, Dickens ("The printed word got me").

Despite his love for books, Constantine dropped out of school the first time around ("I was a piss-poor student"). An English composition teacher flunked him twice, said he didn't know how to make an English sentence. For a while, in his late teens and early 20s, he got in trouble; he was jailed four times, once for as long as 21 hours ("It scared me so bad!"). The printed word, and the woman he met and later married, saved him.

In the Marines, with plenty of time on his hands again and no money, he'd have a few beers at the service club and then go to the library on the second floor, where he discovered Eric Hoffer's *A Passionate State of Mind*. It "blew my mind. Here was a guy talking about having a taste for making sentences, and I was wrestling with that idea and, at the same time, was bored crazy. Boredom is one of the greatest motivators there is," Constantine believes, and it drove him "to see if I could make a sentence."

Next time around, he did better at school—he graduated—and he got married ("the best move I ever made"). He began to write and eventually found an agent: "You can write only so long, and then it's like a professional soldier who trains and wants to fight. 'cause he wants to find out if all his training is worth it. You want to know, is somebody going to think enough of this to pay you money for it?"

Why mysteries? They sell, and, he thought, "Shit, anybody can do this." He discovered it wasn't so: "You're still talking about at least 50,000 words. Now, what are those 50,000 words going to say? Where do you begin, where do you end and how do you get there? My greatest flaw as a writer before was that I didn't know how to make a plot, and the mystery—the generic word 'mystery,' meaning whatever the hell you think it means—forced you to do something. You went from peace to violation of the peace to

113

peace again. And I found out," he says with a laugh, "it wasn't easy. That's probably what I work hardest at. Dialogue comes very easily." Ultimately he wants to write other things, among them the story of his father, an artist in wood and "a very great man."

Why a cop as central figure? From the late '60s on he heard people say, "We've got to show the youth of America what law and order really means"—and got sick of it. "I needed a place to write about, where somebody's going to say, 'Hey, this is *not* the way it works; it works like this.' "

Mario Balzic is idealized, the kind of cop Constantine would have liked around when he was a kid in trouble. Balzic carries no gun, but his ear and shoulder are always available to distressed citizens. He's lusty, likable and doesn't kowtow to bigwigs. He survives as a cop because he's smart and has a terrific record at solving crimes.

Could a cop like Balzic exist in real life? "I doubt it. I think that the first time he started talking to politicians the way Balzic does, they'd be figuring a way to find something on him to end his career." Many people who think they know about the law, says Constantine, "are almost as dumb as Strohn [the mayor in the new book]. Crimes aren't solved by great detection, but by the use of informers. Somebody always has a body to trade: 'Hey, man, I'm not doing this time; I'll tell ya why I ain't. *He* did *this*. How much do you want him?' So the police, if they're good at anything, it's cultivating snitches. That's what makes a great cop, a cop who's got the smarts enough to understand the psychology of people who want to tell you something."

Constantine's got a great deal to say about the way the law works—and should work—and he says it through Balzic. "I set as a technical goal for myself that I would never tell a story except through Balzic's eyes. I want to tell a story that will come to him, because that's the way life comes to you, and you react to it. I've cheated a couple of times. At the end of *Slow Tomatoes* I did what is called 'a third-person exterior' and said, 'Balzic learned all this.' " This, he laughs again, "was really chickenshit."

He likes *Slow Tomatoes* because he used it to "pay some psychological debts. A lot of the fun of writing fiction is that you can really get on somebody's case." As a youth, he used his fists ("It was very satisfying, also very frightening"); now he fights with his writing: "I get so carried away at times that I distort everything.

That really just screws it up." He's working on a new book, about charity rackets, but has gotten bogged down half a dozen times after about 60 pages. The problem? He's trying to nail a character he doesn't like ("I always get stuck with my emotions interfering with what I know is technically right").

Constantine envisioned 10 Mario Balzic mysteries. There's an appeal to continuing a series: "You start playing a little safe." What he'd like to do is a book "where not only does nobody get killed; nobody even gets hurt."

How have the Mario Balzic books changed? Constantine feels he's gotten better as a writer. And Balzic's "gotten more cynical, more skeptical, really pissed off at so many people taking up his time with dumb stuff." For Constantine, too, there's never enough time. He works a regular job and so can't be as much "around the people and in the places I need to be in order to do better what I want to do. At the pace I work, what I have to do to keep myself in bread and wine, I think four more books this way really's gonna drag my ass down."

What about films or TV? Rocksburgh and its people are so vivid they'd seem natural for these media. With TV, there's the problem of profanity ("People get upset about the things that rhyme with 'duck' "); as for films, there's been one (resistible) offer so far. But Constantine's interested: "God, I wish somebody'd come along and say, 'Look, I'm giving you $100,000 up front, and another $100,000 to mess around with a screenplay, and 2% of the gross.' "

MIRIAM BERKLEY

ROBERT COOVER

Wɪᴛʜ ᴊᴏʜɴ ʙᴀʀᴛʜ, William Gaddis, William Gass, John Hawkes and Thomas Pynchon, Robert Coover stands as one of our most serious and daring writers, a master of fictional forms. His work has demonstrated a fierce integrity throughout a writing career that began in 1966 with *The Origin of the Brunists* and has continued with *Pricksongs and Descants; The Universal Baseball Association Inc., J. Henry Waugh, Prop.; The Public Burning; Gerald's Party;* and the collection of interlocking short fictions: *A Night at the Movies, or You Must Remember This,* Coover's reinvention of vintage American films.

Coover greets us at his home in Providence, R.I., wearing jeans and a sweater. He is compact of stature, intense and kindly. We go off with him to a writing class at Brown University; while he tells us he teaches mainly to pay the college tuitions of his own three children, he is an impressive teacher, caring, analytical, vigilant that various pressures don't "round off the eccentric edge" of his students' work.

Back at Coover's home—a house enlivened by the vivid fabrics designed by Coover's Spanish wife, Pilar—we talk about his writing, rich with its own eccentric edges. Coover has spent many of his writing years on the Continent and in England; having recently finished another novel, *Whatever Happened to Gloomy Gus of the Chicago Bears?*—"a burlesque tale of a Richard Nixon whose life took a different turning,"—the author is heading off with his wife for a year-long stint in Europe.

116

But Coover's roots are intensely American. He was born in Charles City, Iowa, in 1932 and grew up in that "small, rural, mid-American classic town—the kind that Reagan and Eisenhower were nostalgic for," then moved to Indiana and Illinois. "Illinois was a kind of culture shock for me. I was suddenly in a coalmining community, Herrin, a violent town, quite ugly in many ways." As an adolescent working on his father's newspaper, Coover "began to deal with a feeling of alienness"—all of it eventually becoming material for his first novel.

After college, he began to do his "first serious reading" as a naval officer in the Korean War. Then as a 25-year-old civilian, he holed up in a cabin in Canada to do his first serious writing. "I found my mentor in Beckett, in the way he erased the slate, allowed everything to start over again. I saw the novel as finished, and he described how that was so and what one might do next. He also gave me a sense of writing as a true vocation, not just something that one does to earn a buck."

Coover went to graduate school at the University of Chicago, concentrating in philosophy and history. American mythology and the American fairy tale have been abiding interests. "We need myths to get by," Coover has said. "We need story; otherwise the tremendous randomness of experience overwhelms us. Story is what penetrates."

A Night at the Movies deals with the movies as both reflector and creator of myth and fairy tale. "It's one of the books most dear to my heart," he tells us, "which probably means nobody will like it." Coover reconjures and reexamines some of our favorite myths, movies and movie stars, themselves now mythic figures. There are, among other things, the western fairy tale (a take on the *High Noon* shootout); tributes to the comedy of Keaton and Chaplin; a new look at Astaire in *Top Hat* ("I always found it startling to see this sweet man pull out a machine gun and mow guys down"); and a stunningly erotic rewrite of the ending of *Casablanca*, the book's "romance." Coover's own brand of magic realism permeates the book; as in his other writing, reality is a slippery business.

"I am both curious about and disturbed by the way our minds are warped by filmic syntax. Flicking channels on a TV is an amazing thing: I can sit and watch people dying and situation comedy at the same time. I'm concerned about that—concerned, interested, fascinated, not of a single mind about it.

"My central concern has to do with structure and form, and the way it reflects the world. I probably am less interested in some things that people do care about deeply—personal relationships and how one survives in a meaningless world. My concerns really focus on the larger issues, larger in spatial terms, not necessarily in terms of profundity or importance—of societies and how their art forms reflect their structures, how myths grow and shape action and how action converts myth into something new, how one simply rises up and says 'no' to it and destroys it. Because I'm always thinking about form, structure, and how it relates to social forms and structures, everything I write has a kind of organic interconnectedness. When I write about the world, I'm writing about my own writing."

Coover says he does his best writing between midnight and five a.m. He rewrites "*In-tensely*. Everything. From the first line, I'm revising. It's a kind of dialogue with the self, and I find this dialogue to be more interesting on the computer than it ever was before; it exists as a reality. I work from a kind of structural overview, so I usually get hasty at some point, impatient to fill up the structure that I have in mind so that I know what it's going to come to in the end." Sometimes, he tells us, he skips whole chapters along the way, sections he confronts in the rewrite. Coover tells us about getting stuck in the middle of *Gerald's Party*, a book done more line by line than with an overview. In the catastrophic party Gerald gives, dead bodies are strewn about the house, sexuality and scatology, theatrics and satire abound. ("The large metaphors that sustain novels," Coover reminds us, "contain the world: religion, sex, family, history, politics.") "There was a moment in that story when I thought, 'Jeeze, I'll never get out of here.' It was a funny moment, a wonderful moment, actually. I was absolutely at a loss, and Gerald was expressing this: 'What's going to happen next?' *I* didn't even know. My wife walks up and says, 'I think I'll put coffee on.' That's the line I was looking for."

Coover is often referred to as an experimentalist, and we ask him why he chooses experimentalism over any other kind of writing he might do. He tells us our question "has a variety of answers, depending on my mood, and one of them is that I'm not experimental. I am really, truly, in pursuit of the mainstream. Much of what we think of as mainstream writing is not. It's a collapse into the banality of something that was important a century ago, but isn't important now. Our minds are set for it—it doesn't seem strange to us, and we can read it without difficulty. But this is not the mainstream. The mainstream keeps moving, and the mainstream, after all, isn't preexistent: it cuts its own path, and only appears to be mainstream later on when we look back and set the route it took. The route it's been taking, since World War II, has been what people have called experimental, but what is only quite, quite traditional, quite *profoundly* traditional.

"The most traditional writers we have amongst us are people like Hawkes, Barth, and Pynchon. Most of what we call experimental actually has been precisely traditional in the sense that it's gone back to old forms to find its new form—to folk tale, to all the pre-Cervantean, prenovelistic narrative possibilities. It's not going back in a regressive way, not to imitate something. It's a rediscovery of that total range of what narrative can be, what it is when we put words and sentences in a sequential order to create a sense of movement—narrative always moves.

"But at the same time, I also think of myself as experimental in the sense that I want to test out these forms all the time. I'm willing to take a lot of chances. It's not paradoxical, and it isn't contradictory either; it's the two sides of the same coin."

Coover's work is often erotic and deliberately, disturbingly so. "Art finds its metaphors in the most vulnerable areas of human outreach. We are never more susceptible to our own doubts and fears and anxieties than when we are approaching the erotic, and so are most apt—and part of art is process—to discover something going that route and not being too programmatic and selfcensoring. Understanding the self, approaching 'the other' by way of its erotic impulses is a way of understanding everything— philosophy, religion, history. But this is what has led me over and over to the use of it. And I think it's led *all* artists to it, in a way that is ultimately not prurient but revelatory."

Coover has had what he characterizes as "a tough publishing career. I have just broken the record with my newest publisher and editor, Joni Evans and Allen Peacock [at Linden Press, Simon & Schuster, who bought out a two-book option from Viking

119

for *Gerald's Party* and a book of short stories]. This must be my 10th or 11th book, but it's the first one that will be published without first having been rejected. Rejections usually have come about for reasons not to do with the quality of the text, but to do with political questions, obscenity questions sometimes. And questions of, Will it make money? That's always been a problem, but now giants have swallowed up minnows in the business, at tremendous expense of variety and competition."

Coover's *The Public Burning*— his satirical "political romance," whose most prominent characters are Nixon and Julius and Ethel Rosenberg—was considered so potentially libelous that it was read first not by the editors in various publishing houses, but by the houses' lawyers. Eventually, Richard Seaver, then at Viking, saw it through. "Seaver is to me one of the most unique figures in the whole industry, a man with great integrity. He was so involved in the text and so loving of it, supportive and loyal to it; and editorial sessions with him, important in that book, were always extremely amicable and even insightful for me. I was listening to a man whose mind I really respect, especially as it approached the text. If it hadn't been for him, I don't think the book would have appeared. He was the last straw; Georges Borchardt—more than an agent, a close and important friend— and I had been through the whole industry by this time. And the lawyer fought me tooth and nail. The first thing he wanted to do was take out all living persons, for starters. 'I don't mean to eviscerate your text,' he would say, 'but. . . .' He threatened me with legal suits if I didn't follow his instructions. I had to get my own lawyer. I didn't make any money on the book; I spent it all on legal fees, just getting the book into print.

"My whole objective became to have copies existent, like having a birth certificate. The day I knew that happened, I was finished with it. I disappeared about that time, went off to Barcelona, near my wife's hometown. We settled in and began new work, watched a lot of soccer, went to the Barcelona Football Club games. It was the wonderful season of the return of Catalan autonomy, and we were there for the Diada, the first national holiday celebrated since before Franco. We had a joyous autumn, and I didn't pay any attention to what was going on back in New York. It was over. I had a copy of the book. That was all I wanted.

"If I were *not* having difficulties, I'd have some doubts about myself. My next book's probably going to be conventional by historical standards, probably a sequel to the first novel—not because I'm regressing, but because I feel everything's possible and I want to do all these things and I feel pretty sure of myself— happy as to my current publishing situation, and in many ways I'm grateful. A recent review of one of my books was kind of horrific. It described my work as some sort of terrorist mission— and yet I *like* it, I like to be controversial in that way. It's proof I'm alive."

AMANDA SMITH

HARRY CREWS

HARRY CREWS MIGHT be a character he created for one of his own bizarrely offbeat—and lately upbeat—novels. The piercing scowl that stares out of his photograph quickly gives way to self-deprecating asides and a good-old-boy friendliness that is a legacy of his hardscrabble boyhood in South Georgia. And his body, though centered by the beginning of a middle-age paunch, moves with the athletic grace of someone who has known his way around a gym all his life.

"I go crazy—I'm prone to craziness anyway—if I don't get into a gym every day and break a sweat," says the 52-year-old writer as he eases his pickup into traffic and heads for lunch at Gainesville, Florida's Lafitte's, a favorite restaurant. He orders a large seafood salad, Cajun-spiced soup and freshly baked bread, and exclaims when it arrives: "Man, this stuff is good! Your body will applaud you for eating it."

He is feeling the pangs, however, of what he describes as "a postpartum depression" after finishing *The Knockout Artist*, a novel about boxing with a New Orleans setting. "Harry Crews has been into some heavy scenes in his time," he candidly admits. "Alcohol, drugs, fighting, you name it—I can't deny it. As I told my son"—a 23-year-old rock musician in Gainesville—"if you're going to lie, and I hope you won't, make sure you don't lie to yourself."

Nevertheless, he is wary of those who want to talk about things other than his work as a writer. A recent interviewer, Crews notes, "went out of her way" to write about his apartment and what he had in his refrigerator. "That didn't make sense to me. I've written some journalism"—his *Esquire, Playboy* and other magazine pieces from the '70s are collected in *Blood and Grits,* one of his three books in Harper's Perennial Library paperback line—"and I know how that works. But if you're going to write about a writer, stick close to his writing. That's the only claim the public has on him."

Still, he understands the curiosity of those motivated to poke into his personal life. "That's human nature, the way people are. You see, people—even those you think of as friends, probably even your wife, lover, whatever—are all waiting to see you knock yourself out," he contends, an echo of dialogue spoken by one of the central characters in his new novel. "Yes, I know that seems a dreadful view of things. But if that weren't true, when someone is standing on an eighth-floor ledge in New York waiting to jump, there wouldn't be a crowd down on the street shouting, 'Jump, Jump!' "

So is that what the hard-edged novel is really about? "Well, that and other things," he replies. A happy ending (for a Crews novel) balances the kinkiness, betrayals and other sordidness. But a good book, he thinks, is more than what is seen on the surface. "If a book of mine doesn't work for me as a metaphor, it just doesn't work."

Crew's first novel, published in 1968, was *The Gospel Singer,* which Harper reissued in the Perennial Library. Nine other novels followed, a lineup still characterized by critic Jean Stafford's general description of his early novels: "Macabre and slapstick, howlingly funny and sad as a zoo," she once wrote in the *New York Times Book Review.* "Harry Crews' work is southern Gothic at its best, a Hieronymus Bosch landscape in Dixie. . . ."

"It's fair to say my books are kind of strange," Crews surmises. "I've been asked a million times why that is so, and I still don't know the answer." He recalls that when his ex-wife read the manuscript for *This Thing Don't Lead to Heaven,* his third novel, she asked, "You don't intend, do you, to make a career of midgets?" There had been midgets in the first two novels, and there was another in the next one. "But until she asked me that, it had not occurred to me that I was writing about very different people."

His focus on the grotesque, Crews is certain, is the reason a wider reading public, as well as some reviewers and editors, has not taken to his books. "I'm asked, 'Why don't you write different books than you write?' Well, I don't know that either," he says, indicating that it is an unfair question. He writes about his native South Georgia as well as North Florida—*The Knockout Artist* is the first of his novels to be set elsewhere—because, he explains, "in the words of Flannery O'Connor, I know 'the manners of my people.' " Asking a writer to be different than he is, he adds, "is like asking him to have different colored eyes. You don't chose your eyes, they're just there."

Whatever might be said about him, Crews thinks no one can legitimately find fault with his storytelling, a skill he learned from the works of Graham Greene. "I have always been a indefatigable reader, even as a child. There weren't many books to find in Macon County when I was growing up there, but I found more when I went to Jacksonville to school. Then in the Marine Corps"—he served a three-year tour of duty—"they could get me almost anything I asked for." But those by Greene had the greatest impact. "When you look at my books, including the nonfiction, you will find, I think, a clean narrative line. If I've got a strong suit, that's it. I learned hot to do that from him."

Greene's influence, nevertheless, was secondary to that of Andrew Lytle, a leader in the Agrarian movement that shaped much of the South's intellectual life in the '30s and '40s and a pivotal figure to two generations of writers. A teacher of writing at the University of Florida when Crews enrolled there on the GI Bill after leaving the Marines, Lytle gave the young man his first look at what it meant to be a writer.

Crews always knew he would be a writer. In *A Childhood: The Biography of a Place*, an elegiac memoir of his Macon County years, he told of writing a novel "with a soft pencil on lined paper," an outgrowth, he believes, of the stories he used to make up from the pictures in the Sears, Roebuck catalogue. Later, he wrote stories in the Marines, and when he entered the university he did so thinking he would have four years—at Uncle Sam's expense—to write. But he didn't expect to find what Lytle made it possible for him to see.

"I've always wanted to dedicate a book to Mr. Lytle," he says, "but I never thought I had written one on which he would want to see his name. He was—still is—a man who asked for perfection; he knew he wouldn't find it, but that's what he wanted.

Most of what I wrote for him, I don't think he read. He would hand it back and say, 'Burn it, son, burn it. Fire is a great refiner.' And I did. But he gave me a mark to reach for, he showed me the discipline of writing, and he held up examples of good writing, such as *Madame Bovary*, which I read every year, sometimes twice. Mr. Lytle showed me what writing ought to be."

When Crews returned to the University of Florida to teach in 1968, after losing a son in a drowning accident and teaching elsewhere in the state, he adopted a method perhaps patterned on Lytle's example. In *Florida Frenzy*, an anthology of some of his nonfiction and fiction about the state published by the University Presses of Florida, he wrote in an essay titled "Teaching and Writing at the University" that he refrained "from writing anything on a story a student gives me. Rather, we have a conference about it. I try to do for him what a good editor would do if he had a good editor. . . . A good editor always leaves the writer with the feeling that what he wants to do, has been trying to do, is possible. A teacher of writing has the same responsibility."

But teaching, for Crews, will soon be in his past. Other than concentrating on his writing, however, he has not set long-range plans. "I don't know where I'm going—maybe back to New Orleans. I like it there. I think it's probably the closest you can get to being outside the country while being inside it." The apartment in which Eugene Talmadge Biggs, the Georgia-born boxer in *The Knockout Artist*, lives facing Audubon Park, Crews points out, was the one he lived in before moving to a friend's cabin in northern Louisiana to finish the novel.

He will remain in Gainesville, though, until he completes a play commissioned by the Humana Foundation for the nationally regarded Actors Theatre of Louisville's Annual Festival of New American Plays next spring. Also, he is three chapters into a novel he calls *Body*. "It's about the world of female bodybuilding," is the way he summarily describes it, a world he learned about the way he learned about boxing—from firsthand experience.

"I couldn't have written *The Knockout Artist* if I hadn't spent much of my youth in a fight gymnasium," Crews explains, adding that his brother was a professional boxer. Similarly, he soaked up the atmosphere of women's bodybuilding when he trained "a great lady"—Maggie Powell, now the director of the Wellness Center at the West Jefferson Hospital in suburban New

Orleans—for the Ms. Gainesville and Southeastern United States contests, both of which she won.

Crews does not have the same kind of admiration for bodybuilding, however, that he has for boxing. "I particularly love fighting," he exclaims. "I know some people say it's a stupid, ugly, bloody sport. Well, I don't defend it; neither does Joyce Carol Oates. I just say I have done it, I love the people who do it, and I love to watch it."

Searching for a deeper relationship between his writing and boxing/bodybuilding, he says, "What it comes down to is my respect for discipline, for wanting something bad enough that you push everything aside to achieve it. See, I hate people who just talk a good game. I hate people who just talk about my sport, which, in this instance, is writing," a phobia that may have developed during the six years in the '70s, when he was on the faculty of the Bread Loaf Writers Conference. "You hear writers say, 'I'm gone write this, I'm gone write that.' Don't tell me what you're 'gone write,' man! Go ahead and write it, and then we'll talk about it."

Following his own advice, Crews says he is at his typewriter every morning by 4:00 or 4:30 a.m., and that he tries to get 500 "good words" out during the next three hours or so. But sometimes he has to start over again the next day, he continues, and sometimes he may go for a long time when nothing satisfactory comes, a reference, maybe, to the nine years that lapsed between *A Childhood* and *All We Need of Hell*.

One of the lessons he learned from Lytle was that persistence is a cardinal virtue for a writer, a precept Crews tested in getting his first novel published. He sent it to "everyone in the world," he says, before he found a publisher (Morrow) and an agent (John Hawkins). In looking back, he thinks that what that teacher was saying was, in effect, " 'Here is this thing, son, you ought to be. I won't love you if you're not. But if you fail, just keep trying.' And that's what I'm doing, just trying."

BOB SUMMER

PETE DEXTER

GENERALLY SPEAKING, THERE are two things authors of serious fiction can do to support their frequently unremunerative habit: they can teach, or they can write screenplays. Although he's only been screenwriting for two years—since he was invited to provide a script for his National Book Award–winning third novel, *Paris Trout*—Pete Dexter has always belonged, in philosophical terms, to the second group. He'd much rather be writing than talking about it. He's wary of analyzing his work and hostile to sweeping generalizations about the writing process.

With his spare, scrappy physique and a face that looks as though it had run into a few fists in its time, Dexter just isn't someone you can imagine standing in front of a class outlining the symbolism of *Adam Bede*. In fact, he cheerfully admits that during the eight years it took him to get a B.A. from the University of South Dakota ("I quit school when it got cold, and it got cold every year in South Dakota"), he resorted to Cliff's Notes more often than he did to the classics.

This determinedly unanalytic attitude came under some pressure during the writing of *Brotherly Love* (Random House). The novel originally began with a scene that now opens part five, more than halfway through the finished book, in which protagonist Pete Flood jumps off a roof. "I realized about a month into this thing that this wasn't where it was actually going to start," Dexter remembers, in a voice whose cadences frequently shift to take on the different rhythms of the many regions he's lived in. "But instead of turning around and starting from scratch, I

127

finished the book and then went back and tried to put the front end on it. Don't ever do that!

"When you're writing in a chronological order, or the natural order of the novel, you don't have to stop and ask if you're bullshitting yourself, because it's true and it's coming the way it's supposed to come. This way, because you know you've got to end up at this part of the book on that rooftop, you start wondering if you're stacking the deck. That bothered me through the whole thing. When I look at the finished product, my sense is that it's all right, but I did a lot more analysis and second-guessing, and I don't like any of that. I just like to do it and get things done."

Dexter got a lot done in the 1980s, when he finally gave up the roistering lifestyle that had made him a legend at the *Philadelphia Daily News*, where he worked for more than a decade. His first novel, an atmospheric portrait of a tough Philadelphia neighborhood called *God's Pocket*, was published in 1984. *Deadwood*, an idiosyncratic retelling of the story of Wild Bill Hickok's last year, followed in 1986. Bob Loomis at Random House steadfastly continued to edit and publish Dexter despite minimal sales for both titles; his faith was justified with *Paris Trout*, a chilling tale of a psychotic businessman and the havoc he wreaks in a small Southern town.

Paris Trout got good reviews, but those were nothing new for Dexter; more to the point, the National Book Award pushed hardcover sales above 30,000 copies and brought him wider recognition. Screenwriting offers made it possible to give up magazine articles, which he found time-consuming and usually frustrating, and concentrate on his fiction, though he continues to write a weekly column for the *Sacramento Bee*. He now lives, with his wife and daughter, on an island north of Seattle in Washington State.

As Dexter likes to tell it, his career happened more or less by accident. At 48, his drinking days long behind him, he still spins the kind of elaborate, half-funny, half-scary stories you're most likely to hear when perched on a bar stool. How much is fact, how much fiction? Let's just say that the facts are artfully arranged to present his listener with a persona that's been years in the making.

Take his account of how he got into the newspaper business. "I was in Fort Lauderdale, and I was walking home from one of those boring, miserable jobs—I've had a lot of them. It was real hot, and I was tired, and I walked by the *Sun-Sentinel* office. It was air-conditioned, and not only was everybody in there obviously almost freezing to death, but everybody looked good, everybody looked happy. So I went in and filled out an application, and they hired me as a reporter. It was a little easier in those days; that was before Woodward and Bernstein made this job desirable."

Dexter enjoys portraying himself as "a pain in the ass as a reporter; I didn't want to do anything they wanted me to do." Moving to the *Philadelphia Daily News*, his freewheeling ways put him in such conflict with the city editor that once at a party Dexter "threatened to drown the guy in his own chili." Fortunately for all concerned, a new editor arrived at the paper and figured out that Dexter would be better off as a columnist.

The format suited him perfectly. Even now, he spends only about three hours a day working on a novel, because "I go 800 or 900 words and that's it—column length, and then it gets stale." The personal nature of a column, "just writing whatever's on your mind that day," is something he values. "Because the deadline's two hours away, not two years, you can't hide who you are, which I think maybe you can a little bit in a novel. It's a shock when you see that some very good novelists can really be small, jealous and ungracious—and some of them write pretty well; it's got nothing to do with it. But I promise you, if they were newspaper columnists and had to put it out there three or four times a week for five years, they might still have the job at the end of five years, but people would understand what they were; there'd be no sense of, God, what a wonderful person."

One of Dexter's columns led to the incident, fictionalized in *God's Pocket*, that prompted the writer to give up drinking and get serious with his life. "I wrote a column on drugs, and some guy called up and said he was going to break my legs. In those days, if you said that to me—maybe you will and maybe you won't, but we'll find out." Those words come out with a trace of the macho swagger Dexter cloaked himself in back then, but he adds with a grin, "I think maybe that night I was trying to explore just how stupid it was possible for a human being to be!" Not content with getting himself beaten up once by the angry reader and his buddies ("I got banged up a little bit, lost some teeth, but I wasn't really hurt"), Dexter came back into the same rough part of town later that night, bringing a heavyweight boxer freind with him, and confronted his assailants in a bar.

"I just wanted them to understand that even though they're sitting there in this neighborhood with a real bad reputation, in the heart of their own place in their own social system, they weren't safe either. Nobody was going to get hurt, but then some little fat guy ran out the side door, and that place just filled up with people with baseball bats and crowbars."

"My back and my leg were broken, my head was banged enough so that it changed the way. . . . At any rate, among the things it did was change the way things tasted; I can't to this day put alcohol in my mouth. I wasn't drinking that night, but I used to drink a lot. I was never somebody who sat in bars drinking alone or because I was sad; I just did it for fun—fun stuff happened in bars. But it's no fun to sit there drinking Cokes, and if you don't hang out anymore, you've got an extra 30 hours a week. I'd written a lot of magazine pieces, and some agent in New York [Dexter prefers not to mention the agent's name] called and said he had people who would be interested if I wrote a book. So I sat down and wrote God's Pocket, and he sold it to Bob Loomis at Random House, who's been my editor ever since."

Although he's now represented by a new agent, Esther Newberg, Dexter never felt the impulse to change publishers or editors, "Bob and I have a real good working relationship. When I give him the book, he'll call, and we'll have a two-hour conversation where he'll go through all his notes. I pay a lot of attention to the things he says, because he doesn't say many things; when he does, he has my complete attention. Then I fix it and send it to him. The end process doesn't take long; from the time Bob gets to it to the time it's finished is maybe a month. I don't do a lot of rewriting."

He has also been pleased with Random House's handling of his books, despite the disappointing sales of God's Pocket and Deadwood. "When you've spent a year of your life writing a book and fewer people read it than read a newspaper column, it can be discouraging. But I never felt it was Random House's fault. They're very careful—I don't think there's a typo in any of my books—they spend a lot of time doing cover after cover, and there's a kind of gentlemanliness about the place."

130

It's a bit surprising to hear Dexter describe gentlemanliness as a quality he values, for it's clear from his account of his life that he's familiar at first hand with the violence and anger that permeate his novels. When asked why he has been preoccupied in his writing with the darker side of human nature, however, he's reluctant to make any general pronouncements.

"It's always gets me when you see an interview with somebody who writes a book, who will step out there and presume to say anything about what authors are like or what the creative process is. That stuff really—what a bunch of bullshit! 'Cause if you're honest at all, you know that it changes from day to day. The whole process of categorizing it or explaining it—even if it exists and even if you could say things about it that are true for you . . . why talk about how you do it instead of doing it?"

"I can take a sentence apart and tell you why I did it; obviously that's the key to the whole thing, being able to write a sentence, and I've got a sense of what my sentences ought to do." He gives as an example his use of the present tense in the narrative of *Brotherly Love:* "Present tense gives you a different beat and rhythm than the past tense, and there was something about this story that needed that. I could never tell you *why* something like that happens, but your ear tells you that it needs to be a little quicker. I saw right away that I liked it better."

"It's that other thing, this attitude that writers are a special class, that really alienates me. They talk about stress and how awful it is to be a writer—you hear that talk a lot in Hollywood. It's just so removed from real work. I've seen people that actually worked themselves to death, people my age who are all used up from manual labor. I've had some of those jobs—luckily I didn't keep them too long—but I know what they are, and writing is nothing like it. Sitting in a hotel room being interviewed is really not awful. I had to catch a flight out of L.A. at 11 the night before last, so I walk around a little bit goofy for a couple of days 'cause I'm sleepy, but that is nothing like unloading trucks for 20 years."

It's not that Dexter is anti-literature, it's just that he hates pretentiousness—and a lot of things seem pretentious to someone who fancies himself as an ordinary guy who just happens to write. He speaks enthusiastically of contemporaries like Don De-Lillo and Padgett Powell, whose most recent collection of short stories "made me want to start my next novel and made me want

131

to write better." When he can be persuaded to say a few words about his own working process, he describes it as a great adventure: "There's no clear way marked through—there's no way through at all. You just start out at one place, and the only thing you know about the other end is that it's a long way away." He makes the act of writing sound hard, dangerous and exciting—maybe almost as much fun as hanging around in bars used to be.

WENDY SMITH

DON DeLILLO

THE FIRST QUESTION is, of course, where was he on November 22, 1963? "I was in a restaurant on the West Side of Manhattan having lunch with a couple of friends," says Don DeLillo, whose ninth novel, *Libra*, published by Viking is about Lee Harvey Oswald and the Kennedy assassination. "I heard just after lunch, in a bank, that the president had been shot in Dallas. I heard a bank teller tell another customer, and that was the beginning of it. I think that event had been in the back of my mind for a long time, and of course it's moved to the front of my mind since then."

DeLillo says he is "a little less reluctant" to talk about this book than he has been about his eight previous novels, which include the American Book Award-winning *White Noise*, because *Libra* "is grounded in history and because most of the key characters are real people and they come to us with an actual history, which isn't true of the invented characters in my other novels. My characters tend not to have histories, they exist within the margins of the page. It makes for difficult conversation about a book. All you can really do is point back to the writing itself or to the character himself. In this case, however, people like Oswald, Ruby, Marina and Marguerite Oswald and other characters provide a little more solid fare for conversation. And of course the other thing," DeLillo adds, "is that it was such a tragic and crucial event, and I feel a certain responsibility to discuss what led me to write about it and what I tried to put into it."

About himself, the 51-year-old DeLillo prefers not to say much. Perhaps fortuitously for a writer who wants to maintain his privacy, an unfinished front stoop has temporarily barred entrance to his Bronxville home. In the empty office of a Viking editor, DeLillo sips Coke from a sweating aluminum can. The white noise of a small fan's whir is noticeable only during DeLillo's frequent pauses; in conversation, as in his novels, he is careful of making language convey his exact meaning. "Whatever there is about language in my work," he says at one point, "it's simply there, it simply seeps out of me and onto the page."

DeLillo says: "I hear voices, I look at faces, and that's always the starting point, and what flows from that, just flows. . . . *Libra* started with my interest in Oswald, what he looked like, what he sounded like, where he lived. I went to Dallas and Fort Worth and New Orleans just to look at houses he lived in. I found it to be a haunting experience. You get a sense of someone who's lived on the margins of history all his life. Sadness and regret and tragedy kind of hovers over these places. . . .

"Eventually," DeLillo says, "a novel begins to reveal its themes to me, but I might be working on it for a year and a half before I have the faintest idea what it eventually is going to be about, what will sail above the heads of the characters, so to speak. . . . That's how I operate as a writer. In *Libra*, something literally sails above the heads of the characters—the U2 plane, which became a kind of unifying element in the book, and which is a sort of token of mystery—and I think can even be seen as part of that current of elements that stand outside history, which David Ferrie [a character in the novel] refers to when he reveals that what the conspirators want from Oswald is his participation in an assassination, and he talks about the force of things outside history, the force of dreams, intuitions, prayers, of the effect of the astrological forces of the universe [Libra is Oswald's zodiac sign]. Dreams—that's what this novel is about, it's about history and dreams.

"Coincidence is an important element, like those of dreams and prayers," DeLillo adds. "Coincidence informs the whole novel in a sense. How did Oswald feel when he first found out that the Kennedy motorcade would pass right under his window? That, in addition to the point he had arrived at in his life, had to be one of the powerful motivating elements in his decision to take a shot at Kennedy. This is one of the things I'm talking about when I say 'forces outside of history'—something we don't understand, but which motivates many acts that have changed history. No one has ever been able to find the slightest evidence that Oswald's employment at the Texas School Book Depository was anything but innocent. Nobody placed him there, nobody knew the motorcade would be going that way until a few days before it actually occurred. I suppose this is ultimately why coincidence keeps building in the novel until it finally reaches its grotesque fulfillment."

Within *Libra* and all his other books, DeLillo observes, there is "an element of unresolvability" that reflects the psychic confusion the assassination has precipitated in American life and which is "absolutely . . . where my work all began. . . . I don't know exactly how to summarize my work but I would say it's about danger, modern danger." There are connections between *Libra* and its predecessors, DeLillo says, though the links among his novels "are unconscious because I'm not that aware of what the links are myself, it's just the way my mind works and how I perceive the world."

Either, he hypothesizes, "everything I've done has been building toward this, toward this character in particular; or Oswald himself, the assassination itself, was the starting point of my work, although I didn't know it at the time. It's not, I think, that I've been accumulating characters and a particular style and a particular set of experiences that culminate in this novel. It may be that everything I've been doing all along is unwittingly influenced by November 22, and particularly by Oswald. I certainly wasn't aware of it, and I've just begun to think in those terms now, after I've done the novel."

In 1963, DeLillo, who grew up in the Bronx (coincidentally, near where Lee Harvey Oswald once lived, although the two never met), was "working as a copywriter in an ad agency. And that was the next to last year of my advertising career, which was short, uninteresting." Later, as a freelance writer, "I did all sorts of assignments. One day I would be writing about pseudo-colonial furniture, the next day about computers." He began his first novel "around 1966. It took a long time"—*Americana*, in which the assassination figures, was published by Houghton Mifflin in 1971—"because I had to keep interrupting it in order to make a living."

135

Each of his novels, DeLillo says, "is unresolvable, absolutely, and could probably not have been written in the world that existed before the assassination. But I've not been conscious of having been influenced by that event. Still, when people want to know about writers who have influenced other writers, maybe the question ought to be: 'What is there in your life—private or public—that has influenced you?' "

Writing *Libra* took DeLillo three years. "It had never occurred to me before to base a novel on an historic event," he says, "certainly not in a large-scale way. So this novel may in some way be the culmination of ideas in my work, but it also stands a little to the side, because it is so different in that sense and because I was grappling with a real event. It also has had a stronger effect on me for that reason. I'm sure that this novel will be harder to stop thinking about than the others, harder to put into the past and possibly harder to go on from. Surrounded as I am by research materials, in particular by the 26 volumes of the Warren Report, I'll always look at that stuff and think of the strange lonely feeling I had standing in Dealey Plaza one afternoon. A striking sense of mystery, unresolvability, hovers over that little green spot. It seems the loneliest place in the city, even with the cars roaring by constantly. And that's my feeling about the whole experience. I don't think doing a novel about it completes the mystery, not for me, and certainly not for anyone else."

DeLillo says that he "felt a very strong responsibility to fact *where we knew it*. And I made up the rest because we don't know it. If there was a conspiracy, we don't know how it evolved. Oswald is as close as I could make him to what I perceived to be the real person. I really didn't take liberty with fact so much as I invented fresh fact, if you can call it that. I tried very hard to create a unified structure with no seams showing. That was my major technical challenge."

DeLillo depended on the Warren Report and conducted no interviews. He did watch "an extraordinary compilation of amateur footage shot during the motorcade in Dallas [including the Zapruder film as well as other film]. Very crude, powerful footage which as much as anything, I suppose, suggests that the shot that killed Kennedy came from the front instead of from the rear. It's hard seeing that moment of death and blood spurting and then accept the fact that the shot came from the School Book Depository instead of from the grassy knoll. Although I'm sure scientists would find reasons to explain the movement of the president's body, when you see it, it's hard to believe that he wasn't hit from the front. There's no doubt that Oswald hit him, the question is whether he killed him." In *Libra*, Oswald is not a lone gunman.

That the assassination is on film compounds the strangeness of the event and unsettles historical finality: "I think that's one of the things that informed my subsequent work, or all my work," DeLillo says. "The notion of a medium between an event and an audience, film and television in particular. The irony is that we have film of the assassination and yet it is still remote. Because the film is so imperfect. And even if it weren't, I'm sure there are reasons—it's hard not to call them psychological—and anomalies of perception that would still make it difficult to figure out what happened, even if we had expert footage, clear footage, even if we had sound. I think we see different things in the assassination at different periods in our history. We feel a bit differently about it today than we did in the '60s and then in the '70s. But we still don't know what happened, that's the core of it."

DeLillo thinks that "when the authorities quickly determined that Oswald was the lone gunman and an unstable man, people quickly accepted that because it resolved a certain level of anxiety about the very nature of political conspiracy. Some people prefer to believe in conspiracy because they are made anxious by random acts. Believing in conspiracy is almost comforting because, in a sense, a conspiracy is a story we tell each other to ward off the dread of chaotic and random acts. Conspiracy offers coherence.

"The reason so many people think Oswald was not the lone gunman is that the physical evidence, as we know it, argues against it in many respects. But in another way we could interpret the past 25 years as a conspiracy developing in our own minds. Many more people today believe there was a conspiracy than believed it in 1963. Did we invent the conspiracy because it's easier to accept than a random act with no basis in motivation, which is total madness? Is the conspiracy our doing rather than an actual plot against the president's life? That's an unanswerable question,"

DeLillo acknowledges. "I am suggesting that it is possible to make up stories in order to soothe the dissatisfactions of the past, take the edge off the uncertainties. Perhaps we've invented conspiracies for our own psychic well-being, to heal ourselves."

WILLIAM GOLDSTEIN

JAMES DICKEY

JAMES DICKEY OWNS so many different typewriters that a typing pool could move into his home and set to work with simultaneous efficiency. On the dining-room table sits a heavy console, with two portables nestling beside it. Down the hall in his book-crammed office is another one where his secretary, Luke Phillips, types while Dickey dictates. Two or three other typewriters peer out of odd corners; one is almost concealed behind living-room draperies in Dickey's ranch-style house beside a lake in Columbia, S.C.

Dickey, who usually works on half a dozen projects at the same time, has a typewriter always at his fingertips as he moves from poetry to fiction to criticism to screenplays. His novel *Alnilam* represents a lot of typing any way you figure it: 1271 pages in typescript, 792 in the printed book. And it took 36 years to complete!

Dickey started the novel in 1950, worked on it a little, then put it aside. By 1976 he had written just enough of *Alnilam* for *Esquire* to publish a short excerpt, and in the meantime Cahill, the novel's main character, had become blind from diabetes. This character's blindness led Dickey to experiment with an unusual format through much of the novel: he split the page into two columns of print, describing Cahill's perceptions on the left-hand side and "reality," as seen by the other characters, on the right.

Dickey worked full time on the novel only as it neared completion. He took the title from the name of the central star in the constellation Orion: *alnilam*—accented on the last syllable—is Arabic and means "string of pearls." Having signed a contract for the novel with Doubleday 16 years ago, Dickey experienced a battalion of editors. "First was Sandy Richardson, who was a vice-president," he recalls. "I also had Ken McCormick, one of the elder statesmen there. Sam Vaughan, who was sort of overseeing the project, is also gone. Next I had a very bright young guy named Hugh O'Neill; then a senior editor named Kate Medina, with whom I had done another book. Last of all I had Carolyn Blakemore, who worked on the book for about a year. She was assisted by my former student Shaye Areheart, who is also my poetry editor at Doubleday. That's a bunch of people!"

Deliverance, Dickey's first published novel, went quickly compared with *Alnilam:* it took only eight years to complete. Theron Raines, who was later to become Dickey's agent, gave him the idea of writing *Deliverance* in 1962, when Dickey was in Italy on a Guggenheim fellowship. One of his poems with a North Georgia mountains-and-rivers setting had won a prize, and after reading it Raines wrote to Dickey suggesting a novel with a similar milieu. "I was impressed immediately by an agent who reads poetry," Dickey says, "because poetry is so unlucrative for them. Theron wondered if I had any ideas about writing a novel with the same background—he also likes mountains and rivers. I told him I didn't have any ideas at all for a novel. But he had started the wheels turning in my brain."

One day not long after receiving Raines's letter, Dickey lay down to take a siesta in Positano, the village near Naples where he was living. As he drowsed, he thought to himself, "If I did write a novel about the woods and rivers of Georgia, what would it be about?" Nothing surfaced at first—then it struck him: "Wait a minute; what about the time on that canoeing trip. . . ." He got up, made a few notes, then went back to sleep. *Deliverance* had crystallized in his head. "I knew who the people would be, how many there would be, and I knew the events that would happen. I knew everything about the novel," he recalls.

Dickey treated *Deliverance* as "a sort of hobby" for several years, writing five or six other books in the meantime. Then, in a contributors' column of a magazine where some of his poems appeared, he mentioned that he was working on a novel. "Bam! The word 'novel' brings publishers out of the woodwork," Dickey laughs. "Houghton Mifflin bought *Deliverance* on the strength of a skimpy 90-page draft. I took an advance—very modest indeed—but when I had taken the dollar from the drumhead I saw that I was going to have to finish the novel. Then I started working on it full time and completed it in about eight months, I guess."

Meanwhile, according to Dickey, he and his first agent Bob Lescher didn't see things the same way, so he signed up with Raines, and the two have worked together splendidly ever since. Dickey also changed publishers shortly after the success of *Deliverance*. His main reason for going to Doubleday, he reports, is that "they had better plans and more projects" for him.

Although several decades spent on two novels could make Dickey appear unprolific, he is anything but. Beginning with his first book, *Into the Stone and Other Poems* (1960), he has published some two dozen books of poetry; criticism, the best known collection being *Babel to Byzantium* (1968); screenplays (*Deliverance* in 1972; *The Call of the Wild* for NBC-TV in 1976); picture books for Oxmoor House (e.g., *God's Images: The Bible, A New Vision*); two children's books; and a large number of essays, articles and reviews in more than 30 periodicals. His *Buckdancer's Choice* won the National Book Award for poetry in 1966.

Born in Atlanta 64 years ago, Dickey played football at Clemson, flew more than 100 combat missions in World War II, served in the Korean War, wrote advertising copy on the Coca-Cola account in the 1950s and taught at a half dozen universities before becoming professor of English and poet-in-residence at the University of South Carolina in 1969. Despite his action past, Dickey resents media attempts to turn him into "some kind of Hemingway character." His eyes blaze with displeasure when he mentions this kind of journalistic mythmaking, and he stipulates to *PW*, "If I'm going to talk about my books, I want to talk about *them* and not about myself." As soon as he knows we haven't come to pry, he relaxes and talks freely about his writing.

Asked how *Alnilam* began in his mind, Dickey says, "It started as an image, more or less the way I write poetry. For *Alnilam,* it was the image of a training aircraft warming up in the early morning in winter. And *Deliverance* began with the picture of the guy climbing up the cliff, so I wrote that section first"—even though it occurs near the end of the novel.

Although Dickey revises his prose considerably, he reworks his poems even more painstakingly. Showing us what appears to be a

141

ream of paper, whose every sheet is covered with typing and with revisions in ink, he explains that this is one poem—from first images to final shape. "It takes me a long time to write a book of poetry," he says. "A long, long time. I've got some poems that I had in the cooker long before I started *Alnilam*. They go way back to my college days in the late '40s."

Although no poem comes easily to him, he concedes that some come more easily than others. "Those are usually the ones that revolve around an event or something I remember. But for the ones I think have potentially great resonance, I have a horror of messing up something intrinsically good; so I work on such a poem a long time, trying it a lot of different ways until I finally refine it down to what I think is the best I can do."

Although Dickey's fiction is different in every way from his poetry, he claims that the difference is not a conscious one. Rather, he says, "I believe that everybody contains a lot of different people. For my kind of artist, if I may presume to call myself such, it's important to energize as many different personae as you have inside you, or as many as you can discover. There are lots of beings inside everyone that never have a chance to do or say anything. But the writer can galvanize a number of these—at least more than one—and make them talk with different voices."

The various phases of Dickey's personality appear in his conversation as well as in his writing. He can sound fierce when asked if he expects *Alnilam* to be a bestseller: "I don't have any real idea about sitting down deliberately to concoct something that will sell a lot of copies. I've got a statement to make as a writer, and as a human being, and I want to make it as best I can rather than settle for a temporary amount of money, which the government gets anyway."

Dickey's armor dissolves into adoration when his five-year-old daughter Bronwen skips into the room. "Could I have a big kiss, sugar?" he pleads. She obliges, and Dickey's eyes follow her out of the room. Bronwen is Dickey's child with his second wife, Deborah. He has two grown sons by his first wife, Maxine, who died in 1976.

Although he takes writing very seriously, he can see the humor in those who don't. He recalls the time his boss at the advertising agency said in a meeting, "Dickey writes poetry as a hobby." Dickey, having none of that, slammed his hand down on the table and said "Advertising is the hobby!" He grins sardonically as he adds, "Yeah, and I left soon after that."

Despite the length of *Alnilam*, it hasn't really ended. *Crux*, another novel Dickey has been pondering for a long time, is an extension of the *Alnilam* plot. So far, he says, he has only made extensive notes for *Crux*. "I'm an inveterate note taker. I get to know the characters through these notes as well as through the actual writing." He refuses to speculate on when his third novel might be completed. "I don't know if I'll live that long," he says matter-of-factly. "I had brain surgery last summer, and I don't know how long I can hold out."

Nevertheless, "our most public poet," as critic Jonathan Yardley has called Dickey, has as many projects in his typewriters as ever. Despite his successes in various genres and media, he isn't about to fit a cover onto a single keyboard. In addition, Dickey has his teaching and his trips on the college lecture circuit. Although no longer a financial necessity, these readings keep Dickey at the center of his audience—the proper place for a bard. He also admits that he is not immune to lionization: "Being relatively affluent and well known is certainly better than being poverty-stricken and a failure. I've been in that condition, too, and I much prefer this."

SAM STAGGS

ANNIE DILLARD

THE COVER OF Annie Dillard's eighth book, *The Writing Life* (Harper & Row), carries a painting by Albert Pinkham Ryder of a small sailboat alone in a choppy sea. Dillard says she chose this painting (titled *The Toilers of the Sea*) to illustrate *The Writing Life*, as opposed to, say, a Vermeer of a woman quietly writing a letter, because "I wanted the struggle. There's the little sailboat, and there's the big sky, and the sea is up. The boat is solitary and struggling." This is appropriate, she says, because "the book is about danger."

The Writing Life is a narrative filled with metaphors about the process of writing. In seven chapters, Dillard describes, among other things, an erupting typewriter; how she wrote *Pilgrim at Tinker Creek* (which won the Pulitzer Price in 1975, when Dillard was 29) in a dark library; why writing is like splitting wood ("Aim past the wood, aim through the wood; aim for the chopping block"); why writing is like alligator wrestling, climbing a ladder or rowing against the current.

Like Dillard's previous book *An American Childhood* (Harper & Row, 1987), a memoir about growing up in Pittsburgh, *The Writing Life* is about the nature of consciousness.

"Writing has always been one of my subjects. Consciousness interests me, and I've written about it a lot," says Dillard during one of the several chats in Middletown, Conn., where she is writer in residence and adjunct professor at Wesleyan University, and via telephone from her house in South Wellfleet, on Cape Cod, where she spends summers.

From *Pilgrim* to *American Childhood* to *The Writing Life*, Dillard has continually written about what it feels like to be alive. "The first person is a narrator; it's a hand-held camera, an eyeball, a point of view. *An American Childhood* makes the same exploration of the interior life. It's about passion and energy. I don't think I've written a personal book yet. The world is the great subject."

She has always been careful to keep herself out of her writing, and despite the intimacy and power of her narratives, there is an unusually opaque quality to any personal details that are, very rarely, offered along the way. When we suggest that her writing contains reflections, in the literal sense, rather than revelations, Dillard replies, "I don't reflect. I don't meditate. I write *narrative*."

Speaking at the New York Public Library in a series sponsored by Book-of-the-Month-Club in a talk that was later collected in a volume edited by William Zinsser, *Inventing the Truth* (Houghton Mifflin, 1987), Dillard described the process of writing *An American Childhood*. "You have to take pains in a memoir not to hang on the reader's arm, like a drunk, and say, 'And then I did this and it was so interesting.' I don't write for that reason."

In *The Writing Life*, Dillard observes: "It should surprise no one that the life of the writer—such as it is—is colorless to the point of sensory deprivation. Many writers do little else but sit in small rooms recalling the real world. This explains why so many books describe the author's childhood. A writer's childhood may well have been the occasion of his only firsthand experience."

Dillard admits that this is pure self-description, adding that where *An American Childhood* ends "is just about where my experience of the real world ends. I've mostly spent the rest of my time behind a desk."

While the statement suggests a placid existence, Dillard has recently weathered domestic turmoil. She has been married for less than a year to Robert D. Richardson Jr., who she met after writing a fan letter to him about his 1986 book *Henry Thoreau: A Life of the Mind*. Dillard was at the time married to anthropologist Gary Clevidence, father of her five-year-old daughter Cody Rose.

Dillard met Clevidence in 1976, soon after she left the East Coast and her first husband, Richard Dillard, her former writing teacher at Hollins College, whom she married in her sophomore year. After four years in the Pacific Northwest, Dillard and

145

Clevidence moved to Middletown in 1979 when Wesleyan offered Dillard a teaching job.

In addition to teaching and writing, Dillard reads voluminously; since 1966 she has kept a list of all the books she has read, calling it "one of the most valuable things I own." She has managed to do a great many other things as well, from editing *Best American Essays 1988* to serving on the usage panel of the *American Heritage Dictionary*, and on juries for the Bollingen Prize in 1984, the nonfiction Pulitzer Prize in 1985 and, most recently, for the PEN/Martha Albrand Award.

Dillard plays second base on the Wesleyan faculty softball team—"It should be called The Hamstrings"—gives occasional readings, has been a New York Public Library Literary Lion. She was awarded the Appalachian Gold Medallion at the University of Charleston and Boston's St. Botolph's Club Foundation Award.

Seven days a week, Dillard writes all morning before breaking for lunch, which in Middletown means a place at her regular table at the faculty club. She "shovels mail" in the afternoon, either in her office or in her study at home. She refers to herself as a working mother, and is careful to plan for daily time with her daughter.

Requests for Dillard's time are endless. She constantly fends off invitations to serve on juries and panels and boards, and she declines most speaking engagements. Most requests are now met with a printed postcard that reads "Annie Dillard thanks you for your interest and regrets that she cannot accept your kind invitation." Another postcard has been added recently: "Annie Dillard thanks you for your interest and very much regrets that she is no longer able to read manuscripts or galleys, even for friends."

Dillard's writing seems to invite long, heartfelt, even worshipful letters from readers, and a day doesn't pass without mail responding to *Pilgrim*, which has been anthologized in over 40 publications, translated into Swedish, and appears on countless reading lists. The book has given Dillard an identity that she still labors mightily to correct.

"They think I sit under a tree, like Joan of Arc. They think I write unconsciously, that a squirrel whispers into my ear and I write it down."

For the record: although *Pilgrim* is a densely constructed narrative that brims with Dillard's acute and original observations of the natural world and the life of the mind, and Tinker Creek is in Virginia, Dillard is not now and never has been a barefoot, down-home naturalist with a bluebird on her shoulder and a dulcimer in her lap.

What she is, despite some readers' fond fuzzy dreams to the contrary, is an extremely well-read intellectual who grew up in an elegant Pittsburgh household; her ancestors founded American Standard. She chews her fingernails and tries not to smoke, she adores jokes, even dumb ones, likes to dance, cares about her friends, prizing kindness above many other traits, and she comes across as both knowing and deliberately un-chic. She is a self-described "old-timey liberal Democrat" who sometimes works the polls on election day. She is really not an environmentalist first and foremost, she defends hunting, and she is far more concerned about affordable housing than acid rain.

She started out a poet, publishing her only book of poetry, *Tickets for a Prayer Wheel,* earlier in the same year that *Pilgrim* appeared. That switch to prose was "thrilling," Dillard says. "Poetry was a flute, and prose was the whole orchestra. I'm still spending the energy from that shift."

Blanche Gregory has been Dillard's agent from the start, originally because she represented Richard Dillard. Given a couple of chapters of *Pilgrim,* Gregory contacted Lawrence Freundlich, then editor of *Harper's,* who recognized the originality of the material and bought the chapter on praying mantises.

Dillard says that was the best moment of what was to become a sustained success. But after several other magazine excerpts and publication of the book, Dillard found the snowballing acclaim unnerving. There were offers from Hollywood and TV, questions about whether Dillard rode a mule to the post office or if her father was a coal miner. One attempt to lure her into the world of popular culture was lost when an executive taking his doubtful guest to lunch offered her a drink, saying, "Would you like it on the rocks? That means with ice."

Other books that followed *Pilgrim,* which have all, with one exception, been published by HarperCollins, were *Holy the Firm,* a slender and spare narrative; *Living by Fiction,* a volume of literary criticism; *Teaching a Stone to Talk,* her only collection of essays; and *Encounters with Chinese Writers,* published by Wesleyan University Press, a straightforward account of Dillard's experience as a member of a U.S. cultural delegation that traveled to China in 1982.

"I always think books are going to be large and then they're small. *The Writing Life* was about 300 pages, and now it's 128 pages." says Dillard, citing the "delete" button on her word processor as her most helpful editorial aid. One "very black" chapter she deleted from the book concerned the New York publishing scene, and opened with "a drunk man in a business suit crawling across an intersection in the snow, dragging his briefcase behind him."

This and other sections were eliminated because Dillard didn't want the chapters to be too varied. "This isn't a collection," she admonishes. "It's one straight shot."

Certain unnamed flap-copy writers will probably never forget this point. In mid-July, when Dillard received an advance copy of *The Writing Life* complete with four-color jacket, she was taken aback to read flap copy claiming she was "the author of *Teaching a Stone to Talk* and *other books of essays.*"

"I spend too much time fighting the idea that my books are collections of essays when they're not," she says. "It's probably because in *Pilgrim* I was stupid enough to give my chapters separate titles." An erratum slip was considered, but seemed especially unsatisfactory for an error on the jacket.

"I hated to see this misinformation coming from my own publisher. But they said, 'We will reprint the entire dust jacket to the tune of $10,000, just to be nice.' That's what it is to have a publisher! They enjoy my good will and I enjoy their good will. I could probably get more money up front somewhere else, but this is why I haven't yet considered it."

"In view of her unhappiness and our esteem of her, we reprinted the cover and re-jacketed by hand over 50,000 copies of *The Writing Life* at our expense," says Dillard's editor, Buzz Wyeth, who declined to confirm the dollar figure of the cost.

"Annie is one of those wonderful, rare writers who doesn't need a great deal of editing," he says. "At the same time she doesn't say, 'Never tell me to change anything.' She asks for strong copyediting. I can't tell you any horror stories about working with Annie—redoing the jacket was the right decision."

The Writing Life, like all her books, was written "for other writers," says Dillard. It comes "between two big books." *An*

American Childhood is one; Dillard won't identify the other, the one in progress. "It's no use talking about it," she says. "It's going to be five or six years away, and I'm already a good year into it."

Would this next book, by any chance, be a work of fiction? "You bet it is," replies Dillard, ending the conversation because she's off for a short sail with her husband before Rosie's playtime.

KATHARINE WEBER

MARGARET DRABBLE

THE *Oxford Companion to English Literature* has more than a million small-type words on 1155 compact pages, but Margaret Drabble has read it through twice. The reason for this unusual accomplishment is that Drabble, as its editor, had to proofread the volume. "Nobody's ever going to sit down and read it as a novel," she says with a smile. "People are always going to be dipping in." Drabble herself did not even have to read the page proofs from "A" to "Z," since she had already done the cumbersome galleys. "I *could* just make sure the alterations have been put in properly," she comments. "In fact, I can't resist reading through the whole thing again."

It isn't just fascination with her own—and some 80 others'—scholarship and writing that keeps Drabble glued to the page, although she does find most of it "terribly interesting. You suddenly realize there's an interesting cross-reference and you can note that just by putting in an asterisk, or adding a word, and then readers can look up the other entry. Richard Holmes [Thackeray biographer and a contributor] said, when we were planning it, 'A good reference book is like one of those push-ball games where you send a ball round and it lights up one thing, then another, then another, and you just go on reading as the ball goes 'round the board.' "

Editing the *Oxford Companion* (published here by Oxford University Press), which meant deciding what and whom to include, reading and writing at least one-third of the 9000 entries, and copyediting them all, occupied Drabble for five years. We visited her at home in Hampstead, London's chic literary enclave, on two occasions spaced a year apart. The first was in October, in late afternoon of a day Drabble had spent dealing with her taxes, and shortly before she left town for a lecture tour of Turkey (subject: the British novel), with her biographer husband, Michael Holroyd. We next met in November the next year, when she was on her second round of proofreading, which had kept her busy since July. It was early morning—the backyard grass was soaked with dew—following an evening Drabble had spent with the letter "F," due to be picked up by the printers that day. "I hope they've got some more of the alphabet," Drabble says, "because otherwise I'm going to be very out of schedule with the rest of my life."

Margaret Drabble is one of England's best-known literary figures, respected for fiction, criticism and television and film scripts. An attractive woman with a lively face, she wears her brown hair in a Dutch-boy cut, and clothes of interesting texture and a vaguely bohemian cast. She laughs easily, listens attentively, and speaks with enthusiasm in a well-modulated voice. Her 45 years rest lightly upon her. The living room in which we take tea is comfortably appointed, with added splashes of color from a clutch of embroidered pillows (embroidery is a hobby of both Drabble and her father) with geometric design in gros point; an electric guitar leaning against a wall announces the presence in the house of a teenager.

Drabble comes from what she calls "an upper working-class or lower middle-class" background. Her parents both were the first in their families to attend universities; her father became a judge, her mother a schoolteacher. Margaret, like her sisters, was sent to Mount School, a Quaker boarding school that was "more progressive and less class-bound than the conventional public school." She found it a good experience, and its humanist emphasis on "the inner light in every person" has remained with her, although qualified by adult skepticism. Next, a scholarship took her to Newnham College, Cambridge, where she read English, spent a good deal of time acting in university theater groups, and graduated with two Firsts.

She expected to become an actress. After finishing her degree course, Drabble married actor Clive Smith, with him joined the Royal Shakespeare Company, and then became pregnant—which meant very little acting. Instead, she wrote a novel. "Looking

151

back, it was very, very good that it worked out that way. It was as though Providence had given me the free time. I was *furious* at the time, of course." That precocious first novel, *A Summer Bird-Cage*, was published to "very pleasant, very encouraging reviews" when she was 23. By the age of 30, Drabble had four more novels, two literary awards (the Llewellyn Rhys Memorial Prize for *The Millstone* and the James Tait Black Memorial Prize for *Jerusalem the Golden*), two sons and a daughter to her credit. "Writing books," she found, "is a very good way of combining having small children, earning one's living, and filling in the evening."

Early on, Drabble wrote at night, while her husband was out acting and the children slept. Later, she switched to writing in the morning, and reviewing or reading during the afternoon. In the final stages of her most recent novels (*The Ice Age* and *The Middle Ground*) she would go off alone to a hotel room "and really go at it, write an enormous amount very fast. But I can only do it when I see the book coming to an end. I can't do it in the early stages." She compares the build-up of creative momentum to pushing something up an enormous hill, and then having it roll down by itself.

The list of Drabble's publications is substantial, and includes nearly a dozen novels (she has been compared to George Eliot, Virginia Woolf and Doris Lessing), a short critical work on Wordsworth and a biography of Arnold Bennett, and books about Britain in the Victorian Age and the British landscape in literature. In 1980, the Queen dubbed her "Commander of the British Empire."

The *Oxford Companion to English Literature* first appeared in 1932 under the editorship of Sir Paul Harvey; there were three subsequent editions, the last in 1967. In the late 1970s, the Oxford University Press invited Drabble to submit a proposal for a fifth edition. Editing the work, a five-year endeavor, would leave no time for her own novels, but, she says, "I did it partly because I didn't particularly want to write fiction at that time. I felt I'd come to the end of a certain style or *kind* of novel. I wanted to do *something*—psychologically, I have to be working—and I thought it would be very good to concentrate on a different sort of thing. It was a bit of a challenge."

Drabble worked from the first edition, cutting out the general knowledge entries (the term "pieces of eight," the origin of the word "dollar," etc.), the category of classical allusions that were not specifically literary, and only a few no longer relevant writers ("perhaps one or two sports historians"). "I left all the authors in," Drabble explains, "because they're always interesting, and even if they're not read, one needs to know who they were, or a scholar might well need to know. The more obscure, in a way, the more you need them in a reference book."

Some antiquated entries needed to be completely revamped to place them in accord with modern standards of scholarship; authors were also reevaluated. Bulwer-Lytton's entries, for example, have been both reduced and changed, so that "different works of his are now considered important or interesting sociologically," Drabble says. "I don't think it's possible that books like *The Last Days of Pompeii* are going to be taken seriously as novels, but on the other hand, his science-fiction novel, *The Coming Rate,* is terribly interesting to us now."

The foreign author entries in the fifth edition of the *Oxford Companion to English Literature* have been expanded, but, says Drabble, "when I deal with someone like Fennimore Cooper or Emerson or Thoreau I give a European viewpoint of their influence here. I would give more space than your *Companion* does to when they came to England, who they met here and who they influenced. It's not meant to be a full summary of American literature; it's meant to be a sort of cross-fertilization. I get into trouble sometimes with people like Emily Dickinson, who is obviously tremendously important and is very highly regarded here, but because she wasn't published here, didn't have all that much influence." Nonetheless, Dickinson's entry is "quite generous."

With new writers, there was a cutoff date of 1939—anyone born after that year was automatically excluded—and Drabble also decided "they had to have been on the map when I began five years ago. That's my own decision, but I think it's a reasonable one; otherwise one is revising all the time. I had to say, 'This is the moment in history when my book begins'; it would have been impossible to have tried to keep up with people's reputations." Drabble herself, born in 1939, has no entry. "I think if somebody else were writing the book, I'd have been one of the marginal people. There were quite a lot of people in my category, whom I didn't know whether to put in or not."

How did she decide who got in? "Common sense and consensus," Drabble replies. She "read around, read the newspapers, the *Times Literary Supplement*, talked to my friends, asked advice from publishers. I think that if you listen to everybody, you do come up with a sort of consensus. I feel I've become a committee." She started, however, with "people that I admired myself. There are one or two modern novelists who I think did interesting things who are not much spoken of now," she says, and names the 1960s writer B. S. Johnson as an example. "He did something completely new and did it very wittily. I'm sure he will be in the history books in 50 years' time." Drabble gave Johnson a dozen lines "just to register his existence." She has also included "a writer whose work I very much admire, Nell Dunn, a feminist writer not spoken of by the critics with great admiration because she's too readable, she's thought of as being not *quite* literature. I put her in because I think she's very good and again, I think she did something completely new in the English novel."

Drabble also has included a few authors she doesn't care for ("Obviously, I won't tell you who they are!") but who "are important, or other people think they're important, and it's not up to me to tell them who's interesting." She does whisper a name, and exclaims, "Jolly boring!" adding, "I'm sure there will be others that I'm going to think, 'Oh, Lord, they've got to stay.'" On the other hand, Anita Brookner and Russell Hoban are not represented: Brookner began writing too recently for inclusion, while Hoban's reputation has soared really only in the last few years. It is authors such as these Drabble regrets omitting and which lead her to "suddenly wake up in the night."

She tried to maintain a rough kind of equal coverage of major writers, Drabble says. "Oh, we've given 1200 words to George Eliot"—a laugh—"we'd better give a thousands words to Charlotte Brontë." To ensure a uniform, "dispassionate" tone, Drabble copyedited all entries. "My original intention was that there should be no value judgments, no work should be described as 'wonderful' or 'masterly,' but it's impossible to do that, because occasionally there's an obvious example of something that *is* a masterpiece or that *is* a masterly work. Then you just leave it, and say, 'All right.'"

Before she began working on the revision, the Oxford University Press people "did kind of interrogate me as to my intentions. I asked them, 'What about feminist criticism?' to which they responded, 'Oh, no, that's a passing phase.' But in fact they were wrong. The *Oxford Companion* will now have: 'Criticism, School of; Freudian, the New Criticism, Practical Criticism, Feminist Criticism,' and one or two of the major names." Essentially, once she was hired, she was given a free hand, Drabble says.

The last five years have, Drabble claims, "reinforced my feelings about where my own interests lie. It's rather strange that whenever I read the entries on realism or naturalism I feel my pulse quicken. Or my entry on Theodore Dreiser—there's something in his way of writing that's terribly important to me. I think it's possible to fuse it with late 20th century writing. Perhaps it's even being done by people like Norman Mailer, in books like *The Executioner's Song*, which take a huge chunk of reality and treat it in a semi-documentary way. I find that a very interesting way of writing for myself."

When we first spoke with her, Drabble thought that when she finished the *Oxford Companion* she would want to get away from facts for a while. A year later, she has changed her mind. "I think I'm quite interested in sticking to facts now. I've been sitting in libraries, reading all these books—that's one kind of fact. There's another kind of fact involved in the Kent miners' dispute, for example, and I'm keen to go out and find out about that.

"You can't complain in the Western world about our freedom to write; we can write whatever we like now. But we do perhaps seem to have lost some link with the people who don't write or read. I am looking for some way of revitalizing things that have dropped out of the novel a bit, and I think other people are looking for it, too: a sense of being rooted in day-to-day reality, social change, history. I think people are looking for a new way of relating the novel to history."

MIRIAM BERKLEY

UMBERTO ECO

IN 1979 UMBERTO ECO was a professor of semiotics who had just completed his first novel, *The Name of the Rose*, a 500-page metaphysical mystery, set in the Middle Ages, crammed with arcane historical and philosophical material as well as a good dollop of plain old suspense and a fiery finale. His Italian publisher, which had achieved modest success with Eco's scholarly titles, including *The Theory of Semiotics* and *The Aesthetics of Thomas Aquinas*, was enthusiastic about his extracurricular effort and assured him that, based on his reputation, it could probably sell 10,000, maybe even 20,000 copies of his fictional debut.

Just under a decade later, Eco's second novel, *Foucault's Pendulum*, was greeted in Italy with the hysteria usually reserved for touring rock stars. It sold 400,000 copies in its first two months of release, at one point outselling the title just before it on the best-seller list by a margin of 15 to one. The novel's alleged secret meaning became the hot topic of conversation at every fashionable cocktail party. The popular press published plot outlines and glossaries of occult terminology to help readers decipher this playful romp through the history of crackpot theories, with special emphasis on the ancient order of the Knights Templar. Harcourt Brace Jovanovich, which publishes William Weaver's English translation, expects *Foucault's Pendulum* to be just as much of an event in America.

What happened to change an unassuming academic into a brand-name author? Eco's medieval detective story, *The Name of the Rose,* won countless literary prizes and was a surprise bestseller throughout Europe; by the time it was published in America in 1983 it had become an international phenomenon. To date it has sold some nine million copies in 24 languages and been made into a film starring Sean Connery. The author can no longer attend a gallery opening or go to the theater in Italy without being buttonholed by his admiring fans, and though he continues to teach at the University of Bologna, it's for pleasure, not money, "because, you know, the salary can be easily covered by the royalties!"

It's a little strange to be a celebrity, he admits. "As an author I am very happy when I find a good article or a good review, but when the grocer or the conductor on the train recognizes me, I feel embarrassed. I prefer in a train to stay quiet and read my book without being accosted. Selling millions of copies can change your life in a bad way; you lose your privacy. So you try to make a more private life with your friends, not to be disturbed."

Still, success has its pleasant side effects, not all of them financial. "Some of my scholarly books that were not translated have been now. My first book, the one I love more than all the rest, on the aesthetics of Aquinas, was written as a dissertation and because it was very technical was never translated. Now, 30 or 35 years later, it's been published by Harvard University Press. Probably there are 2000 copies, but I am more proud of this book and of those 2000 copies than of all the millions of copies of *The Name of the Rose.*"

Eco is a cheerful, gregarious man of 57 who speaks fluent, if somewhat idiosyncratic, English. He sports a gray-flecked beard, a twinkle in his eye and a figure that suggests he's acquainted with the joys of Italian cuisine. He sits in his American publisher's office, resting between photo sessions on a whirlwind visit to New York to prime the publicity pump for *Foucault's Pendulum.* It's clear that the author can sell books as easily as he plumbs the depths of philosophical treatises: he's witty, charming and gallant in a delightfully old-fashioned way. A publishing veteran—he was an editor at Bompiani in Milan for 17 years before he became its bestselling author—he enjoys telling the story of how his first novel confounded everyone's expectations.

157

Bompiani had already given Eco its estimate of 10,000–20,000 copies when he met with Helen Wolff to discuss the American publication. "Helen said, 'I love your novel, I want to publish it, but you understand, a book like this will probably sell only 3000 copies,' and she paid an advance on the basis of 3000 copies. I gave the book to the [Italian] publisher at the end of January, 1980, and they planned to release it in November. So in April they began the information campaign. In May, they were making one of those meetings with the booksellers, and in two months the booksellers ordered 80,000 copies—without having seen the book! You understand that when you have already sold 80,000 copies six months before publication, you can make a good price, success is already assured, because the booksellers are then obligated to put it in the right window."

Those 80,000 copies, as everyone in publishing now knows, turned out to be only the beginning, and though Eco is grateful to bookstores for their early enthusiasm and to his publishers for their support, he credits readers as the major force behind the success of *The Name of the Rose*. "As a matter of fact, Bompiani didn't make any publicity for the book except the usual small ads. The book marched by itself, by word of mouth. That's an expression I have learned in several languages—word of mouth, *bouche oreille* in France, *bocca a bocca*—because in every country I was told by the booksellers that the book circulated this way."

Given the stratospheric sales of his first novel, Eco might reasonably have looked to the highest bidders for extravagant advances on his second work of fiction. On the contrary, he felt such loyalty to the publishers worldwide who had taken a chance on *The Name of the Rose* that he instructed Bompiani to stick with them whenever possible. In the U.K., paperback rights went to Picador, although a competitor offered more.

"I have always thought the policy of the high advance is negative for the author," Eco explains. "Okay, you get the advance, but if by chance your next book doesn't go so well, the publisher is discouraged, next time you shift to another publisher, then to another publisher . . ."; he shrugs, indicating the futility of this course. "I think that when you stay with the same publisher, they know you and are interested in supporting you. The policy of the high advance is too much adventurous! I understand that the writer who is offered 10 times more by a new publisher can be tempted, but if the difference is not too enormous, it is possible. I told Bompiani, 'Don't pay too much attention to something more or something less.' "

Eco believes in continuity, and he sees it in his work as well. "There is a narrative thrust also in my essays," he comments. "I think that to write a scholarly essay means also to stage the adventure of your research: this is the problem, you tell the reader, now I'll try this solution; this solution cannot work, now I'll try the other one. I think that each of my works—with the exception of *The Theory of Semiotics*, which is by definition systematic— but all the others are the story of how you can arrive at certain conclusions starting from certain problems. Scholarly work is very similar to detection. You start because there is something that doesn't work, there is a problem; you say, so-and-so and so-and-so don't mesh together properly, so it's a story of detection."

Foucault's Pendulum is, in essence, a tale of the detective instinct gone mad. Three editors at Garamond, a Milan publishing house, grow tired of the crazy writers and readers they encounter in the course of their work on a series of occult books called Isis Unveiled. (Eco describes the mechanics of creating a trashy series, and the way Garamond's clandestine vanity press subsidiary lures unwary authors into paying for their publication, with knowledgeable wit that will make publishing insiders smile.) Since the Diabolicals, as the editors call the cranks who besiege them with manuscripts, see mystic links and conspiracies everywhere they look, the trio decided to create a superplot, the Plan. It will explain every supposedly supernatural event in history, from the ancient megaliths to the cryptic intelligence of plants, as manifestations of a single awesome secret known only to the medieval Knights Templar, who created the Plan and prepared to bring it to fruition in the 20th century.

The editors find cynical delight in tying together every strange phenomenon and bizarre philosophy they can think of, taking as their motto, "The Templars have something to do with everything." They are dismayed to discover that the Diabolicals take the Plan seriously—and in fact, invest it with reality through a frenzied search for its purported secrets. The novel's apocalyptic finale drives home Eco's fundamental message: when the natural human quest for meaning degenerates into the paranoid invention of cosmic conspiracies, the results can only be disastrous.

159

"There is a profound human need to find a sense in life," he says. "All the religions and philosophies are efforts to do this. But some explanations are unpleasant, and people try to find another one because they think that a good explanation must be consoling and satisfactory. My book is not against this profound need that we have to find non-obvious explanations; as a semiotician, I am continuously trying to find the meaning of things under the text. It's against the cancer of exaggerated interpretation, in which you are never satisfied, you always want another answer. In the first centuries of Christianity, they had this truth that God is one in three, a trinity; it's a marvelous mystery. But there were immediately all these sects who said, 'No, this is only an allegory for something more secret and more difficult.' It was enough to understand this mystery, but they wanted another one."

Eco offers a lighthearted example of the difference between "healthy suspicion and sick suspicion." Gesturing to the desk in front of him, he says, "I enter this room and try to determine what there is in this ashtray. There are four butts of two different brands. I then suspect that there were here at least two different persons, and since I know that 15 minutes ago this room was empty, I suspect that these two persons are pretty compulsive smokers, since they smoked two cigarettes each in 10 minutes. Okay, this is a good way to interpret it. If I am a paranoid, I start thinking, 'Why four? Maybe they put four butts here to remind me that I had four wives, or that I live at number four.' You can go on *ad infinitum* this way."

Which is exactly what Eco's three editors do. Gradually, they become so enchanted by the convoluted beauty of the Plan that they almost forget it's not real. Eco understands the attraction of "the polyphony of ideas," as one of his characters calls their pastime of yoking every theory together. "As a book collector I have many volumes of lunatic science," he says. "The polyphony of ideas can be very musical, but beyond a certain limit it drives you crazy. That was the reason I had to stop the book, because I was too much fascinated by this polyphony. It can happen with every book you write that at the end you are neurotic, and in this case, using such 'hot' material, I started closing the book and looking around, thinking, 'Why this, and why this?' And you can always find similarities between things. Give me any two objects of your choice, give me $10, and in five seconds I will find a similarity between them."

Lunatic science? Paranoid conspiracy fantasy? Perhaps, but the semiotician-turned-novelist has also given a perfect thumbnail description of the storyteller's art.

WENDY SMITH

CLYDE EDGERTON

CLYDE EDGERTON BURST onto the literary scene in 1983 with *Raney,* an unusually well-received first novel published by the then-new Algonquin Books of Chapel Hill. Two years later came *Walking Across Egypt,* the Algonquin hardcover that was again followed by a Ballantine paperback edition. The brand of individualistic humor integrated into themes of underlying seriousness in both novels brought him a growing audience; the combined hardcover and paperback sales for *Raney* exceed 200,000 copies, and during its first week of publication, *Walking Across Egypt* was #10 on Ingram's paperback list.

But the reception of the previous novels by the 44-year-old North Carolinian already pales in comparison just for *The Floatplane Notebooks,* out from Algonquin in a first printing of 75,000. Ballantine paid a six-figure sum for paperback rights to the new novel, while book club rights went to BOMC and QPBC. After Edgerton charmed a large audience at a recent ABA Sunday Book & Author Breakfast by reading excerpts and singing a song adapted from his Flying Fish Records album, calls came in for interviews on the *Today Show* and with Susan Stamberg on NPR's *Sunday Weekend Edition,* and booksellers began clamoring to get him for in-store autographings.

Not surprisingly, Edgerton is pleased with the attention, but he chuckles at the irony that the first story he ever wrote now appears as a chapter in *The Floatplane Notebooks.* Edgerton and his wife Susan were then living in an old house in the small town of Apex, not far from Durham. One day Edgerton discovered a soft spot in the kitchen floor, crawled under the house to investigate, and found an abandoned well. "That was Christmas '77 vacation," he recalls. "I had completed my dissertation the summer before, so I had finished with all my schooling. I had time, and I sat down and wrote the 'Meredith falling into the well' story—knocked me out!—from start to finish." Eventually he sold the story, the first of his to be published, to *Just Pulp*, a now-defunct magazine of popular fiction.

Edgerton's compulsion to write sneaked up on him. He remembers writing what he describes as "some bad poems" while pursuing his academic specialty, English education, at the University of North Carolina, where he earned each of his three degrees. As an Air Force pilot from 1966–1971, based in Thailand while flying missions over the Ho Chi Minh Trail, he had time to read Hemingway, Twain and Crane. Susan, whom he married in 1975, whetted his enthusiasm for Flannery O'Conner—the Edgerton's three-member Tarwater Band is named for a character in O'Connor's *The Violent Bear It Away.*

"I think I must have been thinking unconsciously about being a writer," he muses. Then the unconscious broke through: "In May—May 14, 1978, I'll never forget it—Susan and I were watching PBS, and there was Eudora Welty reading her story 'Why I Live at the P.O.' We had been in several theater productions of the story; I had been Papa-Daddy, I had been Uncle Rondo, I had been Mama, and I knew the story by heart. I love the story! Susan and I—did then, and still do—quote lines from the story; one is liable to pop out any time!"

Edgerton, an outgoing, genial man, recounts all this information in rapid, occasionally staccato bursts of talk, usually accompanied by an engaging smile.

Edgerton promised himself that the next morning he was going to start writing fiction seriously. Although he was teaching education courses at Campbell College, a Baptist-affiliated school in Buies Creek, he did indeed begin writing, working in such heat that by the end of the summer he had finished four or five stories. When he began submitting his work for publication the following year, he says he must have received "202 rejections" for some dozen stories.

Some of these were the "Raney" stories, and in 1981 he thought he had enough to begin making a novel out of them. He sent 125 pages to novelist Sylvia Wilkinson, a friend, who liked what she read well enough to advise him to write more. Susan advised him to send the manuscript to Louis Rubin, whose classes she had taken at Chapel Hill. "Well, I didn't know," Edgerton says in the soft drawl that marks him as a native of his state's Piedmont region, "I was afraid he wouldn't like it. But then, having read his *Gallery of Southerners,* I thought that what Rubin was talking about in Southern literature was something that somehow was in my past and was what I was writing about. And having been introduced to the works of Flannery O'Connor, Eudora Welty, Lee Smith and others, I had seen that they were writing about people and situations and places that earlier I might have thought not worthy of literature."

Susan had told Edgerton about Rubin's passion for baseball. "Well, I like baseball too," he continues, "and at the time I was reading a baseball book I liked. So I wrote Louis and said if he would read a chapter from *Raney,* I would send him a good baseball book."

Send it, responded Rubin, an invitation whose immediate result was a quandary, laughs Edgerton. "I didn't know which chapter to send. I would pick up one and think it was the best, then pick up another, think *it* was the best. Finally I decided to send him two chapters, and—since I was sending more than the one chapter he had asked to see—a $10 check so he could buy another baseball book."

Rubin replied, advising Edgerton that he had torn up the check. More importantly, he wrote that he was establishing a publishing house, whose editor would be Shannon Ravenel. He asked Edgerton to send the whole *Raney* manuscript to her.

"Well!" Edgerton exclaims, his expressive blue eyes alight with the memory. "I knew Shannon Ravenel edited *Best American Short Stories,* and I had fantasized about sending her a story at some point, but hadn't had the courage to actually do so." Ravenel liked the *Raney* material, thus beginning an editor-writer relationship Edgerton acknowledges to be an essential element in the success of his books. He and Ravenel spent several months working on the manuscript of *Raney*—with Rubin's additional input—before it was published as Algonquin's third book.

Edgerton's pleasure in seeing his first novel published and praised was dampened, however, by the response of administrators at Campbell. In March the acting dean and provost invited him to come by "to discuss a couple of matters of mutual interest," after they had withheld signing his contract.

What was at stake was not Edgerton's job performance—he was and remains a popular teacher—but *Raney* itself, which takes a gently satiric look at some traditional Southern prejudices. "They gave me three specific problems they had with the book," Edgerton remembers. "One, that it was a demeaning characterization of the Baptist Church. Second, that it showed a clash between the old and the new, with the new replacing the old. They also questioned how the book furthered the purposes of the university. I refused to answer that." Ultimately, in May, he resigned after his request for an impartial investigation into his academic freedom was denied. He is now on the faculty at St. Andrew's Presbyterian College in Laurenburg, where Susan, a part-time editor at Algonquin, also edits the *St. Andrew's Review.* Clyde, Susan and their six-year-old daughter Charlotte live in Durham, in a two-story frame house dating from 1900.

When things had settled, Edgerton thought he would get back to work on a still-untitled novel that included both the "Meredith" story and another he had written after seeing a homebuilt floatplane at a local lake in 1980. The floatplane, he says, "blew me away, I guess because I had flown this computerized aircraft for five years. Suddenly here was this thing with a *lawn* chair bolted onto it! I knew I had to use it somehow."

One Saturday he was visiting his mother in Bethesda, the small town that bears a close resemblance to the town of Listre in his novels. His aunts were also visiting, and during the general conversation his mother mentioned that the day before she had sat down in a rocking chair whose bottom had been removed, and had been stuck for 15 minutes. "Well, we thought that was the funniest thing we had ever heard," said Edgerton, "and I wondered how I could use it in a story. Then I said, 'This *is* a story!' So I went home and wrote about 20 pages in no time. Shannon liked it a lot, and she, Susan, and my agent [Liz Darhansoff] thought it might become longer than a short story."

Thus Edgerton detoured into what became *Walking Across Egypt.* "I was just sort of following my nose to see what would happen next to Mattie Rigsbee, and I remembered a juvenile delinquent I had heard about," Edgerton recalls. His next vision was of the on-the-lam character "in the Baptist Choir in a robe standing beside the deputy sheriff, also in a choir robe, who is looking for him. That was a pivotal scene, and, given what I already knew about Mattie, I knew she would have to take him in. Most times, I've never seen an entire novel together. But since this one was so clearly in my mind, I gave myself a daily quota and finished the first draft in seven weeks." The title is that of a hymn he wrote for Mattie after finding the phrase "walking across Egypt" in *The Golden Bough;* as arranged by Edgerton's cousin, the hymn is included at the end of the novel.

Accustomed as he was to writing in quick bursts of creativity, Edgerton found that *The Floatplane Notebooks*, which he describes as "about what wars do to people" and "about persistence, the lingering of a family through the generations," came much harder. He had sent an early draft to Ravenel, but she felt it needed much more work. At that time, Edgerton says, he had 80 pages or so of Vietnam material in the manuscript—"just a lot of stuff I had to work through"—much of which was taken out in later revisions. Edgerton kept at the book for a third try, and a fourth. The biggest problem, he recognized, was point of view; none of the approaches he had used were convincing.

Deep in the Umstead State Park east of Durham hangs a rampaging wisteria vine, inching toward the cemetery where Edgerton's ancestors are buried. It is a place he visits often. Suddenly it came to him: why not have the vine talk, a technique through which he could convey things that had happened in the Copeland family back to 1850, before the experience of the present-day characters. "I thought this was just strange enough that it might work," reasons Edgerton. "And the vine started talking to me: 'I was planted as a seedling by the back steps soon after the first light on the day the field hand died, . .' " Edgerton recites from memory, his resonant voice sending chills up the listener's spine. "I don't know how this [device] is going to be received, though," he confesses. "It might be seen as totally incredible. But it works nicely for me and the purpose of the novel."

Neither is he certain about his reaction to pre-publication talk about the novel being his most mature effort, his Big Book. As he sees it, "there's the author's view, the reader's view, the critic's

166

view, and the scholar's view of a book. It's like the blind man and the elephant. I see *Floatplane* as a more complicated, longer book, and a different story. I think of it as just another child whose birth was more difficult."

BOB SUMMER

STANLEY ELKIN

"I DON'T BELIEVE you," says Stanley Elkin. "In fact, I don't think *you* believe you." There is a collective gasp from the 60-odd students, many of them published writers, crowded into Elkin's fiction workshop at the Bread Loaf Writers Conference, while the young man addressed by the bearish novelist blushes, only to admit a moment later that he indeed did not know what he was talking about. At lunch the next day, the same youth is happily seated at the master's elbow.

Elkin, a gifted teacher who can hold a class spellbound with his exposition of a piece of writing or a lesson on when *not* to describe something, also has a reputation as one of our finest—if as yet popularly unsung—crafters of fiction. The National Book Critics Circle Award given him for his epic *George Mills* was among a dozen honors—including two nominations for the National Book Award, the Paris Review Humor Prize and Guggenheim and Rockefeller fellowships—bestowed on him by his peers. So formidable is his talent and so awesome his persona that even in a place dedicated to the commingling of accomplished and aspiring writers, there are some who keep their distance. Those who venture near tend to find that Stanley Elkin is, as he says of himself, "a pussycat."

Which is to the point. For both personally and in his work, Elkin reveals a complex mix of emotions and attitudes. There is, for instance, his fierce intelligence (the refrain of his *Stanley Elkin's The Magic Kingdom* goes, "Everything has a reasonable explanation"—and he means it, even if the explanation is at times in the realm of magic) coexisting with a superstitious dread involving his pet preoccupations: illness and death. Years ago, as adolescents, Elkin and some friends were fooling around with a Ouija board, and while the other kids all asked for romantic predictions, Elkin's question was, "When will I die?" And the Ouija board said, "1956." And so, says the novelist, for the next dozen years, until 1956, "I was running scared." When 1956 went by, "I breathed a massive sigh of relief. Now I figure it means I'm gonna die when *I'm* 56; I made a mistake." For years, moreover, he observed a lengthy "rigmarole of incredible superstitions," such as pulling his ear whenever someone sneezed or death was mentioned or any of a number of other things happened. Finally, only a few months ago, a friend said to him, "You still do all that stuff? Look at all the things that have happened to you. Has it *helped*?" Elkin, who'd had a heart attack at 38 and suffers from multiple sclerosis, cut out the rituals.

Then there is the ironic, alienated observer sharing his heartbeat with a man so moved by a British television report about seven dying kids going to Disney World that he cries, because "it was just incredibly sad." And, in fact, *Stanley Elkin's The Magic Kingdom*, product as it might seem of an absurdist imagination, was inspired by this newscast; as he dried his tears, Elkin said to his wife, "That would make a terrific novel!" At the same time, he recognized that the subject matter had an inherent danger: the "great temptation to have seven deathbed scenes and just play it for all it's worth, for all the sentimentality that is essentially in it. What would be wrong would be to write a novel that simply sucks a reader's blood and tears—that's manipulative. The real challenge of writing *The Magic Kingdom* was to not make it sentimental and not make it silly. It's not a *realistic* novel—there's an awful lot of stuff in the book that is genuinely supposed to be magic. Why does it snow, for example, just in the park—twice, on the day they come and the day that they leave? Why do Eddy Bale and the Queen of England go into trances? This is a magic kingdom, and I wanted to create magic in the book."

In large measure, the magic that Elkin so successfully creates rests with his gorgeous prose. Through the virtuosic use of sentences structure, rhythm, alliteration, puns and other forms of logodaedaly, of archaisms, nursery words and medical terminology, Elkin seduces the reader into an extraordinarily intimate

169

relationship. One feels embraced by the novel's eloquent but disembodied voice, as if sharing a unique understanding of what our language is all about.

We spoke with Elkin when he was in New York for a few days to sit on an awards committee of the American Academy and Institute of Arts and Letters and to meet with his editor at Dutton, Bill Whitehead, and his agent, Georges Borchardt. The bulk of the year he spends in the St. Louis suburb of University City; he teaches at Washington University.

Elkin, 54 years old and six feet tall, seems both older and shorter, partly due to the MS, which limits his movements and necessitates the use of a cane (which, he says, scares people). "You're intimidated by that sort of prop—in my case, it's literally a prop, since it props me up. The cane makes me more mysterious, as my bad bottom teeth make me more mysterious. And that's what it amounts to finally—when you become a freak, you become a kind of severed head, and people are put off. I am." The impression of greater age is also owed to the crinkly fringe of nearly white hair around his chin, cheeks and balding pate, to the wire-rimmed glasses that frame his watchful eyes, the red suspenders he sports and his air—perhaps illusory—of calm. Stanley Elkin sitting in a New York hotel room looks like a village elder on a country porch.

Born in Brooklyn, Elkin was moved to Chicago's South Side at the age of three, and there he grew up, wanting, for as long as he can remember, to be a writer, but never expecting "it would actually happen." He was an English major at the University of Illinois for his B.A. through his Ph.D. (his dissertation was on Faulkner), with a couple of years out for military service. The Army published his first book, a training manual on forklift trucks ("They tell you, 'All right, in this sentence you will describe the windshield, in *this* sentence you will describe how to take the windshield apart. . . .' "), about the same time as a few of his short stories saw print in the outside world. Doctorate nearly in hand, Elkin went in 1960 to Washington University's English department, where he has been ever since (he now occupies a Chair that permits him to teach during the fall semester only). Not long after he arrived, his mother said, "You want to write? Go write," and gave him a bit more than a year's salary so that he could do so.

170

The Elkins took the money and ran to Rome for seven months. On arrival at their Rome lodgings, they found a telegram from Random House offering a contract on a novel whose first two chapters Elkin had submitted before leaving home. "I don't think I could have written the book if I didn't have a contract," says Elkin, and he adds that that contract, coming when it did, "determined my career, because I still feel that I can't write a book without a contract. The smart thing would be to write a book and then get people to bid it up. It's the idea that I'm working for somebody. Somebody has given me a dollar and a half, so I have to give that somebody a dollar and a half's worth of output. If I didn't have it, I'd scratch myself and watch television." This is related less to the work ethic, he fears, than to "the idea that I'll never be able to sell it if I haven't sold it already," what he calls "the thumb-sucking ethic."

The act of writing itself Elkin used to perform with pen and the ubiquitous blue collegiate exam booklets, until MS made it almost impossible to grasp a pen in 1979. Nowadays, he uses a word processor, a gift from Washington University, which, like any other electrical equipment, he refers to as "the bubble machine," à la Lawrence Welk, who was wont to say on his TV show, "Turn off the bubble machine."

The fact that he has adopted a phrase sired on TV is in keeping with the substantial role this medium, and the other media of popular culture, have played in Elkin's work. "Almost every book I've written has come to me as a kind of gift," he offers. "It's serendipity. I watch a lot of television, and a lot goes on inside that box. From time to time, something that I see triggers something I want to do—and do a lot better than the thing that suggests it." Something in *The Dick Gibson Show* happens on the island of Mauritius, a place suggested when Elkin saw a program about dodo birds, who once lived there. That same book's ending was inspired by a radio call-in show he heard. *George Mills's* eponymous hero has his first adventure in a Polish salt mine, a direct result of the author's viewing of Jacob Bronowski standing in a thousand-year-old Polish salt mine in *The Ascent of Man*.

Similarly, a *Time* magazine profile of Ray Kroc, who built the McDonald's hamburger empire, led to *The Franchiser*, while prehistoric teeth seen at London's Victoria and Albert Museum made their metaphorical way into *The Bail-Bondsman*. As Elkin puts it, "A lot of my stuff is found—sort of found objects—watching the television set, listening to the radio, being in a museum, until the Muse says, 'Hey! Go for it!'"

On the other hand, he does no research before creating the disparate worlds the characters in his novels, novellas and short stories inhabit. What he does sometimes do is *post hoc* validation. About 150 pages into *A Bad Man*, most of which is set in a prison, "it occurred to me," says Elkin, "that I'd be better off if I went to see what a real prison looks like." He was teaching at Smith College that year, and a trip to nearby Walpole State Penitentiary left him "so pleased that I'd gone, because my prison was so much better than their prison; their prison was totally boring. Mine may have been a little bit too Kafkaesque and unrealistic, but their prison did not make for a novel, and mine did."

In *Stanley Elkin's The Magic Kingdom*, the seven fatal diseases suffered by the seven kids are "fairly accurately described," he says, "because I simply picked up the phone and called the Washington U. medical reference library and asked, 'Can you give me the name of seven bad childhood diseases and some information about them?'" But it should be obvious that verisimilitude is not what one reads Elkin for; the truth in his fiction is not to be sought in literal terms. Thus, he did not visit Disney World, which plays a major role in the novel, until he'd already set his own Magic Kingdom in motion. When he did go, along with his younger son and daughter, it was "hoping against hope that it would turn out to be as boring as it finally turned out to be, so that my Magic Kingdom would be *less* boring. If it was overwhelming, if it had been a place you have to go back to 19 times to absorb it all, I would have had to spend too much time simply describing Disney World. Now, I do very little description of Disney World in the book, I mean the *real* Magic Kingdom is Mary Cottle's room. So I use the real world as a kind of baseline. Going down to Disney World reinforced my confidence that I don't *need* Disney World."

A critic once wrote about his work, "'What happens next?' is a question one doesn't usually ask. . . . Plot is not really Mr. Elkin's game." Elkin disagrees. "*The Magic Kingdom* has the most intricate plot and is so carefully structured that you couldn't put a pin in it. In this case, plot is connecting the dots, it's a kind of number painting; you're constantly shooting off surprises." The nonlinearity of his plots perhaps confuses people into thinking that there is *no* plot. In *Stanley Elkin's The Magic Kingdom,* it is, in fact, the plot of which Elkin is most proud (next is his avoidance of the maudlin or sentimental): "The kneebone is connected to the anklebone, and so on."

While he was writing *George Mills,* a six-year undertaking, Elkin was determined that it would be his last book, although, paradoxically, he had just begun, as he says, "to *feel* that I was a writer. I knew that I was a writer about two-thirds of the way into *George Mills.* I'd already written seven or eight books before that, and that's pretty late in the game to feel you're a writer, but I felt I was a *real* writer, not just a writer writer, but a good writer, a very good writer. And it was a wonderful feeling." It was in the thrall of this awareness that Elkin told William Gass, "Anything I say is a part of this novel *is* a part of this novel," which expressed this new confidence in his own vision and voice.

Elkin says frankly, "*George Mills* seems to me a terrific novel, and it seemed to me I couldn't top it, and it seemed to me too much work to write another novel." Although he had seen the news item that inspired *The Magic Kingdom* the year before, he did nothing about it until *George Mills* was finished, and he was sitting around doing nothing. "And when I was writing *The Magic Kingdom,*" he continues, "it seemed to me that that would be the last novel. But again I'm writing a novel"—he's already decided on the title, *The Rabbi of Lud,* for this comic tale of "a kind of pick-up rabbi—because I write good novels. I want to write as many of them as I can before I can't. There may be pens, but there's no ink in the sky. And they don't have word processors in the ground."

MIRIAM BERKLEY

173

LOUISE ERDRICH

W HEN LOUISE ERDRICH was a child in North Dakota, her father encouraged her to write by paying her a nickel a story. Once in a while, a story found its way into a book hand-sewn by her mother. Still, she had no urge to be a writer, she says, "until I got to college and found I wasn't much good at anything else." If Erdrich is, one suspects, being unduly modest about her nonliterary achievements, there can be no doubt about her talent as a writer. Within a single year, when she was 30, her first collection of poetry, *Jacklight,* and her first novel, *Love Medicine*—both published by Holt—received overwhelming acclaim. Laurels for the latter, which depicted the lives of two Chippewa families on and off a North Dakota reservation, included the National Book Critics Circle Award and the Sue Kaufman Prize; it was, in addition, a national bestseller.

With *The Beet Queen,* the second volume in a projected quartet, there is a new flurry of excitement around Erdrich. In addition to her literary output, Erdrich and Michael Dorris, who is her husband, her close collaborator and her agent, have produced two daughters—Persia, two and a half years old, and Pallas, one—the newest members of a family that already had three adopted children raised from infancy by Michael. Life in the public eye, Erdrich finds—she and Michael were profiled in *Life* and feted during the ABA with a mammoth dinner party at Antoine's— is a far cry from their daily existence in an 18th-century New Hampshire farmhouse, which is "consumed with baby details and children details." Says Erdrich, "It's as though we step into a life warp every time we leave our house."

The couple are open with us about their unconventional and profound collaboration. Erdrich, 32, and Dorris, 40, are each part Native American; she French-Chippewa on her mother's side, he Modoc on his father's. Both tall, slim, handsome, brown-haired and brown-eyed, they look as if they could be brother and sister, and recent college graduates rather than parents of a large family. Like newlyweds, they hang on each other's words; like the long-married, they interrupt, echo, complete sentences for each other. Actually, their relationship is both old and new; they have known each other since Erdrich first entered Dartmouth in 1972 as a participant in Dorris's Native American Studies program— and one of the school's first female students—but they have been intimately connected only for the last five years.

Erdrich grew up in Wahpeton, N.D., a small town on the Minn.-N.D. border, which is home to the Bureau of Indian Affairs boarding school, where both her parents worked, as well as to two convents. Her maternal grandfather, Tribal Chairman on the Turtle Mountain Reservation, observed both Catholicism and the traditional Chippewa religion. Erdrich (like Dorris) had a "gothic-Catholic childhood," but never thought about "what was Native American and what wasn't. I think that's the way a lot of people who are of mixed descent regard their lives—you're just a combination of different backgrounds. There wasn't a political climate at the time about Indian rights. I grew up just taking it all in as something that was part of me. It was a small-town life— lots of kids [Erdrich was the eldest of seven] living on a teacher's salary, and we were quite a chaotic, pretty typical family.

It wasn't until she attended Dartmouth that Erdrich began to look at her Native American heritage as something worthy of study. "I remember feeling at different times that the course material was really saying something to me, but sometimes it takes years of your own experience for what you learn in a class to catch up with you." She did not feel a stronger commitment until she got out of college and began to look back and see what was important.

Though she had entertained thoughts of an academic future and was adept at drawing, sometime during her undergraduate years she settled on writing as a career. At Dartmouth she won prizes for poetry and fiction. She illustrated a story that Dorris, then her instructor, had dreamed and written down ("Sometimes Michael just dreams up whole chunks of a story or novel"); it was eventually published in an Indian newspaper.

Erdrich soon became "a fanatic" about writing. "I had a very romantic idea of it. I thought I had to have a lot of experience— you have this notion about what the artist does to pursue the art—and also I had to support myself. I ended up taking some really crazy jobs, and I'm glad I did. They turned out to have been very useful experiences, although I never would have believed it at the time." During college and afterward, she waitressed in Wahpeton, Boston, Syracuse and elsewhere; worked at a Vermont state mental hospital; taught poetry in prisons and schools; lifeguarded; was a flag signaler on a construction site; and edited the *Circle*, a Boston Indian Council newspaper.

She spent nine months in a creative writing M.A. program at Johns Hopkins, alternately teaching and writing. Her degree manuscript included many of the poems later published in *Jacklight*, as well as parts of a "convoluted, unpublishable" novel, *Tracks*, that she compressed into the first chapter of a different book by that name, which will follow *The Beet Queen*. When she started sending out work for publication, she had only sporadic acceptances—first poetry, later a few stories. In Erdrich's parents' house, says Dorris, "are file drawers full of the better rejection slips." I only kept the ones," says Erdrich, "that said, 'Sorry. . . .'" "That actually had," Dorris interjects, "a human being's writing on them." How many rejections? Erdrich estimates, "Between two and three million." More seriously, a ratio of 30 no's to every yes. "I'd say I submitted to every address in the International Directory of Small Presses," she says.

But there were supporters, too, people who read her writing and offered encouragement. Dorris, whom she had met again when she went back to Dartmouth to give a reading, was among them. Although he says he was "not really much into poetry," he attended the event and "was absolutely blown away by the poems. I felt I wanted to get to know her." Erdrich had admired Dorris, she says, "but we just weren't contemporaries."

There was a lot to admire about this unconventional and articulate young man who had attended Georgetown and Yale on scholarship—with a B.A. in English and an M.A. in theater history—and who then, while a graduate student, discovered North American Indian Ethnology in the Yale catalogue and switched majors. Not long after, when Indian studies were being cut from many college budgets, he initiated a course at Dartmouth; he now heads the Native American Studies program there. Moreover, at the age of 22, Dorris, an only child who had always wanted siblings, adopted an infant Indian son. Two other children followed, because he loved and wanted kids but had no immediate plans for a wife.

Erdrich spent the next year or two working in Boston, and attended the MacDowell and Yaddo writers' colonies. Charles Merrill Co. published her textbook, *Imagination*, a learning guide for children, in 1980, and *Redbook* accepted a story she wrote with her sister Heidi under the name "Heidi Louise." Dorris, meanwhile, was in New Zealand, doing field research in anthropology. Free of teaching, he began to write fiction and to send it to Erdrich along with his letters, just as she sent him poems and stories. When Dorris returned to New Hampshire, so did Erdrich; there they began to collaborate on short fiction geared to a popular market. The stories were, as he puts it, "about people who were at crisis points in their lives. We thought they had good values, and they weren't schlock, but they were very accessible." On the level of serious fiction, however, "there was a much bigger barrier. But that eroded over time." Erdrich says, "We've gotten closer and closer in our fiction." They also fell in love and, in 1981, married, although they had to wait until their six-month anniversary for a first date without the kids.

Today, any work published under either of their names— novels, stories, poems or articles—is done in collaboration with the other. "We'll be talking about a character or a scenario and one of us will write a draft: a sentence, a paragraph, a page, a chapter," Erdrich explains. Each writes in solitude, he in a hardback chair at his word processor, she in a soft chair, with pen and pad. "Then the other person takes it and goes over it with a red pencil. The person who wrote the draft takes it back, tries again, sometimes four or five drafts' worth, until in the case of all three books [Erdrich's two novels and Dorris's *A Yellow Raft in Blue Water*], we sit down and read then aloud over a period of a week or so, and do the final paring and achieve consensus, on, literally, every word.

"In the course of it, we'll continuously plot and continuously talk about who the characters are, what they eat, what clothes they wear, what their favorite colors are and what's going to happen to them. In that way, I think it's a true kind of collaboration: we both really influence the course of the book. You can't look back and say which one made it go this way or that way, because you can't remember. You just remember that you had that exciting conversation."

"Nothing goes out of the house," says Dorris, "without the other person concurring that this is the best way to say it and the best way of presenting it. One of the beauties of the collaboration is that you bring two sets of experience to an issue or an idea, and it results in something that is entirely new."

Erdrich adds, "Some people don't believe it's possible to collaborate that closely, although we both have solitude and private anguish as well. You develop this very personal relationship with your work, and it seems fragile; you're afraid to destroy it. But I trust Michael enough so that we can talk about it. And every time I've been afraid to open it up, it has always been better for the work."

Love Medicine started out as a short story, "The World's Greatest Fishermen," written at white heat as an entry in the 1982 Nelson Algren fiction competition, which it won. "Then we got interested in the characters," Dorris says, "and it expanded into a novel. And we got even more interested in the novel, and it expanded into four novels." *Tracks*, the third volume in the quartet, gives the origins of the characters in the first two books. In the final work, the younger characters from *Love Medicine* and *The Beet Queen* will interact. The cross-generational aspect of their fiction owes much to the couple's closeness to their respective grandparents, who lived through the Depression—the period in which the story begins—and made it real to them.

When *Love Medicine* was three-quarters done, Erdrich took her mind off it by writing a short story, "Pounding the Dog," which is now part of *The Beet Queen*. When that was done, they began *Yellow Raft*. "So," says Dorris, "there's a kind of link-over . . ." ". . . which is useful once you finish a book," Erdrich continues, "because then you're already working on another, and you're not so scared about what's going to happen to the last one."

Another thing that takes their minds off writing is babies. According to Erdrich, *"The Beet Queen* was written while either rocking, feeding or changing. . . ." "Or having!" Dorris interjects. "A baby was there all the time," Erdrich agrees. "I was pregnant for two years and then nursing afterwards." "In both *The Beet Queen* and *Yellow Raft,"* says Dorris with a grin, "there are big birth scenes. And that's not an accident."

MIRIAM BERKLEY

HOWARD FAST

Howard fast has been a published novelist for 50 years. He finds this hard to believe himself and says he would never have dreamed it had been that long had not someone at Houghton Mifflin, his current publisher, "ferreted it out."

Having done so, however, the publisher made quite an occasion out of the anniversary: New York executive editor Nan Talese lent her lavish Manhattan townhouse for a crowded party, HM chief executive officer Harold Miller and editor-in-chief Austin Olney flew down specially from Boston, there was a presentation (of the original cover art for *The Immigrants*), kind and sentimental words were spoken and a grand time was had by all. And throughout the festivities, Fast—a gentle, self-effacing person who seems for all the world like an elderly English professor at a small college—remained the soul of low-key modesty.

The quietness of the man is at odds with the often bloody and hectic atmosphere of some of his novels—*Spartacus* and *Freedom Road,* for instance, two of his great early hits—and the unswerving devotion to leftist causes that made him for a time in the 1950s a pariah of the publishing world. But, as he notes gently, "It's impossible to think of myself without being against things like intolerance and injustice." In recent years he has also turned to Buddhism as "the only nonexclusionary religion on earth, and therefore the only one I feel at ease with."

It is hardly a surprise that Fast is not the model of a contemporary author in terms of self-promotion. "I hate to travel and push my own books," he says. A relaxed two-hour chat with us

180

however, was something else again—and proved to be a remarkable overview, from an unusual perspective, of half a century of publishing history.

Fast published his first novel, a forgotten work called *Two Valleys*, in 1933 with Dial. A second followed, and for his third, *Place in the City*, he went to Harcourt, where "I found my first real publisher, Sam Sloan, a man who became my dearest friend, counselor, adviser and father figure." Sloan shortly left to help found Duell, Sloan and Pearce, and Fast went for a time to Simon & Schuster. As he tells it, "They gave me a $1000 advance for my wife and me to go out and live on an Indian reservation in Oklahoma, where I wrote *The Last Frontier*. But when they read it, they wanted their money back." He took it to Sloan at his new firm, rewrote it for him and stayed with the firm until Sloan died in 1944.

The Last Frontier turned out to be Fast's first book "with some kind of sales and fame. In those days it took only about 25,000 copies to make a bestseller."

Fast's next three books were *The Unvanquished, Citizen Tom Paine* and *Freedom Road*—books on which a whole generation of radicals was brought up (although it is a cautionary note that when Grove Press recently wanted to reissue *Citizen Tom Paine* in paperback, it couldn't find a copy to print from and had to ask Fast for his own). *Freedom Road* was the big bestseller. According to Fast, "Some have estimated that it's the most widely printed and read book of the 20th century, and there's a bibliography that records editions in 82 languages."

After that, says Fast, "I was deeply involved in the war, first in the Office of War Information, then reporting the fighting for *Coronet* and *Esquire*," With the war over and Sloan dead, a difficult period began for Fast. His unwavering left-wing point of view brought him increasingly into conflict with the Cold War mentality developing in the country—and to add to his troubles, his publishers, he says, "got greedy." For his next book, *The American*, a 100,000-copy printing was ordered, a quantity almost unheard-of then, "and over half of them came back." Then he wrote *Clarkton*, "a real left-wing novel, rather tendentious, but with some good ideas, and that was a disaster."

Angus Cameron, editor-in-chief at Little, Brown, asked Fast to join them. He did a book of stories, *Departure, My Glorious*

Brothers and *The Proud and the Free* there before McCarthyism caught up with him, and he was jailed for three months for contempt of Congress for refusing to testify on his political beliefs. When he came out, he wrote *Spartacus,* "and Angus got very excited with it, saying it was the most significant historical novel he'd ever read. But Hoover sent his FBI agents up to Boston to warn Little, Brown not to publish it. As I heard it, there was a board meeting about it, Angus insisted he wanted to publish and was forced to resign."

At this point Fast became an untouchable within publishing. "So I decided to do *Spartacus* myself. I knew people in the trade, and I got a designer and a jacket artist, took an office, found a printer in Brooklyn, and we put it out. We distributed by direct mail at first, then Citadel agreed to distribute to the trade. We sold almost 50,000 copies in hardcover at $3 apiece."

Further self-publishing was not so profitable; Fast got out another three books, then went bankrupt—"proving, I guess, that a writer who publishes himself is a horse's ass." But at this point his career took another odd turn. He wrote a detective story called *Sylvia* and, because he was still a "nonperson" in publishing terms, sent it to Doubleday under the pseudonym E. V. Cunningham. It did well, became, says Fast, "a very bad movie," but launched Cunningham, under which name Fast has for years written a series of novels for Delacorte starring a Zen Buddhist detective in Beverly Hills. One of life's many ironies, for him, is that although "critics can't stand my mainline books, maybe because they sell so well, they love Cunningham. Even the *New Yorker* has reviewed him, and they've never reviewed me."

As the political atmosphere lightened, Fast found publishers again, including Crown, Morrow and Doubleday—and wrote what he still feels to be his best books, *April Morning* and *The Hessian.* "They're both extraordinary enough to make me wonder how I could ever have written them. They're not the sort of books you can plan to write, and if they happen, you're very fortunate. Twice in a lifetime is more than any writer can expect."

Fast seemed almost to have disappeared from the writing scene for a while in the early 1970s. He became deeply interested in Buddhism, wrote *The Art of Zen Meditation,* a little handbook that he says proudly has sold about 10,000 copies, and a book of Zen stories published with a small California press. Then, once again, his life took a new swerve. "My agent Paul Reynolds retired, and my son Jonathan and my daughter-in-law, Erica Jong, who knew a lot about publishing, took me to Sterling Lord." He in turn took Fast to Houghton Mifflin—"and for the first time since Sam Sloan I was reminded of what publishing used to be."

He decided that "no one in America had ever written a huge, detailed novel about a woman's life in this century, and I decided I'd do it. But first I had to give her some antecedents, and before I paused for breath I'd written 600 pages." The result was *The Immigrants* and a triumphant return to the bestseller list for Fast. It was followed by *Second Generation, The Establishment* and *The Legacy. Max,* his current novel about the movie industry, was an interruption, but now Fast is working on the last volume of his planned five-novel saga. He's finding it harder going, "because I bring Barbara's story right into the present time, and maybe I don't really understand the present time."

Fast is resigned rather than bitter about the fact that critics today don't take his work seriously. "I think I function in the direct tradition of the early American novel, as a storyteller rather than a philosopher or a teacher; so I'm resented by the school of criticism that rejects storytelling as superficial and looks on the novel as basically an examination of the interior life. They automatically see something like *The Legacy* as a soap opera, anything that traces a family over a period of time. . . . That's their way of categorizing things, preventing real thought. They don't choose to examine how *well* you tell a story, and that's what I'm interested in."

In many ways his current position is much like that of Irwin Shaw, and when we point this out, Fast is delighted. "Exactly! Irwin has been around almost as long as I have, and he's got the same problem with the critics. But to me he's writing better than ever."

Fast has by no means given up his leftist convictions: "I still take part in demonstrations and protests, and there's a lot to protest today. And I do a column for my local paper in Greenwich, Connecticut, mostly against the Bomb. Not long ago," he adds with great satisfaction, "the paper got an indignant letter saying: 'Don't you know your columnist is the son of Howard Fast, the Communist, and don't you think it rubs off on him, having a father like that?' "

Fast finds that as he ages, "The writing becomes easier mentally, but tougher physically. My eyes are going, my back is going." A word processor to ease the pain? "I'd need too much energy to figure it out." So he struggles on. And is, finally, philosophical. "I've had a good long run. I've survived, and there were times I never thought I would. And now, when I'm a bestseller again, my kids tell me: 'Dad, you've been recycled. It's all going to work out.' And I believe it will."

JOHN F. BAKER

LESLIE FIEDLER

"I<small>F</small> I <small>HAD</small> to use one word to describe what I think of as my real function in life, it would be 'mediator,' " says critic, novelist and poet Leslie Fiedler. For "mediator" others might substitute "provocateur" or "incendiary." A jury of his peers has hailed *this* critic as "exasperating," "offensive," "an incorrigible rascal" and "a bad boy." At 74, he could be called a senior subversive of contemporary letters.

Yet Fielder is also a good deal more. In his 24th book, *Fiedler on the Roof: Essays on Literature and Jewish Identity* (David R. Godine), the writer contends, sometimes elliptically, with an enduring theme: "my life-long identity crisis." The essays range in subject from the Book of Job to William Styron, but perhaps their true preoccupation is the frankly divided sensibility that guides them.

Some might consider Fiedler's "identity crisis" an insupportable burden. He, though, has made a virtue of it. Or, if not a virtue—the word does not seem native to him—then it is a welcome spur and a fruitfully pugnacious boon companion.

Meeting him and his wife, Sally, for lunch at their large, comfortably old-fashioned house in Buffalo, N.Y., we were struck at once by Fiedler's sanguinity: he seems an uncommonly self-possessed, even leonine man. Other impressions soon follow—of Fiedler's cleverness of phrase, stubbornness of mind and ascendant showmanship. For 50 years he has taught, mocked and fulminated in various ivory towers (and is now Samuel L. Clemens

185

professor of literature at SUNY-Buffalo). But not for nothing is he a veteran, too, of TV talk shows.

"I am essentially perverse," he declares. "I never had any interest, really, in being a teacher. . . . It's a mistake to teach literature at all, I think: the student doesn't have a sense of discovery about it. You have to teach it as if you *weren't* teaching it." And the main trade he plies—scholarly criticism—Fiedler has scornfully dubbed "the undertaker's art." Moreover, "When I was young, I couldn't decide whether to be an actor or a writer. Performers don't know who they are, really; they're the role they play at the time.

"I've made it, you know," Fiedler exults. "I am the only academic I know of who is listed in *Who's Who in Entertainment.*" On the stage, he has played Faust to fellow critic John Simon's Mephistopheles. Half a dozen years ago, he also appeared in *When I Am King,* "a strange little movie" in which he portrayed "the driver of a gypsy caravan circus, wearing tights, with a plume in my hand. A goddamn horse at one point ate my plume."

Born a pharmacist's son in Newark, N.J., from the start Fiedler "wanted to be known, and I wanted to be invisible at the same time. Part of my identity crisis was knowing my own name. When I was young and involved in radical politics, I had many names. For a time, my name was John Simon, of all things. (Since then, I've met at least four John Simons—one of whom I've cordially detested.) Then I called myself Dexter Fellows for a while—he was the PR man for the Ringling Brothers Barnum and Bailey Circus. At another point in my life, I stopped being Leslie A. Fiedler and became just Leslie Fiedler; I dropped the 'A,' which was for Aaron, who is my priestly ancestor." The death of a close boyhood friend who had performed under Fiedler's name in a Harvard production of *Waiting For Lefty* caused Fiedler to be "reborn. There was a new Leslie Fiedler. I took my name back, and from then on I haven't used any other." Incidentally, when he sent his early work out to magazines, Fiedler always used an assumed name—"A. Lazarus," for example.

"Americans *have* no real identity," he maintains. "We're all *déracinés,* uprooted people who came from elsewhere. That's why we are fond of hyphenated titles: Italian-American, African-American, Jewish-American. When I'm in America, I have no doubt that I'm a Jew, but I have strong doubts about whether I'm

186

really an American. And when I go to Israel, I know I'm an American, but I have strong doubts about whether I'm a Jew.

"I used to play a game with my kids when they were little," he offers, grinning, "about what they would inscribe on my tombstone after I was dead. One epitaph was 'Nothing if not ambivalent.' I'm not sure whether I'm convinced that you must believe, but I think you must *believe* that you believe. Yet sometimes I believe that I *don't* believe. It's meaningless to believe unless you have initial doubt.

"I think both Jews and Americans are exiles, rather than natives. But then another voice in me answers, '*Everybody* is a stranger in this world.' I guess the difference is that Jews have known they are strangers and been proud of it. That's one reason why Zionism disturbs me—Jews forget their heritage of being perpetual exiles, think that Zionism is a geographical location, not an abstract notion. Israel is *not* Zion; the Messiah *hasn't* come. This is *not* our home. I really wish I were a deep religious believer. Then I would know why it's good to be a stranger. I'd never forget that the world is just a place of temporary abode.

"Ancestors of mine not so far back made the blind see, raised the dead. The writer prays, but he prays to the muse. You ask for the creative spirit. I *suppose* that's prayer.

"You're so many things in your own lifetime," he reflects. "I had a great freedom to make myself. It's a terrible freedom, a scary freedom, because my family had cut off its ties with the old traditions."

Fiedler was a poet before he was anything else. "When I was in first grade, a poem of mine was read in an assembly before the whole school. You'll see what a learned kid I was when I tell you the title: 'Mercury and the Invention of the Lyre.'" Seven decades later, its author is still laughing. "For the first 20 years of my life, I never got further than 10 miles away from home. Writing was one way of traveling in the world. The way to find your identity, I discovered, was to write." The Newark public library also helped him to find himself, giving Fiedler a well-stocked place to skulk. "I remember walking through the open stacks when I was 14 and noticing a book with a beautiful red binding that turned out to be *Remembrance of Things Past*. Many books just fell into my hands like that. My mother thought my central flaw was an addiction to reading."

187

But books were not all that mattered to him. "When I was very young, I was mostly engaged in an abortive attempt to change the world," Fiedler says. "From the age of 13 to 21, I was a Marxist—first a Stalinist, then a Trotskyist. My dream was of a universal order, and it was not just something I yearned for and agitated for, but something I truly believed I could see happening around me. The great shock of my life is to see that the main political dynamism these days comes from separatist movements."

A peculiarly deep capacity for empathy made itself felt dramatically while he served in World War II as an interrogator of prisoners of war. "Before the war was over, I felt much more identified with the Japanese than I did with my buddies. I remember a prisoner who, when I was shipping him off to go to some other place, said, 'Take me with you. I love you.' The captor identifies with the prisoner, too. I thought of myself much more as the victim, though I had to be cruel."

As he sees it, Fiedler has passed through several incarnations. His view, however, seems judiciously adapted for ready access; one suspects that the real story is decidedly more complex. He earned his B.A. at New York University and his M.A. and Ph.D. at the University of Wisconsin, where his master's thesis was a Marxist analysis of courtly love. "I was thrice-born, I think. World War II made me young again. Then after the war was over, I went back to school at Harvard as a post-doctoral student and felt even younger. Then in the 1960s I decided I wanted to become young *again*—it was my last chance." An early advocate of the legalization of drugs, he allied himself with SUNY-Bufflo students in that cause, and was arrested for possession of marijuana in 1967. Though sentenced to six months in jail, Fiedler was later exonerated by the Court of Appeals of the State of New York—and memorialized the experience in *Being Busted* (Stein & Day, 1969).

Fiedler's debut as a writer of books occurred "late" by his own estimation—in 1955, when he was 38. *An End to Innocence: Essays on Culture and Politics* was published by Beacon Press at the urging of Beacon's consulting editor, Sol Stein; Fiedler was then chairman of the department of English at Montana Sate University in Missoula. At that point a short story writer as well as a published poet, he had wandered into the essay form because "occasionally when a story was turned down, the editors of a magazine would say, 'We can't use this, but would you be willing to review such-and-such a book for us?' Fiedler's single best-known essay, "Come Back to the Raft Ag'in, Huck Honey!," collected in *An End to Innocence*, was originally published in *Partisan Review*, where editor Philip Rahv "was sorry, later, that he'd published it. We had a total falling out." Stein, however, went on to publish many of Fiedler's future books under the Stein & Day imprint.

At *Partisan* Fiedler became acquainted with "a very great editor—Catharine Carver," who edited many of his books on a freelance basis. He has never had an agent. "I feel about agents the way medieval Christians felt about usurers." The sale of *Freaks* (1978) to Simon & Schuster, however, was handled by Tom Collins, whom Fiedler calls "a middleman." His other books include criticism, novels, collections of short stories, and anthologies. *Fiedler on the Roof* is the first volume of a projected trilogy. The second volume will contain essays written outside the field of literature—"I want to talk to everybody," Fiedler says—and the third, tentatively titled *Back to Innocence*, will collect essays on popular culture.

Fiedler claims, " 'Come Back to the Raft Ag'in, Huck Honey!' is really a poem. It's a short, lyric expression of the emotions, with a specific peg in the real world—the specific peg being another book." But a conventional critic would more likely term it an examination of underlying homoerotic currents between Huck Finn and Jim in Mark Twain's previously inviolable classic. As for his magnum opus, *Love and Death in the American Novel*, Fiedler calls it "a gothic novel disguised as a work of criticism.

"I don't make the traditional distinctions between fiction and criticism," he clarifies. "I am profoundly anti-methodological. My fiction is critical, and my criticism is fictional. I'm very different from academic scholars. All of the critics I admire have also been imaginative writers—Coleridge, Eliot, Pound, Lawrence, Poe. I don't think you can ever know what a work of fiction is unless you have constructed one yourself.

"Lawrence thought of literature as apocalyptic text. It's better to think of it as scripture, in a scholastic or Talmudic way.

"Many critics spend their lives wondering, 'How will this go over?' or, 'Is this the fashionable thing to do?' " Fiedler prefers to wield what he calls "the power to disturb. But it drives me crazy

189

that what I've been doing all my life has suddenly become fashionable. Everybody's talking about the canon; they've now invented something called cultural studies, which is what I've been practicing all along, seeing literature in its social context.

"I want to change people's *minds* with the revolution of the word," Fiedler says. "Yet one of my deep beliefs is that literature never really changes anything—it only makes you feel for a moment as though the world has changed. Maybe that's the best we can do. There's no flood prevention in literature. You can't even change the direction of the stream."

MOLLY MCQUADE

KEN FOLLETT

To THE BOOK world, Ken Follett seems to have sprung, fully armed, into bestsellerdom with *The Eye of the Needle* in 1978; in fact, things were by no means that simple, and the book, far from being a highly commercial debut novel, was the cumulation of years of practice—and frustration.

Relaxing in the offices of William Morrow, publisher of his last three books, including *Lie Down with Lions*, Follett, a youthful-looking 36, talks with disarming frankness about his publishing career to date, from the time he left "the only respectable job I ever had"—as a junior reporter on London's now-defunct *Evening News*—to his current eminence alongside such seniors as Robert Ludlum and Alistair Maclean as an automatic bestseller in the international action mode.

His introduction to American readers came about by way of Don Fine, then head of Arbor House, and although the two men had their difficulties, resulting at one point in mutual lawsuits, Follett still thinks of him with reluctant admiration in many ways. The young author received $20,000 for *The Eye of the Needle*, which, Follett says (and contrary to popular belief), did not require a major rewrite: "The second half was not rewritten at all, though there were certainly some changes in the first half." There was far more conflict over *Triple*, his second book, which Follett says *did* go through major rewriting by Fine. After that, their relations went from bad to worse. A "true-life" French crime caper book, on which Follett had served as a rewrite man ("Not a good book, not a rotten book," he says, "but one I didn't

191

want my name on at that stage"), became a bone of contention with Fine, who wanted to publish it with Follett's byline to capitalize on his new-minted fame. Lawsuits flew, a compromise was ultimately reached, and Follett took his act elsewhere.

Looking back on that introduction to American publishing, Follett is philosophical. "Don Fine had a big impact on my life, for better or for worse. He's given me a lot of headaches, but *Eye of the Needle* was safe in his hands—it was published with extraordinary enthusiasm and skill."

At that stage his agent Al Zuckerman (whom Follett describes as "virtually my collaborator") began introducing him around to other interested editors—including, especially, Pat Golbitz at Morrow. In the end, a contract was signed with New American Library, with Morrow as the hardcover publisher for his work, an arrangement that still continues. Golbitz, says Follett, "is an ideal editor because, although she has lots of good suggestions, she doesn't feel the need to claim she's written the book."

For Follett, the outline is central to his work methods. "I rewrite it many times trying to solve the problems at that stage. Most authors, I think, try to solve them as they go along. Then, although I may later rewire many big scenes, I do two drafts."

This was the way he worked on *The Key to Rebecca, The Man from St. Petersburg* and now *Lie Down with Lions.* An intervening book, *On Wings of Eagles,* was something altogether different. Follett recalls: "I was approached by the PR director at Electronic Data Systems in Dallas, who wanted to do a book on how his boss, the multimillionaire H. Ross Perot, had ransomed some of his key men from Iran at the time of the revolution. They wanted an authorized book because they were afraid someone would do an unauthorized one. It seems that Perot's wife, Margot, recommended me because she liked my stuff, but she didn't realize I wasn't an American. I was interested because I'd just done three novels in quick succession, and I was tired of it and looking for something different.

In any case, he went to meet Perot, and after initial reservations—"I thought at first he'd be too strong for me, would just want me to be a typist"—found they worked well together. "The real problem in doing the book was in how to explain all the preliminary negotiations without boring the reader. In the end, I did it by having people make phone calls to Perot reporting on developments and did it all in dialogue, with him asking the right questions. I learned a whole new way of writing for *Eagles,* and I could easily imagine doing another nonfiction book, in order to acquire new skills I could use again."

The young writer who found himself creating a paperback bestseller out of a peculiarly American adventure was born a long way from Dallas, "in a little terrace house in Cardiff in 1949." He explains: "It was very much a petit-bourgeois background. My dad was a clerk in the Inland Revenue [English equivalent of the IRS], and I went to state schools." When he was 10, the family moved to London, where he eventually took a degree in philosophy at University College. "At that time I wanted to be a captain of industry, then later I thought I'd be a great reporter." So he took a job with a London paper, and in his spare time began to write short stories.

He sold one or two, but nothing much came of them. Then came an epochal event. Driving in the country one day, his car broke down. "It was going to cost 200 quid to fix it, and I just couldn't afford it. I knew one of my fellow reporters had written a thriller on the side and sold it, so I decided to try my hand." Working furiously, he wrote a mystery thriller called *The Big Needle* and sold it—for £200—and fixed the car.

But he wasn't satisfied. "I read Forsyth's *Day of the Jackal* to see why it had sold so many copies, and I realized I was writing with the wrong attitude. What was in the book didn't *matter* enough to me. I had to know more, be more attentive to detail." He did 10 more books before *Eye*—"not good enough to be multi-million bestsellers, but not bad. Now we're bringing them out in a low key, like *The Modigliani Scandal* recently."

Eye was such a big success that for the first and only time Follett went to live abroad for a while to avoid English income taxes. "I thought it might be the most money I'd ever make in my life, and I wanted to keep it." He chose the traditional English refuge of the South of France. "I worked there well enough, and liked it, but I never thought of settling down there forever; I had no say in what was happening at home, which was the bloody Thatcher government." So he came home and now lives overlooking the Thames in London with a new wife, Barbara.

Follett also sees *Eye* as a turning point because for the first time it was an adventure story and a romance as well as a plain suspense story, with a strong female character. And in that sense, it is kin to Follett's latest, a thriller set against the unusual background of the civil war in Afghanistan, in which Jane, his enormously likable heroine, finds herself torn between her former lover, a CIA man, and her husband, a French doctor working clandestinely for the Soviets. "I chose Afghanistan because there, at least, most people could identify who were the good guys and who were the bad guys. In Nicaragua, say, it's not so easy, nor even always in the Middle East." As usual in preparing a book, he read a lot of newspapers and magazines and consulted available books. In fact, he offers a bibliography at the end. (And it's typical of the evenhandedness with which he approaches tough issues that he had Jane in the novel complain that an Afghanistan run by Moslem fundamentalists, if the rebels won, would not be so much better than one occupied by the Soviet Union.)

But it is probably in the climax of the book that Follett's rather offbeat approach to adventure fiction comes into its own. Faced with a moral dilemma seldom even hinted at in conventional swashbucklers, Jane acts out of her deepest feminist convictions at a crucial moment in the action, and nearly throws the whole story off course. And it was a change that only occurred to Follett after the first draft. "I had her acting the first time around as you might expect a heroine to act," he says (details omitted for the sake of the would-be reader). "Then it occurred to me that if she was really to be consistent with the character I had written, she simply wouldn't have done that." As a result, he had to write a whole new ending—and one that he acknowledges is a slight letdown in terms of tension. One of his villains also lives to fight another day. But will he? "I doubt it," says Follett wistfully. "But it would be good to create a cast of characters I could use again and again, without having to start from scratch every time."

It takes Follett about two years to produce a book; he acknowledges that he is somewhat slower than some of his bestseller rivals, but "I can't substantially hurry that up." He hardly needs to write to fix his car anymore, of course. "No, the pressure on me is simply the consciousness of not having written lately," he says, noting uneasily that he has been idle since finishing *Eagles*.

Oddly, he is one of those English writers (John Fowles is another) who do much better abroad than in their native land. "I do better in Italy, even—*Lions* is number one there at the moment, for instance—but America is certainly my best market."

He gives his engagingly boyish grin. "Naturally, I think the Americans are right."

JOHN F. BAKER

RICHARD FORD

In RICHARD FORD's fiction, characters wince at a painful moment, extract its grudging truth, and scramble to survive. Ford, whose fourth novel, *Wildlife*, is out from Atlantic Monthly Press, writes about "the smaller lives," their redeeming aches, and the luck or grit his people need to know themselves.

"I'm an optimist," Ford insists, but is rueful about what he calls, with amused chagrin, his "solemnity." It is something that permeates his stories and novels and also makes it presence felt in the author's soft-spoken yet hard-bitten Southern drawl. "I would rather be the guy who says 'I'm happy,' " Ford avows, "but I'm not much of a hoper. Rather than hope, I try to *do* something."

Since 1968, doing something has meant writing and it came about fairly innocently. "When I decided to write, it wasn't larky, yet it was quixotic," Ford says. "I didn't have any notions of making a life out of it. I had the idea of writing stories, one at a time." Briefly a law student at Washington University in St. Louis, he had grown dissatisfied with the "answers" the law prescribed. Having been away for a spell from his home in the South—he was raised a salesman's son in Jackson, Miss., and Little Rock, Ark.—and separated from his Michigan State University sweetheart, Kristina Hensley, whom he later married, Ford felt "itchy and curious." So he left the place where he was living and changed his life.

"Turning my life toward writing books was a pretty strenuous turn. I was wrenched around," Ford concedes. But by temperamental decree, the man seems to need to move. He has been called "peripatetic" with a swaggering romanticism that Ford fights shy of, claiming that such talk is "very tedious to me. I don't think I'm restless. I live in the U.S., and wherever I am, I am." (These places have included New York City, Chicago, Ann Arbor, Princeton, Missoula and now New Orleans.) Protesting that "your preconceptions about a place are not exactly what happens," he explains his roving by stating, "I need to be certain that I have new stimulus. New places give me something I can use." But the self-described fatalist grew up with "an awe of the unknown" that may have predisposed him to rapid transits. His awe, Ford says, "was useful. There were a lot of things I didn't understand, and I got accustomed to living with that. I discovered that the virtue of writing can extinguish the vice of ignorance."

Ford swears that "I wasn't an extraordinary young man at all, and I didn't strive to be. I liked to write because I could do it by myself." But he acknowledges the help he got—and the salutary boot out the door he received—from such mentors as E. L. Doctorow, with whom he studied at the University of California at Irvine, earning an M.F.A. in 1970.

Doctorow proved a useful teacher because, Ford says, he taught his students that once class ended, they had to make their own way in the world. "It seems like you're getting left out in the cold, yet you're supposed to be left out in the cold—and get your work done." A popular writing instructor himself at Princeton, Williams College and the University of Michigan during the '70s, Ford quit in 1981 because his yen for "the cold"—and his wish to concentrate his energies on writing—got the best of him.

"I was always a hard worker when I was young, and my ethic was to work hard at writing. But to make literature your life's habit is a fairly fragile habit," Ford observes. "You get to the point where you're doing it the best you can, and then you can't do much else. It's like walking down a road that gets narrower and narrower. As you get further out on that limb, it becomes precarious, but writing *is* a precarious life—and all life is precarious." Or, as a character in Ford's acclaimed short story collection *Rock Springs* put it, "The most important things of your life can change so suddenly, so unrecoverably, that you can forget even the most important of them and their connections, you are so taken up by the chanciness of all that's happened and by all that could and will happen next."

Ford broods, "Writing is the only thing I've done with persistence, except for being married to Kristina—and yet it's such an inessential thing. Nobody cares if you do it, and nobody cares if you don't. And the way you 'make yourself up' to be the author of your books, especially when you're young, depends on the stars coming into alignment. Life tugs at you. It's not as if there's a profession for writers out there; there isn't even a fraternity. You may have friends who are writers, but they can't write your books. I don't think writers *have* careers—my work doesn't exist separately from my life.

Ford's first book was *A Piece of My Heart,* brought out by Harper & Row in 1976, and nominated for the Ernest Hemingway Award for Best First Novel. *The Ultimate Good Luck* followed five years later; *The Sportswriter* was published in 1986. *Rock Springs* came out in 1987. All have been issued in trade paperback by Vintage.

As he has roamed, so have Ford's books. *A Piece of My Heart* was hailed by the *Boston Globe* as a Faulknerian "collision course with destiny set in the swamp-ridden Mississippi Delta." *The Ultimate Good Luck,* called by one critic "a bruiser of a novel replete with gunmetal dialogue and drug deals gone sour," takes place in Oaxaca, Mexico, and was completed while the Fords were living in Cuernavaca and Yahualica. *The Sportswriter* has New Jersey as its locale; Ford came to know Princeton well while teaching there. The backdrop of *Rock Springs* and *Wildlife* is Montana, where Ford moved in 1983 when his wife accepted a job as planning director of Missoula.

While Ford has changed addresses often, much of *The Sportswriter* and some of *Rock Springs* were written in a house in the Mississippi Delta, one of Ford's longtime favorite spots despite his reluctance to be classed as a Southern writer. Jackson, Miss., his boyhood home, continues to hold his affection—as does Jackson resident Eudora Welty—and many of his relatives are in northwestern Arkansas. Though Ford's attachment to Mississippi may be circumstantial (his parents settled there because it was located at the center of his father's sales territory), his ties to the South are such that his 1987 Mississippi Academy of Arts and Letters' Literature Award came as a special pleasure. Still, regardless of where he is, Ford aims "to write a literature that is good enough for America."

But no literature can be good enough for everyone. Ford recalls, with impenitent cheer, the reaction of "a famous New York editor" to the first hundred pages of *The Sportswriter*, later to sell upwards of 50,000 copies: "He told me I was wasting my life." Ford concludes, "I got bit there. But you'll always get bit." When his publisher, Simon & Schuster—for whom Morgan Entrekin had acquired *The Sportswriter* before leaving S & S—requested changes in the novel, Ford resisted. Gary Fisketjon, then at Random House, now Ford's editor at Atlantic—and soon to join Knopf—finally acquired the book as a Vintage Contemporaries Original. Agent Amanda Urban's entreaty—"You need a book that's going to do well"—was thus satisfied.

Not all critical response to *The Sportswriter* was ardent, but sportswriters made their enthusiasm known, writing fan letters to Ford (who, after college, had hoped to be a sportswriter for the *Arkansas Gazette*). Their testimonials? " 'I lay in bed with my wife and we read your book back and forth for a month,' " reports the author bashfully. "It hasn't made me rich, but it's made me read." Somewhat less gratifying was critic James Wolcott's fierce sally at Ford's accomplishments to date in the August 1989 issue of *Vanity Fair*. Deemed "a totally nasty piece of work" by Ford's publisher, "Guns and Poses: A Revisionist View of Richard Ford, the Lauded Novelist" was read by Kristina Ford, who told her husband not to try it. After letting fly with a few choice bits of invective, Ford philosophizes, "There are certain things that people are going to say about you that you can't redeem—you have to get used to it."

It was easier to get used to the praise of *Rock Springs* offered by such critics as the *New York Times*'s Michiko Kakutani, who cited his "wholly distinctive narrative voice . . . that can move effortlessly between neat, staccato descriptions and rich, lyrical passages," and novelist John Wideman, who lauded the way Ford fashioned a "concentrated, supple, ironic" prose style from "everyday speech."

In fact, some of the credit for that style should go, Ford says, to the poets he has read and admired over the years. Once merely "mysterious" to Ford, poetry became clarified when "I saw people *doing* it"—James Wright, Galway Kinnell, Gregory

Orr, Charles Wright, Donald Hall. "I saw how useful it could be to exercise such care over phrases and utterances and lines." In his own sentences Ford seeks a comparable "level of intensity, an economy of language and maximum effect."

Ford's "maximum effect" will soon extend to film; he has just finished wrapping up post-production work on *Bright Angel*, an adaptation of two stories (and a new one) from *Rock Springs*. Starring Sam Shepard and Valerie Perrine, the movie was directed by Michael Fields and shot on location in Montana.

Also an essayist, Ford served as guest editor of Houghton Mifflin's *Best American Short Stories 1990*. With typically gentle self-mockery, he recalls trying to say no to his first essay assignment, from Rust Hills of *Esquire*. The year was 1983, the magazine's 50th-anniversary issue was in the planning stages, and Hills approached Ford with the idea of writing a piece on Faulkner, Hemingway and Fitzgerald. "Oh, you're making a big mistake," Ford dodged. "That's just an opportunity to hang myself." "Well," Hills countered, "you've been likened to Faulkner, you've been likened to Hemingway, you've been likened to Fitzgerald." Besides, he added, "Philip Roth turned it down."

Other recent projects include Ford's introduction to *Juke Joints*, a collection of photographer-friend Birney Imes's work published by the University Press of Mississippi. And Ford was recognized for his lifetime achievements with an American Academy and Institute of Arts and Letters Award for Literature.

So he sits and works in his New Orleans townhouse, where the crime of the French Quarter is "scary." With his reputation as a "tough guy"—hotly disputed by Ford himself—and as a skillful evoker of male voices and violence, perhaps it's not surprising to hear Ford talk of a recent near-fistfight. "This man was threatening to beat up his girlfriend in front of our house. I just kind of stepped out the door and asked him to quit. So there we were, nose to nose. And the police came and wanted to arrest *me*. We settled it, though." Ford pauses. "Maybe I am a primitive and don't know it." He hunts and fishes "to forget about what's bugging me, because my father and grandfather did it, because Kristina likes to do it," and for the fun of raising bird dogs.

"Writer's lives are such pedestrian affairs," Ford complains. "You want to mine out everything you can, but then broaden your ways. In an effort to be demanding on myself, I create an aura of difficulty, in which things won't turn out right. But I would like language to be, in some secular way, redemptive. Writing *is* an act of optimism: you make a thing, make it well, give it to someone, and it has a use. They need it—though they didn't know they did."

MOLLY MCQUADE

PAULA FOX

ONE OF THE paradoxes of Paula Fox's professional life is her visibility as an acclaimed, prize-winning author of 17 books for children, and her relatively lower profile as a writer of six adult novels, all of them equally praised by critics but known to a smaller audience of discriminating readers. Yet her novels, with their finely honed, poetically compressed prose, resonating imagery, tensile energy and unsparing appraisals of life's struggles and rewards, would for another author be a sufficient oeuvre on which to build an enduring reputation. The latest of these is *The God of Nightmares* (North Point Press).

As in her previous books, the characters in Fox's latest novel are quiet people living ordinary but emotionally rich, complex lives against a subtly integrated backdrop of world and national events, art and politics. Generally they sustain a sometimes inchoate yearning to find meaning in the vicissitudes of human relationships and their troubling—and often ennobling—consequences. Fox's novels are existentialist questions, reflecting dark shadows as well as the moments of clarity and transcendence that lead to cautiously affirmative denouements.

The author's own life has been anything but ordinary; "unconventional," is her understated appraisal. Born in New York some 60-odd years ago to a young woman of aristocratic Spanish/Cuban descent and an Irish/English father who was a playwright and Hollywood scriptwriter, she did not live with her parents. Fox is unwilling to elaborate except to say that her mother was very young, and could not assume the responsibility for a child. One

202

senses more than a need for privacy in Fox's reticence; it is a desire to spare feelings and not rake up old hurts. Young Paula was sent to live in the home of a minister in upper New York State. "He was the great person of my childhood," she says; among other things, he taught her to read. When that arrangement ended, she was "rescued" by her maternal grandmother, who took her first to New York and then, when she was seven or eight, to Cuba, where the grandmother was a companion to an elderly relative who owned a plantation. They left during the 1932 revolution, when Batista achieved power. Living for short periods here and there, Fox found her schooling "terribly interrupted"—she attended nine different institutions by age 12, and was forced to leave school to support herself at 16.

"I had a very difficult, complicated childhood—as most people have in one way or another," Fox says with no trace of self-pity. "As a child I was very wary of adults. They tended to leave you behind in train stations." Once in a while she had a visit with a treasured uncle, who brought the possibility of another life, the world outside. "He was a kind of angel, but a fallen angel, the brightest spot of those bleak years. One of the benefits of having a disruptive and painful childhood, *if you're lucky,* is that you see there are other possibilities."

"What I feel now, looking back, is that the plate is in front of one that one is born to. You feed on it, as bitter as it is and as sweet as it is. God knows, I've had both. And then you don't want to undo your life after a while, not because it's wonderful or not wonderful, but because it's what you have."

The handsome, forthright woman Fox has become has a strong face, blue eyes that hold one in a steady, candid gaze, fashionably short hair worn in a chic flip to one side of her brow, and a deep, sometimes rueful laugh. Whatever the previous instability in her life—and indeed perhaps because of it—the house in Brooklyn's Cobble Hill that she shares with her second husband, critic, translator and former editor of *Commentary* Martin Greenberg, bespeaks order, warmth and welcome. A four-story brownstone, beautifully furnished with antiques and Oriental rugs on gleaming wood floors, it was built in 1860 and acquired by Fox with the money she earned for screen rights to one of her novels, *Desperate Characters.* Her husband's study on the top floor fronts on the quiet street; hers overlooks the back garden.

203

Her childhood experiences as a peripatetic, perennial outsider imbued her with a writer's sensibility, Fox declares. "It makes a sentry out of you. You're on guard; you're watching all the time. You swim in your own life like a fish most of the time. But then if you're thrown out of the fishbowl, you have to take into account a lot of other things. It's no virtue that's inherent in you. You become aware of the medium more than you might have if it's thrown into question all the time."

Before she began to write, Fox held a series of jobs too numerous to enumerate; a quick rundown reveals that she was a salesgirl, a model, and worked in a rivet-sorting shop and as a lathe operator at Bethlehem Steel during WWII. She went to California at 16, where she read books for Warner Brothers, including Spanish novels, since she was bilingual. A "terrific break" when she was 21 sent her to Europe right after the war, as a stringer for Telepress, a small English wire service; to make ends meet, she also read for Victor Golancz. On her return to Manhattan she found a job in a public relations agency and married Richard Sigerson, the father of her two sons.

At 30, divorced, Fox determined to finish her education. Though "not quite an elementary school dropout and not a high school graduate," she got into Columbia by dint of her wide acquaintance with literature, though her inveterate reading had left her largely ignorant of math or the sciences. She managed to complete almost the entire four years, simultaneously working at a full-time job and raising her sons, until debt forced her to quit. Though she laughs at her lack of diplomas, during her conversation with us, Fox easily and unpretentiously quotes Proust, Montaigne, Emily Dickinson, Thomas Mann, Trollope and Balzac with the authority of a scholar and the ardor of a lover of words.

A job teaching troubled children ("I developed a certain skill, probably because I'd had a tough time myself") led to positions at two prestigious Manhattan private schools. During that time she started writing seriously, which she had wanted to do since childhood. "That, I'm sure, had something to do with my absent father, whom I thought of as a writer, but it also had to do with an ineradicable tendency to tell stories and listen to them. Reading was everything to me. Wherever I went—except in Cuba—there was a library. Even though my schools changed, I'd always find a library."

In the late '60s everything came together for Fox. Her husband's Guggenheim took the family to Greece for six months, where she worked on a novel that became *Poor George*. Then she wrote—very quickly—her first children's book, *Maurice's Room*. She was teaching a fifth-grade class when she got a call from Harcourt Brace accepting *Poor George*. Shortly thereafter, Macmillan's Richard Jackson bought *Maurice's Room* and began a close professional association that has endured almost without interruption, Fox following Jackson to Bradbury Press, and recently to Orchard Books.

Despite her prolific output and her loyalty to editors, Fox has had some lean years. Harcourt Brace published her first three novels, but then "everybody was fired," including William B. Goodman, her editor there. The beloved, legendary Henry Robbins at Dutton bought her next novel, *The Widow's Children*, and her children's book *The Little Swineherd*, which had been turned down by 18 publishers; his premature death ended that association. An "endless" number of publishers rejected her stunning novel *A Servant's Tale* before North Point took it; she chose to stay with that house and her editor Jenny McDonald for *The God of Nightmares*.

Fox says she has been "terribly fortunate" in her editors. She would follow Jackson anywhere, she says. Goodman is now at Godine, which has just re-released *Desperate Characters* in what Irving Howe has called "one of those small triumphs of literary resurrection that can only bring pleasure." She is equally grateful for her longtime agent, Robert Lescher.

Though publishers did not always come forward immediately, once brought to fruition, her books for young people have been recognized for their ability to convey children's secret interior lives. Fox won the Newbery Medal for *The Slave Dancer*, a Newbery Honor for *One-Eyed Cat*, and the American Book Award for *A Place Apart*. The prestigious Hans Christian Andersen Medal, an international award bestowed for an author's entire body of work, went to her in 1978. She also has been the recipient of awards from the National Institute of Arts and Letters and the National Endowment for the Arts, and earned a Brandeis Fiction Citation.

Alternating between genres does not involve a conscious decision as much as some inner prompting, an idea waiting to be realized, Fox says; the nature of the problem dictates the book that ensues. "Most writing is the questions one asks oneself. What has happened to me? Does it have meaning? Is this its meaning? It's a peculiar process. I begin to think obsessively about certain things, but they come forth in their own time. I've been thinking about *The God of Nightmares* for 20 years, experimenting, trying to find the proper form. Sometimes I've interrupted an adult novel to write a children's book. They give me great delight, but I'm a little tired now; I've done four in the last 10 years, and that's a lot, because writing them takes exactly the same intensity and seriousness as a novel does.

"The timing of it is very tricky. Sometimes I force myself to begin a new book when I'm not ready. But there's a point when you can't wait any longer. Then I go to my room every day, even if I play solitaire or do crossword puzzles. Antonioni said that inspiration begins with images that haunt you, and a writer has to make these images speak verbally. Once I begin to work I find that I'm thinking about it all the time."

Because her books are written with a realist's eye, some critics have accused Fox of being downbeat, pessimistic. The charge raises her ire. "The American idea is that everything can be solved. Our lives are not problems to be solved! They're to be *lived*. One of the worst aspects of our country is that we like happy tragedies. Children are given liar's clothes early on. It's a way of not looking. One can't blame any of us for not looking sometimes, but it's a sad thing that children are given the means to corrupt themselves so young," she says heatedly.

The discrepancy between the reputation she now holds as a writer of children's books and the smaller core of readers who wait eagerly for her novels elicits from Fox the sturdy stoicism that has seen her through other vicissitudes. "One always has the feeling that there's a party going on to which one hasn't been invited. And do you know what? It's true. And do you know what else? It doesn't matter."

Her voice surges with intensity. "At the core of everything I write is the feeling that the denial of the truth imprisons us even further in ourselves. Of course there's no one 'truth.' The great things, the insights that happen to you, come to you in some internal way.

"I feel that every book has a kind of joy that approximates life. There's the joy of beginning; then the erosion and the wearing down, but ultimately it's the doing of it, the *living* that matters." And the talent that makes it possible for her to convey this philosophic blend of patient endurance and cautious optimism, the belief that meaning and happiness can be found, even in the face of what she calls "the implacable forces of time and loss." Fox is fervent: "How *glad* I am that it's been given to me!"

SYBIL S. STEINBERG

EDUARDO GALEANO

Although eduardo galeano claims to have been "a wretched history student," his latest book is the third volume in a trilogy that chronicles the awesome history of America from the Creation through 1984. (When Galeano says "America," he means every square mile from Alaska to Tierra del Fuego.) The trilogy, published by Pantheon and collectively titled *Memory of Fire*, comprises *Genesis* (1985), *Faces and Masks* (1987) and, recently, *Century of the Wind*. Galeano spent nine years writing the three volumes, using an anecdotal style replete with vignettes, songs, myths, reportage—indeed, every conceivable device except the traditional narrative of most histories. And, since he is Uruguayan, he stressed the history of Latin America, "that despised and beloved land."

Galeano's poetic prose is haunting, and, as his narrative moves from the remove past to our inevitable present, political horrors and prodigious violence become nearly unbearable. But Galeano the engagé artist transmutes brutality into beauty, championing the overthrow of unjust powers. In person, he is far more subdued. His English is fluent but heavily accented, and his sentences often sound like early drafts of poems. His flinty blue eyes betray a long and constant bombardment of pain.

"In *Memory of Fire*," he says, "the voice of my conscience and the will of my hand coincide absolutely. I was looking for little stories that would reveal the great ones, the universe seen through a keyhole. The little things about little people reveal the history of America—the *masked history*, not a history officially

208

reduced to figures of bronze or marble. I was looking for the other side of it, which is the daily life of common people.

"I was looking for stories with electricity. I was looking also for those magic moments when history speaks a perfect language of symbols, for history expresses itself as a poet through metaphors." Galeano gives as an example of such a metaphor Juan José Castelli, an early-19th-century revolutionary/orator in Argentina. Just when the push for independence from Spain faltered, Castelli got cancer of the mouth, and his tongue was removed. "That's what I mean," says Galeano triumphantly. "In the moment when the revolution became mute, its speaker lost his tongue. This is precisely what I was looking for."

To fill three volumes with such striking metaphors of history, Galeano consulted thousands of books, periodicals and documents. He also drew upon his memory and those of his friends. Although he included bibliographies of several hundred sources at the end of each volume, he admits that these are only the main ones. "I didn't make the list longer because it would seem arrogant," he says.

The 47-year-old author concedes that his work is difficult to classify. "It's not an objective book of history," he says, "and yet my intention is that it may be used as a history text in universities. But it's also a poetic novel and a long chronicle of life in America. It has elements of the essay, of the novel, of the short story, of testimony—everything at once. I'm trying to create a synthesis of all the different ways of expressing life and reality. And, when I speak about reality, I am speaking about dreams also. Perhaps they are the most important part of reality."

Galeano had already perfected his style, which Gregory Rabassa has called a "verbal collage," before starting *Memory of Fire*. "I discovered this way of expression through *Days and Nights of Love and War*" (an autobiographical volume published in Spanish in 1978 and in English in 1983). As a political exile in Spain in the late '70s, Galeano was, he says, "broken in pieces." Speaking hesitantly, as though experiencing anew some of the anguish of those years, he explains how, upon his arrival in Spain, he had "a strong need to bring together my broken pieces. So I began writing that short text, which was, in a manner of speaking, the pieces of myself. I tried to create a structure from all the broken pieces of myself, like putting together a puzzle. *Days and*

Nights of Love and War resulted from this open, free conversation with my own memory, as I tried to understand what had really happened and to guess who I really was."

What had happened was a military coup in Uruguay in 1973 that forced Galeano to flee across the border into Argentina. Three years later, a coup in Argentina sent him into exile in Spain. Galeano, a leftist journalist with high visibility, was persona non grata to the military dictators. Although he was still in his early 30s when the military took over in Uruguay, he had been an influential member of the left-wing press for almost two decades. At age 13, in 1953, he began publishing cartoons in *El Sol*, the weekly paper of the socialist party in Uruguay.

In his late teens, Galeano began writing for *Marcha*, a weekly journal of opinion that he considers "the most important Latin American publication in all of history." *Marcha* published his drawings as well as his articles, and, in 1961, he became editor-in-chief. In 1964, he was appointed director of the daily newspaper *Epoca;* two years later, he assumed the position of editor-in-chief at the University Press of Montevideo.

Soon after his arrival in Argentina, Galeano founded the magazine *Crisis*. "At its peak," he says, "it sold almost 40,000 copies a month, which was the highest circulation of any Spanish-language cultural publication ever." Galeano describes *Crisis* as "showing the best of Latin American literature, arts and popular culture." He emphasizes that the magazine tried "to *show* popular culture alive and powerful, not merely to speak about it."

Despite his crowded life in the '60s and '70s, Galeano wrote several books, including novels, short story collections and nonfiction works on China and Guatemala. The latter was the first of Galeano's books translated into English; Monthly Review Press published it in 1969 as *Guatemala: Occupied Country*. Galeano had met Paul Sweezy and Leo Huberman of Monthly Review a few years earlier in Uruguay. When his book on Guatemala came out, he sent them a copy, and "they found it interesting enough to publish it in the U.S."

Monthly Review chose Cedric Belfrage to translate the book, an auspicious choice both for the publisher and for Galeano. Belfrage also translated Galeano's *Open Veins of Latin America* for Monthly Review in 1973, and by the time Galeano began work on *Memory of Fire*, he considered Belfrage indispensable. "We are very much identified with each other," says Galeano. "I feel that I wrote his English version of *Memory of Fire*, and he, I'm sure, feels that he wrote my Spanish version. This is the dream of any writer—to have such a relationship with a translator. And, especially with one who is himself a fine writer, as Cedric is." (Born in London in 1904, Belfrage came to the U.S. in 1925. He was a cofounder of the *National Guardian* in 1948 and its editor until 1955, when a brush with McCarthyism led to his deportation. He has written 10 books, both fiction and nonfiction, and now lives in Mexico.)

"Cedric is not at all a passive translator," Galeano says with a smile. "While he was translating *Memory of Fire*, he identified so strongly with my way of writing that he became angry each time I didn't write what he would have written. He felt I was betraying him." Galeano usually makes photocopies of his first draft of a book and sends them to a dozen or so friends. When he collects all their opinions, he starts to revise his manuscript. Belfrage, of course, always receives one of these photocopies. The resulting collaboration is far more intimate than it would be if Belfrage merely received the completed book to translate. According to Galeano, "He not only suggests changes, he fights for them. Sometimes when I didn't make the change he wanted, he got angry." Galeano and Belfrage have more than a friendship; Galeano calls it "our brothership."

In addition to his outstanding translation, Belfrage did Galeano an enormous service by introducing him to his own agent, Susan Bergholz. "Until I knew Susan," Galeano says, "I was more or less lost in U.S. publishing. Then she appeared like an angel, exactly as angels appear in the Bible. Sometimes I tell her, 'It's a mystery to me how you can be so enthusiastic about my work.'" Galeano also feels fortunate to have Tom Engelhardt as his editor at Pantheon. "He handles my books with such delicacy," he says.

In Uruguay, Galeano publishes his own work, but, with the international success of his books, he finds himself signing contracts with more and more foreign publishers. Besides the North and South American editions of *Memory of Fire*, the trilogy has been published in Germany, France, Greece, Scandinavia, Spain and the U.K.

The critical success of *Memory of Fire* has made readers and publishers eager to see Galeano's earlier works. Although *Open*

211

Veins of Latin America sold slowly at first, it has turned into what he calls "a lucky book," with 55 printings of the original Spanish version. In the early '60s, Galeano visited China. His book on the Sino-Soviet split came out in 1964 but has never been translated into English. Now, however, there is a particularly timely reason for a translation, since it includes Galeano's interview with Pu Yi, the "Last Emperor." "The Bertolucci film has made him a big shot now," Galeano says, "but then no one paid any attention to him. We spoke for two hours, and he was enthusiastic; no one else was interested in what he had to say." The emperor could have conversed with Galeano in English or French, but, instead, chose to speak Chinese through an interpreter. He uttered only two words of English during the interview. While they were discussing the Japanese period, during which Pu Yi was in power in Manchuria, Galeano asked him, "Puppet?" and the emperor replied, "Yes, puppet." Even as a young journalist, Galeano was already seeing the universe through a keyhole.

By 1984, the military government of Uruguay had weakened, so Galeano made a two-day visit to his country to test the political climate. Since he wasn't threatened by the authorities, he made plans to leave Spain and return home. While preparing to end his exile, however, he suffered a heart attack and had to postpone his homecoming for several months. He wrote in a letter to a friend at the time, "My heart broke because I used it too much."

And no wonder. Galeano declares, "I was never outside my material, never. So I suffered a lot. But I also had very happy days, because I was inside a joyful and terrible history." His empathy is evident on every page of *Memory of Fire*. One does not feel he is overstating when he says, "I identified so strongly with the history I was telling that it came to feel like my autobiography." On the last page of the final volume of *Memory of Fire*, he himself jumps into history, as it were, by making the final "scene" a personal letter to Cedric Belfrage. Galeano concludes with the affirmation, "Now I feel more than ever proud of having been born in America, during the century of the wind."

SAM STAGGS

GEORGE GARRETT

A CONVERSATION WITH George Garrett is a merry experience. His pink-flushed, cherubic countenance alive with fun, he regales the listener with an inexhaustible series of literary anecdotes, delivered with gleeful grins and punctuated with appropriate gestures, superbly mimicked voices and even, at one point, an illustrative dash across the room. It is sometimes difficult to believe that this witty raconteur, who could make many a standup comic gasp with admiration, is the author of numerous works praised for their fidelity to historical detail, an authenticity that can be achieved only through assiduous, painstaking scholarly research.

Beneath the genial patter and animated delivery, however, lies the soul of a perfectionist. Garrett's book *The Succession* is an example. Years ago Garrett signed a contract with Doubleday for what he meant to be "a nice, skinny little book" to be finished in one year, as a companion to his highly acclaimed novel *Death of the Fox*. The volume he delivered more than a decade later is not "skinny" at all; it is robust in size, scope and concept, and it evokes the complex, dramatic, paradoxical world of Elizabethan England with a remarkable breadth of imagination and in a rich, rhythmic prose.

Initially intended to be a crystallization of the letters between Elizabeth I of England and James VI of Scotland, the book changed its form several times. By the time it was finished, "practically everyone at Doubleday was dead or gone except Sam Vaughan," Garrett says. "Sam had been very patient, till about the 10th year. Then I began to get very crisp letters sprinkled with legal phrases." Even now, Garrett admits, "I would have liked to have spent another 10 years on it. There are many things I didn't get to," he observes.

Garrett's interest in the Elizabethan period dates back to a childhood fascination with his mother's brass dinner bell embossed with a picture of the Queen. Born in Orlando, Fla. (traces of a southern accent soften his speech), he was already writing poetry after his graduation from Princeton in the 1950s when he came across "a quite wonderful book" by Agnes Latham, in which she had put together for the first time the correct text of all of Sir Walter Raleigh's poetry. "It was my first experience of real detective work, a scholarly job," Garrett muses. In her introduction, Latham mentioned that an authoritative biography of Raleigh had yet to be written. "I thought: *I* noticed that but no one else will, and I decided I would be the man to do it." The Korean War intervened, and by the time Garrett came out of the army, several Raleigh biographies had appeared. "So I started thinking about a novel." But *Death of the Fox* had an even longer gestation period than *The Succession;* Garrett worked on it for 20 years.

Throughout his career, however, Garrett has devoted himself to many projects simultaneously. His literary output is impressive: six volumes of poetry, six collections of short stories, four novels, two plays and assorted filmscripts. Poetry was the field he initially intended to pursue. It took him quite a while, he says, to realize that he "wasn't quite doing what other people were doing in poetry. People said, 'Hmmm, this is very strange. No one writes like this.' I took it as a compliment."

With typical self-deprecatory humor, Garrett relates the advice he received from R. P. Blackmur at Princeton. "He said: 'Someday you'll be wanting to send your poems around to magazines. Don't be discouraged. At first they'll reject everything, particularly in *your* case. What you do is keep sending the same poems to the same people, after a decent interval, of course. After about the fourth or fifth time they will actually read them, and they will hear a little bell ring that they'll call the shock of recognition, and they'll take one.' "

Garrett claims that's exactly what did happen. "I never even retyped them. I just moved the paper clip so it wouldn't get rusty." Although he swears that one of his submissions to the *New*

Yorker was returned the same day he sent it, eventually the literary magazines began accepting his work.

In the interim, Garrett attended graduate school after being mustered out of the service, on a fellowship designed to bring Princeton graduates back to the English department. He never did turn in his dissertation, however, being waylaid by the long gestation of *Death of the Fox*. While that project languished in turn, he published several volumes of short stories and poetry and two novels, before confidently submitting his third novel, *Do, Lord, Remember Me*. "Everybody rejected it, some with real enthusiasm, including Little, Brown, which had published my previous two novels. I remember I got their letter on Christmas Eve. It began: 'This book is both scabrous and orotund.' I had to look up both those words. Ever since I have seen them as my blurb: 'This author is both scabrous and orotund.'"

The publishing woes of *Do, Lord, Remember Me* take on a saga-like quality in Garrett's jocose rendition. The novel next went to Charles Duell, of Duell, Sloan and Pearce, who bought it. Soon afterward, however, the company merged with Meredith Press. According to Garrett, during the final negotiations on the merger, Meredith promised Duell "absolute editorial discretion, *except* for one thing. They would not publish *Do, Lord*. Meredith is, of course, *Better Homes & Gardens,* and they thought my book was trash." Duell compromised by getting Meredith to agree to publish another book by Garrett, and phoned him directly from the meeting. "He said, 'Give me, on the phone now, any title, any subject, and you have a contract.' I said, 'How does Sir Walter Raleigh strike you?' He said, 'Done!'" But Duell died before Garrett finished *Death of the Fox,* and when he finally turned in the manuscript to Meredith, the house was no longer doing trade books and was less than eager to publish it. Garrett eventually went to Doubleday, where Sam Vaughan had meanwhile brought out a truncated version of *Do, Lord,* and Vaughan took it "after everyone else in town had rejected it," Garrett says.

Garrett's main means of support in addition to his writing has always been teaching. After a peripatetic career, he is now professor of English and senior creative writer at the University of Michigan. "I used to think when I got straightened out I'd quit teaching, but I'm still doing it," he says, with wonder rather than regret in his voice.

215

To augment his income Garrett began giving poetry readings early on, and now is much sought after on the lecture circuit. In the early '50s, Marianne Moore heard him read, and sponsored him as one of the participants in a well-publicized symposium at the Museum of Modern Art in New York City. "I thought it was going to be easy," Garrett says. "I had never had anything published yet, and there I was reading at the MoMA!" The reality was far less glittering; there were many years during which his readings were the only means of exposing his poetry to the public, years during which Garrett claims that he "earned the world's record for performing before a minimal audience." He cites the experience of reading "to an audience of one—a ferocious lady—in a huge auditorium in Knoxville, Tennessee. Her husband makes two, actually. She said, 'He stayed up late last night writing your introduction. Now you *read!*' "

Between delivering *The Succession* to Doubleday and its publication date, Garrett has been involved in several projects. He has completed a short biography of James Jones for the Harcourt Brace Jovanovich series on writers. "I had no idea it would be so much fun," he says. "Neither Gloria [Jones's widow] nor Frank MacShane [Jones's official biographer] knew about all the stuff in the trunks up at Yale. There were furious letters to magazine editors, along the lines of: 'You fool! I'll punch you in the nose if you don't publish this.' "

Garrett also put the finishing touches on a volume of his collected poems to be published by the University of Arkansas Press, and a collection of short stories for Doubleday. He has promised Doubleday another "skinny short novel" based on the character of an actor in *The Succession*. "It will be a kind of little Elizabethan detective story," he says, "on the murder of Christopher Marlowe. People have a lot of theories about it, but right now I don't have any theory at all. We'll see what happens."

Juggling many assignments is a way of life for Garrett. Despite his accounts of his experiences as a series of humorous contretemps, one senses that hard times have come a-knocking more than once. During the long period of writing *The Succession* "things had gotten quite severe in our lives," he admits. Though his wife Susan and his three children "had made all the sacrifices," they never complained, he says. "But this novel had to be done right for Susan. She changed her whole life for me." An excellent classical guitarist and lutanist, according to her husband, "and a great teacher with the potential for a fine career," Susan Garrett gave up her profession during the lean years. After paying off his debts when *Death of a Fox* was published, Garrett had "just enough money to have a real concert guitar made for her." Midway during *The Succession* she sold it, went back to school and became a health administrator. "She was one of the first women in the U.S. to run a hospital," Garrett claims.

Aside from the financial pressures, writing *The Succession* was "the most exciting experience in my life," Garrett says. "There were moments that overcame everything else, times when I really had this feeling of *presences* around me as I wrote. I kept thinking: How lucky I am to be doing this! Here I am getting to do exactly what I want to do!"

He has two rules for writing historical fiction, Garrett tells us. One comes from his "mentor and guide" Shelby Foote. "Getting his approval was very important to me. He doesn't like historical novels at all, although he wrote one brilliant one—*Shiloh*—and then the magnificent three-volume history of the Civil War." Foote can be "very eloquent and persuasive about why one shouldn't write historical novels," Garrett says, "but he has come around in the case of the Elizabethans. He thinks they were people so concerned with imagery and the fictive life that it's all right to write about them in fictional form. But I am concerned not to cheapen them, that's my first rule," Garrett says.

His second guideline is "never knowingly to violate the world of fact. It's complicated because I don't know enough," he says modestly. "I may do it by mistake, but *never* on purpose. It's almost a moral code for me," says this exuberant author, quite serious at last.

SYBIL S. STEINBERG

NADINE GORDIMER

"RIGHT FROM THE beginning," says Nadine Gordimer, "I used my own background. Everything that I wrote was related to what I knew." For nearly half a century, since she began to write as a young girl, Gordimer's fiction has delineated meticulously the many different realities of her native South Africa.

In nine novels and nearly as many collections of short stories, this writer, winner of the Nobel Prize in Literature, has made palpable the pernicious, pervasive character of that country's race laws, which not only deny basic human rights to most people but poison many relationships. As South African political and social conditions have deteriorated, her writing has taken on a heightened sense of urgency. Her 1981 novel *July's People* drew a frightening picture of civil war in the near future. Her novel *A Sport of Nature* may well be considered her masterpiece. A BOMC and Quality Paperback selection, the novel features a heroine whose development into a leading figure of emerging Africa is set against the last few decades of her country's, and her continent's, history; it ends, also in the indefinite future, with South Africa under black majority rule.

Despite the opportunity to emigrate, and to live and work under more secure conditions abroad, Gordimer has chosen to remain in Johannesburg, where she continues, as she puts it, "to oppose apartheid with might and main." We spoke with Gordimer, a slim, small woman with an unusually expressive face and a clear, finely nuanced voice, on two occasions: first, when she was in New York for last year's PEN conference—she is vice-president of International PEN—and again recently. In the interval, Gordimer's activities have included the completion of *A Sport of Nature*, which took her three and a half years to write; lectures and readings in Germany; the acceptance of honorary degrees from Harvard and Yale, and publishing *Lifetimes: Under Apartheid*, which couples selections from her prose with photographs by David Goldblatt. She has helped to organize the Anti-Censorship Action Group (ACAG), in response to increased censorship imposed in South Africa with the second State of Emergency, and is also involved in planning a national writer's conference, "South Africa—Beyond the Platitudes."

Nadine Gordimer was born in 1923 in the small mining town of Springs, in the Johannesburg area of the Transvaal, the second of Isidore and Nan Gordimer's two daughters. Her father had come to South Africa as a 13-year-old fleeing poverty and anti-Semitic oppression in czarist Lithuania and gradually built up a jewelry business. He was, she explains, "like many people who've had a tremendous struggle when they're very young, only concerned with his own survival." Her mother, from a long line of London Jews, was "a generous-hearted woman with a genuine feeling for people," whose social conscience led her to perform "good works" but not to question the basic order of things. "She didn't see that you have to carry it to political action."

Gordimer and her sister were day students at a convent school, which her parents believed provided a better education than the state school. Their younger daughter was, however, "a bolter," continually running away. "I had very claustrophobic feelings about school. I'm lucky to be a writer. I seem able to discipline myself, but from a very early age have been unable to be disciplined by other people," Gordimer says.

As a child she was vaguely conscious of antagonism between Afrikaners and English-speakers, but it wasn't until adolescence that she became aware of racial injustice and began to question what she saw. She found the process "a shattering one, because you realize that your whole life, your whole inheritance, is based on something that is wrong. My father had come from exactly the same kind of family situation that blacks were living under: his parents couldn't afford to live with their own children, the children were restricted from schooling, and so on. And then he became the overlord and white master. He was acceding to, if not actively taking part in, the administration of repression of another people."

By this time, Gordimer had become the family intellectual, although, she says, "It wasn't noticeable. When you do things that other people in your family are not doing, you become very secretive about it." At 10 she began writing stories for the children's corner of the local newspaper.

Books (" 'Literature' seems a big word to put on a child's plate," she notes), were her passion, and she read widely in the local library. "I was like a pig in clover. Nobody said, 'These are the hundred best books in the world, and you've got to read them,' so I read an extraordinary mixture of things—at the age of 12, *Doctor Dolittle* and Thucydides and Pepys's *Diary.* That's an ideal way for a writer to grow up."

Gordimer bought a Hermes "Baby" [typewriter] at 14 or 15 and, not long after, published her first adult story, "Come Again Tomorrow," in a Johannesburg weekly. Other stories, which reflected her burgeoning social awareness, followed; one dealt with a police raid on the backyard quarters of a black servant who brewed illegal liquor; it "exposed not so much brutality, but the tremendous sense of authority of the police.

"I invented my characters from things I knew well. I'd been living among these policemen, I'd seen them arresting people in the street. That particular kind of incident became my subject then. I wasn't saying, 'I must do something about it.' I was saying, 'This is what's happening. What does it mean in my life? And what does it mean in the life of the country that I'm born into?' "

At 25, Gordimer published her first collection of stories, *Face to Face,* and embarked on a short-lived marriage, which produced a daughter. In 1950 her work began to appear in the *Yale Review* and other American literary magazines. A *New Yorker* story the next year led to query letters from American publishers, then Simon & Schuster's 1952 publication of a collection of her stories, *The Soft Voice of the Serpent* and, a year or two later, of her first novel, *The Lying Days.* Living modestly—"but doing what I wanted, which was a great luxury"—she was able from the start to subsist on her writing. In 1954 she married Reinhold Cassirer, with whom she has a son.

Gordimer has had three books banned by the South African government but otherwise seems to have been left surprisingly alone. "It's rather different here from the way it is in Eastern Europe. There is a slight difference with black writers, but even with them it is not the *writing* [that causes problems]," Gordimer says. She mentions an article in the *New York Times* reporting Breyten Breytenbach's imprisonment for expressing opposition to apartheid. "Breytenbach's books are all available in South Africa, even the book about South African prisons. That's how marginal we writers are. He went to prison because he became an active revolutionary. We must be fair: no writer has gone to prison in South Africa for what he has written. All honor to the writers who have put writing aside and had the courage to do other things as well."

Perhaps more surprisingly, Gordimer is read not only by those who share her views but by those who oppose them as well. "The paradox again is that the standard of reviewing in the English-language papers is unspeakable. But in the Afrikaner newspapers, which are mostly pro-government or to the right of the government, they have got serious pages on literature and a quite remarkable standard of reviewing. Simply as literature, they'll review anything that isn't banned."

Why were her books banned? "They're not obliged to give you a reason," she says, but she supposes that *A World of Strangers* (1958) was banned because "there was still at that time this fruitless attempt to discourage the idea that there could be absolutely equal human contact, that if you wanted to, you could defy the law, go in or out of the townships, have love affairs, have close friendships. There was a close friendship in the novel that showed up the cruelty and idiocy of apartheid and the dangers of daily life for blacks. It would never have been banned 10 years later, and, indeed, it was banned for 10 years.

"Then I wrote a book in the mid-'60s called *The Late Bourgeois World*, and that had much more reason to be banned. It arose out of a time after the big liberation movements—the African National Congress and the Pan-Africanist Congress—were banned and small liberation movements had sprung up. There were young people in the universities, not just students, but academic people of the Left, who tried to start a movement which would work in a loose way with blacks and would try selective violence, since passive resistance seemed to have failed or been crushed. It was a story of people of that time, and it was perhaps a savage picture of their parents, because my feeling was that their ineffectuality had produced this desperation. That book was banned for 12 years."

Of *Burger's Daughter*, published in 1979, Gordimer says, "As soon as I knew what I was going to write about, I thought, 'Impossible, this book will not be read here.' It was banned immediately. But by then I had become pretty well known in the outside world, and I did my only bit of vanity publishing, with a little, semi-underground publishing house—rebel Afrikaners, God bless them. I wanted to publish a little pamphlet, 'What Happened to *Burger's Daughter*.' I had discovered that the writer had a right to get the opinions of the people on the board who said it should be banned. I published these, which were staggering reading for most people—the intellectual level of people who were judging books!—with some of the reviews the book had been getting abroad, and objections from other writers, among them Heinrich Böll.

"As a result, that book was banned for only four months, and then they released it. And they released several other books as well by white writers. Then we, the white writers, made a fuss and said, 'We're not thanking you. You're using us. Until you release [certain] banned books by black writers, it's not even a crack in the wall of censorship.' And they did release an extraordinary book, an anthology put together by a black writer."

How does she see South Africa's future? "It's very difficult to say," she replies, her voice, as she continues to speak, beginning to shake with distress. "Now you're seeing quite a lot of white people like my couple Maureen and Bam [in *July's People*], who are not ill-intentioned people, and who genuinely believed they were doing everything, and perhaps they were, to prepare their lives in a different way, but who found out about it too late, and all the time were under a delusion about the things they were doing and the way they were being understood. And I think this is true for all of us living there. We are, unfortunately, terribly ill-prepared for the future that is coming.

"It's awful to think that people do not know how to live, even if they have the best intentions—they will not know how to live in a decent way when the opportunity is given to them. There are many people who say, 'It's a shock to think of living under a black majority government' and are running around asking for minority guarantees and all the things they should be able to see only perpetuate racial differentiation, instead of looking at their own country and looking for the best way to run their own country.

"The whites wouldn't see that their structures were bursting at the joints . . . the edifice of white justice, big enough only for a minority, could not hold," Gordimer writes toward the end of *A Sport of Nature*. "It is all one country now, there are no homelands, but only a homeland."

MIRIAM BERKLEY

DORIS GRUMBACH

AFTER YEARS OF big-city life—as a child and young woman in New York City and its environs, a wife, mother and teacher in Albany, N.Y., literary editor of the *New Republic* and then freelance critic and novelist in Washington, D.C.—Doris Grumbach has fled an urban environment she finds increasingly hostile and settled in rural Maine. Here, she writes in *Coming into the End Zone* (recently published by Norton), "I have recovered the sight of the horizon." Her memoir chronicles in intimate detail the feelings of futility and anger that engulfed her during much of the year that followed her 70th birthday in July of 1988, but ends on a note of hope as she finds tranquility and renewal in a new landscape.

A visitor to Grumbach's home in Sargentville, Maine, can easily understand her pleasure in it. The small, shingled house overlooks a pretty cove where gentle waters, protected from the ocean currents, sparkle in the summer sun; from her study window, the writer can see the family of ducks that make their home there. Across the driveway is the building that houses Wayward Books, the "used and medium-rare" bookstore run by Grumbach's companion, Sybil Pike. Though the weather is unusually warm for Maine, the screened porch to which she guides us is refreshingly cool, sheltered from the sun and fanned by a light breeze.

Author of six novels, a critical study of Mary McCarthy and now a memoir, known in the literary community as a generous and astute critic, Grumbach at 73 remains vigorous and active, with several works either in progress or awaiting her decision on whether they deserve further effort. She considers herself primarily a fiction writer—in fact, has cut down on reviewing to give herself more time for it—but decided to take the series of notes that became *Coming into the End Zone* in hopes of resolving a personal crisis.

"My 70th birthday was an occasion of real despair," she explains. "I've never felt worse. So I thought, well, perhaps it would help if I just take notes on this year; whatever happens may throw some light on why I'm still here, make some sense out of living so long. The death of Bill Whitehead, whom I loved a great deal both as a friend and a caring, sensitive editor, made an even sharper contrast between being granted the gift of living as long as I have and the terrible injustice of dying of AIDS.

"I looked at Bill and my friend Richard Lucas and the young men in the AIDS ward where I volunteered at Capitol Hill Hospital, and it seemed so cruel that their lives and their great talents should be blighted in that way, while I, who I've never really thought of as having a major talent—being a second-string writer and critic who made a certain wave but not a great splash—should be spared. I was trying to see some reason into it."

Her craft helped her. "I think writing is an act of healing. It's an exorcism of sorts, to put into words and symbols this almost inexpressible anguish. That was why I started, to try and alleviate the despair. Writing shapes experience for me; it isn't ever the experience that gives any shape to the prose. It's by looking for the words and formulating the sentences that you give some kind of order to it that raw experience never has—and in the process, I guess, reduce it to a manageable emotion.

"There's one thing about autobiography, though. When I re-read the galleys of this memoir, I realized it was no more fact than my fictions are. In doing an autobiography, you think you're dealing with fact—that of course is not so. The view one has of me, of Sybil, of our lives, is just as much a fiction. A fiction writer writes fiction about everything; even the laundry list has fiction in it! When language takes over, fiction enters. So I don't really think I've moved away from fiction in this; I think I've sort of pressed it into a new mold."

An intriguing point, for in her novels Grumbach has often played with the relationship between life and art, anchoring the entirely imaginary interior existences of her characters with details from the lives of real people: the founders of the Mac-Dowell Colony in *Chamber Music;* Marilyn Monroe in *The Missing Person;* two actual 18th-century aristocrats in *The Ladies;* Diane Arbus, Sylvia Plath and Ezra Pound in *The Magician's Girl.* "I was interested in seeing what you could do, given a cat-afalque of fact that I assumed might be known to any literate person who came to the book," she explains. "I wanted to fantasize about it, to imagine things that probably were not so, and by that process make them true. I thought you could make that move and people would forget what the catafalque was, but they don't; they superimpose what they know, or think they know, upon what you've written, and they become critical about it."

This was particularly true, she feels, with *The Missing Person,* a book whose generally poor reception she attributes to the fact that "there's such a cult of Marilyn Monroe in this country. I tried to supersede that, but I couldn't manage—although I love that book the way you love a retarded child among three or four healthy ones. And I still believe it works better than most people think. I liked the idea of trying to take reality, move it through unreality and create a new reality. That idea fascinated me for a long time, from 1979 down until now, but my new novel has none of those fact/fiction alliances."

Grumbach considers herself fortunate to have worked with a succession of distinguished editors who "all have the same quality: they care about the writer." When she resumed her career as a novelist with *Chamber Music* in the 1970s (two apprentice efforts appears in the early '60s), she sent it to Henry Robbins, whom she had met while she was at the *New Republic.* He called four days later to say he wanted to publish it.

"Henry was so sensitive to me," she says. "He had sent me a request to write four or five more paragraphs that he felt were needed at some point in the book. I steamed over those paragraphs, couldn't get back into the book to make them sound the same. Two weeks later he called me and said, 'I have a feeling that you must be having problems.' We talked about it for a long time, and he said something that gave me an idea of how to do it. But it wasn't *that* I valued, it was the fact that he sat in his office in New York and thought, I'm going to call her in Washington and see if she's having problems. That was Henry; he was a remarkable fellow."

Faith Sale, then Robbins's associate, copyedited *Chamber Music*. "As in every case with a good copy editor, there was one of those pink flags on every page, some pages had four—it was terrible! I put it off, then I had to do it because there was a deadline. The phone rang; it was Henry. He said, 'I know what you're doing right now. You're looking at those pages and thinking, What does this stupid woman think she's doing to my pristine, pure manuscript? Well, just look at them as if you don't have to make any changes if you don't want to, but look at them as something that stopped the reader.' And of course the more I looked at it, the more I realized what a good editor she was and how I should be grateful for her acumen and not sit there rebelling against it. After Henry's death I went to her at Putnam. I've always thought that a writer should not look at the house; if you're lucky enough to get a good editor, you ought to go with her."

Although she remains friendly with Sale, the publication of *The Missing Person* was an unhappy experience, for reasons she prefers not to discuss on the record. She took *The Ladies* to Bill Whitehead, "who turned out to be, like my other editors, very concerned with detail and accuracy, a reader with sensitivity. Gerry Howard is like that," she adds, referring to her editor at Norton. "For the fourth time I've been blessed. He's smart, astute, well-educated, he writes very well himself, has a beautiful style and a very good eye. He found things that I never saw, so that when I get a manuscript back from him, I know, having conquered my horror of those pink flags, that it's going to be done with taste and care. I feel very lucky to have him."

Despite the fact that she feels "publishing is less a craft, less an art, it's become a business," Grumbach finds "there are still editors of the caliber of the ones I've been privileged to know, still publishers like Bob Giroux and James Laughlin at New Directions and Bill Turnbull, who tried to do the same thing at North Point Press. I'll name another editor: Alice Mayhew. There's a woman who's made books out of raw material, and even if that little, snide creature attacked her in the *New Republic*, he had no right to do so; he just doesn't know enough about what Alice Mayhew does. Because of the publicity for big books and big advances, people forget how much these commercial houses devote to second-string books or the short story writer of talent. I'm a judge for the PEN/Faulkner award, I get boxes of novels every week, and I'm amazed by how many of them are good, reputable pieces of writing that come out of commercial houses like Simon & Schuster—maybe out of the back door, but they're there."

Grumbach herself takes no part in the high-stakes end of publishing. "I'm into a book now that I have faith in, but I would never say to my agent, 'Let's send out five chapters and a summary and see how much money we can get.' It's too late for that merchandising for me; I don't see publishing in those terms. I get a great deal of pleasure out of finishing a work, deciding that it's the best I can do and says as best I can what the work has to say. What happens to it after that doesn't even interest me very much. I've never gone on a tour to promote a book; I find all that avidity that writers have to, as Jean Stafford says, push the book, a sign of lack of faith. I have faith that a good book makes its way and a bad or mediocre book falls into that great heap of the stuff that doesn't matter."

This belief can be seen in her work habits. She has done years of research for a biography of Willa Cather, but is unsure she will ever write it. "I've gone from uncritical admiration through a long period in which I was highly critical of her as both a person and a writer. I now know that she was a good writer despite her very real faults, but I've never gotten to like her as a person again. It's just as bad to be wildly enthusiastic—like this new Eric Lax biography of Woody Allen, which is so effusive—but I don't think it's right if you're not at least favorably disposed to the subject."

She prefers to concentrate on fiction. *Camp,* a novella about a 14-year-old girl's summer in the Catskills, awaits a companion piece to bring it up to publishable book length—"Sybil says it needs a stablemate!" She has cannibalized portions of *The Habit,* a novel she decided didn't work, to provide a character for one of her books in progress, which also contains a segment about her childhood in Far Rockaway, N.Y., that was originally a separate novella.

"I should have a need to publish," she admits. "I should say, 'Well, you've only got a short time; publish, publish, publish!' But I don't; I'm willing to wait. Neither the publishing nor the reception is important to me, although like everyone I sweat out the reviews. What I care about is the time and thought it takes to produce a book. After that, maybe the publishers will do something about it and maybe they won't, maybe the critics will like it and maybe they won't, maybe the public will buy it and maybe it won't. That doesn't change the nature of the thing you've done. People say, 'Yes, but it's three years of your life!' Well, what would I have done with those three years anyway? You do what you want and do it the best that you can. If it makes it, then you celebrate with it, and if it doesn't—well, you haven't wasted your life."

WENDY SMITH

ALLAN GURGANUS

"I would be extremely happy if my book were seen as one of the nails in the coffin of minimalism," Allan Gurganus says, in a quiet voice that has lost much of its original North Carolina accent. "The flat, affectless language of minimalism has even less color than the language of newspaper reporting. In minimalism, you take out all the modifiers and the active verbs, and end up with industrial gray, high-tech prose that eliminates the drama by knocking out the beginning and the end, presenting only the middle of a story. This is not what I want to read, nor what I want to write. I think there is a great appetite, and a great need, for Stories with a capital S. And a great longing for sentences full of sensation, full of stained-glass colors and shaded by the time of day. The language has been anorectic too long."

Referring to his first novel, *Oldest Living Confederate Widow Tells All* (Knopf), Gurganus says, "My book is full of war and blinding and rape and sadness, but it's also full of meals and local color and consolations and a great deal of love between the characters. I hope it will coincide with readers' appetites for big, fat, beautiful, historical novels."

Gurganus is a talker, but his talk has not a trace of good-ol'-boy posturing, nor of television-nourished New South chic. He sounds more like a favorite teacher whose sensible classroom voice echoes years later in the mind. From afar, almost inaudible in his well-shaped conversations but constantly impinging on his writing, come reverberations of mythic visions. "I wanted more than anything to write the burning of a plantation," he says, "because the presence of these ruins was one of the central images of my childhood.

"Sherman burned most of the great houses in my part of North Carolina," he continues. (To Southerners, it's never "General Sherman" but always "Sherman," stark and terrible.) "Ruins were very important to me. On Sunday afternoons we went for rides in the country, passing one former plantation after another whose six or seven standing chimneys, three to four stories high, were now filled with mice, swallows and bats. Sunday after Sunday, I would ask my parents, 'What did it look like before?' As they tried to answer my questions, they revealed images of how unbelievably grand the houses had been."

Gurganus has incorporated those images, and countless others, in the life of Lucy Marsden, the 99-year-old narrator of his novel. She, too, is a talker; from her bed in a nursing home, she does indeed tell all, or certainly as much as time permits. When the novel ends after 752 pages, this Southern Scheherazade shows no signs of winding down.

"Stories about Sherman and the Civil War and battles are the bread and butter of a Southern childhood," Gurganus says. "They seem to me as mythic as the realm of García Márquez." The influence of *One Hundred Years of Solitude* is apparent throughout Gurganus's novel. "I'm repaying a debt to García Márquez in a way," he says. "In doing so, I'm also paying a kind of homage to Faulkner. It's no accident that García Márquez considers Faulkner the most influential writer for himself and for all of South American magical realism. The tropical density and the exaggerated mythic component of the culture of the South is very much like that of Central and South America." Gurganus mentions two other novels that influenced his writing: Günter Grass's *The Tin Drum* and Elsa Morante's *History: A Novel.*

In blending realism and myth, Gurganus was less interested in dates and literal facts than in "what could and could not have happened, what might and might not have occurred." Nevertheless, he tried to avoid anachronisms. One of the many books he used for verification of daily life in the 19th century was a reprint of the 1888 Montgomery Ward catalogue. Far more important than research, however, was his contention that "growing up in

231

North Carolina in the 1950s was in some ways like growing up there in the 1880s."

Gurganus, 42, says, "My family went to visit my grandparents every Sunday afternoon, no exceptions made, which is exactly how my grandparents had grown up, and theirs before them. There was an enormous amount of continuity. So I know a lot about the 19th century from growing up in a small town that had been affected only outwardly by such 20th-century inventions as television. Family structures remained very much of the 19th century."

Gurganus knows many of Lucy's traditions at first hand. Storytelling, for example. He says, "I'm trying to replicate the 19th-century sensibility that it is the responsibility, and the joy, of an individual to tell stories. And to improve them with repeated telling. Before the days of radio and television, people provided their own entertainment."

During the seven years he worked on his novel, Gurganus entertained himself most days from 6:30 a.m. until the early afternoon by using Lucy Marsden as the mouthpiece for stories remembered and made up. "I don't own a television set, I don't subscribe to any magazine. I don't have a vacuum cleaner or an iron. That has given me lots of time to concentrate on her," he says, sounding like a Luddite or hermit.

But living on Manhattan's Upper West Side and teaching at Sarah Lawrence, Gurganus was never far removed from the late 20th century. He often sounds intentionally old-fashioned, however. While his peers may quote Freud, Derrida or the thinker *du jour,* Gurganus says, "I didn't have to look up the biblical epigraphs that begin each chapter; they were on tap, from too many Sunday school classes at the Presbyterian church. There is a great love of the Bible in Lucy and in my family and in me." But his next statement might sound dismayingly secular to those pious Sunday school teachers for whom the Bible is a fearsome and all-enveloping garment: "The South is called the Bible Belt, but I think the predominant religion is a love of conversation, almost a sense of competitive talking."

Asked if he ever rebelled against the weight of Southern traditions, Gurganus answers, "Well, I moved away from the South, didn't I? It was only when I came to New York 12 years ago that the South became available to me as a writer. In the classic expatriate way, I couldn't write about the South while I lived in it.

232

When I left, I realized how much a part of the South I was—and am."

In the summer of 1982, while at Yaddo, Gurganus read a brief item in the *New York Times* about the handful of Confederate widows still receiving government pensions. The article included the phrase "oldest living Confederate widow."

"When I saw that," Gurganus says, "I felt as though a sledge hammer had hit me over the head. I was on my way to swim, but instead I went back to my room and typed for four hours. When I stood up, I had written the first 30 pages of the novel, which remain almost unchanged from that first inspiration. I thought it would be a 35-page story, then a 60-page story, then a novella of 100 pages. Twelve hundred manuscript pages later, I realized it was not just Lucy's story, it was everybody's story."

Before "everybody's story" entered his life, Gurganus had published about a dozen short stories in *Harper's*, the *Atlantic, Paris Review* and elsewhere. "Minor Heroism," the first one that he considered a major finished story, was also the first to be published. John Cheever, who was Gurganus's teacher at the Iowa Writers Workshop in 1973, sent it to the *New Yorker.*

When William Maxwell, then an editor at the magazine, phoned to tell Gurganus that the story had been bought, the latter was sure that it was a friend playing a joke. As he recalls it, the conversation began like this: "Hello, this is William Maxwell at the *New Yorker.*" "Yeah, and I'm Mae West." "Oh, I assure you this is really William Maxwell." The confusion was soon cleared up, and the story appeared in 1974. It was the first *New Yorker* story to deal with homosexuality, breaking the taboo that Harold Ross had established years earlier when he wrote in a memo that, as far as the magazine was concerned, there was no such thing as homosexuality.

Years later, when Cheever was dying, he sent Gurganus a valedictory letter of recommendation, addressed "To Whom It May Concern." He wrote: "I consider Allan Gurganus the most morally responsive and technically brilliant writer of his generation." Referring to Cheever's letter, Gurganus calls it "an enormously touching and beautiful gesture."

Asked what he thinks Cheever meant by the phrase "morally responsive," Gurganus says, "Our times are amoral. In recent years, we have turned away from a sense that we are all responsible for each other. But I believe we are. That moral frame, which is visible in novels, shows how the deeds of one member of a community have a continuing impact on the lives of other members. This moral vision has been out of fashion for a long time, but it is essential. It is the cornerstone of what a novel is all about. [I wanted to] show the outspreading implications of the killing of a 13-year-old boy during the Civil War. His death affects the lives of people 100 years later who, of course, never knew him."

During the seven years he worked on his novel, Gurganus never entertained the notion that his publisher would push it as a major commercial event. "I'm as surprised as anyone," he says. "I thought I was writing a highly literary, vocally experimental work that would be recognized by a certain kind of literary reader. I also wanted to write a very good yarn."

Robert Gottlieb bought the novel before he left Knopf to become editor of the *New Yorker*. "I don't know what his plans were for my book," Gurganus says. But last year, Sonny Mehta, editor-in-chief at Knopf, and Elisabeth Sifton, Gurganus's editor, enticed the author with the promise that, if he could finish the novel by the end of July 1988, it would lead the spring list. He did so and, following one postponement because the book was selected by BOMC, the novel heads Knopf's list for the fall.

Surpassing the standard publicity hoopla for a first novel, Knopf scheduled a 20-city author tour, T-shirts plugging the title and cardboard posters showing a homey cross-stitched sampler.

Gurganus has a lot more work completed and ready for publication, although he has not signed a contract yet; his agent, Amanda Urban, advised waiting to see what happened with *Confederate Widow*. Also ready to go is a short novel, *Blessed Assurance*, and three novellas about famous people—Joan Crawford, Elvis Presley and Billie Holiday—which he plans to group together for publication. The Joan Crawford novella is purported to be her autobiography from beyond the grave; in it she answers the charges that her daughter Christina made in *Mommie Dearest*. The Presley story deals with the singer's documented necrophilia, and the first line of the third novella is, "My father asked Billie Holiday for a date."

Before they meet these characters, however, readers are likely to spend a long time at the bedside of the oldest living Confederate widow. Gurganus, a considerate host and storyteller, has done everything possible to make his audience stay in the book. Waxing expansive and metaphorical, he says, "I want my readers to have every advantage; that's why I make a comfortable place for them, give them a couch, a lap robe and bowls of cherries and pistachios."

SAM STAGGS

JIM HARRISON

THOUGH HE SPENT brief periods in New York and Boston during his restless youth and though his riotous visits to Key West, Fla., and Hollywood with his friend Tom McGuane have been the subject of numerous journalistic accounts, Jim Harrison's home has always been in northern Michigan. He and his wife, Linda, live on a farm about 50 miles as the crow flies from Grayling, where he grew up. It's only a short drive from their house to Lake Michigan, across which lies the Upper Peninsula, even more rural and remote, where Harrison has a cabin he retreats to in the warmer weather—"Summer," wisecracks a character in his recent book *The Woman Lit by Fireflies* (Houghton Mifflin/Seymour Lawrence), "being known locally as three months of bad sledding."

The initial reason Harrison decided to return to the Midwest was financial. "After my first book was published [the poetry collection *Plain Song*, in 1965] we had nearly 15 years where I averaged only 10 grand a year," he says candidly. "I needed a place with a low overhead."

But there was more to it than that; when *Legends of the Fall*, a trio of novellas released in 1979, added a measure of economic security to his already established critical reputation, he chose to remain in Michigan. "Ever since I was seven and had my eye put out, I'd turn for solace to rivers, rain, trees, birds, lakes, animals," he explains. "If things are terrible beyond conception and I walk for 25 miles in the forest, they tend to go away for a while. Whereas if I lived in Manhattan I couldn't escape them."

236

He steers clear of urban literary life for the same reason he has steadfastly turned down academic jobs. "I had this whole heroic notion of being a novelist," he says. "I wanted to be a writer in the old sense of staying on the outside. I can live for about a year on the proceeds from the first draft of a screenplay, which sometimes takes only six weeks, and I think that's more fun than hanging around some fucking college town for 10 months waiting for summer vacation."

Like his characters, the author is blunt and outspoken, with an earthy sense of humor and a boundless supply of charm that take the sting out of his sallies. When he's said something especially outrageous, he glances slyly at us, inviting us to share his enjoyment of how wicked he is. Yet he also sprinkles his conversation with quotes from Yeats, Camus, Santayana and Wittgenstein— Harrison is a complex man, by no means the macho figure some critics have taken him for.

This complexity can be seen in his work, both in the poetry collected in such volumes as *Returning to Earth* and, most recently, *The Theory and Practice of Rivers*, and in the series of novels and novellas for which he is best known, including *A Good Day to Die, Warlock, Sundog*, the remarkable *Dalva*—in which he definitively refuted the claim that he couldn't create believable women—and his latest. Though Harrison writes of such contemporary subjects as the rape of the natural landscape and the search for a meaning beyond materialism, none of his books can be reduced to a simple, one-sentence thesis. There is a mystery at the heart of each, a sense that beneath his beautiful, deceptively simple language lie deeper truths that can only be hinted at with words.

All of his ideas, he says, come to him in the form of images. The heroine of the title story in *The Woman Lit by Fireflies* first appeared as "a lady of about 49 climbing a fence behind a Welcome Center in tennis shoes. I had been thinking about Clare for years, worrying about her—you make somebody up and then you worry if she's going to be okay. I usually think about a novella or a novel for three or four years; all these images collect—Wallace Stevens said that images tend to collect in pools in your brain— and then when it's no longer bearable not to write it down, I start writing."

"The images emerge from dreams, or the period at 5:30 in the morning between sleeping and waking when you have that single durable image, like 'Nordstrom had taken to dancing alone' [the opening line of "The Man Who Gave Up His Name" in *Legends of the Fall*], which totally concentrates the character. I think you try *not* to figure out what they mean at that point, because what you're trying to do in fiction is reinvent the form; I want every fictional experience I have to be new. Once it gets didactic, than I say, Well, why not just write an essay? You don't create something so that people can draw conclusions, but to enlarge them, just as you have been enlarged by the experience of making it up. Art should be a process of discovery, or it's boring."

Harrison's own life has been a process of discovery. At age 16, in 1954, he decided he wanted to be a writer and headed for New York City, where he stumbled on "what I at the time called Green-wich Village," he says, pronouncing it like the color and laughing. "That's when I knew I wanted to be a bohemian; I wanted to meet a girl with black hair and a black turtleneck—and I did! Then I lived in Boston when I was 19; I went up there because I'd heard Boston was America's St. Petersburg, and my biggest enthusiasm in my teens was for Russian literature." He managed to squeeze in an education around his voyages, graduating from Michigan State in 1960, the same year he got married.

"I started out as a prose writer," he says. "Prose, poetry, I never separated them. But in your first notebook stage you tend toward poetry, because it's easier at that age, I tried to write prose, but I was never any good at the short story." In his mid-20s, while living in Cambridge, Mass., with his wife and baby daughter, "I discovered the Grolier Bookstore, where I used to hang out with other poets. I'd written some poems and sent them to Denise Levertov, who was the only poet I'd ever met. My friends at Grolier had mixed feelings when I arrived one Saturday with my first contract for a book of poems—that wasn't supposed to happen for a long time!"

But the proceeds from poetry weren't sufficient to keep Harrison in the East after a year at Stony Brook convinced him he wasn't cut out to be a teacher. By 1966 he and his family were settled in Michigan. It was nearly five years before he made another try at prose, prompted by his friend and fellow Michigan State grad, novelist Tom McGuane. "I fell off a cliff bird-hunting and hurt my back. Tom said—he barely remembers this—'Well, you're not doing anything else, so why not write a novel?' I thought, Yeah, that's the ticket, and so I wrote *Wolf*; I had a Guggenheim, which made it easier. I sent my only copy to my brother, who was the science librarian at Yale, because I didn't want to pay to have it copied, but I sent it away two days before the mail strike, and it was lost. He went down to the main post office and finally dug it up. I had a book of poems [*Outlyer and Ghazals*, 1971] coming out with Simon & Schuster at the time, and they took the novel too, so I started out with a bang."

Alix Nelson at S & S was the first in a long line of nurturing women editors for Harrison. He speaks warmly of Pat Irving at Viking, who published his third novel, *Farmer*, and Pat Ryan, "who saved my neck, because she would give me assignments to write outdoor pieces for *Sports Illustrated*, and they paid well enough for us to live up here for several months."

The period after *Farmer* was published in 1976 was a difficult one, however. "It sold only a couple thousand copies—it sold 10 times as many copies last year as when it came out—and it was a terrible disappointment. I thought, If this is the best I can do, and it's utterly and totally rejected, then I don't know where I'm even supposed to be. There didn't seem to be any room for what I wanted to do; what I valued most, no one in the literary community valued. I went into a long clinical depression, but I gradually recovered."

Professional salvation came in the form of Seymour Lawrence, then affiliated with Delacorte, who made *Legends of the Fall* Harrison's first commercially successful book. "I had written these three novellas, and my agent at the time said, 'No one's going to publish these; they're not short stories, and they're not novels.' I thought, Sam Lawrence has a good record for taking literary writers and giving them a shot, so I sent them to him. Then Clay Felker did the whole of "Legends of the Fall" and three-quarters of "Revenge" [the third novella] in *Esquire*."

If *Legends* didn't exactly make Harrison rich, it did make him much more widely known; the sale of film rights to all three novellas enabled him to buy land in Michigan and launched the screenwriting career that now allows him to attend to his real writing with a minimum of distractions. Since that book, Harrison has followed Lawrence from house to house. "Sam's mostly a publisher and a very acute reader," he says. "The kind of author he wants is someone who knows his stuff."

For the line work every novel needs, the author has relied on his eldest daughter, who reads his manuscripts before anyone else, and two editors associated with Lawrence. "Leslie Wells edited *Dalva* at Dutton, and she is so pointed. I tend to organize something dramatic and then back away from it, and she can always see it. The first sexual scene between Duane and Dalva was too emotional for me to write, and both Leslie and my daughter said, 'Hey, let's let 'em really do it!' Now there's a wonderful girl who works for Sam, Camille Hykes, who's a good editor too." His financial negotiations are handled by "my Sicilian agent, Bob Dattila, which obviously means 'from Attila'—so he has always been my main protector!"

In recent years, Harrison's ride on what he describes as "this shuddering elevator that is the writer's life" has been relatively smooth. Though he considers poetry and fiction his primary work, he doesn't disdain the movies. "I'll keep writing screenplays even if I don't need the money, because I want to write one really good one. You can't write novels all the time, and I'm intrigued by the screenplay form." He is polite about the recent film made from "Revenge" starring Kevin Costner. "John Huston wanted to direct it 12 years ago, with Jack Nicholson, and Warner Brothers turned him down. It was disappointing to me at the time, but when they finally made it, it was almost a real good movie—almost. It did well in California, the South and the Midwest, but not in New York. I doubt your average yuppie would think much of somebody dying for love—it would be out the question."

There's a certain combativeness in Harrison's attitude toward the New York literary establishment but, he says, "it would be pompous of me to feel ignored when all nine of my books are in print. It's just that the nature of my books isn't by and large the kind of thing that interests Upper East Side New Yorkers.

"I like grit, I like love and death, I'm tired of irony. As we know from the Russians, a lot of good fiction is sentimental. I had this argument in Hollywood; I said, 'You guys out here in Glitzville don't realize that life is Dickensian.' Everywhere you look people are deeply totemistic without knowing it: they have their lucky objects and secret feelings from childhood. The trouble in

New York is, urban novelists don't want to give people the dimensions they deserve.

"The novelist who refuses sentiment refuses the full spectrum of human behavior, and then he just dries up. Irony is always scratching your tired ass, whatever way you look at it. I would rather give full vent to all human loves and disappointments, and take a chance on being corny, than die a smartass."

WENDY SMITH

SHIRLEY HAZZARD

Shirley Hazzard simply will not sit still for a conventional interview. It's not that the distinguished novelist (*The Transit of Venus, The Bay of Noon*) is literally on the move; in fact, after ushering us into the sunny living room of the New York apartment she shares with her husband, critic and biographer Francis Steegmuller, and providing a glass of lemonade, she remains firmly planted on the sofa for the next two and a half hours, except for a few trips to the overflowing bookshelves to find a favorite quotation that makes her point more precisely.

But in words Hazzard roams the world. The variety of subjects which prompt her forthright indignation or excited approval is enormous; the nimbleness and speed with which she leaps among them would be intimidating if her opinions weren't delivered with such warmth and charm. The usual question-and-answer procedure is impossible—her interlocutor barely has a chance to draw breath before she's on to the next topic. Nonetheless, a coherent self-portrait emerges from this verbal torrent: the impromptu connections that make her conversation so dizzying are the result of a clearly defined personal philosophy that brings her again and again to the same central issues.

Hazzard's book *Countenance of Truth: The United Nations and the Waldheim Case* (Viking) is a case in point. For the second time she has reluctantly put aside fiction to write about the organization where she worked for 10 years, because she believes it essential that the public understand the reasons for the U.N.'s failure to live up to its ideals and because she doesn't see anyone in the news media providing that information.

As early as 1980, in an article in the *New Republic*, Hazzard asserted that then–U.N. Secretary-General Kurt Waldheim's links to the Nazi Party had been much closer than he'd ever admitted; although Waldheim threatened a libel suit he never challenged her assertion in court. But, she remarks, "Do you think any of these U.N. correspondents came around and asked, How could you say this? Where is the information? It was six years before it all came out. When Waldheim was at the U.N., no questions were asked. When he went out into the real world— they call it that themselves at the U.N., 'the real world'—then they found out immediately. The information was there.

"The great powers had knowledge of his background," she says bluntly. "It was impossible that they didn't." The larger point she makes in *Countenance of Truth* is that, far from being a shocking anomaly, Waldheim was exactly the kind of U.N. official the world powers wanted. "Since the moment of the United Nations' inception," she writes in her introduction, "untold energies have been expended by governments not only toward the exclusion of persons of principle and distinction from the organization's leading positions, but toward the installation of men whose character and affiliations would as far as possible preclude any serious challenge to governmental sovereignty."

In her 1973 study of the U.N., *Defeat of an Ideal*, Hazzard detailed the ways in which the principle of an independent international civil service was compromised from the beginning by the organization's leaders. She repeats some of this material in *Countenance of Truth* because "it places a very different perspective on the Waldheim affair; it brings the pieces of the puzzle together in a rather alarming way. That's why we couldn't get any leadership; we got people who were not going to be courageous or independent. And it's become a habit; the idea of the U.N. actually doing anything is inconceivable now. We had a General Assembly meeting here in New York while the most important events in 40 years were taking place in Eastern Europe, events the U.N. had done nothing whatever to nurture, was totally detached from—in fact, hardly able to make a lucid comment on."

The consequence of having filled the U.N. with self-serving bureaucrats, says Hazzard, is that the organization lacks the moral courage to take a stand in world affairs. "U.N. officials always say, We can't say anything about the Vietnam War or human rights in the Soviet Union, because it wouldn't do any good. Well, it's not to us that they should say these things; they should be required to go to the people who have suffered in Cambodia or the Gulag. I think even they would know they couldn't say these things there without being greeted by a roar of helpless laughter. I often feel that a roar of helpless laughter would be very healthy for our leaders." Hazzard quotes a passage from Alexander Pope's *Satires* which states that those not afraid of God are yet shamed by ridicule. "There's so little of it now—oh, satire, where are you when we need you?" She laughs, but as she later says, "laughter is not merriment."

Another English poet provided the title of her new book. " 'Countenance of truth' is from an essay by Milton, who was incensed by the corruption of the clergy in his day. He was criticized for writing essays against the Church, and in reply he says something to the effect of 'I have a work that I love, as a poet—as if I would turn away from that bright countenance of truth to mix up with antipathetic matters of this kind if I didn't feel that I could not forbear to do it.' Well, I had information about the U.N. just by the circumstance of having worked there, and as years go by with nobody else doing it, I feel some obligation.

"But I can't go on with it. If this book doesn't make any immediate impression, at least it's on the record of history, and I suppose the ultimate reason for writing it is to tell the truth. In the beginning I hoped to change things, but one loses that expectation. But I think that a truth set out takes on a life of its own. These aren't private truths, they belong to everybody, although they always come back to personal conduct. People talk in categories; even I have to use this phrase 'the leadership of the U.N.,' but these are single men—we can use the word 'men' because there are so few women in the leadership—human beings who should be answerable for their actions. We should be asking, as I've said in the book, What matter of men were these who supported Waldheim and now say that he was destroying the U.N.?"

Hazzard turns with relief to the subject of fiction. She's working on a new novel and hopes to finish it this year. "I've thrown it away four times, because it wasn't the tone or the feeling I wanted. Of course I salvaged something every time, but that's why it's taken so long. Now, I can't wait—it's beautiful to get back to art, because finally if there's truth in it, that's what remains."

Her bright blue eyes, which had flashed with indignation over the sorry state of the U.N., shine with pleasure when she speaks of fiction. At 59, she still remembers the joy of discovering Italy and a creative profession in the mid-1950s. "I felt restored to life and power after years in this bureaucratic world. My imagination began to work again. I spent some summers with an Italian family, and they took it for granted that what was humanly interesting and lovable was what mattered in life. I also had believed this, but I'd buried it—it was in the underground, and I was part of the resistance! Now I didn't have to be in the underground anymore, and I began to write." In 1962 she left the U.N. to devote herself to fiction.

Publishing came easily to Hazzard—her first stories were promptly accepted by the *New Yorker*, and she speaks warmly of the encouragement of William Shawn and fiction editor William Maxwell—but writing, though deeply satisfying, was and remains difficult. She admits with dismay that she's become less fluent over the years. Her short story collection, *Cliffs of Fall*, appeared in 1963, followed in fairly rapid succession by three novels: *The Evening of the Holiday* (1966); *People in Glass Houses* (1967); and *The Bay of Noon* (1970). *Defeat of an Ideal* took her away from fiction for three years, and *The Transit of Venus* consumed seven more before it was published in 1980, winning the 1981 National Book Critics Circle Award.

Hazzard's beautifully wrought prose, each word charged with layers of meaning and emotion, takes time to craft. "Something that plays a part for me in every phrase and sentence is the sound. The weight of sound, the kinds of syllables that are there—these influence the way something is read. When one becomes interested in that, it can become a trap. Peter Quennell said in his memoirs that he became obsessed with this to such a degree that he would try, in a paragraph of some length, not to repeat a preposition. Well, I never got to that stage, but on some days I recognize this incipient preposition phobia! You know that word is there, and it's your business somehow to find it. And when you do find exactly the word you want, this is a lovely moment. I'm not advocating the degree of it that I've sometimes got into, but one does try to do something more difficult each time. Also, there are so many books, and one becomes a little apprehensive that one is going to write another book which may be all right and may even give pleasure to somebody, but that's perhaps not all one wants to do. You want to satisfy yourself."

She doesn't agonize over every word in quite the same way with nonfiction, but the genre poses a philosophical challenge. "It's almost impossible to speak of individuals. You remain always conscious that a system isn't just an abstraction, it is made up of individual human beings who are responsible for themselves and the rest of us. We can see at this moment in history, goodness knows, the difference one determined person can make."

Nonetheless, she feels that "the kind of difficulty in fiction is unique. I won't say it's more important, because a man who's written a great history has also dealt with this question of humanity; all important books come to this. But writing fiction or poetry, you have a blank sheet and absolutely nothing to put there except what's going to come out of you. You have to invent everything—even the prepositions! There's no substance until you invent it. You're not given a theme or a period or a personality; you have to make all these things and frame them in some kind of believable existence. If you have at all achieved what you set out to achieve, then you feel that your characters go on with their lives; you don't know what those lives are, but they haven't stopped, they're not dead. That's really what one hopes for, that when the book is closed they aren't defunct.

"But I like the feeling of completion," she continues. "People say they hate to finish a book and how terrible it is to let it go. Well, you can see that I haven't been eager to let this novel go, in the sense that I've been rewriting, but that was because I didn't think it was right. But I don't have that feeling of 'Oh, it's my book and I don't want to part with it.' When I get near the end, I go like this"—she pantomimes gleefully riffling the pages of the hefty manuscript. "I'm thinking, 'So now it will be complete,' because when you write the last word it becomes a different thing, it becomes an integer. It has its own existence, and that's a rather thrilling thing. Those last words, if done right, come as a complement to the book's first words; one always takes

246

great care with the beginning and the end. Then you see: So, after all, it came round, it met, it's enclosed in a circle. And that's a lovely moment. I'm not at all against finishing a book—I wish I'd finished many more!"

WENDY SMITH

MARK HELPRIN

JUDGING BY THE range of experiences and geographical settings depicted in his fiction, we imagine Mark Helprin to be a middle-aged man with a face lined by dangerous living, vagabond traveling and frequent glimpses of the infinite.

We are wrong.

Encountered at his publisher's office, Helprin is a slight figure who seems at first glance to be a college undergraduate or slightly aging Eagle Scout. Dressed in plaid lumber shirt, baggy tweed trousers and hiking boots augmented by tortoiseshell glasses and a diffident air, Helprin has a decidedly boyish appearance. Further belying the image of a writer entitled to rest on his dignity by virtue of critical kudos, Helprin dashes out into the frigid afternoon to replace the batteries in our ailing tape recorder. He returns so quickly it's as though he has conjured up new batteries as mysteriously as some of the mystical events in his stories.

Thoroughly disarmed, we settle down to a cozy interview—and find a man of decided opinions and a will of steel.

First off, Helprin resists our attempt to elicit biographical data, to match up his experiences in the British Merchant Navy and in the Israeli Infantry and Air Force with events that befall his fictional characters.

"I've always thought that a writer's work should stand independently of his life," Helprin tells us firmly. "If your product is what you're interested in getting across, then naturally you're reluctant to be biographical in an interview."

Although he concedes that his life could summon up a somewhat extravagant vision ("I'm thinking of Hemingway, of course, because I've done more stuff than Hemingway ever did"), Helprin insists that he doesn't want to build around himself "a fake theatrical image."

This established, he reveals the genesis of his determined pursuit of exceptional experiences. "I've always tried to pack a lot in," he says. "Very early I made up my mind to see as much as I could see."

Like the character Marshall Pearl in his novel *Refiner's Fire*, Helprin says he vowed not to be constrained by fences and proudly claims to have been hauled in by the police "many times" for trespassing. "I feel it's my duty to observe," he says. This philosophy, and the purposeful energy he radiates even sitting still, probably account for a mastery of skills and intellectual disciplines (mountain climbing and reading Dante in the original Italian are two) that most people do not achieve in a lifetime.

Having declined to be forthcoming about his personal life, Helprin is eager to talk about other subjects. When asked about a recent article in the *New York Times* characterizing him as an exception to the usual rule of "short story poverty," and calling him an "aggressive salesman" of his work, Helprin reacts with vehemence: "I am anything but an aggressive salesman!"

He does not deny a thorough familiarity with the publishing industry, or that sales of some stories from *Ellis Island* (Delacorte) have already earned him an appreciable amount of money in advance of the book's publication. His involvement with the selling and marketing of his work, he insists, is no more than a natural and sensible one. "I've taught myself the publishing business so that I would have more ability to maneuver. I perceive it as being alert rather than aggressive."

To this end, Helprin seems to have established a mutually respectful relationship with Seymour Lawrence at Delacorte. "We sat down, and he showed me the figures. We talked about the budgets," he says. Admiration of his publisher's methods is unequivocal. "Sam is what every publisher ought to be. He never promises anything that he doesn't do. He never does anything that he doesn't say. He's fast, he's honest, he's straight and he's vigorous."

Helprin credits his own vigorous business acumen to his father, a motion picture executive who got his start during the industry's infancy. His son grew up quite aware of the huckstering aspects of marketing entertainment. According to Helprin, his father's prodigious film output (26 features a year) mandated the purchase of hundreds of properties. "Once he bought the entire rights to Jules Verne—the whole thing! Later he gave *Around the World in 80 Days* to Mike Todd as a gift."

This background apparently conditioned Helprin's view of the publishing industry. "I don't feel awe for publishers as such. I understand the business and how it works, so I think it's perfectly legitimate for me to be in on some of the decisions."

Ever since he sold his first short story to the *New Yorker* when he was 21 and still at Harvard (using the proceeds to buy himself a suit in the boys' department of Brooks Brothers), Helprin has enjoyed a more than adequate income from his work. He no longer teaches to augment his earnings, now that he is in the high tax bracket. The latter fact seems to bemuse him, since he acknowledges, "I haven't even really started to catch on yet. I'm still in the minor leagues."

Indeed, Helprin expresses a desire to reach other than an elite audience. He hopes for a mass readership, he says, because "I come from a family of immigrants—farmers, storekeepers, seamstresses, tailors, carnival men and a master lock technician and vault-opener named S. S. Smith. Accidents of fortune have not made my values different from theirs, and I want people like my own to read me."

If financial security at a young age—without the sacrifice of literary integrity—makes him somewhat of an exception to the general breed of penurious writers, Helprin is not surprised. "I'm used to being an exception," he asserts equably and, by way of explanation, goes on to expound the military theories of B. H. Liddell-Hart, whom he calls the "greatest military strategist of the 20th century." In his book *The Strategy of the Indirect Approach*, Liddell-Hart reviewed the course of military history and proved, according to Helprin, that the victor "always comes around from behind—or from the side or below or underneath or above." After reading Liddell-Hart, Helprin discovered that the indirect approach typifies his whole life. Initially by temperament, now by determination, he claims to achieve his objectives via an oblique method that puts him slightly outside the general run of humanity. He speaks of a "protective shell" he has fashioned in order to "overcome disadvantages" and adds that his Jewish heritage has been a factor. Although he spent 10 years at Harvard as undergraduate, graduate student and teacher, Helprin says that he never was at ease there. "I never felt I belonged there—or anywhere else, for that matter—but that's a good thing for a writer."

That he would be a writer was evident to Helprin from the time he was a child, living in a huge old carriage house in the Hudson Valley. In speaking of his childhood, Helprin seems to relax for the first time, his voice growing husky.

"The house was surrounded by land owned by the Church and railroad—1000 acres of forest. It wasn't our property, of course, but as a child, I owned it all. The man who wrote *The Night Before Christmas* [Clement Clark Moore] lived right across the gully, and right up the gully was the factory that made Brandreth's pills, mentioned by Melville in *Moby-Dick*."

The family enjoyed the services of a "superb" French chef, Helprin further relates. His description of the chef's Cordon Bleu creations ("steaming delicacies") and the nightly routine in the ornate dining room begins to resemble the slightly fantastical cast of some of his stories.

"My father wouldn't let me eat unless I could earn my way to the table. He would always make me stand away from the table and would say: 'Tell me a story.' Every night I would have to tell another story. Sometimes the story wasn't good enough, and my father would say, 'That's not convincing,' and cut himself another slice of steak. It was like Scheherazade—with a slightly different twist."

As he evokes this mythic scene, Helprin's eyes take on an antic sparkle and his voice a mesmerizing tone. He is a natural storyteller, warming to his task.

SYBIL S. STEINBERG

JOHN HERSEY

"A WRITER SHOULD speak only through his work," says John Hersey. It's a principle that the Pulitzer Prize–winning novelist and journalist holds dear: Hersey does not give interviews, preferring to let his 12 novels and seven nonfiction books "speak for themselves." Amidst preparations to close his winter home in Key West—a modest, clapboard house in an Old Village compound whose other residents include John Ciardi, Ralph Ellison and Richard Wilbur—he did, however, take time to discuss his career with a former student, a reminder of the 18 years he spent as College Master and writing instructor at Yale, his alma mater.

The occasion is the publication of *The Call* by Knopf, an epic account of Christian missionaries in China. Structured as the biography of a fictional character, the novel chronicles the sweeping forces of political struggle and social change that marked the first half of the 20th century in China, as seen through the eyes of David Treadup, who forsakes his New England roots to spread the "social gospel" of the YMCA in the East.

His first book in eight years (he says he was writing it the last six), *The Call* represents something of a return for Hersey, recalling some of the formal and thematic concerns addressed in his earlier, best-known works. Treadup's central dilemma—how to instill an appropriate measure of American values in a sometimes unreceptive foreign culture—is reminiscent of the problem facing Major Joppolo, the well-meaning leader of Allied occupation troops in Italy in *A Bell for Adano*, the debut novel that won a

Pulitzer for Hersey in 1944. As he did in Adano and The Wall, the 1950 bestseller about the destruction of the Warsaw ghetto, Hersey bases his latest novel in extensive firsthand reporting and research, and uses the novel form to examine some of the most important events of the 20th century. And the setting marks a return to the Eastern milieu Hersey examined in his novels *A Single Pebble* and *White Lotus*, as well as the essay *Hiroshima*.

But *The Call* constitutes a very personal return for Hersey as well. His father, to whose memory the book is dedicated, was himself a YMCA missionary in China (he appears as a minor character in the novel), and it was during his father's stay there that Hersey was born in 1914, in Tientsin, where the family remained until they returned to America in 1925. Hersey says that his unique heritage—as part of a physically and economically dominant minority race—naturally had a lot to do with his interest in the topic of his latest novel. But, he continues, it also shaped his perspective on themes of individuality and nationality expressed in his writing throughout his career.

"I was born a foreigner," he says. "I was born in China, and I think in some ways I have been an outsider in America because of that." At 70, Hersey looks fit and tan, the dignity with which he carries his six-foot, two-inch frame adding weight to his tales of growing up a white giant in China, and of the "sense of confusion that came, for example, when I was a very small boy, of being pulled to school in a rickshaw by a human being, and paying him a very few cents for that service."

That sense of dislocation—he's not Chinese, he's not American—is reflected in his work, most obviously in the fact that few of his novels are situated in contemporary America. Rather, they present a view of the world as a global community; the events he chronicles, despite their distance from the reader, are depicted not only as historically significant, but as representative of a shared humanity that supersedes nationality. "In the long run," he says, "the qualities of human character break through ideologies."

A recognition of this universal bond, Hersey feels, is imperative in today's world. "One of the major happenings of the 20th century has been a shrinking of the earth," he says. "That has brought many difficulties as well as benefits." Some of his greatest works have focused on these difficulties—the Holocaust, the atomic bomb—because, he says, they "have made us have to face the necessity of learning how to live on this smaller and smaller planet."

The American response to that shrinking, he says, is paradoxical, characterized by "a very deep urge to help others in the world," which itself has a "dark side" that can turn these beneficent ventures destructive, as happened in Vietnam. "*The Call* is an effort to picture that American urge that's very deep in our psyche," he says.

This, too, is familiar territory for Hersey, dating back to *A Bell for Adano*, in which the benevolent impulses of Major Joppolo are juxtaposed against the militaristic megalomania of his superior, General Marvin. That contrast was a resonant one for readers in 1944, and the book was a commercial success. "It was not Major Joppolo but General Marvin who attracted attention," Hersey says. "This was the first book that suggested that an American general might not be everything we stand for. I think that that was a shocking idea at a time when the war was still far from won."

That shocking idea obviously found favor with the Pulitzer Prize committee. While some young writers dream of having their first novel meet such recognition, and may indeed strive for it, Hersey's attitude, looking back on the award, is characteristically humble. "I was lucky in a way to be hit by that very early," Hersey says, "because I learned that writing is its own reward." That lesson, he says, also "made it possible for me to go on, from work to work, really enjoying what I do."

Like his two previous books (he had already published two nonfiction accounts of World War II) and all that have followed, *A Bell for Adano* was published by Knopf. His relationship with the firm, Hersey says, has been "without exception comfortable." About founder Alfred A. Knopf himself, at whose memorial service he spoke, Hersey speaks with affection and respect: "He was one of the last of that generation of publishers that included Charles Scribner Sr., Alfred Harcourt, and others, who were book men, who cared really more about authors than they did about individual books. They nurtured writers in whom they believed and cared about their entire careers."

Perhaps because of that nurturing, Hersey was able to pursue his career in the direction he saw fit, and he chose to follow up

254

his debut novel by returning, as he has occasionally throughout his career, to the nonfiction genre. The work was *Hiroshima*, the book-length essay chronicling the plight of six survivors of the nuclear holocaust to which the *New Yorker* devoted the entire issue of August 31, 1946. An account of the Hiroshima residents' struggles to survive in the days immediately following the explosion, the piece was the immediate focus of national attention: the issue of the *New Yorker* quickly sold out, and the essay was reprinted in newspapers and read over radio stations nationwide. Knopf published the essay in book form later that year, and it is now in its 18th printing.

While *Hiroshima* is technically nonfiction—every word was subjected to the *New Yorker*'s renowned fact-checking procedure— Hersey brought to the subject not only the reportorial skills he had honed as a *Time* war correspondent, but also the novelist's talent for conveying the characters and their situation in a few simple, powerful strokes. What makes the reality of *Hiroshima* heartbreaking is its intimacy: the survivors are depicted with a clarity and sympathy we expect only from a fictional characterization.

The use of techniques from one genre while working in another is characteristic of Hersey's work, and few contemporary writers have found such success as both a journalist and a novelist. Though he says that he feels "very strongly that dividing line between fact that you hear and see with your ears and eyes—and fiction that you fabricate with your imagination," he has always believed that the devices of fiction can help journalism convey real life and, conversely, that a grounding in fact can lend a piece of fiction greater reality. The genre he chooses to work in, Hersey explains, depends on the subject about which he is writing.

But not surprisingly, considering that his novels outnumber his nonfiction works, he says that he prefers working in the fictional mode. "I think the challenge of fiction in dealing with the realities of life is for the author to try to afford the reader identification with the people who took part in the events about which you're writing," he says. "Fiction gives that kind of access more deeply than journalism can.

"The journalist is always a mediator between the material and the reader," Hersey explains. "And the reader is always conscious of the journalist interpreting and reporting events. If the novelist is successful, he vanishes from the reader's perception except through his voice in the work, and the reader has direct access to experiences. So, to me, fiction is much the more challenging and desirable medium for dealing with the real world than journalism. But there are also things that ask for a direct account while the material is still too hot for fiction. In those cases I resort to reportage."

After *Hiroshima,* he returned to fiction with *The Wall,* but with a strong foundation in fact and comprehensive historical research of a scope that rivals that in evidence in *The Call.* Like its two predecessors, *The Wall* was an enormous critical and commercial success. But in subsequent novels Hersey ventured away from this form of journalistic or historical fiction, experimenting in allegory and satire, and consequently he began to lose the critical and commercial audience he had won with his earlier books.

Hersey speaks about his career fluctuations without bitterness or regret. "*Hiroshima* was a book at the right time," he says, "and *The Wall* was a very early shock to American sensibilities about what had happened to Jews in Europe. They came at the right moment. From then on I was writing books that didn't have their exact moment. Some have had a life of their own, and some haven't, and that's the ways things go."

While *The Call*'s similarities to his earlier, more successful works do not go unnoticed by him, Hersey focuses more on the differences. "I was 27 when I wrote *A Bell for Adano* and I'm 70 now. I've lived a lot, seen a lot, learned a lot—I hope learned something about writing too." Readers familiar with both works may feel that the years between them were disillusioning. *PW* found the book "unflinchingly pessimistic," due to the apparent failure of Treadup's efforts and the bitter irony of the novel's conclusion. Hersey concedes that the darker side of the American presence in foreign cultures is perhaps given more play in *The Call* than in *A Bell for Adano*. "In some ways *A Bell for Adano* was a much easier book to read—much more attractive, and it probably sold more copies than *The Call* will ever sell," he says. "But it's a shallower book, less true to life, I think."

The pessimism is balanced with hope, in his perception. He felt "buoyed" by Treadup's persistence and dedication, in light of the endless obstacles he faced, he says. And, he points out, history demonstrates that the efforts of Treadup and others were not all lost. While the Chinese communists once dismissed the missionaries as "running dogs of imperialism," they have recently begun to acknowledge that missionaries made substantial contributions to the modernization of that country. Thus, he concludes, "the work of a Treadup, though it appears to him and to us to have been a failure, had its elements of success as well."

The formal and thematic return suggested by *The Call* will be even more evident in his next project. Hersey is scheduled to spend three weeks in Japan, where he will prepare an update to *Hiroshima*, examining the lives of the six original survivors in the years since the bomb. The project is an exciting one for Hersey; he has kept in contact with the four subjects of his original tract who still survive, and he welcomes the opportunity to work again with William Shawn at the *New Yorker*, whom he describes as "a kind of editorial Zelig [the chameleon-like character in Woody Allen's movie of that name]. Shawn's great gift is that he becomes each writer he deals with. He has the extraordinary ability to think the way the writer thinks."

And after that, another book, on a topic he won't disclose. With characteristic reticence, Hersey refuses to comment on it, again preferring to let it speak for itself. When it does, will it be fiction or journalism? "I don't know yet," he says, smiling. "It's too early to tell."

TOM SPAIN

OSCAR HIJUELOS

OSCAR HIJUELOS LIVES in an apartment building on Duke Ellington Boulevard (106th Street) in Manhattan. He greets us with slightly embarrassed apologies about some untended things—a phone call he must make, and other ministrations that eventually turn up as plates of mozzarella in olive oil with crisp Italian bread. Hijuelos is on the fair side of Hispanic—"a Gallego," he explains, with ancestors going back to Spain's Celtic province of Galicia. He has reddish hair and a pale complexion, the former lightened, the other freckled by the summer's sun.

Hijuelos' 12th-floor apartment looks north over a range of rooftops into the heart of Harlem, and provides him with visual reminders of his life as a New Yorker: there is St. Luke's Hospital, where Hijuelos was born in 1951; there is the Cathedral of St. John the Divine (currently imprisoned in gaunt scaffolding), where, on the back of a palm reader's flier, Hijuelos wrote the opening page of his first book; slightly to the north and west is Riverside Church, in the basement of which a younger Hijuelos practiced the art of boxing. Although admitting that sometimes he sees New York as "a city of churches," Hijuelos is quick to point out its more profane elements—"that block over there where the cops busted 30 crack dealers the other night," and rooftops where naked girls (he swears) sunbathe.

The visual composition of urban and spiritual imagery mixed with personal biography is more than a New York view for Hijuelos; it is also an apt description of his second book, *The Mambo Kings Play Songs of Love*.

The novel, which is the lead title for its publisher, Farrar, Straus & Giroux, tells the story of the brothers Cesar and Nestor Castillo, Cuban-born musicians who come to New York in 1949 to find their fortunes, or perhaps to escape them. In any event, their exploits—musical, amorous and gustatory—taking place as they do in Latin nightclubs, crowded kitchens and lonely hotel rooms, provide a lively narrative upon which the author hangs his sometimes somber meditations.

Although *Mambo Kings* has many themes—music, sex and love, pain and death, not to mention TV—Hijuelos's inspirations clearly spring from the self-awareness won through family and friends.

"I was born in New York. I grew up on 118th Street, just a few blocks from here. I was always in a band, mostly with Puerto Rican guys; we played Top-40 stuff and some Latin things," he says of his teenage years and early 20s. As for schooling, Hijuelos describes it in a somewhat dismissive fashion: "Catholic school, public school, public school." He finished at City College of New York.

His parents hail from Oriente province, "the easternmost province in Cuba, home to Desi Arnaz, Fidel Castro, Batista, Jose Lima, Alejo Carpentier. They came here in the 1940s, which is what my first novel, *Our House in the Last World* [Persea], was about—an ambitious people from a nonprofessional class coming to America."

That first book, published in 1983, was roundly praised for its tender portrait of émigré life. *Mambo Kings*, though not centered on Hijuelos's family, had its origins nonetheless in the details of his life.

"Basically, the first image I had for the book was of a superintendent who played music," says Hijuelos. "I got that image from Pedro, one of the elevator operators in this building who used to come up and play music with me. He was a wonderful bolero singer. I'd listen to him and think, 'This guy could be famous. What happened?' " In the novel, the elder brother, Cesar, after a long career as a modestly successful bandleader, humbles himself by accepting the superintendent position in his building, only to dignify the post with disarming pride.

"I also have a cousin named Angel who was a bolero singer in Cuba, although I didn't know it. I was at his house and he started singing, and he was beautiful. And he became a mechanic. So I had this idea of incredibly talented people who never made it.

"In a way," he adds, "the whole book was formed by listening to music and dwelling on personalities."

The sharply drawn figures of the Mambo King brothers are more than mere amalgams of real people, however. "Cesar and Nestor are archetypes. There's the flamboyant Cesar who's really very troubled, and there's the troubled Nestor who's really very soulful. I guess it's mostly invention rather than portraiture. I hope that anyone who has the greater lust for living can relate to Cesar, and anyone who has lost a love can relate to Nestor."

And anyone who has seen *I Love Lucy* will be able to relate to an event that wends its way throughout the book—a guest appearance by Cesar and Nestor on the then-top-rated TV show featuring America's favorite Cuban bandleader and his madcap comedienne wife. From their knock on Lucy and Ricky Ricardo's apartment door (to which Lucy responds "I'm commmmmming") to Ricky's "Gee, it's swell you fellas could make it up from Havana," to their performance—as Ricky's Cuban cousins—at the Copacabana, a legend, at least among family and friends, is made. Nephews of Cesar and Nestor are called to the TV whenever neighbors spot the Mambo Kings episode coming on; from such a brief event posterity is born, and it occasions one of the books's more philosophical, or perhaps spiritual, themes.

"I was really thinking of the TV appearance as being about memory, and memory being about immortality," says Hijuelos. "And the thing about a book is that it should have a cumulative effect; some novels go for the quick knockout, and I wanted to write a book where, at the end, you would know what someone feels like who really cares for someone and thinks about them. In the end of the book, when I replay the appearance of the brothers on the *Lucy* show, for me, that's what memory is about—you love someone, you feel for them, you remember them. It's like a rerun in your head.

"Desi and Lucy themselves have become cultural icons," he continues. "Desi is very typically Cuban to me, and I was very interested in the uniting of American and Cuban culture. When I used to watch the show I thought that Desi was the star! I was in Italy when he died and I couldn't continue the book for awhile. And now Lucy is gone. And just yesterday in the Albany train station, I found a 'poor-Lucy-we-loved-you' magazine on the seat. There's a quote in there by Bob Hope: 'One of the greatest gifts to mankind is laughter and one of the greatest gifts to laughter is Lucille Ball. God has her now, but thanks to television we'll have her forever.' "

In *Mambo Kings*, considerations of the hereafter barely hold their own against the enticements of the here-and-now—the book's atmosphere is thick with sexual desire.

"I intended a little bit of parody of the super-sexual virility that men are obsessed with in the macho cultures," says Hijuelos. "I was having fun with it. Also, for me, it's a play on mortality, and on the body and how one can be hyperphallic—built like the Empire State Building—and it won't make any difference to the ultimate issues of love or family or death. I wanted to write a book that had meat in it," he says with a laugh, "but which was also nourishing, with a provocative understructure. A lot of themes are repressed in the book but sex is not; it actually covers other layers. The sex balances the pain of the book."

Clearly, the challenge of structuring a novel to incorporate Hijuelos's many passions must have been daunting. But Hijuelos knew what he *didn't* want to do—"an elaborate plot—ABCDEFG, with atmosphere, character introduction, dramatic tension, denouement, all that. In a way, I think I avoided it, and honored the idea that life doesn't always work that way."

Instead, Hijuelos settled upon a simple, open organization, one that is familiar to anyone who listens to music—the book has two parts, Side A and Side B.

"The formal idea was sort of like having a record going round and round. You know how sometimes when you listen to music and the song cuts off and you're into another feeling? I wanted to move atmospherically. I saw the chapters as different songs. That's why I needed the device of the hotel, with Cesar sitting in The Hotel Splendour at the end of his life, listening to an old Mambo Kings record, and as different songs come on he has different thoughts, going forward, going back. It does drift around, I have to admit; the reader is not always aware of being with Cesar, but I wanted that improvisational feel in part of the book, like a horn line."

Choosing this structure also allowed Hijuelos to promote another of his passions—the music itself. "It is *the most fun* music

261

in the world," he says, hopping up and into another room to turn on his electric keyboard. "It is soulful, it combines Spanish lyric beauty and almost maudlinness with a sort of hipness. I was listening to a Talking Heads record, *Naked*, and the hippest track on the whole album is a straight mambo vamp. If people listened to the source of that stuff, they'd go nuts."

Hijuelos leans seriously into his keyboard playing. "If you've read the book, you've at least heard *of* this tune." He plays "Beautiful Maria of My Soul," the song that, in the novel, is rewritten 22 times by the long-suffering Nestor in memory of a lost love; it is the Mambo Kings' only hit, and the song that grabbed Desi Arnaz's attention. Indeed, it is soulful to this listener's ear. To the question of composition (the words and music appear in the book), Hijuelos admits co-authorship with a friend. "I write songs all the time."

The strains of seeing this book through publication have been hard on Hijuelos. "After a while you become indistinguishable from your book," he laments. "I'm getting out of the country—to Portugal—so I can think again." As for his next book, he says that, "Surprisingly, at least to me, writing this book made me want to write a book about women. My next book is about 14 sisters."

There is a particular atmosphere in *Mambo Kings* that fascinated Hijuelos even as he was writing. Certain of the female characters, like the cooly independent Dolores—who suffers through a rape attempt by a gum salesman before becoming Nestor's wife—completely grabbed him. "I was sorry to have to leave Dolores. I could have written an entire book about her," he says.

Despite the male bravado, and the decidedly male melancholy in the book, *The Mambo Kings* has a convincing female camaraderie, in which the women seem to outwit the fates that all the men fall prey to. Hijuelos attributes those scenes to a period in his life just after college.

"When I got out of school I worked in an office researching trends in advertising. Some of the atmosphere in the book came from that job. The women's gossip was distilled from hanging out with the girls from the office. Women often go through incredible trips with men. For some reason they used to tell me about it. I love that whole life—the gin mill life. We used to go to clubs at night. Disco was the craze, not the mambo, but it's all the same. People want to go out and have fun—they want to find magic and romance and they want to find poetry and fall in love and be loved to death. People live this dream and then they hit real life again. And there are arbiters of that dream—that's what entertainers are about. They are that dream all the time. And I think novelists and poets, or the worlds inside their works, are too. What I want to do is entertain and give readers something that can help them live more happily, just like characters in a song of love."

MICHAEL COFFEY

TONY HILLERMAN

On the tough, sweaty scramble to the giant alcove in Chinle Wash, Tony Hillerman pauses to catch his breath, rest his knee. Far above him the Navajo boatman scampers like a housefly up the sheer, wind-carved cliff. At 62, with his gouty toe, bum left ankle and loose right knee, Hillerman has trouble enough just getting to the cave. Yet writer's itch has kept him going: he wants to check out his impressions of this crucial locale in a brewing first chapter of a mystery he's writing.

For six days, floating with Hillerman down Utah's San Juan River, we are having a rare chance to watch the author at work. His uniquely habit-forming novels about a pair of Navajo tribal policemen, Lt. Joe Leaphorn and Officer Jim Chee, break every rule of publishing success: they're crammed with exotic characters and magic—but virtually no money or sex, and precious little violence. The eighth and latest novel, *A Thief of Time*, is out from Harper & Row.

Hillerman is no more glamorous than his books. A portly ex-newspaperman, he's devoutly Catholic, a doting grandfather of nine with slow, courtly ways, an irrepressible sense of humor and an unfashionable contempt for money.

His novels are marked by a deep-rooted sense of place and people. The Native American characters he creates are soaked up from anthropological lore, scholarly dissertations and his own experts, including two Navajos he met in an ethnology course—one a female shaman. He also spends time on the scene, hanging out

264

at trading posts. "On some books all I have done is go out and take a look at canyon country, sit around and feel it and smell it." he says.

Joan Kahn, the editor who bought his first novel in 1970 for $3500, told him: "Mr. Hillerman, I hope you don't think you're going to make any money on this book." He didn't, but later "the money kind of built up" with foreign rights and movie options. His novels have remained in print, each book selling better than the previous one.

Hillerman rarely bothers to read his six-month royalty statements. "I just look at the numbers on the checks." His wife Marie still shops around for cheaper potatoes. He doesn't want anyone to think of them as affluent. "I don't particularly like or understand those people who measure success by numbers," he says. The Hillermans have lived in the same big Albuquerque house for 25 years, and Hillerman drives a secondhand Isuzu Trooper. He and Marie laugh about not knowing what his gross income is.

Hillerman was born in 1925 in the Oklahoma dust bowl, where "the Joads were the ones who had enough money to move to California." His father ran a small general store in Sacred Heart, stocking "overalls and pig feed," and worked a hardscrabble farm with an outhouse, no tractor and no electricity. The nearest library was 35 miles away; the once-a-week movie, too expensive. The battery radio was "a big deal when it was operating. Growing up where I did, high value and respect were attached to being able to tell a story, to interest or entertain people." The two-room school, however, was so bad that Hillerman was tolerated (just barely) at St. Mary's Academy, a boarding school for Potawatomie and Seminole girls. But he was a motivated student. "If you grow up surrounded by poverty, everyone shares one ambition: get the hell out."

At 18 he ran to the army and World War II. "It was a way to get some adventure and see the world." In his two years on the front lines in Europe, his original 212 riflemen shrank to eight survivors. In his letters home, he "tried to write stuff I knew would interest my mother"; his V-mail made the hometown paper. In '45 he was hit by a grenade behind German lines in Austria; he had two broken legs, was burned and partially blinded.

When the bandages came off three weeks later, he could see light, "a big step forward."

Home on convalescent leave with eye patch and cane, Hillerman was delivering drilling equipment outside Crownpoint, N.M., when he saw "12 or 13 men in ceremonial attire, the horses all duded up." Someone explained that this was a Navajo Enemy Way ceremony, a curing ritual for a soldier just back from the war. "To see people with a living culture still affecting how they live—that interested me. I'm drawn to people who believe in something enough that their lives are affected by it."

A local reporter who had read Hillerman's wartime letters told him he could be a writer, an idea that had never occurred to him. At the University of Oklahoma Hillerman crammed a journalism B.A. into two and a half years, edited the humor magazine and met his future wife, Marie Unzer, a Phi Beta Kappa bacteriology major.

From his first journalism job as police reporter in Borger, Texas, he leapfrogged to political reporter in UPI's Oklahoma City bureau, where a good editor often made him cut his stories 40% without leaving anything out. "Before long I learned to write a 500-word story in 275 words," Hillerman says.

At 27 he was UPI bureau manager in Santa Fe. He and Marie had one child, then adopted five more. He wound up as executive editor of the Santa Fe *New Mexican*, but an itch to try other types of writing persisted. In 1962, with Marie's encouragement, he quit to troubleshoot for the president of the University of New Mexico, simultaneously picking up an M.A. in English literature.

For 22 years he taught ethnic and writing courses at UNM and became an authority on the Southwest. He has written *The Spell of New Mexico* and *Rio Grande;* a children's book based on Zuni legend, *The Boy Who Made Dragonfly;* and a Fodor's guide to New Mexico. His first book, *The Great Taos Bank Robbery,* was inspired by a call he got as city editor from a Taos stringer, who said, "We're going to have a bank robbery in 15 minutes." Somebody had spotted a hairy-legged man, dressed as a woman, with a gun, standing in line for a teller, and sure enough. . . .

Yet Hillerman's "number-one ambition was to have my name on a piece of published fiction." To him, nonfiction had "the strength of credibility, but you have to dig out the truth. It's inflexible material. I thought: Wouldn't it be wonderful to work

266

in plastic instead of flint; make your own imagination drive the writing."

Increasingly fascinated with Indian culture, he decided to try capturing it in a mystery novel, "a shorter form that has shape and flexibility, a story line with a lot of narrative." In the late '60s he steeped himself in Graham Greene, Raymond Chandler and G. K. Chesterton "to see if there was anything I could steal," and spent three years writing *The Blessing Way*. In '70 he sent it to the New York agent (he will not reveal her name) who had handled his magazine articles. Her one-sentence verdict: "If you insist on rewriting this, get rid of all that Indian stuff."

The "Indian stuff," 70% of the book, happened to be what Hillerman wanted to write about. "I thought the hell with that. I've got three years' work in this. I was either going to publish the book or feel like a failure." After seeing an article about Harper & Row mystery editor Joan Kahn, he sent the manuscript directly to her. A week later she said she'd buy it if he came up with a better last chapter. Hillerman complied, and he credits Kahn for much of his success. When Kahn left for St. Martin's Press, Hillerman remained under contract with Harper—"kind of like a child of divorce"—and was inherited by Larry Ashmead, with whom he has enjoyed "a good relationship from the very beginning." Hillerman says that his publisher has always treated him well, citing the fact that print runs and publicity bookings have risen with each new mystery.

Hillerman loyally stuck with his original agent until a clause she left in a movie option contract resulted in a L.A. producer owning all the rights to one of Hillerman's characters. "The same month the Ayatollah took the hostages, Bob Banner took Joe Leaphorn," he says. Hillerman eventually spent $21,000 to ransom Joe "out of slavery"—and switched agents; he is now represented by Perry Knowlton at Curtis Brown.

Over the years Hillerman has seen some "incredibly bad" filmscripts spun from his books, including one he wrote himself. "I used to pray that nobody would ever make a movie," so that he wouldn't have to "spend the rest of my life explaining that I didn't have a damn thing to do with it." Recently his prayers were answered in a more satisfactory way: Robert Redford's Wildwood Films picked up the options to all of the Indian novels. Hillerman admits to being pleased. "Having a guy like Redford, with his track record of being sensitive to the people—that's different."

Hillerman "quit a long time ago trying to outline a new book," since he finds "they don't come out at all like I intended." He confesses that he spends "an awful lot of time sprawled on the sofa watching TV, trying to think through a problem." He tries to tackle the hard parts first: "Then it's easier to start again. If I could write three pages every day I'd be happy, but before I write a scene I have to get somewhere quiet and daydream my way into it. I imagine all the sensory feeling, where the sun is, what you see, hear, smell, the dust in the air—I really see it in my mind."

Although he has written about other tribes, he says that his affinity is with the Navajos. They share with him strong family ties, storytelling conventions and a tradition that reveres language for its power, importance and precision. And also a sense of humor and a horror of obscenity. "The worst thing you can be called in Navajo is a ghost or a coyote. The worst insult is 'He acts like he doesn't have any relatives.' There's this sense that what counts first is the human being, not money."

He speaks of the whole vast Colorado plateau as "my parish. This is my territorial imperative, obviously not designed for human occupancy. You can't make a living out of it, but you could certainly die here. I feel at home in it." He says he wouldn't write his novels "if I didn't think of them as moral books. But you can sell the moral only if you give the reader his money's worth of entertainment."

In the rush of his hard-won success, his most valued accolades still come from those who discover their own roots in his pages. Like the Navajo boys who tell him they've "either got to read me or drop out of school." Or the old people who say the books "got their grandkids reading and interested in their culture, asking questions." Or the librarian who put it this way: "When we read others, we say yes, that's us and it's so sad. When we read you, we say yes, that's us and we win."

In the Southwest Hillerman is often recognized on the street now. "Lots of Navajo kids bring me raggedy books to sign—that's the ideal kind. I've had dozens of them look surprised and say, 'I thought you were a Navajo.'" He is "an honorary redskin" anyhow, since the tribal council honored him last fall at Window

Rock's Navajo Fair. While he says he "had no missionary impulse when I started, now I do, a little, when I become aware of the possibilities."

Hillerman sometimes grouses that if he was 25 or 30 he would "drop everything and learn how to use videotape." But he also admits that he "wouldn't write if it wasn't fun. I really do think each book reflects what I've learned, and is technically better. Otherwise I'd quit, because writing is really hard to do, and it doesn't get any easier."

CATHERINE BRESLIN

LAURA Z. HOBSON

THE SHEER FORCE of her personality envelopes the visitor to Laura Z. Hobson's Fifth Avenue apartment. Although she is candid about her age in her autobiography, *Laura Z: A Life* (Arbor House), Hobson in no way looks or acts her 83 years. Exuding energy and joie de vivre, a tall, slim, very attractive woman with a commanding presence, Hobson exhibits the animated drive that fueled several careers, numerous love affairs and a lifestyle daringly ahead of her times. One quickly senses as well the strength of character that has brought her through uncommon vicissitudes.

Those who have read Hobson's nine novels already know a great deal about Laura Z. Hobson, although they may be generally unaware that all were based on episodes from the author's own life. The offspring of radical Socialists (*First Papers*), Hobson was a topnotch advertising copywriter (*Untold Millions*); an unwed mother (*The Tenth Month*); the parent of a homosexual son (*Consenting Adult*); an outspoken political activist and foe of fascism (*The Trespassers*); and a crusader for civil rights (*Gentleman's Agreement*).

Why, then, write an autobiography, when she has previously mined these experiences in other works? Will her readers have a sense of *déjà vu* as they encounter events already described in her fiction? Hobson admits it was just that fear that for a long time prevented her from revealing the details of her life. "I have always said to my two sons, 'I'll *never* write an autobiography. I'm not an egotist enough to write my life as if it were terribly important.' Besides, I have taken the biggest chunks of my life and based novels on them."

As she recounts in *Laura Z*, however, Don Fine, president of Arbor House, broached the subject of her autobiography during a lunch date with Hobson's son Mike, himself a publishing executive. Hobson debated the pitfalls of telling her life story without the protecting cloak of fiction. Her novels, she says, are "the curious amalgam of what happened and what you wish had happened," and the difference is crucial. "People say to you, 'How much is true?' Take *Untold Millions*. When you tell the basis of it as I do in my autobiography, it took 20 pages. *Untold Millions* was a 500-page manuscript. How much is true? Come *on!*"

Warming to her subject, Hobson goes on: "Let's take *Gentleman's Agreement*. Was I ever a young man, a reporter on a magazine? I was never. Was I ever a young widow? Never. Was I ever living in California and suddenly a stranger in New York? *No!* Yet *nothing* is made up—except the stuff that doesn't matter."

As Hobson speaks, her voice grows resonant with feeling, and she gestures often, sometimes absently adjusting the heavy gold chain she wears around the neck of a chic red-and-black patterned silk dress. She is prone to rhetorical questions to which she delivers the vehement answer in the next breath. "If you're writing a murder mystery, you don't have to be a murderer. Correct? If you're writing espionage, you don't have to be in the CIA or the foreign service. Correct? If you're writing about a divorce, however, you have to have been divorced, to have lived though the pain and grief, or you will *never* write a serious novel about it."

In her fiction, Hobson concludes, she is like an archaeologist on a dig, who comes upon a fossil bone and creates a whole dinosaur out of it. "I take a part of my life and create a whole other creature around it."

The demands of nonfiction were different, however. Researching her own life "killed me at times," Hobson confesses. "At times I would sit there at the typewriter and be writing steadily and strongly and suddenly dissolve into tears and be right back where I was 35 years ago. I would weep—and then go on. That's when you know you've got it right.

"There are very few honest autobiographies; I'm convinced of it. And as for memoirs, don't ask me because I'll get livid.

Memoirs are things that pick and choose. I put in things that I wish I hadn't had to."

One realizes, reading *Laura Z*, that Hobson's reputation for tackling controversial themes in her novels was the result of an independent, liberated lifestyle long before feminism was a catchword, and before it was fashionable to speak out against social and political injustices, a commitment that still motivates her today. She shares with us the reprint of an article on the *All in the Family* TV show, which she wrote for the Arts and Leisure section of the *New York Times* a few years back, in which she cogently criticized the dissemination of racial prejudice under the guise of comedy. Her spirited attack touched off a furor of letters to the *Times*. She says proudly, "That article is the culmination of how I feel.

"I don't think I would be my kind of novelist if I hadn't been terribly active in the things I care about, like civil rights, like politics, like the Author's League. (I was a member of the National Council for 27 years.) If I hadn't involved myself in all those things, would I have been more prolific, written a novel every year? Never!"

She has never thought of herself as a crusader, however. "When you're going through something, you don't think in terms of history, of other people's labels. Only years later do you begin to evaluate. Then it's nice when you can give yourself a pat on the back, of course." Galvanized to social action by the Nazi book burning in 1933, Hobson endeavored to call attention to the atrocities in Germany early on, writing the copy for a full-page protest in the *Times* to denounce Charles Lindbergh's "America First" credo. She sponsored the escape of two (non-Jewish) psychiatrists and their children from Vienna. She never hesitated to reveal her own Jewish origins when she encountered anti-Semitism in the social world in which she moved in the '30s as the wife of Francis Thayer Hobson, then a vice-president of William Morrow. The Hobsons and the Henry Luces were close friends, a circumstance that provided Hobson with an entrée to Time Inc., but talent alone propelled her to the position of director of promotion for *Time*, the only woman among the 30 top executives. She had also been a reporter on the New York *Post*, had published short stories and had collaborated on two westerns. All this before she wrote her first novel at the age of 43, when she was the single mother of two adopted children, one of them actually her own son born out of wedlock and "adopted" under another name.

Her decision to become a novelist inaugurated for Hobson a career that she says is both immensely satisfying and a form of psychoanalysis, enabling her to relive experiences with a new perspective. "Researching my own life was a fantastic revelation!" Hobson says. "But then I'm always happiest when I'm writing, being totally, absolutely absorbed in it." She welcomes what she calls "happy insomnia, when you sleep a few hours and wake up writing a scene in your head."

Hobson wrote her first novel, *The Trespassers*, at the suggestion of Richard Simon, and maintained an amicable relationship with Simon & Schuster through her next three books, including the classic *Gentleman's Agreement*. When she came to write *First Papers*, her account of a radical childhood, she asked Dick Simon's permission to go to Random House to work with the revered Saxe Commins. "He was an editor of Faulkner and Eugene O'Neill, but the reason I wanted to go there was very simple: he knew my period; he was the nephew of Emma Goldman."

A long hiatus of writer's block followed *Final Papers*, however, and when Hobson was ready to write again, she took *Consenting Adult* to Doubleday. "Betty Prashker was my editor, and she was marvelous, and they were marvelous because it was a very successful book. But when they got to *Over and Above* [her next novel], they saw it wasn't going to be a big thing. They had precisely one ad for it and dropped it like a rock," Hobson says, her voice ringing with displeasure. "All of us being very civilized and decent," she recalls, she got out of her option clause with Doubleday and went to Harper and Row, where her editor for *Untold Millions* was Larry Ashmead. ("*There's* a nice man for you!") The invitation from Arbor House to publish her autobiography was a cliffhanger for a while, while her agent Robert Lantz talked with both houses.

To give an idea of the progress of the negotiations, Hobson goes to the handsome, S-shaped desk-cum-bookcase that dominates the corner of her living room and retrieves one of the red leatherbound volumes of the date books she has been keeping faithfully for many years. Brief entries in a neat, ladylike hand detail the evolution of the agreement whereby Harper and Row

273

will retain first option on her novels but both volumes of her autobiography will come from Arbor House.

How she came to the decision to recount her life in two volumes is related with gusto. Realizing that she could not meet her deadline and compress all her experiences into one book, Hobson (with some trepidation) suggested to Don Fine that she end the book in 1947, the year of the publication of *Gentleman's Agreement*. "I said to him, 'Listen, the best book of the year is *Growing Up* by Russell Baker; it only took *him* to age 21. Why do I have to do it in one massive volume?' And I could see he was excited; his eyes just flamed. He said he'd think about it over the weekend, and he called on Monday and said, 'The book is in production.' Now you know it usually takes a whole year [between delivery of the manuscript and the publication date]. Here is the proof that if a man wants to publish a book quickly, it can be done."

Hobson adds that she has the "highest regard" for Fine. "He's an aggressive publisher. *He's* not going to print a book and drop it; *he's* going to push the living hell out of it!"

She won't even hint at what happens in the next volume, telling us only that "there are some fascinating things coming up in the second part of my life." She will, however, share some of the details of her life today.

"It's a very good life, really, for somebody who's not young. I'm very rarely bored. I have so many resources. I love music. I love reading. I love the Yankees. I love bridge. I love British crossword puzzles. I love doublecrostics [she was editor of the *Saturday Review*'s doublecrostics for 24 years]. I love biking; I rode eight miles in Central Park today, my girl! I love my two sons. I love my grandchildren. You know, life can be so full, if you use it."

SYBIL S. STEINBERG

WILLIAM HUMPHREY

WILLIAM HUMPHREY'S VARIED writings—fiction, memoirs, essays—are so intimately connected with the facts of his life that it should come as no surprise that his recent novel *No Resting Place* (Delacorte/Seymour Lawrence), which deals with the exodus of the Cherokee nation from Georgia, was inspired by his having a Native American Indian ancestor. "No one knew much about him," Humphrey tells us, "but I decided he was a Cherokee." This decision was not a whim, however: the story of the forced march of the Cherokees in the days of the Jackson presidency and their subsequent mistreatment at the hands of the Texans is this native Texan's way of paying tribute to a people more unjustly treated than history has let us believe.

In his research—"I have read every book on the subject," Humphrey says—he discovered that "the Trail of Tears," as the march from Georgia is called, was followed by a similarly tragic experience in Texas after the territory broke off from Mexico. It was a particularly egregious betrayal, since the Battle of San Jacinto, the decisive conflict in Texas's war with Mexico, could not have been won without the benevolent neutrality of the Cherokees. All this makes for a dark period in American history, and Humphrey pursues it with the same meticulous passion that he brought to the hard life of Northeastern Texans in *The Ordways*, *Home from the Hill* and *Farther Off from Heaven*.

Having left Texas before he finished college, Humphrey did not return to his hometown of Clarksville until 34 years later. His welcome was genial—though one citizen commented, "You were

275

pretty rough on us"—but he did not mean to stay. ("Who would I have to talk to?" he asks.) Very soon after coming to New York at the age of 21, he met his wife of over four decades, a figurative painter, and they lived abroad, mostly in Italy, for seven years, and before settling in Hudson, N.Y., where they have lived for the last 24. But the heart of his fiction is tied to Clarksville, and since it was his father, dead since Humphrey was 13, who taught him to hunt and fish, once could say that his sportsmen essays (Delta has issued *Open Season* in paperback) have their genesis in Texas, too.

Humphrey is not skittish about the autobiographical element in his work—unlike many writers who expound aesthetic demurrals when the subject is raised—and talks with pleasure about the real counterparts of his characters, a pleasure sometimes mixed with wonder. "My mother was very much hurt by that book," he says of his masterful *Farther Off from Heaven*, with the puzzlement authors feel when a truthful but loving portrait meets with disapproval. He can be gleeful when the reader "gets" the meanness subtly depicted in seemingly loving characters, as in the passages about his maternal grandparents in the same book.

As we drive from the station by the river in Hudson into the hilly countryside where the Humphreys live, the sight of one of the houses reminds him of a short story he has recently finished, based on the lives of old acquaintances, but he confesses, "I shall have to wait until they are dead to publish it." This need to anchor his stories in actual and often personally experienced situations perhaps explains his impatience with nonrealistic fiction and with writers primarily concerned with style. He also puts a distance between himself and writers like Faulkner, to whom he has been compared, by his insistence that he is interested in the passions of normal people, not in abnormal psychology.

He has struggled, with each of his books, he says, to discover the form that the subject demands. Having often been told that his books are quite different from each other—*No Resting Place*, for example, is his first historical novel—he likes to quote his reply to an interviewer who said that were it not for the title page he would not know that the same man had written each of his books. "If my books differ from one another," Humphrey recalls saying, "it is because I do not want to tell myself the same story again and again. It was Tolstoy who defended his apparent self-contradictions with, 'What am I?—a cricket that I should make the same noise all the time!' "

He also likes to say that a writer is someone to whom writing comes harder than to most people. He begins each day at the typewriter in his study; later he decamps to the kitchen downstairs, where he writes with a pencil until he cannot read his scribbles any more; then he shuttles back to the typewriter. Though the typewriter is an electric one "that can do almost anything" (he does not think he will ever take to a word processor), its virtuosity does not make writing any easier. Half a page is still a good day's work. "But toward the end of a book," his wife Dorothy adds, "you do a little more than that," and he agrees.

"I get up in the morning and I see a scene in my head. I don't know where it goes . . . and very often it doesn't go." But he writes the scene, although it may not follow upon the previous day's work. "You think sometimes you've got a pretty good idea of what you're going to do, but you've got to be ready to abandon that idea or any other idea at once if the characters start saying to you, 'We're not gonna go down that way, we're gonna go down this way—and you're coming with us!' "

He can look at his own work coolly and critically, he says, revealing that, in the case of *No Resting Place,* he retrieved the first version from his American, English and French publishers before they could comment because he had decided that the history it contained was not sufficiently "digested." This ability to stand back from a manuscript helps to make him impatient with contemporary editors, and he can still talk bitterly of the first story he published in the *New Yorker.* He had already spent the magazine's check to rent a place better than his cramped accommodations at Bard College, where he was teaching, when he received galleys replete with the considerable editing for which the magazine has long been famous.

There ensued much argument with his editor about the changes. At one point the editor said, "Mr. Ross is in the hospital and he is very unhappy about the stubbornness you're showing— he would like to make you one of our stable." "I am not a horse," Humphrey replied; now he whinnies at his remembered effrontery. He was pleased to see in the final galley that a sentence was circled and a comment in the margin said: "This sticks out like a sore thumb." He recalls that he had the satisfaction of writing: "That's what I told you when *you* put it in there!"

Despite such stories, his relationships with the three houses with whom he has published—Morrow, Knopf and, at present, Delacorte—have been personal ones, and he deplores the loss of that relationship in the mechanisms of publishing today. As a young man first starting out, he made personal appeals to established figures in the arts. He came to New York with a five-act play about Benjamin Franklin, and brashly knocked on Broadway producer Brock Pemberton's door. "It had a cast of 350. Needless to say, it was not produced. I then fell in with a crowd of Village bohemians and learned that my attitude toward the arts was dated and I'd better catch up with the avant-garde. I never did."

He was more desperate and less impulsive when he approached W. H. Auden and Randall Jarrell. After four years of what he calls being "on the lam," in order to retain custody of a child of his wife's first marriage, he desperately needed some reassurance about his work. Each writer said that he thought the piece in question was a mistake but that, yes, he had talent.

"Auden bought me lunch too," he said, recollecting "the dear man's" generosity and his own penuriousness. Jarrell suggested he read Katherine Anne Porter, a writer from his part of the country, and with some of his last cash he bought a used copy of *Flowering Judas* and was carried away by it. "That good simple direct prose opened up a whole world to me," Humphrey remembers.

Heartened by these encounters, he went back to writing. He got a job in upstate New York, milking goats and caring for a vegetable garden. With the job came a one-room house, and it was there he wrote his first story. *Accent* paid him $15 for it. His second was bought by *Sewanee Review* for $190.

After Morrow published his collected short stories, they asked him for a novel. He recalls replying that he did not have one and did not mean to write any novels. To his own surprise, his next book turned out to be a novel: the moving *Home from the Hill,* which made the bestseller list and became a movie. *The Ordways* was also a bestseller and was bought by Hollywood, but this has not been the case with his later books. When asked about that, he says that what would really bother him is if they all did as well.

He fears that today "cost accounting has taken over the publishing industry, since the field no longer belongs to publishers. In the old days, Alfred Knopf, whom I did not like but whom I did admire, would have said, 'What does it matter that this title of Humphrey's won't sell all that much—the important thing is to keep him alive.' " About reviewers he is not much kinder. "I used to hang eagerly on the verdict of reviewers, but I don't anymore. I've got a thick skin. . . . Imperceptive praise is the most discouraging."

Humphrey taught at Bard for seven years, and later for a term each at Smith and Yale, but he has never been part of academia or the New York literary set. The grants and honors that accompany a successful literary life have largely not come his way, surprising for a writer of his stature. Many years ago, Katherine Anne Porter told him that if he wanted she could get him into the National Institute of Arts and Letters "in two days." He replied, "If that's how you get in it, I don't want it." And that is how his relations with the literary establishment have remained.

And yet, as his conversation inadvertently reveals, he has known many literary figures. He often visited Leonard Woolf, and they would sit up late talking, mostly about music. One time, however, Woolf told him of the occasion when he and Tom ("Tawm," Humphrey says, in parody of the Bloomsbury accent) and Virginia were out for a walk on the downs. Eliot and Virginia walked ahead and at one point they paused and looked back for Woolf. "Leonard is pissing against a tree. This so embarrasses Tom that he averts his face quickly and Virginia, who was possibly a bit more than a prude herself, asks, 'What is the matter, Tom?' She does not see anything particularly wrong but adds, 'Does it upset you?'; 'Certainly,' he replied, 'I wouldn't let anybody see me *shave!*' That says a lot about Tawm and his poetry."

Humphrey has no patience for Eliot, observing that his "*fin de siècle* weariness with the world was an affectation." He does not accept as evidence in Eliot's defense our belated knowledge that he had known despair in his personal life. "That's no excuse!" Humphrey exclaims. "Who hasn't?"

He adds, "Of course, one can forgive this sort of thing in a person if that's what you are. But I find this same streak in his poetry." Obviously, Humphrey believes that for a man to revel in weariness, "to say at 40, the aged eagle has clipped his wings," is something of a sin. It is not that at 65 he is a pollyanna, but rather that Humphrey—in the novel *No Resting Place* as in so many of his family stories of Clarksville—celebrates the indomitable and the unyielding and looks at life with unblinking honesty.

JOSÉ YGLESIAS

JOSEPHINE HUMPHREYS

JOSEPHINE HUMPHREYS' BRIGHT, high-ceilinged office in Charleston's Confederate Home is a clue to her relationship to a city busy accommodating the old to the new, a state of flux captured in both *Dreams of Sleep,* the PEN/Hemingway Award–winning novel, and *Rich in Love,* her second book (Viking).

Built around 1800, the large building became a home for Confederate widows and orphans. When some apartments there were made available to professionals and artists for work spaces, Humphreys moved in her word processor, desk and wicker sofa and set up shop. The writing office, she explains in the soft speech patterns of native Charlestonians, "gives me the isolation I need." Located in the business district, the space nevertheless is private as well as accessible. Not far away is the mid-19th-century home where she lives with her husband, a bond lawyer, and two teenage sons. And it's only a short drive across the Cooper River and through the sprawling suburb of Mt. Pleasant—the setting for *Rich in Love*—to their summer house on Sullivans Island.

Nearby also are the houses in which she grew up, that of Neta, her much beloved grandmother, and the one into which Humphreys' parents later moved their three daughters. Not only is everything on "the peninsula"—the site on which Charleston was contained until not long ago—close to everything else, but people who live there tend to be part of a close-knit community. Many of the women who live in the Confederate Home had known Neta, whom Humphreys recalled in an essay she wrote for

A World Unsuspected (UNC Press), an album of childhood recollections by 11 contemporary southern writers. At one of the residents' social gatherings, she read the remembrance (titled "My Real Invisible Self") about an episode that happened when she was 13, one that culminates in self-recognition: " 'I want you to write some stories for me,' [Neta] says, nodding, 'Why didn't I think of it before?' . . . My dense and sullen heart lifts at the suggestion. *Write some stories for me.* I have stories ready to go. I have been making them up for years! And I have, as I will later discover, a quality that serves writers well: self-doubt so deep it is indistinguishable from vanity. Neta saw it and nurtured it."

But although she thought of herself as a writer from an early age, actual commitment to the craft didn't come until later. Instead, Humphreys remembers, she was "pulled along" through her teens by "feelings of being unusual, left out, and unpopular." Her family, though not wealthy, belonged to Charleston Society—her great-great grandfather was George Trenholm, the Confederacy's Secretary of the Treasury—and she made her debut into that rarefied milieu. "I wish I had known then that there was no need to be unhappy about those things. But try telling that to a young girl. It's impossible."

Lucille, the new novel's central character, suffers from a similar uneasiness, and at one point says, "Things happen that you are unable to halt or moderate." When Humphreys began thinking about the novel, she wanted to find a character like Irish, the teenage babysitter who was her favorite character in *Dreams of Sleep.* "It was easy for me to imagine a girl so connected to her place that it becomes more than a setting," Lucille's creator notes. The development, however, was more difficult. "A lot of what she turned out to be came slowly, and I was often unhappy in her company. I think I was rehabilitating my own image of the teenage girl and reexamining what I was when I was one." The first-person viewpoint she chose, a departure from the third person of *Dreams of Sleep,* had much to do with that. "I didn't realize how big a difference it would be, and I had to get much more involved with the inner self of the character. It was claustrophobic for me at first."

Humphreys' novels include vividly realized black characters, but the ability to create them also came slowly. The public and private schools she attended in Charleston were not integrated.

Neither did she have any contact with blacks in her age group until she went to Duke in 1963, the first year that undergraduate classes were integrated there. Looking back, she finds it "incredibly bizarre that we lived like this, that I could grow up here without speaking to even one black person my own age. That's one of the ways Charleston has changed. There's not that deep rift now between black and white children, and there is a degree of integration" at private as well as public schools, she adds. And when she returned to Charleston to teach at Baptist College, after pursuing a Ph.D. at the University of Texas at Austin, her classes were integrated.

But the first black friend she had was at Duke, the university her father picked out. "I had longings for New England. My mother had gone to Vassar, but my father felt if I went there I would never return. He thought Duke was the great university of the South, a place filled with southerners. Little did he know," she interjects with a laugh, "that most of the people there were from the North." But she knew she wanted to study creative writing, and when she saw a photograph of Reynolds Price in an article about where the good college teachers were, she knew Duke was for her. "Reynolds's *Long and Happy Life* had just been published and had made a big impact. The article said he was also a brilliant teacher, and it was right."

The writing program at Duke was headed by William Blackburn, whose students have included William Styron, Mac Hyman, Fred Chappell, Anne Tyler and Price, among others, and to whom Humphreys dedicated *Dreams of Sleep*. She passed the audition for Price's class—"He gave us the first sentence of a story that we then had to complete," she recalls. Each student wrote a story a week thereafter, and Blackburn would read each story aloud to the class. "He didn't criticize and take them apart, like some creative writing teachers do. Mostly he told his students how wonderful their stories were, and that was very encouraging." But he did offer advice that she thinks is worthwhile for all aspiring writers to follow. "He told us to choose an author, read everything he wrote, and study how he did it."

Following graduation in 1967, however, Humphreys began "slipping" into an academic life. She enrolled at Yale for a graduate degree in English literature, because at that time, one didn't have to commit to a specialty until the selection of a dissertation topic. "It was a broad, general program, the most sane of the graduate programs I know of. The teaching was brilliant, and it wasn't too rigorous academically." But because she didn't know anyone in New Haven and felt isolated, she was unhappy. "I got a master's degree, which was considered shameful because it was an admission you weren't going to be around for a whole Ph.D. So one afternoon, another person and myself sneaked in and paid our $5, which is all that was required after completion of a year of classes. Soon after that, Yale stopped giving master's degrees."

Austin was much more to her liking. Not only did she feel a kinship to Texas, since Neta and Humphreys' mother's family came from there, but a classmate from Duke, the Chicago native she later married, was at the university's law school. She had worked toward a Ph.D. on the poet William Cowper through the oral exams and about a third of the way into a dissertation when the couple decided to move to Charleston. Writing again took second place to her teaching duties at Baptist College, where she carried a course load that included 17th-century and Romantic poetry, a survey of English literature, American and world literature courses, plus her favorite, remedial English. Both her sons were born during that time. "One day I ended up in the doctor's office with terrible chest pains, and I took offense at his suggestion that I was doing too much. But I realized he was right, and that I wasn't doing the one big thing that I really wanted to do. So I dropped everything—except the children, of course—and started writing." She was 33.

Although she had not been writing, she had nonetheless been storing things in her mind and knew she wanted to write about the changing social fabric of a city in transition. She began *Dreams of Sleep* to show the interrelatedness of the various kinds of people composing the community's social strata. "In that story," says Humphreys, "Iris and her mother in the housing project are the last of the poor white people living in the [redeveloped] area tourists come to see." Because it's the place where Charleston's recent prosperity is most evident, poor people are being forced out to less visible parts of the city. "When I was growing up, we were much more economically integrated," Humphreys says.

284

Does Humphreys create her characters with specific people in mind? "I try not to use real people," she says. "I think that writers have to be good at imagining other people's experiences strongly enough to understand it. It was quite a shock to me when reviewers spoke of the novel's characters as though they were flesh and blood. I never—never!—looked at them that way. I was much more interested in the words." Storytelling is not my biggest talent, I'm afraid. It's necessary, of course, but I think of the story as a vehicle for words."

When she finished the novel, however, Humphreys had no idea what to do with it. She wrote Price asking for advice but used an address she later discovered was one he had not been at for years. "It's amazing that he even received the letter. But he did, and asked me to send about 50 pages. He liked what he read, and sent it on to his agent"—which is how Price's agent, Harriet Wasserman, came to represent Humphreys.

When Wasserman asked Humphreys which publisher she would prefer, she went to the library to see who had published the books she liked best. One of her favorite authors is Josephine Pinckney, a Charlestonian whose novels, published by Viking, were quite popular in the '40s and '50s. The idea of having the same publisher as Pinckney greatly appealed to the younger Josephine.

Three O'Clock Dinner, Pinckney's biggest success, is also about contemporary Charleston and families there, which for some may add weight to the argument that women writers have one theme, the family and its relationships. But, Humphreys asks, what else is there for a novelist to write about? "There are many, many men who write about family relationships. In a lot of ways, fiction is based on the family story, and I think that there is a deep narrative structure within that story. Adam and Eve, Cain and Abel—those are family stories, our first stories. And they didn't come out of a woman's book."

BOB SUMMER

JOYCE JOHNSON

"Has it become my own madness not to have outgrown those years when the door first swung open on a world I never managed to explore as completely as I longed to?" writes Joyce Johnson in her absorbing memoir *Minor Characters*. The book evokes a legendary period in the 1950s, the years of the Beat generation. Jack Kerouac, Allen Ginsberg and other Beats play supporting roles in Johnson's story, although she was herself a "minor character" in their celebrated lives. Revisiting one's youth generally arouses complex memories and emotions, and in Johnson's case these are augmented by her recollections of active participation in an era of cultural and social ferment and her illuminating insights into the personalities of several significant figures in modern American literature.

Johnson was Joyce Glassman, a student at Barnard, when she met Jack Kerouac (on a blind date arranged by Allen Ginsberg) and immediately became Kerouac's mistress. The product of a firmly conventional middle-class family, she had previously shocked her parents by moving out of their home (a sign of a "bad" girl in the '50s) and into a succession of grungy apartments in Greenwich Village and the Lower East Side, in pursuit of a bohemian lifestyle.

Today the executive editor of Dial Press, Johnson looks anything but the stereotypical bohemian one encounters in her book. The requisite all-black outfit, sandals and dangling earrings are no longer her uniform, but Johnson has not succumbed to chic. Dressed in a bottle-green blouse and beige skirt topped by a

286

tweed jacket, she looks more like a tidy surburban housewife than either a former Beat or a successful editor. Fine muted-blond hair frames a mild, full face on which the dabs of blue eyeshadow seem to strike a false note of sophistication. Soft-spoken and earnest, Johnson conveys an impression of gentle vulnerability and self-effacement, not the sort of person one would expect to have been in the vanguard of a controversial social movement.

But in conversation, as in the pages of her memoir, Johnson is acute and articulate. "It was an exciting period of my life," she remembers, "a time of enormous hope and energy and the feeling that anything was possible . . . that four people sitting around a table could change the world." Although she always knew she would someday write a book about those years of social and literary upheaval, she instinctively felt she must have some perspective on both Kerouac and the Beat generation he came to represent. She also did not want to go though the rest of her life "labeled 'the girl who knew Kerouac.' I wanted to establish myself as a person in my own right first," she says.

After many years of incubation, *Minor Characters* had an odd catalyst. About three years ago, when Johnson was in England on business, she went with friends to a London pub called The Pizza Express. A group of old Kansas City jazz musicians were playing there—"wonderful old men with gold teeth and impeccable suits with diamond stickpins, septuagenarians who were on the road. Something about the place—a cellar, dimly lit—reminded me of the jazz places I had been to in the '50s. I started reflecting on how extraordinary it was, these old guys in their 70s still on the road, whereas as lot of younger musicians had died. I thought of the writers I had known, and I thought of Jack. Suddenly I realized that enough time had gone by. I had enough perspective on it all." In addition, she was curious about what had happened to the other players in the Beats' dramatic era.

Working with the remnants of a sporadic journal and a trove of letters ("Jack was a great letter writer; we *all* wrote letters in those days"), Johnson began writing her book a few hours each morning before going to work, a habit she has had for many years. "I'm metabolically fortunate; I can get up quickly, my mind is clear, there are no distractions," she says. She manages a slow but steady output, a page or two a day, and is often rewarded with new ideas on the bus on the way to her office.

"Some people feel enormous anguish to have to split their time between writing and a job," she comments. "They've been sold a bill of goods that you have to have perfect conditions in order to accomplish anything. That's not true."

She ran into an unexpected obstacle when Kerouac's last wife, a woman he married 11 years after he and Johnson had ended their relationship, categorically refused to grant Johnson permission to quote directly from the letters he had sent to her. Johnson is dismayed by the fact that documents she possesses, letters that were so much a part of her own life story, could be controlled by a person who had nothing to do with this period in Kerouac's life. "It's a complicated issue of personal involvement," she muses, "and one that other authors may well encounter."

"I wanted to do several things in this book," Johnson goes on. "I wanted to give a picture of Jack as he was as a person." Even in well-researched biographies of Kerouac she has always had the feeling that the essence of the man was not conveyed: "I felt I could give a better sense of him by zeroing in on a little piece of his life," she says. "I was also trying to address the myth of Kerouac. There is the person I knew then, the person I now remember after 25 years, and the myth. These pictures are sometimes conflicting, and I tried to sort them out."

She had another purpose, too. "It is more a book about a certain kind of young woman of the '50s and our attempts to escape to a different kind of life. We were involved in a struggle to break away from home, to have our own apartments, to stay out all night if we wished. It was a struggle to achieve things that young people today take for granted."

Yet for all their hard-won independence, Johnson, her friends Elise Cowan (who was in love with Allen Ginsberg) and Hettie Cohen Jones (married to LeRoi Jones, now known as Amiri Baraka) and others lived primarily through the men in their lives. "We were attracted to men who represented unconventional values, who were rebels. We had the illusion that we could establish relationships with these men that would be different from anything that had gone before, that we would be comrades. We did not see ourselves as conventional wives. They wanted us in conventional roles, but at the same time they didn't want the traditional responsibilities. They wanted to be free." (The relationship is serendipitously symbolized in the photograph on the jacket cover of *Minor Characters*. Retrieved from a magazine's archives, the photo shows a somber, slightly pugnacious Kerouac in the foreground and a retiring Johnson in the shadows behind him.)

While the young women companions of the Beats paid a considerable emotional price for this mixed privilege, Johnson on balance considers that portion of her life an exhilarating episode. "It was a remarkably rich period. To be part of this extraordinary convergence of painting and writing was a heady experience," she muses. "Except that if you were a woman in the group, you were watching all these wonderful things. You were off to one side. Even if you were doing some writing yourself, none of these people was very interested in your work. You didn't discuss it with anyone—not even other women in the circle whom you admired. At times it could be very lonely."

Johnson was indeed writing at this time—a novel about her Barnard years, developed during a writing workshop taught by Hiram Haydn at the New School for Social Research and accepted by Random House on the basis of its opening chapters. Titled *Come Join the Dance*, it was published in 1962, when Johnson was 26. By the time the turbulent decade came to an end, Johnson had also experienced an abortion (Kerouac was not the father) and a brief marriage to a painter, Jim Johnson, who soon afterwards was killed in a motorcycle accident—almost a metaphor for the intensity of life as the Beats conceived it.

Thereafter her life became more conventional: a second husband (from whom she is now divorced); a son, Daniel Pinchbeck, to whom *Minor Characters* is dedicated; and a second novel, *Bad Connections*, published in 1978 (Putnam). Having worked in publishing since the day she left Barnard, starting as a secretary to a literary agent and moving on to Farrar, Straus and Cudahy; Morrow; Dial ("in the days of Ed Doctorow"); and McGraw-Hill, Johnson returned to Dial about six years ago. The roster of authors she has worked with over the years is impressive. At the beginning of her career she seemed a "natural for radical books," she confesses, editing Abbie Hoffman's *Revolution for the Hell of It*, books by LeRoi Jones and Ann Moody's *Coming of Age in Mississippi*. She was also the editor of Judith Rossner's first three novels, *Free to Be You and Me* and Ron Kovic's *Born on the*

Fourth of July. At Dial Johnson was responsible for *Photographs for the Tsar, The Romanovs* and Catherine Breslin's *Unholy Child.* She also edits the Virago series there.

As one who has experienced both sides of the publishing process, Johnson reflects about the kind of instant fame Kerouac achieved when *On the Road* created a furor in 1957. As she recounts in *Minor Characters,* it was a profoundly destructive experience for Kerouac, terrible to witness. "No other author up to that time had become famous in precisely the same way," she recalls. "The TV talk show was in its infancy, and Kerouac was one of the first to get that treatment which authors now take for granted and demand." Kerouac had no perspective on fame, she goes on, and when as a result of the media blitz he became a celebrity virtually overnight, he could not handle the phenomenon. "It's my belief that media saturation is probably very destructive to art," Johnson says. "New movements get overexposed and exhausted before they have a chance to grow, and they turn to ashes in a short time. Some degree of time and obscurity is often very necessary to artists."

Although her own first novel was accepted for publication with astonishing ease, Johnson feels her literary *rite de passage* was safeguarded by a certain irony. "I was a Beat, but I had a split existence. I got up every morning and went to work, no matter what had happened the night before," she recalls.

The legacy of the Beat generation was an impetus to a general freeing up of social conventions, Johnson feels, but many tenets of their lifestyle have vanished. "The Beats had a belief in the goodness of a certain kind of poverty," she says. "Now it's no longer possible to be bohemian, to be poor with grace. It's no longer possible for someone to come to New York and find an apartment for $60 a month and feed themselves on $15 a week." Gone, too, is the "enormous feeling of mutual support among a community of people. People all helped each other in those days. Older artists looked out for younger ones. They were accessible. It was not a hierarchical situation."

Johnson recalls a newsletter called the *Floating Bear,* with each issue consisting of about eight mimeographed sheets. It went to a mailing list of about 100 people and found an audience for a lot of new, experimental writing. Hettie and LeRoi Jones published what Johnson calls a "very influential" little magazine named *Yu-*

290

gen, which Hettie financed from her salary of $75 a week from her job on the *Partisan Review*. "She paid for it and typed it," Johnson says, "and distributed it after we all got together and stapled the pages."

Johnson deplores the fact that most of this interdependence has vanished from writers' lives. "People are more passive today," she says. "They sit around hoping for grants. I think some of that do-it-yourself spirit had better come back into literary life. That artists were very much in touch with each other was one of the invigorating aspects of that whole period. It was a very intense time. Nobody did anything lightly. And it was wonderful."

SYBIL S. STEINBERG

WARD JUST

Snow has begun to fall as we make our way up the winding avenue that leads to the summit of Montmartre, past small houses with large windows built as artists' studios, to the incongruous Art Deco apartment house—all in loggias and patios—where novelist Ward Just hangs out these days. We find the author puzzling over the just-received jacket of his novel *The American Ambassador* (Houghton Mifflin), the lettering of which, in a strange burst of coincidence, could easily have been created by the designer of the apartment building. Just hasn't been living here very long, but it has been long enough to realize that his immediate neighbor is a professional soprano and most of the other tenants are photographers (how else to explain the frequent projections of strobe lights from windows giving on to the courtyard?), but so far he hasn't seen a painter or a sculptor. Nevertheless, Just seems relaxed in these surroundings: he's an erstwhile foreign correspondent, an American who travels well, like the ambassadorial family he writes about in *Ambassador*.

In the publisher's blurb on the book jacket, Just is identified as a former reporter, a current author, who "lives in Paris and on Martha's Vineyard." How does one do that? A mild-mannered man with comfortable eyeglasses and a receding hairline, Just has to go back a way in time to explain. As son and grandson of publishers of the *Waukegan* (Ill.) *Sun*, Just spent his formative teen years at nearby Lake Forest. After working for his father at the *Sun*, he went on to *Newsweek*'s Chicago bureau, then to that magazine's Washington bureau during the Kennedy administra-

292

tion, when Ben Bradlee was boss; from there he put in a stint as *Newsweek*'s man in London. Then when Bradlee, who had been something of a mentor to him, went over to the *Washington Post* in 1965, he took Just with him, and that year Just was assigned to cover Vietnam (it was a true Christmas present, for he flew to Saigon on December 25). He remained there until May 1967, on return requesting leave to stop over in Ireland while he wrote a memoir of his experiences. *To What End* became his first book, published by Houghton Mifflin.

"It shouldn't need saying that Vietnam was a crucible for any-one who was there," Just comments. "And I was wounded in ac-tion, which tends to concentrate the mind." He was on a reconnaissance patrol with the 101st Airborne Division when they found themselves, as he puts it, where they "shouldn't have been." It wasn't an ambush; the proper military term was "meet-ing engagement." A hand grenade put Just in a succession of hos-pitals and gave him material for more than one work of fiction.

"Vietnam had its advantages, all the same. You were covering America's number-one story, in the days when the American commitment was growing every day. After that any other journal-istic assignment was a pale brew."

When Just returned to Washington late in 1967, the pale brew was domestic politics: he was assigned to the presidential cam-paigns of Richard Nixon and Eugene McCarthy. Next thing Just knew he was an editorial writer. "But there was always a novel in my desk drawer," he remembers, quickly adding: "I have a feel-ing that doesn't happen nowadays," because, he thinks, fiction doesn't have the same attraction for today's young reporters. Ac-tually he took a summer off to draft his first novel, *A Soldier of the Revolution,* whose central character, involved in a charitable organization in Latin America, gets caught up in a guerrilla movement. It was well published (by Knopf) and well reviewed, but the author now says of it: "I wish I had it back to do again."

By then he was fed up with editorials. "I felt silly commenting on news instead of digging it out," Just remembers. And the *Post* management was confused by this man who was always on leave to write his own thing. A friendly separation ensued. "I was so involved with that paper that there are people who still think I work there—and it's been 17 years." He did a two-part piece for the *Atlantic* on the Army—"what Vietnam had done to it, which

293

was to goddamn near destroy it." Knopf published it as *Military Men*, but Just comments: "Two pieces in the *Atlantic* do not a book make."

Then there were short stories—most published in the *Atlantic* before seeing book covers (as *The Congressman Who Loved Flaubert, and Other Wartime Stories*, done by Atlantic–Little, Brown). Several novels followed, the next to last entitled *In The City of Fear* (Viking)—the city being Washington, which is virtually a character in the novel.

Here *PW* injects an impertinent question: Why has Just changed imprints so often? He pauses to think about that, then says, "Mutual disappointment, I suppose. I don't believe in asking for an advance before I sit down to write. I bring in a complete manuscript, and by that time the sales of the previous work have convinced both sides that we're not made for each other. That doesn't mean I'm mad at my previous publishers, nor are they with me. If one hasn't had a success on one's own terms or theirs, one tends to move on."

In a sense, *In the City of Fear* can also be seen as an introduction to *The American Ambassador*. Both novels, and indeed most of Just's fiction, turn on the contrast between Washington appearance and Washington reality—the finality being disillusion. "There is a collapse of ethics, which seems to get worse as our century goes on. Every time I return to Washington I'm impressed with the power of money there, and at every level—among journalists as well as lawyers and lobbyists. Power used to be the big game; now money has to be included. The town is for sale."

Just would like readers to approach his Washington as they do the Chicago of Theodore Dreiser, Frank Norris or Upton Sinclair. Among writers who have influenced him, he places F. Scott Fitzgerald at the top of the list. "The romance of money is not all that different from the romance of power," he says. Just also ruminates a good deal about Henry James and his recurrent theme, "the collision of values between Europe and America."

Does Just feel more comfortable with fiction than with fact now? He answers that question with a story. "At the *Atlantic*, Robert Manning asked me to do a media column which we called 'Newspaper Days.' I wrote it for six issues of the magazine and then stopped. One reason was that I kept making errors—errors

294

I had never made as a reporter. I retired from the field quite bloody. I'd been accurate in journalism, but in the intervening years I'd lost the use of the muscle. My work tends to puzzle readers because it sounds like fact. In *The American Ambassador* that's rarely the case. If you weight fiction down with too much factual material it always seems to me dead on the page. What we don't need is one more *roman à clef.*"

In *The American Ambassador,* Just comes to grips with the regrettable side of American power once again, but he also tackles the supreme enigma of our day, the terrorist mentality. The American ambassador's son is a terrorist, and Just depicts his cold-blooded fury with chilling effect. The novel is set in Africa and Germany as well as in Washington, but more important than persons or places is the theme, a central concern that Just sees as underlying all of his writings: loyalty. The ambassador must choose between his son and his country. "It's a choice no one should be asked to make, and yet we're expected to make it all the time," Just says.

He admits that his book has a number of peculiarities. One of them is his portrait of a long-lasting happy marriage. But he also shows a consequence: the child of such a union can feel very excluded. After he finished the manuscript someone showed him a quote from Robert Louis Stevenson to the effect that "the children of lovers are always orphans." That's at least part of the reason Ambassador North's son Bill slips into the German underground.

Just's fictional family is part of an American establishment with global responsibilities and a global reach—until things begin to go wrong. Early readers like its pace, and the author agrees it is better plotted than his previous books. Readers looking for parallels with other writers dealing in disillusion may reject le Carré and Graham Greene, for they work within a system that includes those private "public schools" and class warfare: we note more of a resemblance with another Washington novelist, Charles McCarry. "If you write about Hollywood, readers will look for real names behind your characters: you have terrible difficulty getting people to forget Marilyn Monroe. When you write about Washington, readers look for keys, expecting composite characters— one of the components has to be Henry Kissinger. Perhaps that's why there is little good fiction on our government."

The writing of the *The American Ambassador* took place while Just was writer-in-residence at Phillips Academy in Andover, Mass. His wife, Sarah, was then working for a local public radio station. Her assignment ended when Just's residency was over and their son Ian graduated from high school. They were all free of responsibilities, didn't have to be anywhere—a heady situation. So they packed to come to Paris. Apart from the crazy apartment building, their only roof is at Lambert's Cove on Martha's Vineyard; it's actually only a summer house. When we pursue this matter, Just realizes he's a nomad now. (Sarah puts in: "People think of you as a Washington writer, but you're not.") So Paris remains their home of choice, not the least because "it's affordable," Just explains. More so than New York or Boston, and much depends on how well the new novel does in the stores. For the moment the Justs are too enchanted with Paris to know or to care what the falling dollar is doing to its affordability. Nomadism is made easy by the fact that Just works with a manual typewriter. His interest in things French was recently enhanced by the sale of the French rights to *The American Ambassador* to Flammarion— his first-ever sale to France. Just definitely intends to be around for publication.

When he arrived in Paris last year, Just had what he remembers as a tremendous burst of energy, during which he drafted a long novella and then a briefer story. Since then? "I'm in my receiving mode and not in a sending mode," he replies, adding the excuse: "Paris is an easy city not to work in." In any case, *PW*'s envoy muses as he skids over the courtyard tiles on his way out to the slippery sidewalk, there's always next summer on the Vineyard.

HERBERT R. LOTTMAN

GARRISON KEILLOR

GARRISON KEILLOR WASN'T always Garrison Keillor. In 1956, when a boy named Gary Keillor was in the eighth grade, he submitted his poetry to the school paper. "It was in a school and at a time when boys didn't write poetry. So I used the name Garrison. It sounded a little stiffer, a little bigger. Flags flying. I think I was trying to hide behind a name that meant strength and 'don't give me a hard time about this.'"

Nowadays no one would think of giving Keillor a hard time about his writing. The humorist is a regular contributor to the *New Yorker* and the *Atlantic,* author of *Happy to Be Here* and *Lake Wobegon Days.*

Keillor is best known, however, for creating and hosting *A Prairie Home Companion,* a national two-hour live radio show produced by Minnesota Public Radio. He has been doing the program since 1974, and has built a following of an estimated two million listeners who tune in every Saturday night. Sometimes billed as "America's tallest radio comedian," he broadcasts from the fictional town of Lake Wobegon, Minn., which he introduces as "the little town that time forgot, that the decades cannot improve."

Each week Keillor presents a variety of musical guests (including fiddlers, guitarists, singers and jug bands), and participates in skits, fake commercials and funny songs. But the highlight of the show comes when he stops the music and fills listeners in on "the news from Lake Wobegon." These monologues, often with no specific beginning or end, present loving portraits of the inhabitants of Lake Wobegon, while also poking fun at their foibles and their insignificant triumphs. Keillor has taken these stories and expanded them into *Lake Wobegon Days*.

When we meet with Keillor early one morning, he's on what he calls his "preseason exhibition," a preliminary interview before his book tour begins. We spot him almost instantly as he steps out of the elevator at the Algonquin Hotel; standing six feet three inches tall, wearing an off-white suit and a jaunty red tie, Keillor cuts a distinctive figure. His voice is even more distinctive: deep, rich, mellifluous, with a touch of broad Minnesota accent. Keillor speaks slowly and deliberately, caressing certain words and phrases and letting them hang in the air.

Over breakfast at a nearby coffee shop, we discuss how Keillor accommodates his love for radio and for writing. After he graduated from the University of Minnesota, he switched back and forth for many years between the two, with alternating stints of a year and a half to two years for each. "Part of this had to do with money—it's not easy to earn a living freelancing humorous fiction—but also with an attraction to radio. There's a wonderful simplicity about radio which cuts through my own pretenses.

"I had a early-morning radio show. You sit at a microphone with your favorite music, talk to people and wish them a happy birthday and try to create something pleasant and happy for them. Seemed to me to be a simple, decent service to mankind. Whereas sitting at a typewriter and writing often seems to me to be particularly ambitious, in sort of a scheming, crafty way. So much in humor and comedy is manipulative. But I love to write, I do it every day and I have since I was a little kid. So I've had to resolve these things somehow."

A Prairie Home Companion strikes what Keillor considers a good balance between writing and performing. He enjoys the "craziness and unpredictability" of live radio, and though he writes his monologues ahead of time, he leaves the script backstage.

"Radio is a powerful invention," he comments. "A single voice talking into the radio and speaking in concrete images is very powerful, and when it is done live it is even more powerful: knowing that this person who is talking to you is standing out on a stage not reading from notes. It makes it possible for me to do monologues that are sometimes flat. People forgive that, because the ones that move them, move them very much. When people tell me they laughed and cried at the same time, I believe them, because I do sometimes myself."

Keillor grew up in the small town of Anoka, Minn., raised by strict, fundamentalist parents. "I am a shy person," Keillor readily points out, a trait going back to his childhood that has prompted many monologues on the problems shy persons face. In high school Keillor saw his first copy of the *New Yorker*, and he decided then and there that his goal was to be a *New Yorker* writer ("E. B. White is still my hero in the writing biz," he states). His determination—along with his talent—helped to sell his first story to the magazine in 1970. He's been writing humorous pieces for them ever since.

"I still love the *New Yorker* and love writing for them, and want to write anything I can for them. But there's another style of writing that I cannot do for them, which is to me more Midwestern, more colloquial. My Lake Wobegon monologues, which all start out as writing, are humor that is also sentimental. They have an emotional base you don't have in short, satirical fiction. Satire to me has a moral base but not an emotional base. And the monologues always do. So my writing this book is an attempt to take this form of writing that I developed through the radio, and see if I can't turn it around into book form."

Readers of *Lake Wobegon Days* may wonder to what extent Keillor's material is autobiographical. Clearly, the events and the people are described too intimately, too sympathetically, for them to be completely invented. "Most of the book is based on people I have known, and things that happened or things that might have happened to them," Keillor says. "But I would have a hard time saying who, what and where. I don't believe I invent anything—everything comes from experience. But it all sits around for 25 or 30 years and simmers. Marinates in its juices."

Keillor's book resonates with the same warm humor that fills his monologues: humor that's regionally specific but universal in its appeal. Minnesotans hold a special place in Keillor's heart. "I've lived all of my life in Minnesota. As a child, the Laura Ingalls Wilder books were special to me because they were set so close by. These stories led me to other books written by Minnesota authors, and later I read Sinclair Lewis and F. Scott Fitzgerald.

I've loved all kinds of books—including books that are far better than anything Lewis or Fitzgerald ever wrote—but it amazed me as a boy that people could make books out of the terrain and population where I lived. It just amazed me, to think that you could write books that would be set in Minnesota."

Though he considers the actual process of writing "not only difficult but often impossible," he recalls that he had a lot of "childlike fun" creating the many jokes and digressions sprinkled throughout *Lake Wobegon Days*. "Some secondary characters were based directly on pals of mine. There are names of people in there who are real people, but I use them as part of a wonderful old literary tradition—to put your pals in your work in an incidental, humorous way.

"The book also has what I believe to be the longest footnote in American fiction [a 12-page parody of Martin Luther's 95 theses]. I was pleased with the footnotes in the book and that one in particular. I think footnotes have a place in fiction. There is supporting material which can be read in sequence or earlier or just glanced at or eliminated entirely, and that can go into footnotes. It really allows a person freedom of digression that you want in a book. And I like the idea of a book being packed and rich and having layers."

Keillor is both amused by and resigned to the way reviewers often categorize his humor. "I predict that a minimum of 15 reviews of this book will refer to me as 'a modern-day Mark Twain.' Anyone who writes anything humorous who comes from anywhere west of Eighth Avenue is 'another Mark Twain.' To a great many people who live and work and write in New York, those of us who live out there in 'fly-over land' look the same to them. They see no essential difference between Tennessee, Minnesota, Nebraska—it's all that 'strong beating heart of the Midwest' and they can't distinguish among the different voices."

The editing stage was, for Keillor, "one of the great pleasures of the book." His editor, Kathryn Court, went out to St. Paul for a few days last winter to work with him. Keillor recalls, "We sat in my living room in front of the fireplace and went over the manuscript. It's fascinating to go over your own work and see it through someone else's eyes and have their help on it."

He came to New York for a week this past June to help get the book ready for the press. "I stayed at the Algonquin and took the

Sixth Avenue subway down to Viking every day. They gave me a little office. It was a joy: poring over the drawings spread out on the floor, looking at the jacket and end papers. I loved the camaraderie of working on a project with other people. The book was written in a series of small, dark rooms. So it felt good coming out here for the last week—like getting a place on the basketball team."

Keillor wrote *Lake Wobegon Days* on a word processor, which he has just begun to use. "I'm sure I could have written the book without one, but it would have been such an act of character. I never used a typist all those years. And this machine eliminates all of the retyping." Though he acknowledges its usefulness, he's still not a complete convert to the new technology. "I think word processors can be responsible for producing a good deal of flabby writing. The words come out of you like toothpaste sometimes. There's no shortage of sheer wordage in America; more sentences are not what this country needs."

Though his book was finished months ago and Keillor has since moved on to other projects, his mind still wanders back over *Lake Wobegon Days* and thinks of ways it could be better. "I don't know why—I shouldn't. But it's deeply depressing to let go of a piece of work that's taken so much of your time and thoughts. I felt very good about a lot of it when I wrote it, but that was a long time ago sitting in a room a long ways from here.

"I've never been particularly satisfied with anything that I've done. Well, a few things. I made a catch once in center field when I was 19 that I've thought of many times. I was playing too deep and had to come in for the ball. It was a combination of a long run and fighting the urge to pull up and take it on the bounce. I was either going to get it or it would go right through me and I'd be a fool. I caught it and made a sidearm throw to second as I was hurtling forward that doubled up a runner. You only need to make one of those plays once."

Viking has high hopes for the success of *Lake Wobegon Days;* the book has a 190,000-copy first printing and is a Book-of-the-Month Club dual main selection. Keillor remarks, "I come from religious people who do not admire success. Although I sometimes feel successful, I think that my upbringing doesn't really allow me to enjoy it. Or doesn't allow me to admit it."

He is also ambivalent about growing older. His 25th high school reunion this summer, coming right on the heels of his 43rd birthday, provoked some introspection. "I'm a little past the mid-point of life now, and it's a tender age in some ways. I don't want to be 18 again, not really, but you accumulate a lot of regrets by the age of 43. The capacity for foolishness remains as high as ever, though. Being 43 doesn't mean I'm entirely grown up yet."

Keillor is set to embark on a two-week, 12-city publicity swing for *Lake Wobegon Days*. "The tour starts the week after Labor Day," he observes. "Kids go back to school and authors hit the road." When that concludes, he will return to the house he shares in St. Paul with his 16-year-old son (Keillor is divorced). He'll resume broadcasting *A Prairie Home Companion*, and work on more stories and a new project with a photographer friend. They're collaborating on a book of photos from places around America, accompanied by letters sent by Lake Wobegon residents who have visited these sites, or Lake Wobegon exiles who have moved there. "It's kind of a travel book, but it's all based on Lake Wobegon, because that's where they're from," he explains.

So even in his next book he'll be writing about his favorite subject, "the little town that time forgot." Keillor once said, "From Lake Wobegon I get my voice." For him, the town is not simply a setting for humorous stories, but a necessary part of the way he expresses his view of the world. When Keillor describes the residents of Lake Wobegon, he is also describing the influences that helped shape his world view.

"As I get older, more and more often I hear my father's voice coming out of me, and I find myself saying things he would say. I write things that seem to be something my father would have said, or my Uncle Lou would have said—sort of an apotheosis of what they would have said if they had been writers. I find the satisfaction in doing that, that I don't get from writing funny stories."

DIANE ROBACK

TRACY KIDDER

WHEN WE START to arrange an interview with Tracy Kidder, we discover the man who won the Pulitzer Prize for a book called *The Soul of a New Machine* doesn't have a telephone answering machine. That drawback overcome—his publisher, Houghton Mifflin, has just bought him one—and communications established, we find that to talk to Kidder, we have to go to coastal Maine, where he's building a summer—perhaps someday a permanent—residence. He is again working with two of the men, Jim Locke and Richard Gougeon, who constructed the house described in *House*, the best-seller in which he charted the building of a home for a Massachusetts family—and the complex personal relationships that went with it.

When we arrive at the building site, Kidder is cutting part of the roof with one member of his construction team. It's a beautiful afternoon; the sea sparkles beyond the pine trees and, when the construction noises stop, birds sing through the silence and the clear air. Kidder is trim and suntanned. We perch on what will be a window looking out to sea in the skeleton of the house and talk about his provocative new book, *Among Schoolchildren*, which chronicles a year in the life of a fifth-grade class in Holyoke, Mass. The book is, as well, an ode to their remarkable, energetic teacher, Christine Zajac, and to unsung teachers everywhere.

Where did the new book start? we ask. "Two schoolteachers, friends, suggested it, almost simultaneously," Kidder tells us. "At first I didn't think it would be such a great idea. I began to notice something, though, as I turned this over in my mind. I know

303

quite a few schoolteachers, and they're almost all female. I'd find myself at parties with these women; they would start talking about their classes with real animation, and they had a lot of good stories to tell. It made me feel that there was really some gold here, that this was something worth looking at, that it would have intrinsic narrative interest."

Kidder wanted to write about a city school, and he wanted a city near his home in western Massachusetts. The state has been the locale of his previous two books, both of them about people in the workplace as well: *House* was set in Amherst, and Westborough is the location of Data General, the corporation Kidder portrayed in *The Soul of a New Machine*, his book about computers. For *Among Schoolchildren*, Holyoke was perfect. "Holyoke is, as one local reporter—a good one—put it, an ark of humanity," he says. "It's always been an immigrant city. All of Europe at one time had outposts there." Kidder approached the Holyoke superintendent of schools; he liked the idea, "understood he couldn't control what I wrote" and provided a list of the five best elementary school teachers. From that list ("They were all terrific") Kidder picked Chris Zajac.

"To manage a classroom alone is a feat, one that she is particularly gifted at. Really astonished me, that woman. She likes what she is doing, that's the main thing. She is also a humorous person. And she likes kids. It was quite an eventful year, one of her more eventful, I suspect. She had the most difficult she'd ever had, and she had the brightest."

We ask Kidder if he compiled the material for his book by sitting in Chris Zajac's classroom every day. "I missed two days all year. One I just played hooky, and the other one, I was sick. For the most part, I was silent," Kidder says. He took 10,000 pages of notes, however. "We had a deal, Mrs. Zajac and I, that I would never be left in charge of the class. I didn't want ever to be in the position of having to discipline them. God knows, I don't think I could have. There was one occasion, when, for some reason or other, she had to leave the room, and I was left reading to them. But it wasn't for very long, and nothing had happened." Happened to whom? we inquire. "Neither party suffered very much," Kidder grins.

"But I did talk to the children, and I was *constantly* talking to Mrs. Zajac. One of the biggest problems that a writer has is point of view, that is, where you stand as the storyteller. I didn't want to do it, but finally, with help from my editor, Richard Todd, I realized that the only place I could stand was right over Mrs. Zajac's shoulder. I had been with her so many days, and she had spoken so openly to me, that I think I really knew what she was thinking, and also she *told* me what she was thinking. This is a woman of enormous candor and honesty. So I thought finally, in certain places I'm just going to say, 'This is what she was thinking.' I wanted to keep that focus narrowly right on her."

Kidder is passionate about education. "One of the things that's interesting about education is that, discussed in the abstract, I find it extremely dull. But described or experienced in the particular, in the places where formal education actually takes place, it's very interesting. It's impossible to generalize about because most of what's going on is, it seems to me, a very subtle, very complicated set of relationships which are changing and being formed, growing and coming to the verge of falling apart. A classroom really is like a little village. The teacher presumably is mayor—sometimes village idiot, I suppose—but not in the case of Mrs. Zajac."

"My sense is that most efforts at reform usually are conducted independently of the experience, knowledge, wishes of teachers. And that's a *terrible* mistake, of course, since for better or worse, education *is* what happens in these little rooms. Countless little rooms, millions of them. For better or worse, it's usually a room that's presided over by a woman who's usually alone.

"To be as good a teacher as Mrs. Zajac does not require a Ph.D. in physics. It requires, first of all, the *desire* to be a good teacher. And obviously some skills that not everybody has, but many of them are ones that can be cultivated. But I think you really, genuinely, have to like children, first of all, and you have to be interested in them, and you have to have an open mind. The ideal of having a nation where all teachers are good teachers or where some enormous percentage are really good teachers isn't completely realistic. It is unrealistic under the present circumstances—under the pay and working conditions that generally prevail. Mrs. Zajac was making, what, $25,550, or something like that. I can't remember exactly. That's *terrible*. That was after 13 years of experience and a master's degree. Now, *really*.

"What I hope is clear from the book is that a good teacher does make an enormous difference. But you never really know if you've succeeded in any long-term sense. Sometimes children come back as adults to tell you. But more often than not, the effects of good teaching are incalculable, particularly for the teacher. My book is not the Hollywood kind of story where children suddenly blossom into something they weren't before. There is some blossoming here. But there's also some remarkably sad stuff. I wanted the reader to come away feeling sad but glad that Mrs. Zajac was around."

Building his own home, it seems, has continued Kidder's personal education while allowing him to maintain a certain idealism. He chose white cedar shingles because "I want an absolutely zero maintenance house," he says, optimistically. Despite his knowledge and experience of homebuilding, to his chagrin, the new floor joists don't meet their specifications, and the floor is sagging before the walls are even framed in. In some respects he is simultaneously expert and layman: suddenly lifting his hand from a piece of wood, he exclaims, "Did I just get a splinter? I did. *Another* one. I think I'm going to start wearing gloves on this job."

Kidder was born in New York City, son of a lawyer and a schoolteacher mother, to whom *Among Schoolchildren* is dedicated. "My mother's been a high-school teacher for 20 years—a very good one, I'm told, but I never saw her teach. But I've run into old students of hers who always have nice things to say about her. She likes the book, of course. And that's important to me. But most people wouldn't take that seriously as a testimonial—that it's a good book because your mother liked it."

Married to an artist and the father of a girl, 10, and a boy, 15, Kidder shortcuts his biography: "I'm 43, grew up on Long Island. Then I went to Harvard, I went to Vietnam, I went to the University of Iowa Writers Workshop, and after that, I just wrote, and then I had a successful book, my second." His first, *The Road to Yuba City*, was about a murder case.

Kidder majored in English at Harvard. "I started majoring in political science. I quit in the middle of a lecture by Henry Kissinger. It had nothing to do with politics. It's just that I was bored." Drafted? "No, I joined up." A protest of some sort? "No.

306

Just stupidity." In Vietnam, Kidder did his stint in Army Intelligence, a job that did not "involve much combat experience. I received information which I took to a colonel. That's basically what I did. In Vietnam, as in any war, only a very small percentage of soldiers were in combat."

Speaking of his nonfiction, Kidder explains: "The thing that I concern myself with is narrative and characters. The ingredients of a good narrative are characters, bringing people to life on the page, and the sense of plot, as E. M. Forster defined it. 'The king died and the queen died' is a story; 'the king died and the queen died of grief' is a plot. The engine of narrative is human motivation. With nonfiction, of course, you're stuck with what is, what was. I don't like to invent quotes. I try to make it as accurate as I can. But within those boundaries, what really interests me is some kind of marriage of all these things."

I try to look behind at what's deep and engaging about the topic. Education will always be a big subject. I didn't set out to write a tract about education. I set out to tell what I thought would be a pretty interesting, complicated story.

"Nonfiction writers who are interested in narrative tend to look for intersections, for places where lots of issues get joined. You could write about the entire world starting from a classroom. I believe in approaching from the particular instead of the general. Part of the problem that America has had in trying to reform its educational system has been that the approach is general, it's always from the top, always these august committees, and always looking for grand solutions, to problems that couldn't be more particular. But I really think that this thirst for the grand solution is part of the problem. I hoped that looking at one class closely, I could say a lot about education generally, and that I wouldn't have to say it, it would all be there."

About to leave to join his family and house-building comrades for dinner, Kidder says, "The writing ought to be in service of subject and vice versa. It's complicated but may be really very simple. My *intentions* were to tell an engaging story, to try to bring people to life on the page and re-create the atmosphere of that city, which is so palpable to me. To do a lot of the things that novels do, but it's a piece of nonfiction, and it's about a subject that's very real and very important. But many novels are too.

This one just happens to be factually accurate, I hope. I'm pleased with it. I think I like it better than anything else I've written. But then again, that's the way I ought to feel. I think it's a lot sadder and there's a lot more emotion in it. I think it has more heart to it than the other pieces."

AMANDA SMITH

BARBARA KINGSOLVER

ACROSS THE SCORCHED desert toward the lower Tucson Mountains, up a gravel-covered dirt road identifiable only by two weather-bleached yellow pillars, lies a house almost hidden by native cacti and scrub. Here Barbara Kingsolver, author of *The Bean Trees, Homeland and Other Stories* and the HarperCollins release *Animal Dreams,* weaves her stories of plucky, sometimes downtrodden, characters "ecologically" placed in a world of issues—the U.S. involvement in Central America, Native American traditions, feminism, the environment. Her office is reached through a courtyard draped with grapevines and flourishing with squash. The window looks out across a terrain that to many seems inhospitable but to Kingsolver brings inspiration and solace. On the bulletin board above her computer are several fliers announcing speakers on the underground railroad for South American refugees. On her desk is a paintbrush. When the writing gets tough she takes the brush out to the courtyard, where she hand-pollinates her squash blossoms.

Kingsolver and her husband, a chemist at the University of Arizona, have been remodeling this cabin for five years, incorporating original beams into a practical and beautiful modern design. The couple did all the work themselves, consulting how-to's from the local library. Complimented on the extensive tile work, much of which she laid herself, Kingsolver quips, "It represents about 12 nervous breakdowns."

Raised in rural Kentucky, she grew up among farmers. "Our county didn't have a swimming pool, and I didn't see a tennis court until I went to DePauw," says Kingsolver, 35. "I didn't grow up among the suburban middle class. If I wrote a novel with that background, I'd have to do research. It's not that I try to write about poor people or rural people, I am one myself. It's important to illuminate the lives of people who haven't been considered glorious or noteworthy."

Some critics contend that Kingsolver's characters live on the margins of society. "That's a shock to me," she bristles. "I write about people who are living in the dead center of life. The people who are actually living on the margins of society are those you see on *Lifestyles of the Rich and Famous*. I like to remind people that there's nothing wrong with living where we *are*. We're not living 'lives of quiet desperation,' but living in the joyful noise of trying to get through life."

Kingsolver claims she was always a writer. "Eudora Welty, Carson McCullers and Flannery O'Connor were the stars in my sky as a child," she says. Later she was influenced by Doris Lessing and Ursula LeGuin, with Faulkner as the one male admitted into her personal constellation. "But I couldn't figure out how you could manage to get paid for being a writer or that you could do it for a living," she says. Beginning in college and through two years traveling in Europe, she took a number of jobs: typesetter, X-ray technician, copy editor, biological researcher and translator of medical documents. After graduate school at the University of Arizona, she became a science writer. Armed with a single creative writing course at DePauw and later a class with author Francine Prose in Arizona, Kingsolver "sneaked" slowly into freelance journalism, selling pieces to the *Progressive*, the *Sonora Review, Smithsonian* and gradually into short story writing for *Mademoiselle* and *Redbook*.

In 1983, Kingsolver began a book on the long, bitter copper strike against the Phelps Dodge Corporation in Arizona, focusing on the women—mostly union wives—in the isolated company town of Clifton. "People's internal landscapes turned out to be so interesting. The women earned a sense of themselves and their own value and personal power. When I first interviewed them, they'd say things like they didn't go out of the house without their husband's permission. By the end of the strike, these same women were going on national speaking tours." A year later, she'd written half of the book, but her agent was having a hard time placing it.

Kingsolver went back to freelance work. In 1985, she found herself pregnant and suffering from terrible insomnia. Her doctor recommended that she scrub the bathroom tiles with a toothbrush. Instead she sat in a closet and began to write *The Bean Trees*—about a woman who leaves a rural life in Kentucky for the urban world of Tuscon, where she encounters the sanctuary movement. "I saw that book as a catalogue of all the things I believe in, and not in any way commercial." If baby Camille hadn't been three weeks late, Kingsolver observes, she might not have finished the novel. Her agent, Frances Goldin, read the book overnight and called in the morning to say she wanted to auction it. "I look back on that time as a never-never land," says Kingsolver. "To be able to write with no one looking over your shoulder! Now I try to pretend I'm back in that closet."

She took her advance from *The Bean Trees*, finished *Holding the Line* (published by ILR Press of Cornell University in 1989) and began a book of short stories that she was determined would be different from her first novel. "People always say that a first novel sounds so much like the author," says Kingsolver. "I think that's certainly true of *The Bean Trees*. The voice of Taylor, the main character, was very strong, and she wanted to tell all of my stories. I've had to lock her away." In *Homeland and Other Stories*, Kingsolver again dealt with many of the same political themes, but seen through the eyes of a menopausal woman, a male biology teacher, an old Native American woman and other so-called "marginal" characters. "In *Homeland*, I was really stretching my voice and trying to break into the land of real fiction," she says.

In *Animal Dreams*, the author has taken all of her previous themes—Native Americans, U.S. involvement in Nicaragua, environmental issues, parental relationships, women's taking charge of their own lives—tossed them into a literary pot and created a perfectly constructed novel. In the book, Codi Noline—bereft of her sister, who's left for Nicaragua to fight for social justice—returns to her hometown, where she confronts her painful past, a father afflicted with Alzheimer's, family tragedy and an environmental disaster. "*Animal Dreams* is about five novels," concedes

Kingsolver. "About two-thirds of the way through I realized I wasn't *just* a fool; I had jumped out of a plane and the parachute wouldn't open. I wanted to go back to bed, but Harper had already designed the book jacket." She turned on the answering machine, yelled at her family, pollinated the squash and set about answering the questions she had asked.

While Kingsolver has, in fact, answered all of them admirably, her subjects and themes won't disappear. "Those issues will keep turning up in everything I write. They're central to my reason for living. The only authentic and moving fiction you can write about is about things that are the most urgent to you and worth disturbing the universe over. If you're willing to get up and face a blank page every day for a year or more, then it has to be an idea you're willing to be married to."

"The issues are fundamentally related, fundamentally the same. I wasn't really trying to drive five horses, but one horse. I don't want to be reductionist, but all of the issues can be reduced to a certain central idea—seeing ourselves as part of something larger. The individual issues are all aberrations that stem from a central disease of failing to respect the world and our place in it."

In *Animal Dreams*, Codi learns to place herself within her family, then the community, then the political world. The Stitch and Bitch Club, a group of women who have spent years making hand towels and gossiping, harnesses its talents to save the fictional town of Grace, so much like the real-life strike-stricken community of Clifton. "The women knew how to fight to save their town. They knew how to do ordinary things to maintain life. I like stories about ordinary people doing heroic things that are heroic only if you look close enough."

Can a novelist truly educate and change the world about man's basic inhumanity to man? "I have to believe that, don't I?" she answers. "What keeps me going is the hope that I might be able to leave the world a little more reasonable and just. I grew up in the '60s, when convictions were fashionable. We believed we could end the war just by raising a ruckus. I've been raising a ruckus ever since." Ten years ago, Kingsolver was writing mimeographed leaflets on the "outright villainy" of what was happening in El Salvador or on the building of the Palo Verde Nuclear Power Plant; she believes that her job description hasn't changed

312

much. But with fiction, Kingsolver maintains, the author must both refrain from diatribe and respect the reader.

That balance may have its origins in Kingsolver's own choice of physical environment and habitat. After years of what she terms a "rolling stone existence," Kingsolver—liking the sound of Tucson but knowing absolutely nothing about it—went there for what she thought would be a few weeks. "The Southwest appealed to me on hearsay," she says. "I though it would be a wide open place that would allow for some eccentricity." That was 14 years ago.

"I probably would have become a writer no matter where I was, but the Southwest has informed my subjects. Culturally, the Southwest is so rich. I can drive from here to Albuquerque and pass through a half-dozen nations." The Central American issues that infuse her work come from living in an area that derives its cultural plurality both from the people who've been there for hundreds of years and from the refugees who come from the south. "A lot of my friends are refugees, and they got here because our government dropped phosphorus bombs on their villages. How can you not do something about that?"

Kingsolver's "anthropologist's heart" has compelled her to seek out different world views. "For research, I look for open doors, read what there is, depend on friends." For *Animal Dreams*, that meant poring over doctoral dissertations on kinship relations, as well as visiting a pueblo. Kingsolver believes that Americans have a lot to learn from cultures like those of the Navaho and Pueblo tribes, whose cultural myths have less to do with conquest and more to do with cooperation. "I don't even like to use a word like 'religion,' because all Pueblo life is religious. It's about keeping this appointment with humility which reminds us of our kinship with the natural world. I was trained as a biologist, so I know intellectually that human beings are one of a number in the animal and plant family. We are only as healthy as our food chain and the environment. The Pueblo corn dances say the same things, only spiritually. Whereas in our culture, we think we're *it*. The Earth was put here as a garden for us to conquer and use. That way of thought was productive for years, but it's beginning to do us in now."

In her new novel, backed by a 45,000-copy first printing, first serial rights to *Confetti* and a 15-city tour, Kingsolver isn't about to lose the casual reader over ideas, ideals or philosophy. "If

313

people are provided with information, then they can draw their own conclusions," she says. "A novel can educate to some extent. But first, a novel has to entertain—that's the contract with the reader: you give me 10 hours and I'll give you a reason to turn the page. I have a commitment to accessibility. I believe in plot. I want an English professor to understand the symbolism while at the same time I want one of my relatives—who's never read anything but the Sears catalogue—to read my books."

LISA SEE

DAVID LEAVITT

DAVID LEAVITT DISCUSSES his work dispassionately. He sounds rather like an essayist preparing a critical appraisal of— David Leavitt. Speaking of his collection of short stories *A Place I've Never Been* (Viking), he hesitates a moment, then sums up his career so far: "I see the new book as the first one in stage two. My first three books were The Early Work, and the new one is the first book of The Middle Years."

He says it without sounding lofty or self-important; on the contrary, his neat evaluation is both ingenuous and wry. Reviewers are likely to agree with his assessment. The stories in Leavitt's new collection show a maturity only glimpsed in his earlier work. His fictional voice has grown deeper; the prodigy has been left behind.

Phrases such as "The Early Work" and "The Middle Years" of course recall Henry James, and the allusion is apt. Leavitt, like James, has discovered Europe, or more specifically, Americans in Europe, as a prodigious theme which he exploits in several excellent stories in *A Place I've Never Been*.

Europe discovered Leavitt some time ago. His previous books have been bestsellers in Italy, Spain, and elsewhere (although not in the U.S.), and *Place* has been published in Italy by Mondadori. Leavitt says the two stories with Italian settings are his favorites in the new book. Italian reviewers, however, disagree. According to Leavitt, "They called it 'a wonderful book except for the Italian stories.'" Asked to speculate on reasons for their disdain, he says, "I think they feel I'm intruding on territory I don't know. Perhaps, too, they dislike my portrayals of Italians as quite crazy. I think Italians really are that way, but they don't like to admit it about themselves. Perhaps, too, the Italian critics confuse my perspective with that of my characters, who tend to be far more callow about Italy than I am. These characters have romantic expectations of Italy. I don't, at least not any longer, having spent a lot of time there."

Chatting with us on the patio behind his two-story house in East Hampton, N.Y., on Long Island, he talks about writing short stories and writing novels.

"I suspect I'll continue to do both. But if I were forced to choose, I would write only short stories rather than novels. That's because I feel more confident as a short story writer. Writing a novel is like a marriage—you must live with it every day. Some days you're madly in love, while other days you hate it and you want a divorce. A short story, on the other hand, is like a wild, passionate affair that lasts for a couple of weeks and then it's finished. Or else it lasts for a few intense weeks, then you leave it and come back six months later for another fling."

Leavitt is now a veteran of two such literary "affairs" and two "marriages." His short story collection *Family Dancing* (1984) was praised by reviewers and was nominated for both the PEN/ Faulkner Prize and the National Book Critics Circle Award. His first novel, *The Lost Language of Cranes* (1986), was less well received; Leavitt calls it "something of a critical flop in this country." In 1989, his second novel, *Equal Affections*, received mixed reviews.

Reviewers and interviewers made much of Leavitt's age when *Family Dancing* was published. He was 23. Leavitt's youth is still often mentioned in reviews of his books; last year Beverly Lowry's *New York Times* review of *Equal Affections* ended with these words: "And Lord, he is still so young." Does he still consider the harping on age a form of condescension? "Sometimes. It was even worse when I was younger. Being young has its advantages and disadvantages in the horrifying world of public relations. When my first book came out, the public was obsessed with early achievement. Wall Street investment bankers were making their first million by age 25. In a literary way, I fit right into that whole fascination with early achievement. Subsequently it all changed to resentment. My second book suffered from the turnaround, I think, in terms of journalists' reactions to it."

316

Leavitt, who grew up in Palo Alto, Calif., explains his precocity this way: "In retrospect, I'm amazed a how young I was when my first book came out. But it makes perfect sense in terms of my own psychology. I was a youngest child, with a brother and a sister nine and 10 years older. So I grew up being the child in the room whose presence everyone forgot about. By the time I was 20, therefore, I had absorbed an enormous amount, but I had experienced almost nothing. As my shrink put it to me at the time, I was like a perfectly unclouded mirror that reflected everything I had seen and heard."

Leavitt's mother had cancer for many years while he was growing up. Her disease, and eventual death, are recurrent themes in his fiction. "The enormity of that experience cannot be minimalized," he says. "It has all gone into my work. Most of what I know about living and dying I learned from my mother." He calls *Family Dancing* "the book of a frighteningly articulate child." The subsequent books, however, are those of a writer "who had lived the things which, up until then, he had only seen and heard about."

Leavitt has been criticized for writing too much too fast. His response is, "I don't have the security of knowing that I have the rest of my life to write fiction. I say that not so much in the literal sense of fear of AIDS, as in a metaphysical sense. I don't think young people today, especially young gay people, ever feel they have an endless future. They've experienced so much death and loss at a young age. That's one reason I've written a lot, and perhaps more quickly than I would have in a less threatened time."

Leavitt says he has sometimes been criticized by reviewers in the gay press for writing about cancer rather than AIDS. "As if, being gay, I had an obligation to write about AIDS," he says. "That is always troubling to me. Even though I think it's fair to say people have obligations as political beings to *do something* to fight AIDS, I don't think it's fair to say that writers have an obligation to write about any particular subject. A writer's only obligation is to write well."

He continues, "Having said that, I find myself writing more and more about AIDS. What got me started was my involvement with ACT-UP." Leavitt considers the activist group ACT-UP (AIDS Coalition to Unleash Power) and the memorial quilt the

317

two most important cultural responses to AIDS, because "the quilt provides an outlet for grief, and ACT-UP gives people a way to express their rage."

"Gravity," a five-page story about a man with AIDS and his indomitable mother, is one of the most memorable entries in *A Place I've Never Been*. Leavitt is also writing a screenplay about AIDS for director John Schlesinger. Although "sworn to secrecy" about the plot, he reveals that the film is "quite political, and it attempts to be very much about living and not about dying."

Although Leavitt is often thought of as a *New Yorker* writer, only two of his stories have appeared in the magazine, the most recent one in 1983. The first, however, was the one that launched his career.

About 10 years ago, Mary D. Kierstead, an editor at the *New Yorker*, received a copy of the Yale *Quarterly*, the undergraduate literary magazine, from a friend in New Haven. "She read a story of mine," Leavitt recounts, "which was a very early version of 'Counting Months.' She wrote me saying she liked the story and asking me to send her my work. When this letter appeared in my mailbox at Yale, I was completely floored. I promptly sent her everything I had ever written, and she promptly rejected it all. But I kept writing, and eventually I wrote the story 'Territory,' which she accepted."

When the story was published in 1981, Leavitt received letters from a number of agents. Among his correspondents was Andrew Wylie, whom Leavitt chose over the others because " he was the only one who didn't tell me I had to write a novel before I could publish a book of short stories."

Knopf published *Family Dancing* and *The Lost Language of Cranes*. Leavitt calls Bobbie Bristol, his editor there, "one of the best I've encountered." He describes the editing process with her as "very intense, almost like psychiatry. For days we would sit in her office, going over every page. Not only points of grammar and the like; Bobbie is able to go inside the writer's mind, suggesting, 'I think what you want to say here is not X but Y.' "

Explaining why he no longer publishes with Knopf, Leavitt says, "It was a confusing time; Robert Gottlieb had just left. Andrew and I decided it was certainly worth approaching other

318

publishers if Knopf didn't offer as much money as we would have liked, which initially they didn't. Eventually Weidenfeld & Nicholson offered a lot more money for *Equal Affections,* as well as the promise of strong publicity. At that point it seemed there was no other choice, although in retrospect I'm not sure it was the wisest decision."

Leavitt says he was pleased with Weidenfeld's treatment of his second novel and left only because the house "fell apart." He also praises his new publisher, Viking. He first met his editor, Dawn Seferian, when he worked as a slush reader at Viking in the mid-'80s.

Although Leavitt has often been placed in two dissimilar "schools" of writing—minimalism and the Brat Pack—he says he has made "a fierce effort to disassociate myself from both." Referring to minimalism as "that terrifying brand, the scarlet M," he says he has never understood why the label was applied to his work. "My stories are long, so you can't say they're minimal in the sense of being short. I also think they're explicitly emotional, which seems to me to contradict the traditional definition of minimalism. And they're also quite descriptive."

Leavitt has obviously thought about the subject a great deal. "I think it's possible to interpret this whole matter in feminist terms, because so many of the writers called 'minimalists' are women. The term is applied to very few men. I wonder if there is an implicit idea that to be male is to be maximalist, to thrust out in this big male way, and women, whose work is more quiet, intimate or concentrated, are not good enough because their writing is too small."

As for the so-called Brat Pack, Leavitt seems relieved that journalists have stopped naming him as a member. "That's because I aggressively told people I wasn't," he says. "I never trusted the whole thing. I knew there would be a backlash."

He is also irritated when people try to match his fictional characters with members of his family. "I suppose it's a natural impulse," he says, "but it doesn't lead very far. If a particular character resembles my mother or my sister, so what? It's just gossip, and not even very interesting gossip."

As Leavitt's Middle Period progresses, perhaps commentators will tire of writing about extraneous matters and consider his

319

work in the terms by which he judges other writers: "As a reader, I look for a sense of urgency, a sense of something at stake. I'm a great admirer of risk-taking in fiction, whether it's a formal risk-taking or taking risks in which you dare to write about."

SAM STAGGS

MARIO VARGAS LLOSA

MARIO VARGAS LLOSA is that rarest of rare creatures in Latin America—a moderate. The Peruvian writer deplores right-wing military dictatorships and left-wing Marxist terrorists. He believes in democratically elected government and cautious economic reform. Above all, he detests the fanaticism that imposes rigid ideological order on complex situations: inability to look reality in the face, he believes, causes the spiraling violence that plagues Latin America.

Though based on a historical incident and set in the 19th century, *The War of the End of the World* (Farrar, Straus & Giroux) takes as its central theme this distinctively modern problem. "I wanted to show how fanaticism, religious or political, is a tremendous obstacle to real progress," he says. "Fanaticism is the root of violence in Latin America; we haven't overcome this Manicheistic vision of society, of men, of solutions to problems. When I discovered the story of Canudos [the event on which his novel is based, a bloody suppression by the military of an apocalyptic religious movement] in a history book, I got the impression that I had been looking for something like that ever since I started writing. Canudos presents a limited situation in which you can see clearly. Everything is there: a society in which on the one hand people are living a very old-fashioned life and have an archaic way of thinking, and on the other hand progressives want to impose modernism on society with guns. This creates a total lack of communication, of dialogue, and when there is no communication, war or repression or upheaval comes immediately."

321

Seated in a comfortable New York hotel room, on his way to London for a three-month stay, a handsome, well-dressed man of 48 looking very much a member of the prosperous middle class, Vargas Llosa seems far away from the bleak social and political landscape of his native land. But though he lived in Europe for many years, he returned to Peru in 1974 and hopes never to leave again. "Living almost 17 years abroad, I started to feel I was losing contact with my world, my reality, the Peruvian language," he says. "For the kind of writing I do, this close contact is very important. I need to be excited or irritated by what is happening at home; it gives me not only material for my writing but the psychological mood I need to write. In spite of the fact that I admire Flaubert enormously, I don't like the ideal of a writer completely isolated in his cabinet, surrounded only by books. Literature *must* be submerged in life, otherwise it becomes a specialization that I think is the negation of literature. I love the 19th century because literature was so intimately related to the daily experience of life. Faulkner too, I think, was closely connected to his period: there is great imagination, great invention, and at the same time real life is there. Experimentation is important, but if literature becomes only experimentation, if it's cut off from the main source of life, it will die. It will become an exquisite name for the elite, and I don't want that. Literature can help people live, and to do that it must be committed to everything that is happening.

"I had a television program, *The Tower of Babel*, for about six months," he continues. "I wanted to demonstrate that a culture program is not necessarily boring, but can be very alive. The idea of culture on television in our society is a man talking about very strange and difficult things. I tried to show that culture is everything: you can talk about sports, you can talk about dancing, you can talk about anything from a cultural point of view. I liked it very much, but it was too absorbing. I couldn't write, I couldn't read, I was taken 24 hours a day."

His intense engagement in the culture and politics of Peru, paradoxically, is the reason Vargas Llosa spends three months of every year in London. "I go there like other people go to the countryside—to be completely alone," he says, laughing. "In Lima I am always so invaded. It's a problem, because literature demands great dedication, and this political involvement is so distracting. There's a great risk of endangering your vocation. On the other hand, it's difficult to avoid; if you think what is at stake is really essential, you have an obligation to participate. I hope to live in Peru until the very end, and for that reason it's important to me that it become a free country. I couldn't live in Peru if it became a kind of Pinochet regime. Probably that is one of the reasons I involve myself in the political debate, because I need my country to be an open society. If I can't write there, then of course I'll go abroad, because writing is essential for me, but I want to stay.

"If you are a writer, I think you're particularly well situated to understand how important freedom is," the novelist continues. "If there is no freedom, there is no creation, there is no real culture. Reforms are essential in Latin America, but reforms with freedom, respecting criticism. Otherwise, we'll keep having what we've had our whole history: brutality, corruption and fake culture. This is my problem with writers who defend totalitarian solutions. [Though once a Marxist, he has been critical in recent years of writers who ally themselves with the left, including his old friend Gabriel García Márquez, who supports Castro.] Why do people try to escape Cuba? Why is there turmoil? How can you, a writer, defend this model of society as a solution for our problems? I think there is a lot of opportunism in this position: I can't really believe that a writer is in favor of this kind of authoritarian system. Life is less uncomfortable if you have set solutions and you accept these clichés—left means progress, left means being in favor of the poor. Trying to defend a moderate position is very difficult. You can make a lot of mistakes, and you risk being manipulated by right-wing interests, so you must be very vigilant all the time. But an intellectual must try to look deeper than the surface."

Whatever his differences of opinion with other Latin American writers, Vargas Llosa is inextricably linked with them by his prominent role in the continent's extraordinary literary flowering of the past three decades. Queried as to the causes of "el boom" (as it is somewhat patronizingly called), he offers a typically complex answer that cites both historical and literary factors. "The transformation of Latin American culture from a rural world to an urban one, this explosion of the cities in the last 30 or 40 years, has been very important," he says. "Now in most Latin American countries the majority of the population lives in cities, and historically this has always produced the flourishing of novels, of narrative. Also, the social crisis is very good for writing. Nobody wants to stay as we were, but we are not sure what we would like to have in place of what's dying or disappearing. This incertitude is very favorable for the creation of literary myths: when you're looking for something but you don't know what it is, literature becomes very important. Also, the identity crisis of Latin America is a great stimulus for literature: we don't know exactly what we are, and literature gives us a personality."

Like many other Latin American writers, Vargas Llosa stumbled on this literary identity during his years in exile. "I discovered Peru and Latin America in Europe," he says. "I realized abroad that I was a writer profoundly linked to Peruvian experience, Peruvian language. I hadn't this idea when I was living in Peru. I remember when I was at school we read foreign writers, but now there is a Latin American public following its own writers very closely and with interest."

The author who most strongly affected Vargas Llosa's generation, however, was neither Latin American nor precisely foreign. "The influence of Faulkner on Latin American literature has been enormous," he comments. "There is no Latin American writer so influential, from Mexico to Chile. I remember what it meant for myself to read Faulkner in the '50s; it was incredible. He was the first novelist I read with a pen and paper, trying to establish the structure he gave to a story, its complexity, mystery, subtlety, ambiguity. I think Latin American writers discovered that form was essential in fiction through Faulkner.

"On the other hand, the mythology of Faulkner, the world he created, is very Latin American. We too have a society in which different cultures are coexisting in a very tense and difficult way—black and white in some countries, Indian and white in Peru—a love-hate relationship creating the same kind of clashes as in Faulkner. Also, his references to a mythical past, a civil war hanging over the present, traditional values being destroyed by modernity, this agrarian world of nostalgia and ritual—all this is so Latin American! We can identify very easily with Faulkner's world. Someone once wrote a beautiful essay saying that Yoknapatawpha County has its limits in the Caribbean, so it's a Latin American country."

Watching Vargas Llosa's animated gestures and listening to his excited, rapid-fire delivery of these thoughts, it's clear that no matter how deep his political commitments are, his greatest love will always be reserved for literature. He even writes criticism, the true mark of an addict. "Not academic criticism," he explains. "Free criticism, criticism as an exercise of the imagination. I admire very much Edmund Wilson, for example. I remember his *To the Finland Station* [a book examining the evolution of socialist and communist thought] as a novel; it's so *marvelously* narrated, the characters are so alive, it's like a wonderful novel."

In fact, having recently finished a novel of his own, which will appear in Spanish, Vargas Llosa will turn his attention to criticism for a while; his next project is an essay on *Les Misérables*. The just-completed novel, *The Story of Mayta*, draws its inspiration from a factual episode and points much the same moral as *The War of the End of the World*, but the author insists the two books are quite different. "This one is short," he says, laughing (*The War of the End of the World* runs 568 pages). "I love long novels, heavy novels, but they're not very popular nowadays. This is concentrated in one character and his search. It's inspired by something that happened in a small village in the Andes in the 1950s. A group of students led a rebellion that lasted just a few hours, trying to establish a socialist country. They didn't know anything about socialism—they had heard of it, that's all—and they weren't in contact with any political party. It was a farce and a tragedy. The book is about fiction as a source of violence. I think fiction in literature is wonderful, but in politics, I think its terrible—you must be realistic."

WENDY SMITH

PAULE MARSHALL

On a chilly, wet, winter day a visitor to Paule Marshall's New York City apartment finds welcome warmth in the rich browns and beiges that dominate the decor. And Marshall herself, dressed in a long caftan of these same colors splashed with orange, radiates a great deal of warmth as she hangs up her caller's dripping raincoat and leads the way into a living room featuring plants large enough to qualify as trees. From the window one looks out over the bare treetops of Central Park, which even in November looks inviting from this vantage point.

Marshall is a beautiful woman. Most striking are her bright eyes and long, lovely hands, which she uses at just the right moments to accent her words. The reason for our visit is the publication of Marshall's *Reena and Other Stories*, a collection of her early short fiction written between 1954 and 1969, out from the Feminist Press.

We wonder if Marshall finds it at all unnerving to be relaunching her early work after so many years, and the author responds with her light, ever ready laugh. "Yes, it is a little odd. On the one hand it is very gratifying that the work has a relevance today, that it is still up to date. On the other hand I tend, as I write over the years, to put things behind me. But what was enjoyable about putting this book together was going back and looking at those early stories, seeing their strengths and of course their flaws, since with the very early stories I was just starting out."

Marshall's very first published story, "The Valley Between," is included in the collection, and in her introductory comments to

326

the story, the author notes that it was written "when I could barely crawl, never mind stand up and walk as a writer. I was a mere babe in terms of craft and technique." Yet the author finds comfort in the fact that, as she puts it, "Even then I was on the right track in terms of what I was trying to say, even if technical things were a little off and my theme was a bit overstated. Still and all, it was firmly grounded in what are some of my main preoccupations as a writer: a woman's need for self-fulfillment, her reaching out for another self and the kinds of opposition and resistance that she runs into. These are themes that really only came into their own in the early 1970s, when there was a flowering of writing by women. But way back then in the '50s I was aware of all the constraints placed upon women, and in particular upon women writers, and I felt so strongly about this that I began writing about it then."

Marshall discusses several other influences that led her to become a writer. She was born in Brooklyn, of parents who had come to New York from Barbados in the 1920s, and some of her strongest early memories are of her mother and her mother's West Indian friends, sitting around a kitchen table after a long day's work. Marshall speaks of the "insight, irony, wit and humor" that emerged from the conversations among these women, and of their "poet's inventiveness and daring with language."

The author sits forward as she recalls these very influential memories; her voice becomes almost a whisper as she slips back in time: "I was that little girl, sitting in the corner of the kitchen, in the company of poets. I was there, seen but not heard, while these marvelous poets carried on. And from way back I always wanted to see if I might not be able to have some of the same power they had with words—their wonderful oral art. I wondered if I could capture some of that same power on paper."

She made her first attempt at writing at the age of 12, when she tried her hand at poetry: "Oh, it was very bad poetry, mainly because I was writing about things that I knew nothing about—apple trees, which I'd never seen growing in Brooklyn; kings and queens. I was trying to get out of myself and out of my world, not knowing then of course that writers should stick with their own worlds."

It was soon after her frustrated attempts at writing poetry that Marshall had a revelation that also fed her urge to write. She made an important discovery in the library, where she spent much time during her adolescence: "The library was a retreat, a wonderful way to discover new worlds," she recalls. "But I remember feeling that there was something missing, and then I came across Paul Laurence Dunbar, and learned that there was a black poet who had produced a thick volume of poems. Although I couldn't have said it consciously back then, he in a sense validated black experience for me. I went to school in Brooklyn during the '40s and '50s, and the black poets and writers—even the great writers of the Harlem Renaissance of the '20s—just weren't taught in the schools. Ironically, they *were* taught in the segregated schools in the South at that time.

"And so Dunbar made me aware that there was a mass body of material by black writers, and that if I ever hoped to write I should start writing about what I knew best, which was what growing up in that tight little island of a world of West Indian Brooklyn was all about. And that maybe there was something important and valid and sacred about that experience of being both Afro-American and West Indian."

Marshall admits that she then spent years thinking about writing, but was terrified to put pen to paper, "because then you commit yourself—you find out if you are good or not." With a laugh, she explains that she had "all kinds of delaying tactics. And then I reached a desperate place: I was working for a second-rate magazine, and I became frightened that I was going to spend my whole life writing mediocre material for this magazine. So I came home one evening and began writing *Brown Girl, Brownstones;* even though I had written stories, it took me a long time to get to the place where I felt strong enough and at the same time desperate enough to start writing a novel."

Brown Girl, Brownstones was first published in 1959 by Random House, where Hiram Hayden was Marshall's editor. In a quiet voice, she recounts an incident that she says made a very strong impression on her: "The day I received my contract from Random House in the mail, I had an appointment with Hiram, and I went off to the lovely neo-Renaissance Villard buildings where the publisher's offices were. There was a magnificent, sweeping marble staircase I had to climb to get Hiram's office, and I remember running up those stairs with my contract in hand, and I can't tell you the feeling of exhilaration I had, thinking that the world had said yes, and that maybe I did have something going for me.

"And there, coming down the stairs, was one Bennett Cerf, and he recognized me as a new addition to Random House, and stopped to say a few words. He ended our polite exchange with words that were just devastating to me. He said: 'Well, you know, nothing usually happens with this kind of book,' and made a kind of dismissing sweeping motion with his hand. I can't tell you how this affected me; I'm sure he didn't intend to be mean, but for a minute or two that contract in my hand felt like a rejection slip. I thought about the incident a lot, and behind his words I think I found what it meant to be a woman in that society, and also of course what it means to be black: that even though my book was going to be published and the publisher found some literary merit in it, I was not really a part of the literary community."

Since her first novel, Marshall has published a book of novellas, *Soul Clap Hands and Sing* (1961), as well as two other novels, *The Chosen Place, The Timeless People* (1969) and *Praise-song for the Widow* (1983). The latter will be released in paperback under Dutton's Obelisk imprint.

Marshall was very pleased that the Feminist Press reissued *Brown Girl, Brownstones* in 1981, and that it has been adapted for numerous courses—Afro-American literature courses, women's studies courses and ("Bennett Cerf should know this," says Marshall with a good-natured laugh) even in ordinary American literature courses. "I find it most gratifying," she says, "that this novel is finding a new audience; a whole new generation is coming to *Brown Girl*, and these readers have found some of their own concerns and ambitions mirrored in the novel."

Between books, Marshall spends much of her time teaching. She has taught creative writing at such schools as Yale, Columbia and the University of Iowa Writer's Workshop, and will soon leave to spend the spring semester at the University of California at Berkeley. Marshall finds that teaching does feed her writing, even though she does not write while she teaches: "Teaching takes over my life, and I can't write at the same time, even though I take notes and think about what I want to write; I become too involved with my students' work and lives. Students give me a great deal, because they are experimenters, which I find exciting and instructive."

329

Experimenting is not new to Marshall the writer. Indeed, she has spent her entire writing life "trying to reconcile the different strains that have gone into making me. What took place in my mother's kitchen as she talked with her friends is my fundamental base, but what that also gave me was a curiosity about other voices. My writing is very concerned with voice in the sense of language. And though I wanted to capture the whole West Indian dialect, I also wanted to capture the black American English that is part of my heritage too. As a child I moved with the utmost ease between these cultures; it was the way the world was for me. With this double exposure, there was the desire in me from early on to play with a variety of voices, to always be stretching and exploring the English language. It has to do with the fact that I come from people for whom language is an art form."

Years later, the inspiration Marshall found in the conversations of her mother and her friends is still with her. Although her mother died before Marshall's first novel was published, and never really knew the influence she'd had on her daughter, Marshall observes that the members of the West Indian community in which she grew up voiced what her mother would have said: "When *Brown Girl, Brownstones* was published, they were on the one hand very proud that a daughter of the sod had written what they called 'the big book.' On the other hand, they were a little annoyed that, as they put it, I had told the truth." One feels that Paule Marshall couldn't ask for higher praise.

SALLY LODGE

BOBBIE ANN MASON

Even **BEFORE ITS** imminent publication, *In Country* by Bobbie Ann Mason was received with great enthusiasm. Advance reviews praised this powerful first novel of a young woman's struggle to understand the Vietnam War and proclaimed Mason a writer of outstanding talent. Harper & Row committed itself to a 40,000-copy first printing, a $40,000 launch campaign and a national author tour. These are fairly standard prepublication indicators of an important release, but *In Country* also inspired an unusually intense affection in its early readers. Mason's sensitive, profound understanding of character and place, her clear-signaled yet compassionate examination of the most divisive issue in recent American history, seemed to strike a deeply sympathetic chord in almost everyone.

Yet the woman who zips into the parking lot of the Carl Bieber Tourways Bus Terminal in rural Pennsylvania just doesn't *look* like a Serious Author; in fact, she strongly resembles this reader's picture of Sam Hughes, the 18-year-old heroine of *In Country*. Wearing jeans with a royal blue shirt belted over them, sporting sandals and socks as footgear, Mason seems far younger than her 40-odd-years. Her favorite topic of conversation is rock 'n' roll (several photographs of her hero, Bruce Springsteen, adorn her study), and she'd rather talk about her seven cats and two dogs than analyze her writing, which she feels "really has to speak for itself." But when Mason sheds her fear of "being pompous and authoritative," she speaks intelligently and cogently about her work. She's not given to chit-chat—occasionally she'll pause after an especially pithy comment and smile apologetically, as if she feels she ought to say more, but can't—but five sentences rendered in Mason's brisk Kentucky accent are worth an hour's talk with a more meandering conversationalist.

Though she began her writing career with short stories (*Shiloh and Other Stories* won the PEW/Hemingway Award in 1983), Mason always intended to be a novelist. "I prefer reading novels," she says, sitting on the porch of her gray house planted among the Pennsylvania hills, "and I tried to write a couple, but then I discovered that short stories were more suited to my style and inclinations, so I got started on those. Making the jump to the current novel was difficult, but it seemed like the right time to do it. I had gotten rather comfortable with the form of a short story, and writing one wasn't very risky because it didn't take that much investment of time or energy. So I guess I didn't want to run away from that challenge; I thought it would be good for me. At first, when you're facing so much that's unknown, it's hard to conjure a novel up, to get it going day after day. It took a long time to get to the point where the material began to overwhelm *me*, where the characters began to live on their own. After that it was very absorbing; I got carried away with it."

One of the reason's *In Country* offers such fresh insights into the tragedy of Vietnam is that the novel's protagonist is a girl too young to remember the war firsthand. When we ask Mason why she chose to write about Vietnam from this perspective, she says, "It didn't come about that way at all. I had almost all the characters in my mind, doing things and going through scenes, long before I had any knowledge that any of it had to do with Vietnam. That was one of the discoveries I made about them, that Sam's father had been killed in Vietnam and her uncle Emmett was a veteran. I had the characters first, in various situations I was exploring, and it took probably a year or more to find out what this was about. Then it took another year to get it focused and get in right. It wasn't deliberate, but I don't think it's any accident that I got onto the subject. I think it came out of my unconscious the same way it's coming out of America's unconscious. It's just time for this to surface.

"You have to understand something about writing," Mason continues. "Things just get written out of the subconscious, and then later you can start to figure it out and add it up, and maybe it makes sense and maybe not. I don't always know." As an example of her exploratory, character-oriented approach, she mentions Irene, the heroine's mother, who wants to forget the war and get on with a new life. "It was like, Irene went off to Lexington, Irene didn't take her records; well, she didn't want to think about the war," Mason remarks, "I didn't say to myself, I've got to have a character who needs to bury her past, or I've got to have a character who represents something pacifistic. Instead, I had this character Irene who went to Lexington, and then later I discovered that she didn't take her records with her. It works backwards. You don't start with an idea."

Does she dislike analyzing her work? "Well, I like to think about it, and I like to try and figure it out," she replies. "When I reread it, or I'm working on a passage and I realize how something comes together, that's a real delight. And it's also delightful when a reader picks out something that fits together that I hadn't quite seen. But I guess I'm just a little leery of telling anybody what it's supposed to mean. I think that in fiction I'm just concerned with portraying the experience; the textures of the experiences are more important than any one-sided vision of things. I don't think fiction should be didactic. Larger themes may come out of it, but I don't want to underline that, I think I'm inherently very shy, modest, and am probably shying away from making large statements because I distrust them."

This distrust of grandiosity is reflected in Mason's prose, which is decidedly and deliberately plain. "I've always written that way, just kind of bluntly," she says. "I think it's a way of being realistic rather than trying to dress something up, which I never learned to do. That comes out of a lot of different ways of talking in the South. One of them is for appearances only, it's just a very polite, social way—the famous southern hospitality. Another is just to cut through the crap, and I tend to think more that way. I think it comes from people who have not learned all the social graces, so they tend to be more blunt when they get the chance."

Mason's characters aren't necessarily without social graces, but they are ordinary, working-class men and women, people often overlooked in American literature, about whom Mason writes with unusual perception and appreciation. "It's important to me," she says, "and I can relate to their problems more easily than I can to more middle-class concerns. I think the lives of people like this have just as much depth and sensitivity as anyone else's. It's the same as Vietnam; I didn't decide to write about the war, and I didn't decide to write about these people. They're the people I'm drawn to. Although there's a way in which I chose them, because I started writing short stories after I finished graduate school, and I was so sick of reading about the alienated hero of superior sensibility that I thought I would write about just the opposite! It helped me to discover my characters, to have been sick of reading about artists."

Mason's respect for her character is evident in the way she treats their culture. Rock 'n' roll is a major presence in *In Country;* it expresses the aspirations and emotions of people who don't always reveal them more openly. (Sam's passionate desire to make contact with her mother by giving her an old Beatles record is one moving example of Mason's use of such detail.) Even more uniquely, Mason refuses to despise television or the people who watch it. The heroine and her uncle spend a great deal of time discussing TV shows and how they apply to Sam's and Emmett's own personal situations. "I guess that's just the way I see popular culture," Mason says. "I think it's very close to people and it reflects what they feel and believe. Certain people denigrate it because it's not high art, but I don't happen to feel that way. I don't want to have an elitist attitude about the culture. It's very real, it means something to a whole lot of people, and I can't ignore that. People have a lot of affection for these images on the screen, names of songs, things that are a familiar part of their lives. If you're writing about people who watch *M*A*S*H* all the time, as I did, then you've got to know why they watch it, what they feel about it, what place it has in their lives. Otherwise, you're putting the characters down. I'm not so interested in what it means ultimately—whether *M*A*S*H* is a good show or not, whether television is ruining our lives, whether we're being manipulated by these images. I'm just after the quality of experience in everyday life. Things like that have significance."

Literature is remote from Mason's characters, as it was from her, growing up in rural Kentucky. "I wrote when I was a kid, but I didn't have any examples to draw from," she says. "I read a lot of Nancy Drew mysteries, but that was about all. [In fact, Mason is the author of a critical study entitled *The Girl Sleuth*.] We had to read stuff in school—*A Tale of Two Cities, Silas*

Marner, The Scarlet Letter—but it didn't make any sense to me. I reread *The Scarlet Letter* this year and I found it such a moving experience. It's a wonderful novel, with incredible tension—the terrible way the town treated Hester Prynne, who was such a hero. And I found myself asking, Why did they teach this in high school? What moral lesson did they expect us to learn? I think they thought they were telling us not to be bad like Hester Prynne, but she was so obviously so much better than anyone else. Finally, in college, I was introduced to some things I could relate to: Hemingway, Salinger, Thomas Wolfe, Fitzgerald. They helped me to understand what it was all about, to have some direction."

Though of the writers she mentions only Wolfe is from the South, Mason feels that "in a certain way" she's a southern writer. "I think the culture I write about is very distinctly southern," she says. When we remark that her work lacks the preoccupation with the past characteristic of much southern fiction, she replies, "Oh, exactly, because I don't know anything about that! I don't think the people I write about are obsessed with the past. I don't think they know anything about the Civil War, and I don't think they care. They're kind of naive and optimistic for the most part: they think better times are coming, and most of them embrace progress. But I think they reflect that tension that's in the culture between hanging onto the past and racing toward the future. It's a very obvious thing you see in that world. One story I wrote, 'Residents and Transients,' really was the focal point for the main theme of the stories: there are some people who would just never leave home, because that's where they're meant to be; and others are, well, born to run." She giggles, looking very much like Sam, as she mentions the title of a Springsteen song.

Despite her stories' strong geographic roots, Mason sees herself as more of a transient. "I've always felt like an outsider since I left Kentucky, because I've moved around a lot," she says. "The way I see the South depends very much on the fact that I've lived in the North for so many years. It was very much of a culture shock to leave the South when I went to graduate school. I think southerners have a very poor image of themselves and tend to be threatened by Yankees. So either they react defensively and become very proud and provincial, or they feel inferior to the North. And I came up here feeling extremely inferior! That monumental shock took up all my energy for a while; it took years to get through that and gain enough confidence to start writing the stories. Also, I needed time to get perspective; I'd lived in such a sheltered world and really didn't know how to see it until I'd broken away for some time. Now I've been trying to move back to Kentucky for years, but it just never worked out. I'd like to, though; I don't want to lose touch with my material."

WENDY SMITH

PETER MATTHIESSEN

For over 30 years, when Peter Matthiessen has returned from the far corners of the earth, whose vanishing landscapes and traditional ways of life he has described in such books as *The Snow Leopard*, he has come home to the eastern end of Long Island. When he moved here in the 1950s, towns like Amagansett and Sagaponack were farming and fishing communities undiscovered by the residents of nearby New York City, which was two hours and about 50 years away. Now urban vacationers flood the area from Memorial Day to Labor Day, and a substantial number of writers and artists inhabit it year-round. Soaring land prices and changing local priorities have endangered the commercial fisheries in which Matthiessen worked as a young writer struggling to support himself, and the families who have drawn their livelihood from the sea since the 17th century are being forced out of the communities their labor created.

This unfortunate state of affairs is the subject of *Men's Lives*, (Random House), one of Matthiessen's two recent books. (Another volume, *Nine-Headed Dragon River*, from Shambhala, chronicles his involvement with Zen Buddhism.) Although it's been nearly three decades since he worked the boats, he would still make a plausible fisherman: he is tall and thin, with cropped gray hair and the permanently tanned face of someone who spends much time outdoors.

On a warm spring day, Matthiessen soaks up the sun as he talks with *PW* out back of his home, an old farmhouse only minutes from the ocean in Sagaponack. Explaining how he became involved in this effort to call attention to the fishermen's plight, he says, "This was a book that was in the back of my mind for later on, but a young photographer who had also worked as a fisherman, Doug Kuntz, wanted to do a photo book now. Adelaide de Menil, another Long Island resident, agreed to sponsor the book, and she felt there should be text to go with it and approached me about it. We hope that most of the profits will go to help the fishermen. They would never take direct charity, but some things would be acceptable: we're working on a project to develop some alternate fish processing factories, and another to reseed the shellfish beds."

How did the proud, fiercely independent fishermen, so distrustful of outsiders, react to Matthiessen's desire to write a book about their lives? "Naturally they were wary, especially the ones that didn't know me," he answers. "But there are a group of us who were the first outsiders who were ever let on the crews, and everyone remembers us because we were kind of a curiosity at the time, so I had a certain amount of acceptance. They weren't wary so much of me as they were of the experience: people taking pictures of them, taking notes and asking questions. Any traditional people are leery of that; I've run across a great deal of it working with American Indian people."

One of the most remarkable aspects of *Men's Lives* is the accuracy with which Matthiessen has captured the fishermen's language, a blunt, salty vernacular that says more about these men than pages of description would. The author caught it all without a tape recorder. "I think I've got a pretty good ear," he comments, "and I had a lot of practice with *Far Tortuga* [his 1975 novel set in the Caribbean], where I did have to use a tape recorder for a while, just to learn how to speak the language. It was must worse than the way I had it; people wondered why I used dialect, but it was actually a very modified version of the way they really speak. So I think I have a good ear"—returning to the subject of *Men's Lives*—"and also I keep a little notebook in my breast pocket. When I hear a special turn of phrase that interests me or that I don't know, I'll put it down and write it up in the evening in a bigger notebook. But mainly I think you can't really write dialect until you can speak it yourself. Otherwise you would have to tape everything, and it would be very stiff."

Matthiessen fears that the traditional way of life reflected in the fishermen's speech will vanish altogether in the next decades. "The oldest and best fishermen will survive," he says. "You're not going to get those guys off the water, they'll stay on until the end of their lives. But the fishermen are not encouraging their kids to go into it. The old guys feel it's too late for them to change, and really they don't want to anyway. And I understand that; I loved it myself. When I was working on the crews and writing, that was the happiest time of my life—not in terms of writing, necessarily, but the life really suited me to a T. And when my hands were all sore and I was worn out, I was very happy to get back to my desk! I like exercise; I write better if I'm tuned up."

Matthiessen respects the fishermen and the values they incarnate. "They know who they are, there's a certain spontaneity and lack of pretense," he comments. "They really live day to day as best they can. I identify with this very strongly. I like the values of traditional people who are closer to the earth. It's an attitude which I think is very precious and is in very serious danger of being lost, stamped out entirely. As it is now, we're on a very material bent."

It's not necessary to read more than one of Matthiessen's many books to know that spiritual matters are always his primary concern. His work's central theme, the relationship between human beings and the natural world, reflects his belief that the material objects with which we surround ourselves in modern society stand in the way of achieving the greater harmony with nature that is the essence of a fulfilled inner life. For Matthiessen, an integral part of that harmony is his practice of Zen Buddhism, the subject of *Nine-Headed Dragon River*. Although he was persuaded to publish the book by his desire to raise funds for a Zen monastery in Riverdale (the book's copyright is held by the Zen Community of New York, to which all profits go), he had grave reservations.

"One is always appalled by the idea of wearing your so-called spirituality on your sleeve," he says. "I never talked about Zen much, and this will be the first book I'm not going to give away to relatives and friends, because I don't want them to feel that they must read it. If people come along and want to talk about Zen, that's wonderful, but I don't want to brandish it. It's just a quiet little practice, not a religion—it's called 'the religion before religion'—just a way of seeing the world that is clearly tied in

339

with the way American Indian people see the world. And I find myself very comfortable with it. People are very suspicious of Zen—it's sort of a catch word for everything that's bizarre and eccentric—but it's the farthest thing from a self-conscious spirituality; that's what teachers call 'the stink of Zen.' On the contrary, Zen is very much a day-to-day, moment-by-moment practice; paying attention to what you do, not constantly living in regret of the past or hope of the future, thereby trampling on this very precious present moment. It's true that if you are truly aware of this moment, then very mysterious and beautiful insights can occur, but that's not the aim of Zen. If you come to it with that purpose, you've missed the point."

Of the simultaneous appearance of *Men's Lives* and *Nine-Headed Dragon River,* the author says, "I didn't plan these to come out at the same time, I just wanted to get them finished and to start on my new novel. I'm extremely happy that I'm back to fiction—it's been a *very* long time—and I hope to stay there. I prefer writing fiction; I find it exhilarating. Your battery is constantly being recharged with the excitement of it. I find that with nonfiction, it may be extremely skillful, it may be cabinetwork rather than carpentry, but it's still assembled from facts, from research, from other people's work. It may be well made or badly made, but it's still an assemblage. *The Snow Leopard,* in a sense, was an exception, because that was a strange kind of mythic trek, and I could be in the landscape, with the wildlife and the people, observing; those parts of the book are fun. Your creative imagination is used in trying to find a way to present the material which is true to it and true to yourself as well. But always, finally, if you're a good journalist, you're confined by the facts; you can't use your imagination all that much. I find it drains my batteries: I'm worn out by nonfiction.

"Whereas with fiction, I never go stale. I worked on *Far Tortuga* for 12 years—I was working on other books at the same time—but I never got sick of it. I had fun fooling with it, trying to make it work, trying to make the pieces resonate, strung out like beads on a string. I had another novel outlined after I finished it, but then I got off on the Indian books [*In the Spirit of Crazy Horse* and *Indian Country*]."

"In a sense, I've always thought of nonfiction as a livelihood, my way of making a living so I could write fiction," Matthiessen comments. "My first novels were very politely received, but they were financial disasters. I was married and had children; I couldn't afford it. Then the *New Yorker* sponsored me on a trip to the wilderness areas of the world, and that launched the whole theme of my life. I had always been interested in nature. My brother and I started with a passion for snakes, and he went into marine biology, while I took courses in various areas right up through college. But I'm not really trained in any of the disciplines; I'm what the 19th century would call a generalist—I have a lot of slack information, and for my work it's been extremely helpful. I've always been interested in wildlife and wild places and wild people. I wanted to see the places that are disappearing— the rain forests, the savannah regions of Africa. I've just come back from the Congo basin of Africa, and I was shocked at how much of the forest has already been knocked down and how little concern there is for conservation of any kind."

The situation is less drastic but essentially the same in his beloved Long Island, where development threatens not just the fishermen but all residents who value the traditional, rural quality of life here "When I first came it was very different," Matthiessen remembers. "It was so beautiful, we all wondered why it was almost undiscovered. Now it's over-discovered, so much so that we're all making frantic noises about leaving, but where can you go where it's different? And it's still awfully nice," he says, gesturing toward the grass and the sea beyond, while the sound of birds singing fills the air.

Earlier, speaking of the essential simplicity of Zen, Matthiessen had said, "Zen is a synonym for life, that's all; Zen practice is life practice. If you can wake up and look around you, if you can knock yourself out of your customary way of thinking and simply see how really miraculous and extraordinary everything around you is, that's Zen." In that completely unmystical sense, this tranquil interview in the spring sunlight, surrounded by a natural beauty not yet extinguished by suburbanism, is a Zen moment.

WENDY SMITH

COLLEEN McCULLOUGH

To MEET WITH Colleen McCullough, one generally must take a 13-hour nonstop flight from Los Angeles to New Zealand, then board another plane to Norfolk Island, in the South Pacific Ocean, a three-by-five-mile bit of land that she calls "a remote speck at the end of the world." Small wonder, then, that we sought out the author at the recent ABA in Las Vegas. The reason was not contiguity alone: McCullough's name is much bandied about, as Morrow issues the first of her five-volume series of historical novels set in the waning days of the Roman Republic. *The First Man in Rome: Marius* would be an achievement on any terms; running 896 pages, with copious notes, a chatty glossary, maps and illustrations all provided by the author, it is yet another departure for the writer who made her name with *The Thorn Birds* and has surprised her readers each time out with a novel quite different from the one before.

As readers of *The First Man in Rome* have discovered, it is not frivolous stuff. Exhaustively researched for historical accuracy and humanized through a plethora of small, telling details that bring Roman politics and society vividly to life, this is a complex story that requires respectful attention. Although she pronounces the book "not daunting for your average novel reader," McCullough admits that "a certain kind of *Thorn Bird* fan won't hack it." On the other hand, she crows, "At least I've written something that men won't be ashamed to be caught reading on the subway."

Nor does she feel that readers will be put off by the characters' cumbersome names, with their similar or identical praenomens

342

and strings of cognomens. "Latin is the major root of our English language," McCullough says firmly. "Metullus is easier to pronounce than Raskolnikov." As for such monikers as Quintus Caecilius Metullus Numidicus and Quintus Lutatius Catulus Caesar, two characters prominent in the first book, McCullough is confident that their sharply delineated personalities will make them spring off the page.

McCullough has never been shy of taking chances. Having dreamed about this saga for 30 years and having researched for a decade, she is confident that it will find an audience commensurate with its 300,000 prepublication printing and status as a BOMC selection. So determined was she to do these books that she left Harper & Row, her longtime publisher, because of its reluctance to guarantee the entire five-book series.

Her fascination with the Roman Republic dates back to her college years in Australia. According to McCullough, she and her five best friends—all boys—had been "brilliant in high school, and when we got to first-year university we were bored dry. We'd all been science-streamed so we decided we'd embark on a program of culture. Amongst other things, we read the Penguin translations of the Greek and Roman classics. I always wanted to read them again, and after *Thorn Birds* I did. I came to the letters and speeches of Cicero and the *Commentaries* of Julius Caesar. And I was fascinated." McCullough pronounces the last word portentously, emphasizing each syllable. She lights another of a chain of cigarettes, smooths her hair, pulled back in a no-nonsense bun.

"One glaring fact hit me square between the eyes. For the first and last time in the history of the world until very recently, these were words written by the men who ran the joint. Not some historian scribbling away after the fact. I was awed! Reading Cicero's letters as he wavers between loyalty to Pompey and the temptation to turn to Caesar, and his glancing references to Cleopatra—whom he loathed—I suddenly saw a world that I wanted to enter as a novelist, desperately. At no other time in the history of the world did so many truly intelligent and talented men walk across a political stage at one time. And the Roman Republic gave us our law, our political systems, our engineering—so much! I thought, it's germane, it's relevant to modern living."

Determined to render the era with exactitude, McCullough assembled in her home on Norfolk Island "the best private library

343

on Republican Rome in private hands anywhere in the world." She enlisted the aid of a full-time researcher, Sheelah Hidden, who is fluent in four languages and who interviewed experts in many countries. Hidden also located portrait busts of the characters, so that McCullough, who had decided that she was "fed up with people thinking that Cleopatra looked like Elizabeth Taylor," could draw the novel's illustrations.

"I did all this research and I put two million words on paper and, of course, being me, I drafted it. Three drafts. This was all nonfiction preparation for the book—a monograph of each of the major characters. Next, I got continuous computer paper, and I made a chronological list of every single thing that happened. I did all that before I started writing the first volume. And I did it for the lot; it is *done!*"

To her surprise, however, Harper & Row was less than eager for the enormous project. "Fred [Mason, her agent] and I couldn't get a contract out of them. They dickered. Money was never at the root of it because we weren't asking for a lot of money. This hemming and hawing went on for six months."

McCullough finally wrote out a précis of each of the five books she contemplated: Marius, Sulla, Pompey the Great, Caesar, Augustus—and sent it to Harper along with a monograph on Cleopatra, so that they would see "how important the women in the books were going to be." The upshot was that Harper pressed her to abandon the first two books and start directly with the events involving Pompey. "When they informed me of this I was 55,000 words into *Marius*. I was *crushed*," McCullough intones dolefully. Though she is recalling a bad time, she is also indulging the raconteur's gift of spinning out a tale.

Convinced that the series should appear as planned, that "in order to understand what happened to the Roman Republic, one must start with Marius," McCullough recalls her anger at Harper's unwillingness to go along with the plan. "A creative artist can't work in that kind of atmosphere. You can't work for a publisher who doesn't want you. Money has never mattered to me, but by God, my work does!"

It was at this point that Carolyn Reidy, President of Avon, which had published all of McCullough's works in paperback, ventured to Norfolk Island to urge the author not to cut Avon out of reprint rights for the projected saga. McCullough, who had always enjoyed working with Reidy, sensed the time was ripe to jump ship to Morrow, and stipulated that Reidy edit all five books. She now professes herself "hugely pleased" at the arrangement.

Quite a lot about McCullough is outsize: her big, comfortable frame, clothed in a muumuu and absent of feminine adornment; her booming, uninhibited laugh; her open friendliness and large, unrestrained smile; her storytelling, delivered with gusto; her ego. But if she doesn't suffer from undue modesty, she is matter-of-fact about her accomplishments.

Born in Australia's outback, she says that she and her brother, who died 25 years ago, were both gifted children of a mean-spirited father and a mother determined to guarantee her children's education: McCullough attended Holy Cross College and the University of Sydney. Possessing what she calls "amazing mathematic and artistic and scientific gifts," as a child of the Depression McCullough decided to opt for security and "do science." An allergy to soap kept her from being a surgeon ("I couldn't scrub, you see"), so she became a medical scientist. Having earned an appointment at Yale as a research assistant in the department of neurophysiology, she arrived in New Haven on April Fools' Day 1967. She loved her job but was very poor, so she decided to write a novel at night to earn extra money. The result was *Tim*, "my bucket of tears book."

McCullough sent *Tim* to agent Freida Fishbein, then "a very ancient lady of 87," who placed the novel with Harper & Row. When McCullough finished *The Thorn Birds*, which was "very loosely based" on her family's history in Australia, she herself delivered the manuscript to editor Ann Harris at Harper. "It was about four times the length of *Tim*, which had earned me $50,000. I thought, with any luck, maybe it would earn me four times that amount."

McCullough then went off to England, where she was due to start nurse's training at London's ancient St. Bartholemew's Hospital, to get background for the hospital novel she was "desperate" to write. "I didn't tell them I wrote books, of course. I was looking forward to some really hard physical labor because I am a workhorse."

Training was due to start on April 11, 1977. On February 27 *The Thorn Birds* made a record sale in paperback auction, and, McCullough recalls, "I hit the headlines everywhere. My cover was sprung. It was manifestly impossible that I go on to nursing. Can you imagine: a millionairess author carrying a bedpan!"

Other major changes in her lifestyle soon proved necessary. "When I became rich and famous, life became very complicated. It was unsafe for me to live on my own on any major landmass; you became prey to all sorts of nuts and bolts in the community." Hearing about tiny Norfolk Island, with its controlled population, she applied to live there. And, soon after, at the age of 46, she married an island native, Ric Robinson, a descendant not only of one of the *Bounty* mutineers (as are many of the island's residents) but also of a Samoan princess and Isaac Newton.

Robinson, who is some years her junior, is "a colonial aristocrat in every way," according to McCullough. A planter of the kentia palm ("it's the very hardy plant you see in all the hotel foyers"), Robinson modeled a reconstructed toga for his wife, providing irrefutable evidence that Romans did not sport underwear when wearing the garment. "It would have been impossible to pee in a toga if you wore anything underneath, you see. There's your left arm, weighted down by an immensity of toga: it's 16' by 9'. You can't possibly lower that hand . . . " McCullough rises from our table in a Las Vegas coffee shop and pantomimes the situation. *PW* is convinced.

On Norfolk Island, McCullough wrote *Indecent Obsession,* which she calls "my whodunit"; *Creed for the Third Millennium,* "my pessimistic novel of the future"; and the novella *Ladies of Missalonghi,* "my fairy tale."

The Roman series is her "bash at the historical novel." Happily embarked on the second volume, she is confident that she will produce the books at the rate of one a year. "The first one's always the hardest, and I got it out in less than a year, from go to whoa. It's not hard to do if you're well organized and well ordered. I'm not short of words. Maybe it's my scientific training, but my feeling is that for a writer, words are tools.

"Nobody expects a neurosurgeon to lay down his tools. I'm good with my tools. I don't mislay them. I'm a fluent writer. I do multiple drafts. Once I start, I'm consumed to finish. I work at a pace a lot of writers couldn't cope with."

McCullough slows her rapid-fire recital. She smiles broadly. "I'm such a nitpicker. I love the little details. If you're going to make it sing, it's the little details that will do it. I found one small detail in Caesar's *Commentaries*. Before a major battle, all the men sit down and make their wills. That's it, you see; that sort of detail makes it a world, and makes the world very real." To McCullough, writing feverishly on her remote island, that world is very real indeed.

SYBIL S. STEINBERG

TOM McGUANE

"THE HEIR TO Hemingway"; "Captain Berserko"; "macho pig"—Thomas McGuane has had plenty of labels to live down and just as many to live up to in his nine-book career, and none of them seems to do him justice.

Barely 30 when he burst onto the literary scene with *The Sporting Club*, he saw his star as a novelist soar with *The Bushwacked Piano* and *92 in the Shade*. Lyrical, coruscating and subtly political, his books made him a media darling—the counterculture cowboy. By 1975 he was writing *and* directing the film of his third novel, and careening toward celebrity and its gossip-page trappings: affairs, divorce, remarriage (to Margot Kidder), another divorce, remarriage, prodigious drinking and a reputation for excess in just about every area but his lean, acute prose. But with his fourth novel, *Panama* (1978), the critics who had made McGuane a hit "couldn't even remember what they had in mind," he recalls. The crash-and-burn reviews were more personal than literary; they took the author to task as much as they did the book.

But McGuane's private life has long been stable, alcohol- and trauma-free, and his critical fortunes have resurged in the last decade. With the novels *Nobody's Angel* (1982) and *Something to Be Desired* (1984) and the short story collection *To Skin a Cat* (1986), the author pursued his concerns with an ever stronger and more reflective voice. His first novel in five years, *Keep the Change* (Houghton Mifflin/Seymour Lawrence), is likely to keep him in the ascendant.

A hunter, avid fisherman and cutting-horse champion rider, McGuane meets *PW* on a stopover in New York City before continuing to Labrador to fish for Atlantic salmon. Settling in for dinner after a long day of flying, he begins with espresso: "I need to get some IQ points back." Six-foot-two, long-limbed and darkly tanned, he approaches what he wryly calls "deep middle age" with undiminished enthusiasm and good humor.

Born in 1939 and raised in Michigan, McGuane felt the desire to write early on; his first attempt at a novel came at age nine, and "by the time I was a junior in high school, it was all I could think about," he recalls. As a young man, he thrived in the company of other writers; his classmates and friends have included Edmund White in high school, Jim Harrison in college and William Hjortsberg at Yale Drama School, where McGuane took an unproductive stab at playwriting.

Until his late 20s, McGuane lived nomadically, spending time in Salinas, Key West, Spain, Italy and Ireland. In the late '60s, longing for a more permanent home, he settled in Montana, where his cattle and horse ranch in tiny McLeod now houses a blended family that includes his wife Laurie, their young daughter and, intermittently, three older children from earlier marriages.

Professionally, he's roved almost as much. First published at Simon & Schuster (where "editors kept leaving *me*"), he decamped for Farrar, Straus, where he stayed for three books with Michael di Capua. What he calls "a business dispute" precipitated a move to Random House, where, he says, "I was just not at home." His last two books have been with the Seymour Lawrence imprint, first at Dutton and, with *Keep the Change*, at Houghton Mifflin. There, he says, "I'm off on another happy relationship, and I hope this one lasts."

Although its tone—a precisely calibrated balance of sensitivity, restiveness, passion and irony—is a departure from much of his previous work, *Keep the Change* will be instantly recognizable as a McGuane novel to his loyalists: its territory, thematically and geographically, is purely his own. With a hero returning to his Western roots to puzzle out his feelings for two wildly different women and a conclusion brought on by no more than a careful unfolding and discovery of desires, the novel reverberates with his past writing to offer a wholly new effect. And characteristically, it's trim—under 250 pages.

"I know it's not exactly in the tradition of post–World War II American writing," says McGuane, "but I think that you should use as few scenes and paragraphs and words to achieve your effects as possible. If you're building fishing rods or shotguns or yachts, the standard is lightness that is as much as possible commensurate with strength. I think that's a universal aesthetic, and the kind of rich overwriting which has become the standard in a certain kind of American fiction is really a mistaken idea. Accretional monument-building as a style is not one I've ever liked."

Unsurprisingly, McGuane's redrafting consists largely of excision. "For me to write a book that ended up being 400 pages, the first draft would have to be 2000. That's part of the excitement of revising, to find something that stands on its own strength rather than depending on the buttressing I thought it had to have."

As for the labels, McGuane ingenuously brushes most aside. The Hemingway comparison (in terms of both writing style and productive/destructive lifestyle) has dogged him throughout his career. Of that persistent identification he says, "either I'm outgrowing the issue or it's going away." On the antics in the 1970s that won him the "Berserko" sobriquet: "By comparison with today's dour, money-crazed climate, it does look like it was one great party. Everyone was in a slightly more festive mood. But in the '70s, I also published four or five books, wrote about eight screenplays and about 40 articles. I was getting a lot done."

Only the accusation of insensitivity (or short shrift) to women in his prose still rankles him, although he laughs when discussing the female editor who'd been "told that I was one of the macho pigs—me and Harry Crews and Jim Harrison." (After reading McGuane's works, she reported to him, "I don't think you're a macho pig at all!")

While not fond of answering for his characters—whose records with women are fairly unenviable—the author admits that "I don't think I'm ever going to make a certain type of women's literature proponent happy. A lot of women are extremely angry. For those people, who are conscious of the depth of the bad debt that has been owed to women for a long time, almost anyone [can] have some of the features they associate with the enemy. It's like having a German accent in 1919. But I have three daughters, and I'm extremely sensitive to what I perceive as their rights in the world."

A hallmark of McGuane's writing is its sense of location; the physical world is deeply important to his characters and his prose. Most frequently, it's been the town of Deadrock (a fictional gloss on Livingston, Mont.). "I require that writing seem to belong somewhere," he says. "If it's floating and I can't attach it to the earth at some point, frustration sets in." Is he a late-arriving regionalist? "I object to the term officially. But in a funny way I sort of like it. Finding people who think of me as a Montana writer reinforces my wish to have succeeded in putting down roots there."

In recent years, McGuane's home state has been the site of a flourishing literary and cultural community—Richard Ford, William Kittredge, James Crumley, David Quammen and a host of other writers, actors and artists make their homes in Paradise Valley and Missoula. While McGuane jokingly refers to the Montana literary renaissance as "five guys with hardcover sales of 8000 each," he admits it pleases him. "I love Montana, but at the same time there's a certain kind of cultural deprivation that I would like to see changed. People who are born and grow up there love it so much they don't ever leave. They aren't liable to produce Márquez characters, and you go around sort of pining for that, wishing that they'd be just a tad more flamboyant."

McGuane's ranch, which keeps him completely busy for about half of every year, has taught him that "there are other circadian rhythms besides the semester system. Like it or not, you get tied into seasons, not just seasons of the planet, but breeding seasons. . . . " During the winter months, when the ranch more or less runs itself, McGuane's schedule is an idyllic-sounding confluence of writing and reading, done in "a comfortable little log house. You're there, you can't go anyplace else and you can just make a pot of coffee, go back to bed and read and read." His passion for literature seasons his conversations, and his enthusiasms are generous and global: Chekhov, Cheever, Raymond Carver, Joyce Cary, Graham Greene and uncountable others. Although he's more reserved in criticism, his assessments can be mercilessly pithy: with scalpel-like precision, he dismisses a contemporary's prize-winning novel as "Micheneresque."

For a time in the 1970s, McGuane was a prolific if almost consistently dissatisfied screenwriter whose credits included *Rancho Deluxe, The Missouri Breaks, Tom Horn* and his own *92 in the*

351

Shade. Last spring his name turned up on the cult comedy *Cold Feet*, which he had written with Jim Harrison in 1976. "I literally couldn't remember what it was about," he admits, and adds that he has no plans to return to film writing. "It's menial work," he says.

McGuane begins his novels with a sense of outline and structure, but all of the big issues in his fiction are resolved in the writing itself. "It's nice to decoy oneself by making outlines and planning, but all the writing you're able to keep comes up just the way phrases come up for musicians. But for some reason, you have to pretend that it's plannable and go through a certain number of mnemonic devices just to get started."

The process was somewhat different when McGuane was younger; writing 92 *in the Shade* in 1973, he says, "I felt as if I had a fuel tank strapped on my back; I felt we were on the cultural nosecone of America, and I had to write about it." While many of his contemporaries became casualties of the era, McGuane survived, and views those years without sentiment or cynicism. "In the mid-'70s, we didn't think in terms of taking a life raft on a boat. A kind of Whitmanesque optimism was afloat," he remembers, "and it's definitely gone. Even then there was a sense that it might end in tragedy, and to some extent it did. There were irreversible misunderstandings between generations that were never repaired, and left an unhealed wound in American life."

That belief resounds in many of his novels, in which wars between sons and their fathers are brutal, futile and fought unto—and after—death. But the fierce cynicism of some of his earlier writing has given way to something more ambiguous, and perhaps hopeful. "I like the more recent novels better," he says bluntly; when he "squints into" his older novels, he "wants to change everything and start rewriting. You say, gee, I wish I saw everything from a constant stance, like a lighthouse. Going back to a 1955 novel is a little like looking at a 1955 Ford—kind of cute, but tailfins just don't mean today what they did then."

In December, the former angry young man of the American West will turn 50. With his family life "semi-euphoric," McGuane can pour his boundless energy into his fiction. "The only thing that fills up the work hole in my sphere of need is writing," he says. "Between me and me in the dark of night, I consider everything else a fib, even my ranching. I love to do that—it gives me a physical grounding in the world and an orderly way to say, I'm not gonna use the old head now; I'm gonna get in the pickup truck and go look at fences. But then I say, That's enough now. My real job is as a writer, and I've got to get back to work."

MARK HARRIS

SUE MILLER

A MEETING WITH Sue Miller, like the experience of reading her novel *The Good Mother*, is at once a surprise and an encounter with the familiar. Until recently an unknown author with a few short stories in print, the Cambridge, Mass., resident has been a single mother and a fairly obscure member of the crowd of Boston-Cambridge writers who keep themselves alive financially by teaching at the area's many academic institutions.

But with her first published novel, Miller burst upon the scene as an extraordinarily accomplished writer who is particularly skilled in the use of visual images and homely detail. She tells a compelling story that takes the tale of an unfulfilled wife and subsequent single parent a giant step beyond the way this situation has been handled in contemporary literature to date.

Because her novel is so powerful and so considered, one expects the author to be serious and perhaps severe. Miller in person, however, projects brightness, animation and verve. She welcomes *PW* to her home of 17 years, located on a side street between the campuses of Harvard University and Radcliffe College (she is in fact an alumna of the latter).

Miller becomes more thoughtful as she describes the impulse from which she derived her narrative. "I objected to a number of postfeminist novels which suggested that all you need to do is shed your husband and then you enter this glorious new life of accomplishment and ease. I have been divorced, and that wasn't my experience or the experience of anyone else I knew. I wanted to trace the development of a character who had a complicated

354

sensibility and watch her begin the process whereby she thinks she can become someone other than the person she's . . . destined to be. The story is told by examining her reactions to events that occur in her life, including events that stem from forces outside her control."

Miller's character, Anna Dunlap, leaves a stifling marriage to make a modest new home and living for herself and her four-year-old daughter, Molly. In a Cambridge laundromat, in an altercation over who is next in line for the dryer, Anna encounters an impulsive artist, Leo, who will provide her with the joy of sexual fulfillment and cause her nearly the deepest anguish a mother can experience: losing custody of her child.

The novel grew out of a short story that appeared in the *North American Review* concerning an adolescent girl's fascination with an older, "exotic" aunt whom she met annually at the family's New England summer home. Agent Maxine Groffsky saw the piece, contacted Miller and was delighted to hear that she had just finished a book evolving from the characters in the story. Miller, about to go off on her honeymoon (with her second husband, writer Doug Bauer), gave Groffsky permission to submit the manuscript to publishers, with the admonition that she didn't want to hear a word about it until she came back. On her return, she was stunned to find that five or six houses were actively interested. Harper & Row, the winner of that contest, is promoting the book with enthusiasm and solid commitment.

The speed and extent of her good fortune has left Miller more than a little stunned. "The whole notion of a commercial success is not something I had *ever* anticipated," she says. "Surprise doesn't begin to describe my reaction."

Because the novel resounds with the ring of truth, it is tempting to conclude that its author might be describing her own experiences. Details, even down to Anna's work as a piano teacher, are vividly drawn. Miller distinguishes the senses in which she identifies with and stands apart from her character. With laughter, she says, "I took piano lessons while I was writing the book. But I'm a terrible piano player at best. I'm not even a *mediocre* pianist! I'm a fumbling beginner, essentially. For the last five years I've played the same repertoire with a few hymns thrown in," she jokes, glancing at her upright piano. Then, more seriously, she says, "I see in Anna moral judgments and those kinds

355

of perceptions that are very close to mine. In that sense she is autobiographical. But the events in her life, outside of being divorced and a single mother living in Cambridge, are nothing that I've experienced, thank God, and were things that I had to research and ponder about."

One setting crucial to the development of Anna's character does come out of Miller's past, however. "The summer camp in Maine is absolutely true to life. And I suppose there is a sense remotely in which the larger family is like mine, in that it is a very achieving, very accomplished family. But my own experience has always been comfortable within that family, even when I was at my worst," she laughs, "which lasted about 10 years! There *is* a general sense in which my understanding of the potential oppressive quality of that kind of family is autobiographical. I have felt it," she says quietly, "but my family is very dear to me."

The first-person narrator of Miller's original story was "a person who thought she could make her life like someone else's, who thought she could be in control of her life. And that seems to me to be a false thing to believe in this world," Miller says. As she developed the story into the novel the author found its theme in her speculations about free will and morality. "I really meant the book to be about God and grace in a sense but didn't want to write a religious book." She had produced two earlier novels, neither of them satisfactory to her. "It really took me a long time to discover what was missing, but I slowly came round to it. What I feel secure in, finally, is a moral viewpoint, and I think without that I simply couldn't be writing. This was hard-won," she admits.

"I think that even in the short stories that I've written I'm interested in a kind of homiletic turn. My family is ecclesiastical on both sides for generations. My father is an ordained minister himself, and both of my grandfathers were also Protestant (Presbyterian and Congregational) clergymen. I've inherited such strong, powerful ideas; right and wrong ways to behave and honor and all that kind of thing. And I feel that these are the true things." Of course, it was hard to live up to an ideal of perfection exemplified by her elders, and Miller admits that she has felt "resentment, and yet at the same time I have a tremendous sense of being glad to be shaped by these values. As far from perfect as I am, I feel that I know clearly what I feel and think about things. It's a hard world to live in, I think, and it seems to me that to be able to be a little judgmental but not unkind is of some value. The ability to see moral patterns in your life and all around you gives you not only a sense of what is wrong; it also gives you a sense of beauty."

It's impossible to think of Miller's rich, complex novel as a didactic tract, but the author freely states, "In fact, that *is* my conception of it. It *is* a didactic book and finally that's the kind of person I am and that's the kind of writer I am." Seeing our surprise, she adds lightly, "I mean, obviously if I wanted simply to preach, I would have done what the rest of my family has done, you know, get a D.Min. and I'd be writing sermons. But I do think that the fiction I care about has that sort of attitude. That's part of the deep pleasure of reading, and that's what I aspire to. It sounds terribly grandiose, but that's *it*, that sense of making a turning that lifts the narrative beyond being 'just a story.' I like that sort of twist, as in a sermon, the point at which it says, 'Even as we do thus and so . . . ,' but that's really where it's all headed."

In terms of her "good mother" Anna, Miller says that it would have been nice to make Anna's life work out comfortably for her. But, she notes, "this wouldn't have been useful to me as a writer, *and* it wouldn't have been the truth in some sense or another" that is important to the author. According to Miller, "She is going to be *something* other than she was before. I really do mean that quite literally and that is exactly where I was headed all the time."

As a child growing up in an integrated suburb near the University of Chicago, where her father taught church history, Miller had no aspirations, except perhaps to get married. When she was a teenager, her parents rented out rooms in their house; one of the tenants was Robert Coover, then a graduate student. Later, while Miller was majoring in English literature at Radcliffe, she heard that Coover's first book had been published. It was then that she gave serious thought to writing herself.

For a long time, however, she did not believe her work was publishable. She had married soon after college, had a son (now 17) and divorced. For eight years she worked in child care, a job she says was useful to her later as a writer in that "it presented me with a window into the lives of families of all sorts. People are very revealing to a day-care person and talk to you a lot. It was also an opportunity, unparalleled in any other kind of work, to learn about communication in a special sense." The children she worked with were one and a half or two years old, "essentially pre-verbal. The teacher had to understand from signals, from gestures, what children were really thinking about. This trained me in observation."

During the years she worked in child care, Miller also earned a master's degree in early childhood education from Harvard and a degree in writing from Boston University, where she now teaches. Only in the last decade has she seen her work as centered and strong enough, anchored at last by its moral viewpoint, to merit publication.

Miller attributes an important part of her security as a writer to her second husband. The author of *Prairie City, Iowa,* an account of his revisit to the farming community where he was raised, Bauer has also written a novel *Dexterity.* Miller says, "I really trust his sensibility and his judgment about my writing. It's terribly important to me to be able to talk to him and for him to be able to enter my fictional world."

Given Miller's extraordinary ability to open her fictional worlds to us, readers will agree that here is an author to watch, enjoy and learn from, although few if any will recognize in her work any hint of sermonizing. In any case, the best of sermons do address the heart, just as *The Good Mother* does, because they are heartfelt.

ROSEMARY HERBERT

TONI MORRISON

"WRITING IS REALLY a way of thinking—not just feeling but thinking about things that are disparate, unresolved, mysterious, problematic or just sweet." Toni Morrison is sitting in the living room of her Rockland County home overlooking the expansive Hudson River above New York City, and contemplating, in her dreamily melodious voice, the matter of writing. Warm, generous, intelligent, knowledgeable and endowed with a wonderful sense of humor, she is awaiting the publication of her fifth novel, an extraordinary work entitled *Beloved* (Knopf), a fierce and heartrending evocation of the horrors of slavery and its complex and often devastating effects on the maternal instinct.

As in her previous works—*The Bluest Eye, Sula, Song of Solomon* and *Tar Baby*—love and family, childhood, the interrelationship between the community and the individual, violence and the historically terrible embrace between the black and white races are at the core of the work. Here the setting is Ohio just after Emancipation, and the central figures are a former slave woman, Sethe, and the incarnation of her dead child, Beloved.

Morrison tells *PW* that her own childhood in an interracial neighborhood in Lorain, Ohio, has been central to her writing. "I use so much of my recollections about childhood as a starting point when I work, as a kind of matrix or wellspring; even if I'm not writing *about* it, it's a place where I start—mostly for a kind of gaze. Our family was large and close and very much dependent on one another. Everything I did as a child was extremely important. If I didn't mind the food on the stove and it burned,

359

there was no second thing to do—food was not all around in refrigerators the way it is now. If you weeded the garden, if you earned any money—everything you did made a difference to the well-being of somebody else.

"All sorts of people cared about me in terms of what I was doing—not just my parents and my aunts and my uncles, but everybody on the street. If I was misbehaving somewhere, put on lipstick too soon, they felt not only free but obliged to tell me not to do it, and I knew I had better, because they were like surrogate parents— this layer upon layer of adults who participated in our lives. That was also something that made me feel, oh, boy, wait till I get out of this place, because I am tired of all these people who can meddle with me." In every book she has written, Morrison points out, "There is this town which is both a support system and a hammer at the same time. And of course having gotten out," she continues, "you'd give anything for your [group of] grown-up women who cared what happened to you. Living in a world of real strangers, you learn that the strangeness is not skin, the strangeness is not jobs—the strangeness is that they really don't care about you."

Morrison says she feels now, as an adult, "very lucky that those requirements were made on us, that there were so many areas of generosities and manners and work and responsibilities that they imposed on us. Approval was not the acquisition of things; approval was given for the maturity and the dignity with which one handled oneself. Most black people in particular were, and still are, very fastidious about manners, very careful about behavior and the rules that operate within the community. The sense of organized activity, what I thought at that time was burdensome, turns out now to have with it a gift—which is, I never had to be taught how to hold a job, how to make it work, how to handle my time."

Morrison has needed that information, since she has juggled single parenthood with—often simultaneously—university teaching, editing and writing. "People used to say, how come you do so many things? It never appeared to me that I was doing very much of anything; really, everything I did was always about one thing, which is books. I was either editing them or writing them or reading them or teaching them, so it was very coherent. It was feeling very responsible for the kind of life you led, because you didn't want to do anything, if you could help it, that you didn't respect, and everything you did made a difference either for the race or the family or the community. That's still very strong in me." She pauses, then says, smiling, "I have to say I wasn't Jeanne d'Arc. I hated it. I didn't want to do anything but read and dream."

Morrison left Lorain to attend Howard University. For a time she toyed with the thought of being a dancer, but in the end she rejected the idea. "It's not as though I were a little perfect dancer with a little blonde topknot. What I did extremely well," Morrison laughs, "was read."

She went to Cornell for an M.A., taught, married, had two sons, Ford and Slade, both now in their 20s. Working as a text-book editor for L. B. Singer, she began to write. "It wasn't really writing—it was sort of doing something at night, rather than cultivating friendships. I found myself very good company, so I never needed a party or a dinner in order to make me wonder on Saturday night, what are you going to do? And besides I had these little children, and so I wrote at night, sporadically, trying to build on a story I had written years before. I found that really wonderful. I liked the authority of being in a place where I was doing it, and I liked how hard it was. And I liked the privacy, the interior world that was all mine, the freedom to explore that in a systematic way."

Morrison didn't however, like textbook editing so much after a while. But luckily, L. B. Singer had been acquired by Random House, and Morrison was asked to make the unusual move from text into trade. She initially favored Knopf: "I thought it would be a great place to work. Bob Gottlieb, on the other hand, didn't think it was such a hot idea. Or rather, what he thought was a hot idea was that he wanted to be my publisher, not my boss. Then I thought, suppose I could work at Random House and publish at Knopf? I'm sure they'd never heard of that, but I can't wait for people to *hear* of things before they get done. I mean, you might not do *anything*."

Morrison had it her way, and in her years at Random House she edited Toni Cade Bambara, Angela Davis, Muhammad Ali, NOW President Karen De Crow and others. She resigned in

1983 to "do like the grownups do—live and write, and only do that." She characterizes Gottlieb's editing of her work—he remained her editor until his shift to the *New Yorker*—as "perfect."

A work she had edited at Random House, *The Black Book*—"a *Whole Earth Catalog* vis-à-vis black people"—would eventually figure prominently in her own writing. The material was supplied by four collectors of memorabilia and included slave letters, folklore, songs, jokes, news-clippings and little-known facts. One story in particular stuck with Morrison, and it eventually became the inspiration for *Beloved:* the story of a young woman who runs away from slavery only to be caught. Morrison elaborates, "There was the Fugitive Slave Bill, which meant that if you ran away and somebody found you, they could take you back. She refused to go back, and in a way that got her a lot of attention—she tried to kill her children. This was a slave who, if she owned anything at all, it certainly wasn't her children. And she claimed them. It's an outrageous claim, not only of property, but rights and sovereignty. She said, 'These are my children, and I own their lives.' She also said, 'Death is better than life under these circumstances, and I can decide that.' All the people who interviewed her kept saying she was very quiet, she was very serene."

Other experiences related in the volume interested Morrison too, and she says, "What emerged was a series of real-life stories which for me said something very special about black women. The desperate need to nurture one's children is what informs everything about them. And the system that prevents that, and what happens to one's intellectual and emotional life when that is misplaced, the lengths to which one goes in order to do it, and the submersion of the individual into that effort. That nurturing quality is so magnificent and so tender and so fierce. I was interested in the excesses of a violent system that would produce this all-consuming effort to love something well. You can't live in this world without loving anything—you just can't do it. It's like hunger."

She continues, "I wanted to explore for myself the interior life of black people under those circumstances. Books about slavery have only one plot: You're in it, and you want to get out of it. I didn't want my head and my life to be enslaved by slavery; I didn't think I had the emotional resources to stay in that world for the length of time it would take to do it, which is usually three, four, five years.

362

"This woman was interesting to me because her story said so much about parenting and being a woman. This is not Medea who kills her children because she's mad at some dude, and she's going to get back at him. Here is something that is *huge* and *very* intimate. I imagined what would those circumstances be if this child could come back and say, 'How do you know death is better for me, since you've never done it?'

"That's where it started. It turned into some other thing. I discovered that this other experience that hadn't been lyricized—the middle passage, coming over on the slave boats. Beloved was also—and it got very exciting for me then—those black slaves whom we don't know, who did not survive that passage, who amounted to a nation who simply left one place, disappeared and didn't show up on the other shores. I had to be dragged, I suppose, by them, kicking and screaming, into this book, because it is just too much. Then I thought to myself, It can't be. It just can't be. If it's too much to write about, then they have won. If it can't be dealt with artistically, then I'm lost.

"Sometimes I have been accused—or complimented, I'm not sure—of writing about people who are bigger than life. I was always befuddled by that observation, and I still am a little bit. But I felt that I was writing about people who were as big as life, not bigger than. Life is very big. There are people who try to make it small, safe, unexamined. If some of my characters are as big as the life they have, they may seem enormous exaggerations, but [only to] a reader whose sense of life is more diminished than mine.

"More importantly, because fiction is, ostensibly, about invented characters, you make these decisions about what is valuable and what is not, what is true—not factual, but true and authentic—and what is not. And that's the best work in the world." Morrison pauses, then says, "This is the best work in the world for me."

AMANDA SMITH

BHARATI MUKHERJEE

LIKE THE NARRATOR of her novel *Jasmine*, Bharati Mukherjee has changed citizenships and cultures with disorienting rapidity. She has written about her several lives in two previous novels, a nonfiction work and two collections of short stories—*The Middleman* collection won the 1988 National Book Critics Circle award for fiction. In *Jasmine* (Grove), she encapsulates many aspects of the immigrant experience in America, in the process revealing the ways in which newcomers from the Third World are being absorbed by, and at the same time are transforming, our society.

Just back from a visit to her family in India, Mukherjee meets us in the Grove offices in lower Manhattan. Intense, elegant and articulate, she is eager to talk about the changes wrought in her life by her nascent celebrity. "The NBCC prize has made an enormous difference, not only in getting my current books into bookstores but also in reviving interest in my earlier work. I've been writing since 1972, and I'd always had a wonderful critical reception. But although my first two books were Book-of-the-Month Club alternates, they never went into paperback. Now for the first time there's a tremendous interest here, in Europe and in India. This has vindicated what I always tell my students: Concentrate on putting out a good word. A good word will not die. Someday it will find an audience."

In Mukherjee's case, the path to her audience was circuitous. Raised in an upper-class Bengali family of Brahmin caste, one of three daughters of a research chemist, she attended private schools in India, London and Switzerland—before a business disaster wiped out the family's fortune. In 1961, she got a scholarship to the University of Iowa Writers Workshop, where she met writer Clark Blaise and married him two years later. The couple lived first in Canada with their two young sons, supporting themselves through a grueling schedule of teaching and other jobs, and writing in the small hours of the morning and weekends. Then a series of near-tragic accidents sent them to Calcutta for a year to recuperate both physically and emotionally. In *Days and Nights in Calcutta* (Doubleday; Penguin paper), the book they wrote about this experience, Mukherjee says, "To be a Third World woman writer in North America is to confine oneself to a narrow, airless, tightly roofed arena."

Financially, too, the outlook was bleak. "I was brought up spectacularly rich—in the Third World sense—and have been spectacularly poor almost all my adult life," Mukherjee says. "At one time, I had to calculate whether I had enough money to buy orange juice as well as milk for breakfast. There was a time when I thought, should I be looking into a job as a chambermaid? But then I remembered I didn't know how to drive, and couldn't get to a motel," she laughs.

"For more than 20 years Clark and I have held three and four jobs per year in order to make ends meet. Now for the first time I'm able to take a semester off from teaching to work on my own novel," Mukherjee continues. "But the momentum of a work-in-progress has always carried me. There's not a single moment when I'm not thinking stories in my head. Sometimes endings will come to me in dreams."

Because she and her husband have shared a peripatetic lifestyle—"I've lived everywhere; that's what happens when you take teaching jobs anyplace that will have you"—Mukherjee has found herself "thrust into adventures. Once I left the very protective, overly nurturing society of India, my life intersected history. The title story in *The Middleman* came about because I happened to be in Costa Rica at a time when American and Central American history was being made."

Mukherjee's characters have always reflected her own circumstances and personal concerns, and one is able to trace her growth in self-confidence and her slowly developing identity as an American through her fiction. When she wrote *The Tiger's Daughter* (Houghton Mifflin, 1972), Mukherjee was living in

Canada, where she was conscious of being "a brown woman in a white society." Commenting on that first book, she says, "It is the wisest of my novels in the sense that I was between both worlds. I was detached enough from India so that I could look back with affection and irony, but I didn't know America enough to feel any conflict. I was like a bridge, poised between two worlds."

Wife, published three years later, "was very much an immigrant book. The wife was going through feminist and immigrant crises. The style was distinctly American in that omniscience was no longer natural to me. I was closer to my character and the material was more passionate. I had sacrificed irony for passion."

The characters in her short story collection titled *Darkness* (Penguin, 1985) were still South Asian immigrants who were trying out new lives. Only three years later, with *The Middleman*, was she confident enough to include a wide range of characters from various countries and strata of society. "With that book I realized that I can enter any gender and any culture, if the character and story excite me," she says.

One of the distinctions of Mukherjee's recent books is her adroit adaptation of the American vernacular. Her characters have urgent, riveting voices; they speak in the contemporary idiom as immigrants handle it, each richly reflecting the cadences of their original language on which they have grafted a new, distinctively regional Americanese. Mukherjee credits her flawless ventriloquism to a very good ear that unconsciously picks up nuances of language and has her talking like a native of whatever region she is in at the moment. "More importantly, it's having married an American writer who has opened up for me an America that is normally closed to immigrants," she says.

Her compact but fluid style is similarly a matter of gradual evolution. "I have lived through so many worlds and have been put in so many odd, momentous situations, accidentally, that all those worlds somehow creep into a single sentence. Mine is not minimalism, which strips away, but compression, which reflects many layers of meaning."

Her newest heroine, Jasmine, starts life as Jyoti in a tiny village in India, is called Jasmine by her husband, comes to America after she is tragically widowed, and becomes Jane Ripplemeyer in Iowa. Jasmine seesaws between her aspirations to make something of her life in America and her belief in an implacable fate.

Though Mukherjee says that "Jasmine contains the shape of my life and my desires, but no incident is at all autobiographical," she admits that, like her heroine, she too coexists between two opposed philosophies. "I do believe in personal striving. Like Jasmine, I want to reposition the stars. At the same time I'm aware of a larger design. My way of solving this is to say that every single moment has a purpose. I want to discover that purpose."

The original Jasmine, in the story of that name in *The Middleman*, was a Trinidadian illegal working in a seedy hotel in Detroit. "The character wouldn't die," Mukherjee confesses. "I am intrigued by that particular kind of survival."

In her second incarnation, Jasmine has a star-shaped scar on her forehead, a mark she has come to think of as her third eye, though in India it is a blemish that reduces her bridal value. The author, too, has a faint scar on her forehead, scarcely noticeable except to one who recognizes the resemblance to her fictional character. At age three, she slipped and smashed her head into a metal ring door knocker. The wound was never sutured, an omission that she now finds "odd, in India, where for a Bengali girl to have a physical imperfection is to be unmarriageable."

While Mukherjee was a student in Iowa, however, her father wrote to say that he had, in fact, found the perfect groom for her, "a nuclear physicist, Bengali, right caste, right background, right education." Plans for marriage were set in motion, but in the meantime, Mukherjee met Clark Blaise. "If I had married this man—who is now very important in the Indian nuclear industry—I would have been a very different kind of person and a different kind of writer," Mukherjee says. "If I had stayed in India, I would have written elegant, ironic, wise stories which would be marked by detachment. But I never could have stayed in India. It was not so much restlessness but enthusiasm and eagerness that has always made me curious about the rest of the world.

"I knew from the moment I got here that I wanted to stay," she continues. "I preferred unpredictability to a privileged but predictable life." But when the couple moved to Canada they experienced a society less open to immigrants than the U.S. "Canada and the U.S. have very different ways of treating newcomers, very different responses to the threat of de-Europeanization. Here diversity is accepted; the melting pot helps the newcomer to feel more welcome." Mukherjee "put the matter of racial discrimination on the public agenda," with an essay called "An Invisible Woman," which appeared in 1981 in Canada's *Saturday Night* magazine. "Bags of mail," much of it hostile, came in response. One reader suggested she change her unpronounceable name. "One said, 'If you didn't play in snow as a child you have no right to regard yourself as a Canadian,'" Mukherjee recalls. Yet the net result of that experience was positive, she feels.

The courage to speak out against prejudice brought Mukherjee to the defense of Salman Rushdie: during the first heated months of the controversy, she sported a large Rushdie button, and she and her husband appeared on Lewis Lapham's TV program *Bookmark* in Rushdie's defense. They too had experienced terrorist pressure in what she calls "a very modest way" after the publication of their 1985 book *The Sorrow and the Terror*, which described the terrorist-directed crash of Air India flight #182. For months afterward the couple received death threats.

The support of other authors has been crucial in Mukherjee's life. Bernard Malamud, who was Blaise's teacher at Harvard, was "a second father to Clark, and he became a second father to me, too," she says fondly. "He was a man of great moral force, and he showered his life on us—sometimes in practical ways, like money, so that we wouldn't starve—other times as role model."

Margaret Atwood also played a pivotal role in Mukherjee's career. It was she who "insisted that we get a good agent and introduced Elaine Markson to us," Mukherjee says. "And Elaine got my material to the right editor"—Walter Bode at Grove. Then there was a long spell of "unfortunate representation," she says. She found herself stereotyped—"I was boxed as a certain kind of elegant woman writer, appealing only to India hands."

During those bad years, her husband's faith buoyed her confidence. "I've really grown up with Clark. We have a special kind of literary marriage, because we're both writers and academics. There's not a moment when we're not talking literature. If I'd married a nuclear physicist, in some way I'd been a lonelier person. This sameness of focus helped us get through extraordinary cultural and religious differences."

Best of all, her marriage has helped her feel American. "Mine is a clear-eyed but definite love of America. I'm aware of the brutalities, the violences here, but in the long run my characters are survivors; they've been helped, as I have, by good strong people of conviction. Like Jasmine, I feel there are people born to be Americans. By American I mean an intensity of spirit and a quality of desire. I feel American in a very fundamental way, whether Americans see me that way or not."

SYBIL S. STEINBERG

ALICE MUNRO

ALICE MUNRO'S COLLECTION of stories *The Progress of Love* appeared four years after her previous book, *The Moons of Jupiter.* Each of her six collections has maintained this steady rhythm of three- or four-year intervals. The gap is agonizingly long for Munro's devoted fans, who can get periodic "fixes" in such magazines as the *New Yorker,* but the cumulative effect gives her work distinctive power. Few people writing today can bring a character, a mood or a scene to life with such economy. And she has an exhilarating ability to make the reader see the familiar and ordinary with fresh insight and compassion.

The Progress of Love, like Munro's other works, is set largely in the towns of southern Ontario, a region akin to Middle America. Her characters may move west to Vancouver or depart for the larger cities of Toronto and Ottawa, where they lead middle-class urban lives, but they are forged by their antecedents. In this collection, Munro has expanded her narrative range. Some of the stories are compressed novels, effortlessly moving back and forth in time or changing point of view. In the hands of other writers, each story could be a saga, but Munro can convey everything a reader needs to know in a few pages.

Although she had struggled for years to write a novel, and thought of the short story as apprenticeship work, she now says, "I no longer feel attracted to the well-made novel. I want to write the story that will zero in and give you intense, but not connected, moments of experience. I guess that's the way I see life.

People remake themselves bit by bit and do things they don't understand. The novel has to have a coherence which I don't see any more in the lives around me."

In the story "White Dump," which concludes *The Progress of Love*, there are three generations who all spend part of their lives at a summer house by a lake. "I wanted not to integrate those versions but to make a mosaic," says Munro. Yet, with her skill and vision, there are no jagged edges and the story has a beautifully conveyed coherence.

It is surprising for someone living in Canada, who has read Munro's stories in literary magazines in the 1960s and 1970s, to hear her recall periods of profound frustration and discouragement. To the observer, she has been an established literary presence for more than 20 years. Her first collection, *Dance of the Happy Shades*, published in Canada by Ryerson Press in 1968, when she was 37, won Canada's prestigious literary prize, the Governor-General's Award. But the seemingly regular publication of stories and collections hid the shaky confidence Munro had in her growth as a writer.

"I became more and more fragile. When I was into my 30s I became increasingly depressed by rejection letters. I had had the feeling that by the time I was 30 I would be established. But I was not at all. By the time of *Lives of Girls and Women*, I was into my 40s and I had become more thin-skinned."

Munro was born in 1931 and grew up "in a fringe community of Wingham," which is itself a small town in southwestern Ontario. She attended the University of Western Ontario in nearby London, Ont., for two years before marrying Jim Munro in 1951 and moving with him to Vancouver. He worked for Eaton's department store, while she was at home with their two young daughters. She was writing all the time, discarding most of it, publishing occasionally; she thought of herself as "promising" for too long. Publicly, however, it was a traditional existence. "I was keeping up appearances as a housewife and mother," she says, "I was not at all a rebel. My energy was going into writing, but it was so often blocked."

Since Munro was supported by her husband, in turn she kept house—a fair trade in her view. "He always wanted a wife who ironed," she says, but he also valued her ambitions and gave her

371

periods alone to "think" about her writing. She credits him and Robert Weaver, who bought her work for his now-defunct literary magazine, *Tamarack Review*, and for CBC Radio, with keeping her alive as a writer.

When Jim Munro wanted a business of his own, she suggested a bookstore where she could help him. In 1963, they found an opportunity in Victoria. For three years, she worked in the store every day and on Sundays scrubbed the floor. "In some ways they were the best times of my life," she says. "When we moved to Victoria the pressure was off. I was no longer working all day trying to write a novel. I was working in the bookstore and it was a wonderful relief. Also, I talked to people all day. God, the isolation of housewives in those days! I love mindless chatter."

In 1966, when she gave birth to their third daughter, Munro was at home again and resumed writing. *Lives of Girls and Women*, her most autobiographical book, was published in 1971. Comprised of linked stories, it is frequently described as a novel. But after that, she feared she had exhausted her material.

"*Lives* is one of those books I should really have written when I was younger. It is the classic childhood, adolescence, breakthrough-into-maturity book. Every beginning writer has that material—and after that you're not sure what you can do. I went through a bleak period. And then I wrote the stories in the third book, *Something I've Been Meaning to Tell You*, almost desperately. I wasn't at all sure they worked."

The fact that *Lives* was winning readers in the U.S., where it was published by McGraw-Hill, doesn't seem to have made much difference to Munro. She recalls with amusement an event that occurred when the book appeared in the U.S. She had dashed to the grocery to buy potatoes for supper. Standing in the checkout line, leafing through *Time* magazine, ("trying to free read"), she spotted a review of *Lives*. "I had only enough money to buy either *Time* or the potatoes. I was so locked into domestic life that I bought the potatoes."

In 1973 she and Jim Munro separated and she returned to Ontario, where her life took two unexpected turns. After her third book, *Something I've Been Meaning to Tell You*, was published in Canada in 1974, she received a letter from U.S. literary agent Virginia Barber asking to represent her. Feeling that she did not have enough material to offer, Munro replied diffidently, but subsequently she sent Barber some stories. The agent immediately sold two of them to the *New Yorker*, and made arrangements with Knopf to publish Munro's future works.

The other turning point presented itself when Munro encountered Gerald Fremlin again. He had been a young World War II veteran completing his studies at the University of Western Ontario when she was a freshman. She recalls writing a short story with the dual objective of getting published and of attracting his attention. By the time her story was published, he had graduated, but he did write her a first, perfect fan letter, comparing her to Chekhov. Thirty years later, when he contacted her during her brief post as writer-in-residence at Western, she was receptive.

In 1975, she moved with Fremlin, a retired cartographer, to Clinton, Ont., (pop. 3200) in Huron County, to the house where he was born. It is only a few miles from Wingham. "I never, never, never, never, never, never thought I would end up there," Munro laughs.

Huron Country is of course, her terrain, fictionally and biographically. Her father, Robert Laidlaw, was a fox farmer and when that failed, he worked as a watchman at the stove foundry and switched to raising turkeys. Her mother, Anna Chamney, was a "school" teacher. "You say 'school' teacher when you mean a rural teacher. Do you notice that?" says Munro, with characteristic attention to the detail and texture of speech.

Munro, the oldest of three children, was 12 when her mother was stricken with Parkinson's Disease. As in her fiction, those facts shield a far more interesting and complex family. Her sister is an artist and her brother is a theoretical chemist. When he was in his 70s, her father wrote a novel of pioneer life titled *The Mc-Gregors*, which Macmillan of Canada published. Munro's eyes fill with tears as she describes his absorption in the revisions in the week prior to his death during cardiac surgery. "I couldn't believe the enormous leap he had made. There was this amazing dormant talent. He had natural skill, and he just knew the things you can't teach."

Munro, a warm, vibrant woman, speaks openly about herself, but she won't allow interviewers to come to her home. Fremlin, now her husband, does not want his privacy invaded, but she also fears it would rob her of herself. Commenting on Canadian TV documentaries that show writers relaxing at home, she says, "I

373

wonder how they could ever do those things again. It's as if they've started living their private life in public, and it would lose its authenticity in some way. It would begin to be a role."

What would a reporter see? "A very ordinary, nice, small town. A white wooden house where we live on the edge of town, with lots of trees—walnut and maple trees—and a big lawn—which I mow." She says it is a modest, comfortable house, with a dining room lined with bookshelves, and a kitchen furnished with a dresser and arm chair. On the second floor, Munro stripped off the wallpaper to reveal the cedar paneling. She uses one of the spare bedrooms as her office, writing at a table facing the wall, working on her first drafts in longhand. "It's like being inside a warm wooden place," she says. Above all, its proportions suit her. "I've lived in a big showplace house and I never want to live again in a house that overshadows me."

For Munro, a story is like a house. When she reads a story, she often starts at a point other than the beginning. "I go into it, and move back and forth and settle here and there, and stay in it for a while," she wrote in an essay about her work. When she writes a story, she continued, "I've got to make, I've got to build up, a house, a story to fit around the indescribable 'feeling' that is like the soul of the story. . . . "

Munro elaborates: "What is important to me about the story is not what happens. . . . It's like a view of reality—a kind of reality that I can go into for a while, and I know right away if I can go into it [further] or not. Then, once I'm into it, I'll find out what happens. It's getting into it that's important, not caring what happens. A story is a spell, rather than a narrative."

Yet things *do* happen in Munro's stories, and there is pleasure in watching revelations and events unfold—never predictable, always inevitable. Those who have not yet read Munro's work are lucky. They now have a feast of collections to discover—and savor.

BEVERLY SLOPEN

TIM O'BRIEN

W HEN NOMINATIONS FOR the 1979 National Book Award for fiction were announced, most observers believed it was a two-horse race between John Irving, for his critically acclaimed and widely popular *The World According to Garp*, and John Cheever, for *The Stories of John Cheever*, a collection that seemed to be his career's crowning achievement. When the winner was announced—32-year-old Tim O'Brien for *Going After Cacciato*, a book that had sold only 12,000 copies in hardcover (compared to 20 times that amount for *Garp*)—the upset not only spelled the end of the NBAs as we'd come to know them (long considered too uncommercial to taste, they were renamed the American Book Awards in 1980, an experiment that itself ended in 1986), but it also thrust a modest, self-effacing writer into the limelight.

"I didn't know how the bullets fired," O'Brien was fond of saying about his 14 months in Vietnam, but clearly he knew how to make sentences. In a laudatory review of *Cacciato*, John Updike sensed that the young author was "reaching for a masterpiece." If O'Brien's publisher, Seymour Lawrence, is to be believed—"This is one of the most original and beautiful books I will ever publish," he says—*The Things They Carried* may be that masterwork.

O'Brien has volunteered to pick up *PW* at Boston's Logan Airport—"The directions to our house would drive you crazy." He rushes into the baggage area, compact and energetic in a short jacket and baseball cap. Ann, his wife of 17 years, is waiting in the car—they met while she was at Little, Brown and he was a grad student at Harvard (she is now production manager at *Sail* magazine). "I was wondering if you'd ask us where our daughter is," O'Brien quips as we hop into the car, referring no doubt to the nine-year-old who challenges the writer O'Brien in the book. His eyes flash as he surmises whether his listener had indeed taken the autobiographical bait.

Called "A Work of Fiction" on the title page, *The Things They Carried* is neither a collection of stories nor a novel. Rather, it is a unified narrative, with chapters that stand perfectly on their own (many were award-winning stories) but which together render deeper continuities of character and thought. Throughout, there are tautly drawn Vietnam vignettes, with "O'Brien" as sergeant; there is the character of "Timmy," a Minnesota fourth-grader who witnesses a schoolmate's slow death by cancer; there are the doubts of a 43-year-old writer with a daughter named Kathleen who tells him, "You keep writing these war stories so I guess you must've killed somebody"; there is a war buddy named Norman Bowker, who implores a famous writer to tell his story and eventually commits suicide. Yet as O'Brien points out as we weave into the traffic leaving the airport, there's no dying little girl, no Norman Bowker, "and we don't have a daughter—it's all made up.

"My own experience has virtually nothing to do with the content of the book," he continues as we settle in over coffee at the O'Brien house in Boxford, Mass., a thickly wooded town half an hour north of Boston. "Every now and then I would draw on my memories or attitudes about Vietnam, but of the whole time I spent there I remember maybe a week's worth of stuff. By and large, in the composition of the book, my attention was on trying to get a feeling of utter authenticity, which meant paying attention to language. My goal was to write something utterly convincing but without any rules as to what's real and what's made up."

O'Brien sees *Cacciato,* his third book, as "an effort to move from realism to a kind of . . . I don't want to say surrealism . . . let's say a plane where the experience of imagining, which was so crucial to me as a soldier and as a person today, formed the body of the book. In this new book I forced myself to try to invent a form. I had never invented form before. Even in *Cacciato,* which people found inventive, the form came through my reading of writers like Faulkner and Joyce, whereas this feels to me as if something has been invented."

After graduating from Macalester College in 1968 with a full graduate scholarship to Harvard, O'Brien was drafted into the army. Near the end of his tour he wrote his first major piece, which was published in *Playboy*. He claims to have suffered none of the readjustment problems that have haunted American vets. "It was land in Seattle—they process you out of the army in about two hours—say the pledge of allegiance, get in a taxicab, get on a plane, take off your uniform in the toilet and fly to Minnesota. It was over, in a day and a half—from Vietnam, to Seattle, to Minnesota. It was fast and effortless, just like gliding out of a nightmare."

O'Brien finally got to Harvard in 1970, where his dissertation was "Case Studies in American Military Interventions" ("I never finished!"). He continued his writing at night, working on short pieces that eventually became part of his first book, the war memoir *If I Die in a Combat Zone* (Delacorte).

"There came a point when I had to decide where I was going to devote my time, and I decided that I wanted to be a writer and not a scholar. I'm glad I didn't pursue it," he says, clearly still relieved.

All but one of O'Brien's five books were published by Seymour Lawrence. *If I Die in a Combat Zone* (1973), *Northern Lights* (1974) and *Cacciato* (1978) were issued under Lawrence's imprint at Delacorte. When Lawrence moved to Dutton in 1982, O'Brien went with him with a new manuscript, *The Nuclear Age*, but a Lawrence book it was not to be.

"When I turned it in," O'Brien says, "the editor-in-chief at Dutton, Joe Kanon, didn't like it that much. The way I understood it was that they would publish it but they wouldn't give it the kind of backing or print run I wanted. It was all quite amiable, and I said I preferred to look around for another house. My agent Lynn Nesbit showed it to Bob Gottlieb at Knopf, who loved the book and said he would get behind it, and did.

"It was very difficult leaving Sam Lawrence," he continues, "but at the time I had a feeling that I would end up going back. And Kanon is now at Houghton and loves the new book, or so I hear. So everything has come full circle."

The Things They Carried was not supposed to be O'Brien's next book. "I've had a novel called *The Lake of the Woods* under contract for a while at Houghton. But in the middle of it I just started amassing this collection." Asked when he conceived of the new book's shape, he says, "All along, I knew I wanted to have a book in which my name, Tim, appeared even though Tim would not be me; that's all I knew. Over the course of, I'd say, 12 years, I was developing courage, which was the whole problem. The conception was pretty clear. But if you can imagine putting your name down doing horrible things you've never done or witnessed, it was something I had to find the guts to do. Even though in the broader sense of the word it's no big act of courage, when you face it in that room"—he points to the large, book-lined study just off the kitchen—"it's a scary feeling."

Although O'Brien admits that "for the rest of my life I'll probably be writing war stories," he contends that it is not out of any obsession with war but rather the imperatives of writing with passion about things that matter that draw him back to the combat experience as a source for storytelling.

"If there is one fundamental thing," he says, "it's that I want to write stories that are good. To do that requires a sense of passion, and my passion as a human being and as a writer intersect in Vietnam, not in the physical stuff but in the issues of Vietnam—of courage, rectitude, enlightenment, holiness, trying to do the right thing in the world."

He also admits to the purely technical allure of war writing. "In a war story there is a built-in life-and-death importance, one that a writer would have to construct otherwise. When you start a story saying, 'It was a hot day,' and you know it's a war story, the hot day has all sorts of reverberations that wouldn't be there if it were set on a beach in Miami."

As O'Brien has grown older and his career has continued, his work has necessarily come under a different scrutiny—from himself and his readers. For example, "Sweetheart of the Song Tra Bong," a chapter in The Things They Carried, "was originally conceived to address the comments I hear from women I know—that they don't like war stories." It concerns a 17-year-old girl from Cincinnati who is flown to Vietnam by her boyfriend only to become enraptured with the most horrific rituals of war. From the innocence of a high school cheerleader she is transformed into a frightening image of war's incalculable madness. When last seen, she is disappearing into the jungle wearing a necklace of human tongues.

"That story is in the center of the collection for a reason," says O'Brien. "It is so far from one's ordinary expectations as to be a fable, unacceptable on the plane of what happens. I *will* say, though, that of all the stories in the book, this one comes the closest to an actual event, not one I witnessed, but one that I had been told about. I had the character Rat Kiley tell that story so I could get into some of the issues of the book itself: his buddies are shaking their heads, saying, 'That just can't be real,' and Kiley gets so furious, saying, 'You accept all this other crap in Vietnam, why can't you accept that some girl comes over here?' And Rat is fighting what I am fighting in this book—this whole problem of trying to make credible what to me was incredible.

"My feeling," he continues, "is that what happened to me as a man in Vietnam could happen to a woman as well. And the reasons it didn't were reasons of sociology and demography, not a difference in spirit."

In *The Things They Carried*, drifting above the reminders that none of it is true, the funereal listings of the "things" the characters indeed carried, and the fantastical flights that call into question the common grounds of sanity, is a sense that the subject of storytelling itself, not only as an act but as an issue, is the thread that binds this collection.

"If there is a theme to the whole book, it has to do with the fact that stories can save our lives," says O'Brien, lighting another Carlton. "I've just read Shelby Foote's trilogy on the Civil War, and the images of Longstreet or Lee or Grant gazing across the battlefield are rendered by Foote as stories. What remains of them all is purely story. What I discovered in the course of writing this book is the reason I love story: not just for its titillation, its instant gratification of what next, what next, but for the livingness that's there as you read and that lingers afterward. Jake Barnes is alive for me. Though he is a fictional character in the taxicab at the end of *The Sun Also Rises*, he is alive in that cab with Brett. That's what I love about writing them and reading them—that quality of immortality that a story *is*—doesn't contain—just is."

O'Brien pauses and struggles as he works through these ideas; the book is not really behind him yet. He apologizes: "This is a hard thing to talk about. It sounds mystical, and I'm not a mystical person. But one has to say what one believes.

379

"My hope is that when you finish the last page of this book, or any book, there is a sense of having experienced a whole life or a constellation of lives; that something has been preserved which, if the book hadn't been written, would have been lost, like most lives are."

MICHAEL COFFEY

TILLIE OLSEN

TILLIE OLSEN'S NAME is revered by some women, excoriated by others. Many women (including some feminists, older women who feel their opinions on life have never really been written about, and a healthy group of young writers) think that Olsen is one of the great unsung geniuses of our time. She captured the voice of a generation in *Yonnindo: From the Thirties,* a book begun when Olsen was 19, then "lost" for 40 years through the birth of four children and having to do "real" work for a living. The four short stories in *Tell Me a Riddle* have been anthologized 72 times. *Silences,* a collection of essays, dealt with the power of class, color and sex in determining whether an artist's creative capacity will ultimately flower or be "silenced." There are some women, however, an equally impassioned group, who feel that when Tillie Olsen gave up her writing to raise all those kids it was a sellout, just an excuse not to sit down and *do the work.*

Instead of a glossy press kit sent to me before our meeting. I receive a series of letters written in Tillie Olsen's minuscule script and a daunting compilation of learned academic papers and books (*Excavations: Tillie Olsen's Reading List; From the Thirties: Tillie Olsen and the Radical Tradition;* and a biographical excerpt from *Portraits and Passages* by Ericka Duncan, published by Schocken Books). And Olsen is unsure about our meeting. When I say that I'm looking forward to the interview, she replies, *"I'm not."* She asks for samples of my work. Although I myself am a woman/writer/mother, it's the first time I've ever had to audition to interview someone.

Then one day there she is, standing on the landing of her San Francisco apartment building encouraging me up three flights of stairs. She remarks that in my profiles I always describe what people wear, but that she hasn't had a chance to get dressed because she spent the morning vacuuming. (Shades of "I Stand Here Ironing"?) She takes me out on her balcony and points out the sights—Japan Town, Bill Graham's Fillmore West and the building that used to house Jim Jones's People's Temple—and says, "This complex is multi-national, multi-hued." (Shades of her past as a '30s leftist?)

Olsen's book *Mother to Daughter, Daughter to Mother*—a collection of excerpts from novels, poetry, gravestone epitaphs and letters—came about in part as a celebration of the 15th anniversary of the Feminist Press. The book includes pieces by such well-known writers as Gwendolyn Brooks, Colette, Emily Dickinson, Harriet Beecher Stowe, Jessamyn West and Virginia Woolf, but also contains stories and letters from people Olsen has met on the lecture circuit (now her primary method of earning a living).

Olsen, 72, sits down in a child's chair and gets straight to work talking about the new book. "*Mother to Daughter, Daughter to Mother* was just one of those happenings and yet it has a long foreground," she explains. "You could say it started when I met Florence Howe during the first stirrings of feminism in academia. Years later [in 1970] she became the publisher of the Feminist Press." Olsen brought to Howe's attention *Life in the Iron Mills* by Rebecca Harding Davis, originally published as a series in *Atlantic Monthly* in 1861. Davis was one of the first to write about what Tillie Olsen calls "the lives of despised people." And she did so under the stresses of motherhood and making a living. The Feminist Press reissued *Life in the Iron Mills*—with an afterword by Olsen—in 1972.

"Last year Florence Howe came to me with the idea of doing a feminist calendar with pictures and a few quotes," Olsen continues. "I opened my big mouth, and the next thing I knew the calendar had turned into a daybook—small enough to be carried in a purse, with room left between the passages for people to keep a diary or use as an appointment calendar. Mainly there was a fever in me to pass on to others what has been of importance to me."

That "passing on to others" is how Olsen has made her reputation. Although she has said of herself that she "may have given in too easily to the demands of family," she followed the rules of her generation, many of which still apply today. Talking with her makes me think of my son's three living great-grandmothers. One is the daughter of Russian immigrants who missed the first grade because she had to stay home and take care of her siblings, eventually married and hasn't "worked" a day since. Another is a member of the DAR, who worked all her life as a secretary in a hick town in the Mojave Desert and now lives happily alone in a trailer park. The third was a feisty Irish girl who married a Chinese when it was against the law and, now 80, still works five days a week. What Tillie Olsen has done in her work is to take *all* such lives and either raise them to art or make them into a paradigm or matrix that we all can recognize. When, after only a half hour of conversation, Olsen begins to cry and says, "We're all dying off, and no one has told our stories," you feel that loss with her, because there's the loss of her own story as well.

Tillie Olsen was born to Russian immigrants. In Nebraska, her father was state secretary of the Socialist Party. As a girl in Omaha, she read *Comrade* magazine and devoured every book in her neighborhood library, commencing with A and reaching the M's. When she was 10 she worked after school selling peanuts. She stuttered. At the age of 18, she joined the Young Communist League. A year later she began *Yonnindo,* and her first baby was born—out of wedlock. She was arrested twice for her leftist activities. The first chapter of *Yonnindo* was published in the *Partisan Review.* In her biography for the magazine she listed her occupations as tie presser, hack writer, model, housemaid, ice cream packer and book clerk. Bennett Cerf at Random House took an interest in the plucky 19-year-old, giving her a monthly stipend of $15. She married and again got pregnant, and somewhere along the line stopped writing.

Motherhood-and-writing is the subject that has haunted Olsen, both personally and professionally. "This has been a consuming concern of mine since I finished the tasks of the race—of perpetuating the species," she says. "It's always been a hard time to be a mother. I remember sitting by a very, very ill child. I was a single mother. I'd tried to take her to nursery school that morning, but they wouldn't accept her. So I had to lie to get off work.

I sat by her crib all day, all night. I was reading *Grandma Brown: Her First Hundred Years,* and I was at the part where her child was dying and she just had to go and work. There were no choices for her. And I thought how lucky I was. Today, the world is a dangerous place. The 'experts' lie to mothers about what they're feeling. They say that a mother feels *guilt* when she leaves her child at a day care center and goes to work. But all that comes from the 'generation of vipers' thinking that began with Freud, who attributed all the ills of the human race to women."

Olsen has her own version of how the problems of mothering have evolved over the years. "In the last century, women/mother/ writers wrote naturally about children. There were many women novelists whose reasons for writing were to support their children. Today you can look back at Harriet Beecher Stowe's work and see her suffering over the babies ripped from the arms of slave mothers. But today in *contemporary* feminist literature and literary criticism, you find a trashing of the last century's 'sentimentality' and tears over the death of a child. This is the first century when we haven't had to accept the death of a child as the will of God. Instead, now you have Mother's Day sentimental shit."

Olsen continues: "There were few women of my mother's generation who had time for their children. They had their hands occupied by all the tasks that kept a family together—all the washing was done by hand, farm chores, cooking from scratch. It was the older children who looked after the babies. During the Depression, although there were more abortions than ever, before or since, children represented the only possibilities of happiness for the human race. During World War II life was totally disrupted. Many women for the first time were running their families. It was the first generation where the majority got through high school. When their husbands came back, the government gave a young family the chance to own a home of its own. For the first time in American history we had the phenomenon of full-time mothers. I believe that the baby boom was not just a result of pushing women back into the home after their few years of independence, but a profound feeling about the preciousness of life on earth."

Olsen goes on to point out that these World War II brides have been unjustly maligned. "They raised daughters who gave birth to the women's movement, and sons—who in other times were raised to carry patriotic fever into battle to be slaughtered like cattle—who instead were raised to feel that their lives were meant for something greater.

"Now, in this generation, we have made a great leap. You have a sense of your possibilities and the chance to exercise them. Frustrations can be laid to your own failures or choosing a wrong course. So here you are. You're marvelously educated and you have all the tools. *You just don't know how lucky you are!*" Olsen's eyes fill with tears again, but she goes on sternly. "And you're being thrown back into a situation generations old. Motherhood is the last refuge of sexism. Women have to obey the patriarchal injunction. They have to choose one or the other. Career women are told to unsex themselves. If you decide to have children, the total responsibility is yours. Standards and aspirations are infinitely higher for ourselves and our children, but human life is not valued. It's not being the best, but besting someone. It still comes down to the children. There is one fundamental question today, and it's the same one I wrote about years ago: 'Who's to care about them if we don't, who?' "

Critics, academicians, feminists and "average" women will argue for years over that question. In a 1971 lecture Olsen said that in all of English and American letters only one out of 12 writers was a woman. A perusal of current bestseller lists shows that Olsen is still right. Perhaps it's because of these insights into the everyday world that Olsen is both revered and disliked. About being disliked, she shrugs. About being revered, she gives a peculiar answer.

"It isn't revered. People respond to you if you don't trash them or put them down. When a woman reads 'I Stand Here Ironing,' she can see that women have all possibilities open to them. Yet critics always write about that story in terms of guilt." Then, cryptically, she says, "On the ninth night after the bombing of Hiroshima a light was seen on earth that was never seen before. It was a moonless night lit up with the strange blue light of radiated bodies. That's the light I have to write in, as opposed to the light of life." She adds, "I have an understanding about things that simply has not been articulated in our time. I know that sounds snotty and self-serving. But I do have certain comprehensions about human life and the hard task of raising a human being in our kind of world. When I first came on the scene, I only had a literary audience. Thanks to Xerox machines I began to have a people audience, because there was a group of teachers who began to put together a living anthology of feminist writers." And finally, "We usually have to accept other people's versions of what is. Most women today still can't harvest 'art' out of their situations. I look back on 'I Stand Here Ironing,' which I wrote in 1957. That's practically prehistoric times, and yet little has been written about motherhood since. Why? Because if you're a mother, every time the phone rings you jump. Is it going to be about the kid? You never have your own complete attention."

LISA SEE

CYNTHIA OZICK

W HEN CYNTHIA OZICK was in her teens, she recalls, "my father looked at my work and said, 'You can't read it, you have to study it.' This line has remained with me as a kind of fate or doom." The 58-year-old stylist of fecund, dazzling prose that is also mandarin and formidable speaks in a calm, softly modulated voice as she patiently elucidates a literary odyssey that has been anything but painless and confident.

"I write in terror," says Ozick, author most recently of *The Messiah of Stockholm* (Knopf, 1987). "I have to talk myself into bravery with every sentence, sometimes every syllable. I have a raven perched on my right shoulder at all times that says, 'That's not good, that's ugly or confusing.' "

Childhood scars, a late-blooming career and a debilitating lawsuit threat have further undermined her confidence. In fact, *The Cannibal Galaxy* (Knopf, 1983) and its antecedent, "The Laughter of Akiva," a novella published in the *New Yorker* in 1980, which cast a caustic eye on "mediocre, philistine, stupid, criminal teachers who undervalue dreamy, artistic children," were drawn from her own "torturous" childhood at P.S. 71 in the Bronx. "I suffered terribly in elementary school. I was writing and reading all the time and was a super speller, but these things had no value because I would get 24 in arithmetic and read the history book as a storybook the first day of school, never open it again and not know the dates for the history test. I went through school dumb and feeling it very deeply," says Ozick, who was to be elected to Phi Beta Kappa at New York University and eventually

387

awarded fellowships by the National Endowment for the Arts and the Guggenheim Foundation.

The author resides in New Rochelle, N.Y., and sets "Laughter," which has the headmaster rabbi impregnating his wife before they are married, in a Westchester Jewish elementary school. The principal of a Westchester yeshiva threatened a lawsuit; the *New Yorker* abrogated its reading agreement with the author for a year, and Knopf pulled "Laughter" from *Levitation: Five Fictions* (1982), which was already in galleys, and held publication until Ozick could write another novella.

"I made some mistakes and I was punished," admits Ozick about her transformation of certain factual material into fiction, "because I believed that fiction is free. The lawsuit threat [never carried out], which was deeply anti-literary and hating of the poetry side of life, frightened me so deeply that it destroyed me as a writer for two years. I was humiliated before my publisher and my community. I was crying day and night."

As a professional writer, Ozick "got a very late start. I always knew I was a writer since the age of five, but I published my first fiction in *Prairie Schooner* when I was already 28. If you've been writing steadily and been rebuffed steadily, since the age of 22, that's late. And if that fiction is an excerpted chapter from a 300,000-word unfinished novel called *Mercy, Pity, Peace and Love*, that's late. Then I published a lot of poems in small literary magazines, each one taking dozens and dozens of submissions."

Although she once wrote advertising copy for Filene's of Boston and has taught a few writing and English composition courses, Ozick is basically a full-time writer, a luxury she says she owes to her husband, attorney Bernard Hallote, who "gave me 24 hours a day for the literary life." (The couple have a daughter, Rachel.) "It was extraordinary, but because all that time I was a failure, I know it was a mistake. I should have gone out into the world of periodicals and journalism. Publish, publish whatever you can as early as possible. Not to be published as a novelist until you are 37 years old is devastating, a kind of living death. I'll never get over it. It has left me with almost an excess of gratitude for any attention I get."

In an interview peppered with Hebrew words and Yiddish aphorisms, Ozick likens the labor she expended on her first two novels to Jacob's courtship of the biblical matriarchs Rachel and

Leah: "Seven years on *MPPL* and another seven years on *Trust*. [The former] was never consummated, but it went on so long it was nicknamed 'Nipple.' I sucked on that 'Nipple' for a very long time. I see it now as a kind of juvenilia; it was much too ambitious and wouldn't have satisfied Proust. It was supposed to be a philosophical novel encompassing all the issues of the age. I didn't know what those philosophical issues were, but I thought I could do that as well as a hundred characters of various kinds."

Trust (NAL, 1966), which, like *Messiah*, focuses on distrust, sat with New American Library's Hal Scharlatt, "who took an option on the novel, gave me $500 and kept me dangling for a year and a half. I finally shamed him into seeing me, and I realized he had begun making quick notes on what should be done to this novel about five minutes before I entered his office. It was intolerable." Ozick was saved by the young NAL editor David Segal ("my knight in shining armor"), who, at Ozick's obstinate insistence, agreed to publish *Trust* as it was, "a moment of astounding glory. But I think he resented it through the rest of our relationship, which was extremely loving." When Segal moved to Knopf, he took Ozick with him.

She approaches her monthly column in the *New York Times Book Review* with a heart full of memories. "When I was in my 20s and 30s, I was reading 16 hours a day like a crazed person. Words were flying out of me and I had no platform." She tried to get book review assignments, but to no avail. "I remember being refused on the same day, at the age of 35, by *Commentary* and the *New York Review of Books*," the latter not allowing her to cross the office's threshhold. "I had been hermitized for many years [writing *MPPL* and *Trust*] and I wanted to embrace the world. I hungered for it and I was turned back repeatedly. Now this dream assignment to write anything I want comes to me at 58. Isn't this the most extraordinary opportunity for the mind?" She sighs. "It's not too late, it's never too late, but it's not when my thirst was."

She is "much attracted" to writers, like her beloved Henry James, "who see imagination as something to be exhausted. I'm bored with the received and the polemical, and I want the utter freedom of the imagination in the deepest literary way." Her newest novel is a "mirror, a book about an imaginary book." In *The Messiah of Stockholm,* she reinvents Bruno Schulz, the

389

Polish-Jewish writer, artist and translator (of Kafka into Polish) who was murdered by the Nazis, as well as his final opus, "The Messiah," a manuscript that in actuality remains lost and unpublished. "The whole idea of an imaginary library is so seductive. Here was an imaginary novel which at the same time wasn't imaginary because we know that Schulz did write that manuscript, we know it existed, we know he gave it to somebody for safekeeping." Although acknowledging that she may indeed revive interest in an "obscure" novelist, she explains that she also "felt the Schulzian ghost angrily at my back—particularly when I saw I needed to reproduce the insides of "The Messiah"—saying 'Who are you? Do you know Polish? Get out of my life!' "

The Messiah of Stockholm is dedicated to Philip Roth, who himself "imagined Anne Frank in *The Ghost Writer,* and here I am, in a sense, following him and imagining Bruno Schulz. But that wasn't in my head at the time I wrote the novel." Rather, as editor of Penguin's Writers From the Other Europe series, Roth personally brought Schulz to Ozick's attention. In 1977, she reviewed Schulz's *Street of Crocodiles* in the *New York Times Book Review* (included in *Art & Ardor,* Knopf, 1983). "He handed me Bruno Schulz, and I'm very grateful to him. Beyond that, I'm an enormous admirer of his." She adds that she "needed very much to ask Roth's permission because in no way did I want to seem to be attaching myself to his fame."

Furthermore, she visited Stockholm in the fall of 1984 because *The Cannibal Galaxy* was coming out in Swedish. "While I was there I heard the lost manuscript of Schulz's 'Messiah' had surfaced in Stockholm. It was only a rumor, of course. When I came home and began to write, I thought it would be a two-week short story, and a year and a quarter later it was this novella. I didn't know it was a novel and wanted to publish it with two other novellas, but Bob Gottlieb said, 'No, this is a novel.' "

She refers to Bob Gottlieb, who became her editor after Segal's untimely death in 1970, as "God Boblieb" and "the extraordinary Bob." She reminisces: "A few days after David's death, on the day Bob's first child was born, he called me from the hospital and said, 'Do not worry. I am going to be your publisher.' He did the same thing on another recent crisis day, the day the *New York Times* announced he was going to the *New Yorker*. On the day the whole world was at his feet clamoring for his attention, he took the trouble of calling me and saying, 'Don't worry. I'm going to be your publisher.' I don't know the details, but that's what he said." Ozick sees Gottlieb infrequently, "for two hours at five-year intervals," but "those two hours go deeply into the roots of all of life. I live on those two hours for the next five years. He has made suggestions and I have taken them: commonsensical things, such as my inability to do arithmetic and getting dates wrong, pragmatic things in the very confused *Cannibal Galaxy* manuscript [that needed revisions to avoid further legal tangles]."

Contending that, with the exception of John Updike, American writers are somewhat parochial, Ozick, who translates Yiddish poems and prose, and pens poems, essays, criticism, novels, novellas and short stories, "attempts to achieve this broad, broad sense of *belles lettres*." After *Trust* she switched to short stories (collected in *The Pagan Rabbi and Other Stories* and *Bloodshed and Three Novellas*, Knopf, 1971 and '76) because she didn't want to again place "all my eggs in one basket" and was exhausted by her "monstrously huge, ambitious, all-consuming" first efforts. Notwithstanding, her favorite fictional art form is "the true, big, fat novel. I long to write a large, many-charactered, many-placed, luxuriously voluptuous novel. I want to do *Middlemarch*. But I don't know whether I have the amplitude or whether the zeitgeist would, in fact, permit that."

She works in a book-lined room that is "tiny as a womb," writing in fountain-penned longhand on a desk "inherited" from her older brother at the age of eight. An electric typewriter sits atop a white marblelike table that was formerly used by patrons of her Uncle Louie's delicatessen. "My first draft is the last. I must perfect each sentence madly before I go on to the next," a method she dismissingly says she devised out of "sheer laziness, because at the end I want to be finished," while also conceding that "the demands I make on a sentence are the same demands I would make on a line of poetry." Adopting the late-night habits of her pharmacist parents, who worked until one in the morning during the Depression, Ozick begins to write late at night and finishes toward dawn, "when the racket of those damn birds comes. The depth of the night is guilt-free, responsibility-free; nobody will telephone you, importune you, make any claims on you. You own the world." Her *Messiah* features Swedish book critics with similar practices.

In this fashion and in this room, she is writing a novel on children of intermarriage, "half Gentiles, half Jews," the first chapter of which, entitled "At Fumicaro," appeared in the *New Yorker* in 1984. "I wonder what it must be like to be thus divided. When you put together two essentially colliding natures, cultures, temperaments, histories, and then you have a child who's bound genetically and loyally to both, what happens in the mind of that child?"

Ozick adds that although "the ironic dimension is always at work [in her fiction], looking at human beings and their pretensions," she hopes that she can begin to "explore the more sympathetic side of my temperament. I want very much to acquire the sympathetic vision of life because I know that as a reader I don't want to read what I write."

PENNY KAGANOFF

GRACE PALEY

GRACE PALEY HAS been a respected name in American letters for years. Her book of short stories *Later the Same Day* (Farrar, Straus & Giroux) confirms her as an utterly original American writer whose work combines personal, political and philosophical themes in a style quite unlike anyone else's.

Paley's characters—women and men who have committed themselves to trying to alleviate some of the world's myriad woes—usually appear in print as activists at demonstrations, marching with upraised fists. She has given them children, friends, lovers, aging parents, financial worries, shopping lists—in short, private lives to go with their public activities. Paley's work is political without being didactic, personal without being isolated from the real world.

This striking individuality accounts for the profound impact of Paley's writing, despite what is to her admirers a distressingly small body of work. Her first book, *The Little Disturbances of Man*, appeared in 1959; readers had to wait 15 years for the next one, *Enormous Changes at the Last Minute*, and just over a decade for *Later the Same Day*. "I do a lot of other things as well," explains the author. "I began to teach in the mid-'60s, and at the same time there was the Vietnam War, which really took up a lot of my time, especially since I had a boy growing towards draft age. And I'm just very distractable. My father used to say, 'You'll never be a writer, because you don't have any *sitzfleisch*,' which means sitting-down meat."

Her father's comment is hard to believe at the moment, as Paley sits tranquilly in a wooden rocking chair in the sunny living room of her Greenwich Village apartment. A small, plump woman in her early 60s, with short, white hair framing a round face, she resembles everyone's image of the ideal grandmother (so long as that image includes slacks, untucked shirttails and sneakers). As she does every Friday, she is simmering soup on the stove in her large, comfortable kitchen; she regrets that it's not ready yet, as she thinks it would be good for her interviewer's cold. She has to content herself with offering orange juice, vitamin C and antihistamines. Many of Paley's stories express her deep love of children; meeting her, one realizes almost immediately that her nurturing instincts extend beyond her own family to include friends and even a brand-new acquaintance. It's this pleasure in caring for others that makes her activisim seem so undogmatic and natural, a logical extension of the kind of work women have always done. It's more complex than that, of course—lifelong political commitments like Paley's don't arise out of anything so simple as a strong maternal instinct—but it helps to explain the matter-of-fact way in which the author and her characters approach political activity as the only possible response to the world's perilous state.

The direction of Paley's work is guided by similarly concrete considerations. One of the reasons she switched from poetry, her first love, to short stories was that she couldn't satisfactorily connect her verse with real life. "I'd been writing poetry until about 1956," she remembers, "and then I just sort of made up my mind that I had to write stories. I loved the whole tradition of poetry, but I couldn't figure out a way to use my own Bronx English tongue in poems. I can now, better, but those early poems were all very literary; they picked up after whatever poet I was reading. They used what I think of as only one ear: you have two ears, one is for the sound of literature and the other is for your neighborhood, for your mother and father's house."

Her parents had a strong influence on Paley, imbuing her with a sense of radical tradition. "I'm always interested in generational things," she says. "I'm interested in history, I'm interested in change, I'm interested in the future; so therefore I'm interested in the past. As the youngest child by a great deal, I grew up among adults talking about their lives. My parents were Russian

394

immigrants. They'd been exiled to Siberia by the czar when they were about 20, but when he had a son, he pardoned everyone under the age of 21, so they got out and came here right away. They didn't stay radical; they began to live the life of the immigrant—extremely patriotic, very hardworking—but they talked a lot about that period of their lives; they really made me feel it and see it, so there is that tradition. All of them were like that; my father's brothers and sister all belonged to different leftist political parties. My grandmother used to describe how they fought every night at the supper table and how hard it was on her!"

As Paley grew older, there were family tensions. "My parents didn't like the direction I was going politically," she recalls. "Although my father, who mistrusted a lot of my politics, came to agree with me about the Vietnam War; he was bitterly opposed to it." Her difficulties with her mother were more personal. "One of the stories in the new book, 'Lavinia,' was told to me by an old black woman, but it's also in a way *my* story," she says. "My mother, who couldn't do what she wanted because she had to help my father all the time, had great hopes for me. She was just disgusted, because all I wanted to do at a certain point was marry and have kids. I looked like a bust to my family, just like the girl Lavinia, who I'm convinced will turn out very well.

"There's no question," she continues, "that children are distracting and that for some of the things women want to do, their sense is right: they shouldn't have children. And they shouldn't feel left out, because the children of the world are their children too. I just feel lucky that I didn't grow up in a generation where it was stylish not to. I only had two—I wish I'd had more."

The experience of her own children confirmed Paley's belief that each generation is shaped by the specific historical events of its time. "I often think of those kids in the Brinks case," she says, referring to the surviving fragments of the SDS, who were involved in the murder of a bank guard during an attempted robbery in the early 1980s, after they had spent years underground. "If they had been born four years later, five years earlier. . . . It really was that particular moment: they were called. In one of the new stories ["Friends"], I talk about that whole beloved generation of our children who were really wrecked. I mean, I lived through the Second World War, and I only knew one person in my generation who died. My children, who are in their early

30s, I can't tell you the number of people they know who have died or gone mad. They're a wonderful generation, though: thoughtful, idealistic, self-giving and honorable. They really gave.

"The idea that mothers and fathers raise their kids is ridiculous," Paley thinks. "You do a little bit—if you're rich, you raise a rich kid, okay—but the outside world is always there, waiting to declare war, to sell drugs, to invade another country, to raise the rents so you can't afford to live someplace—to really color your life. One of the nice things that happens when you have kids," Paley goes on, "is that you really get involved in the neighborhood institutions. If you don't become a local communitarian worker then, I don't know when you do. For instance, when my kids were very little, the city was trying to push a road through Washington Square Park to serve the real estate interests. We fought that and we won; in fact, having won, my friends and I had a kind of optimisim for the next 20 years that we might win something else by luck." She laughs, as amused by her chronic optimism as she is convinced of its necessity. "It took a lot of worry, about the kids and buses going through the park at a terrific rate, to bring us together. You can call it politics or not; it becomes a common concern, and it can't be yours alone any more."

Paley believes such common concerns will shape future political activism. "One of the things that really runs through all the stories, because they're about groups of women, is the sense that what we need now is to bond; we need to say 'we' every now and then instead of 'I' every five minutes," she comments. "We've gone through this period of individualism and have sung that song, but it may not be the important song to sing in the times ahead. The Greenham women [antinuclear demonstrators who set up a permanent camp outside the principal British missile base] are very powerful and interesting. When I went there the first time, I saw six women sitting on wet bales of hay wearing plastic raincoats and looking miserable. It was late November, and they said that on December 12 they were having this giant demonstration. I thought, 'Oh, these poor women. Do they really believe this?' Well, three weeks later, on December 12, they had 30,000 women there. You really have to keep at it," she concludes. "It's vast; it's so huge you can hardly think about it. The power against us is so great and so foolish."

Yet Paley has never despaired—she notes in the story "Ruthy and Edie" that her characters are "ideologically, spiritually and on puritanical principle" against that particular emotion. "People accomplish things," she asserts. "You can't give up. And you can't retreat into personal, personal, personal life, because personal, personal, personal life is *hard:* to live in it without any common feelings for others around you is disheartening. I would think. Some people just fool themselves, decide they have to make a lot of money and then go out and do it, but I can't feel like that." Her voice is low and passionate. "I think these are very rough times. I'm really sorry for people growing up right now, because they have some cockeyed idea that they can get by with their eyes closed; the cane they're tapping is money, and that won't take them in the right direction."

Despite the enormous amount of time and energy political matters absorb in Paley's life, they remain in the background of her fiction. "I feel I haven't written about certain things yet that I probably will at some point," she says. "I've written about the personal lives of these people; I haven't really seen them in political action, and I don't know if I need to especially, for what I'm trying to do. There has to be a way of writing about it that's right and interesting, but I haven't figured it out. I've mainly been interested in this personal political life. But I refer peripherally to things: in 'Living' in *Enormous Changes,* where [the protagonist] is bleeding to death, she remembers praying for peace on Eighth Street with her friend; in 'Zagrowsky Tells' in *Later the Same Day,* he's furious because they picketed his drugstore. That's the way a lot of politics gets in, as part of ordinary people's lives, and that's really the way I want to show it, it seems to me now. What I want is for these political people to really be *seen.*"

The people who aren't seen much in *Later the Same Day* are men: Jack, the live-in lover of Faith (Paley's alter ego among her work's recurring characters), is a fairly well developed presence, but the book's focus is strongly female. "It wasn't that I didn't want to talk about men," Paley explains, "but there is so much female life that has so little to do with men and is *so* not-talked-about. Even though Faith tells Susan [in 'Friends'], 'You still have him-itis, the dread disease of females,' and they all have a little bit of that in them; much of their lives really does not, especially as they get older. I haven't even *begun* to write about really older women; I've only gotten them into their late 40s and early 50s."

Is Paley bringing her characters along to her own current stage of life? "I'm very pressed right now for time to write; I just feel peevish about it," she says. "But I've always felt that all these things have strong pulls: the politics takes from the writing, the children take from the politics, and the writing took from the children, you know. Someone once said, 'How did you manage to do all this with the kids around?' and I made a joke; I said, 'Neglect!' But the truth is, all those things pull from each other, and it makes for a very interesting life. So I really have no complaints at all."

WENDY SMITH

JAY PARINI

"Sometimes I wish Vermont would secede from the Union."
Poet and novelist Jay Parini is cheerfully urging his dusty station
wagon along roads edged by rolling hills. A turtle begins to cross
the highway, its small body lurching forward on a furtive path.
Few houses rest on the surrounding green. And no billboards
rear their ugly heads—Vermonters banned them from the landscape years ago, leaving it to the custody of maples and the simple sleep of dairy cattle.

This New England scene of postcard-proverbial peace has been
Parini's home since he joined the faculty of Middlebury College
in 1982. Vermont, for him a comfortable " '60s enclave," where
nature is not taken for granted and where many New York City
writers bolt for at least part of the year, "makes you feel / the
gravity afoot, the tug of light / particulars, the sway of chosen
hours . . . / life in slow concentric circles," he has observed.

Parini is plainly a writer with a sense of place. His own place is
a "quirky white Victorian" house on a hill in the village of Wey-
bridge, where for the past five years, with his wife and fellow
writer Devon Jersild and young sons Will and Oliver, he has
been at work on *The Last Station* (Holt). Set in Russia of 1910,
the novel concerns the tumultuous final year in the stormy life of
novelist Leo Tolstoy as narrated by Tolstoy himself, his wife, his
physician, his daughter Sasha, his personal secretary Valentin
Bulgakov and other camp followers, including the splendidly
machinating Vladimir Chertkov. A famous, aged, tireless ideo-
logue increasingly dogged by a sense of sin, Tolstoy made a

last-ditch effort to reform at the age of 82, running away from his estate and family, falling ill, and seeking shelter at the home of a railway station master in Astapovo, where he died in November 1910, surrounded by warring disciples, family factions and dozens of newspaper reporters.

The novel's point of view alters with every chapter, each told in the first person and titled with the name of the character in command. Though based on fact, it relies on Parini's powers of invention—and includes excerpts from Tolstoy's writings and reconstructed or imagined conversations. Along wih his chosen personae, Parini lends his own: three poems, addressing the action, are interspersed among the chapters under the sly heading "J.P."

"The novel was more dictated to me than written," Parini insists. "In a sense, I played a role very much like Bulgakov's—I was Tolstoy's secretary. I lived all those lives for several years. I know their voices intimately."

Parini is the author of six previous books: three collections of poetry, two novels and a critical study of the American poet Theodore Roethke. In none of these has Tolstoy figured. Yet this man, born a count, who chose to live as Russia's most renowned would-be peasant, has long preoccupied Parini. "I've spent 25 years reading his novels and stories and essays, and I've read all the Tolstoy critical books and biographies. One day about five years ago, I was reading the diaries of Bulgakov, and something clicked. I said to myself, 'Omigod—everybody was keeping diaries and recording the last year in Tolstoy's life!' His last year struck me as an ideal vehicle for exploring the thing that I'm most interested in: the radical subjectivity of experience, and the impossibility of arriving at anything like objective truth.

"There is no such thing as one clear view of the world," Parini continues. "It's been a great project of modernism to explore subjectivity: Picasso defined cubism as a dance around the object. In many ways, I've tried to write a cubist novel, the object being Tolstoy. And even Tolstoy is 'dancing around the object.'

"At heart, Tolstoy was a fierce Manichaean, dividing the world into good and evil, black and white. But the artist in him was always at war with the moralist. I share with him the Rousseauistic faith in the possibility for an earthly paradise—for human redemption on this earth. Tolstoy's values were egalitarian, ecologically sound;

he believed in education as the key to making things better for the people. But he also had a powerful puritanical streak that ruined his life. I'm scared of Tolstoy's fanaticism—as he was himself. He had a huge ego, and struggled with it, but never resolved it. He had grown up as a traditional 19th-century Russian aristocrat, and a great deal was permitted him that would never be permitted to anyone today. Tolstoy hated the fact that the artist in him was too strong to suppress; almost in spite of himself, he wrote great novels.

"Tolstoy's greatness was his ability to be direct in his writing. He writes *so* directly about the natural world and about people. I think greatness in writing always comes down to the clarity, the openness and the directness of the writing.

"Tolstoy is for me such an important figure because the contradictions in his life are contradictions that we all have to deal with. If we want to be serious, moral people, we have to somehow look around us and feel the paradoxes of living in a country of wealth where there's poverty everywhere. That is what Tolstoy felt about Russia."

Parini is himself no stranger to economic hardship. "I come from a lower-middle-class background, and I have always been very sensitive to class issues," he says. "I grew up in Scranton, Pa., a very impoverished place. My father was an insurance salesman with the Prudential Insurance Company and a part-time Baptist preacher. *His* father was a gangster who abandoned the family when my father was 12. My uncles were coal miners and ditch diggers. We were strained to our economic limits; I was the first person in my extended family ever to graduate from college. So I saw the truth of the country, in some ways: America really is quite a hard place in which to make a living.

"My father was a very moral man, an upstanding fellow and a preacher. I think I may have in me something of the Baptist preacher. And I'm attracted to the preacher in Tolstoy. I'm drawn to figures who are messianic. I grew up listening to Baptist oratory, and understood the power of language to move people."

Attending Lafayette College, Parini spent his junior year abroad at the University of St. Andrews in Scotland, and ended up staying seven years, earning a B.Phil. and a Ph.D. in English. In part, he says he wanted to leave the U.S. behind during an inglorious era of its history—the Vietnam War. But he also "fled Scranton as a barely postadolescent romantic in search of civilization." St. Andrews's "chief advantage was that it was *not* Scranton."

At St. Andrews he also became fast friends with Alastair Reid, the Scots-born poet and *New Yorker* writer. Reid, now a frequent Vermont houseguest, recalls Parini's customary visits at the conclusion of daily runs, when the young man would appear on Reid's doorstep panting and offering up for scrutiny "a limp, sweaty poem."

While in Scotland, Parini wrote his first novel, which he prefers to keep to himself. In 1972 his first book, a collection of poetry entitled *Singing in Time*, was published by "a very small" Scottish press. Three years later, he began teaching English at Dartmouth College. His second book, *Theodore Roethke: An American Romantic*, was published by the University of Massachusetts Press in 1979. Originally Parini's doctoral dissertation, it had been submitted to his "wizened, little" Scottish college tutor and returned unmarked save for a consistent erasure: the word "masturbation" had been blacked out 17 times and replaced by the phrase "self-directed pleasure."

Perhaps diametrically opposite to that effort was Parini's first published novel, *The Love Run*, brought out by Atlantic–Little, Brown in 1980 and edited by former *PW* editor-in-chief Arnold Ehrlich. "One of the reasons I turned to fiction was Erich Segal," Parini remembers. Crowing over the sale of a poem to the *New Yorker* for all of $35, Parini was chagrined to learn from Segal that *Oliver's Story* had earned millions. He then resolved to seek the commercial stratosphere. With the lickety-split, 10-week-long literary collaboration of Reid and Devon Jersild, whom he had met when she was his student at Dartmouth, Parini set off on a jeu d'esprit that led to the loss of his job.

As he explains it today, Parini simply wanted out of Dartmouth's "vicious atmosphere" of the late '70s—"right-wing, smelly, snobby, deeply anti-intellectual and misogynistic." He figured, "Well, if I make a million dollars, I won't have to teach." The undisguised depiction of Dartmouth in his novel as a hypocritical, preppy ivory tower caused a virulent reaction from alumni and administrators, and despite strong support from the Dartmouth faculty, Parini was denied tenure.

However, he debuted first as a character in fiction, not a novelist. While putting the finishing touches on *The Love Run* during the summer of 1979, Parini stayed in the Connecticut home of close friend Ann Beattie, then at work on *Falling in Place*. "We'd have dinner and talk all night. Next day, I'd go into the city and see Arnold, and Ann would work on her novel. I'd come home and read over her shoulder, and she'd read over mine. I'd often see last night's conversation on the page." There Parini also found what he calls "a version of myself"—the frenetic, peripatetic, happily mad poet Bobby, hopeless romantic, ceaseless womanizer and versifier. (The namesake of *Picturing Will*, Beattie's latest novel, is Parini's seven-year-old son.)

Beattie, along with the late Robert Penn Warren, was also responsible for introducing Parini to Rob Cowley, then an editor at Random House, who in 1982 published *Anthracite Country*, Parini's second book of poems. "He is one of the great modern editors," says Parini, heaping praise on Cowley for his skillful editing of *The Patch Boys*, Parini's first "real novel," published by Holt— where Cowley had traveled—in 1986. Rewritten "over, over, over, over and over again," *Patch Boys* tells the largely autobiographical, often comical story of Sammy, a boy growing up in northeastern Pennsylvania during the 1920s as the coal miners' union movement was gathering force. "A lot of the incidents are taken straight from my father's life. He sees it as his own story, and I see it as mine." A third collection of poetry, *Town Life*, appeared from Holt in 1988, edited by Cowley. *The Last Station* was edited by Amy Hertz of Holt, who helped the author cut its length by half.

Parini's days, despite his country setting, are busy. While teaching at Middlebury, he is finishing work on a new book of poems; writing a screenplay; making notes on a projected novel about Christopher Columbus; cohosting an educational cable TV program, *The Classics*; and planning a public TV documentary series on contemporary authors. *The Last Station* is attracting interest from Hollywood—as of this writing, Telly Savalas, among others, is reportedly keen on playing Tolstoy, with hopes for Diane Keaton as his costar. Parini has also agreed to edit four books of poetry a year for Barney Rosset's Blue Moon Books and to lend an editorial hand at the University Press of New England. He is mulling over three possible sequels to *The Patch Boys*.

Yet there are still chances to take long walks over country roads deserted but for the occasional pickup truck, lollygagging basset hound or oddly humorous cow convocation—row upon row of oblivious shanks and heads bobbing at feeding time. Considering the compelling call of Vermont "town life," Parini tells the story of a local old salt he recently encountered. He asked the fellow, "Have you lived in Vermont all your life?' " Brief pause. More briefly still, the gent replied, "Not yet."

MOLLY MCQUADE

ROBERT B. PARKER

Robert B. Parker is the creator of Spenser, that wisecracking, weight-lifting, Boston-based, literary, gourmet cook of a detective whose nature is a combination of toughness and compasssion. Spenser has wit and range: he can describe himself as wearing "a tie asserted by a simple pin" or address an adversary as "Trout Breath." In Parker's novel *Crimson Joy,* Spenser's task is to find a serial murderer before the culprit gets to his longtime love, Susan Silverman.

We talk in the Parker family home, an 1869 Victorian within, as it were, shooting distance of Harvard Square in Cambridge, Mass. The handsome house could be termed fantasy Victorian, eclectically and imaginatively decorated by Parker's wife, Joan: we sit in Parker's study in the front of the house, guarded by his young German short-haired pointer, Pearl. On Parker's desk is a small manual typewriter, and on that rests the next Spenser novel, finished two days previously and ready for the typist— about three months in the writing. "First draft?" we ask. "Also last," says Parker.

At 55, Parker—a burly, irreverent man with a grand sense of humor—is 15 years into his detective-writing career and one of the top names in detective fiction; his titles include *Valediction, A Catskill Eagle, Taming a Sea Horse, Pale Kings and Princes.* The first Spenser novel, *The Godwulf Manuscript,* was written with a typewriter Parker "liberated" from Northeastern University, where he taught before resigning to write full time, and where he also used to "liberate" the English Department's coffee

405

money for bridge tolls to make it home to his wife and two sons, Daniel and David, now an actor and a dancer, respectively, in New York. Since the TV series *Spenser: For Hire* has been canceled, Parker and his wife are pursuing other possibilities; they've just incorporated Pearl Productions for film production and hope to make it a family business.

Parker is primarily a Massachusetts product—born in Springfield, raised there and in New Bedford. He stayed in New England for college (Colby College, in Maine), went to Korea in the service, then came back to Boston University, picking up a Ph.D. by writing a doctoral dissertation on Raymond Chandler, Dashiell Hammett and Ross Macdonald in two weeks. "It went directly from my typewriter to microfilm unseen by the human eye," Parker has said. Then came the teaching stints, the last at Northeastern. Parker doesn't miss the university except for the gym, and he works out at a health club. "Joan and I both belong—she's in better shape than Jane Fonda."

Parker clearly adores his wife, the prototype for the psychologist Susan in the Spenser novels. The dedication to *Wilderness* reads: "This is for Joan, in whom God finally got it right." Together, they wrote *Three Days in Spring*, about the period in 1975 when she discovered that she had breast cancer, from which she is completely recovered. The couple were separated for a time, a fact mirrored in the books. "You write what you've got," Parker says. "One could not make any stab at tracing our relationship by reading the books in any literal way. But estrangement and reunification have taken place in the books and have taken place in my life, and it would be foolhardy to suggest otherwise.

"We were separated for two years. We got ourselves straightened out and found the way to live—which is together and yet apart." Joan has a kitchen and bath and bedroom on the third floor with a separate entrance, "and we cut an entrance through the inside: I didn't want to trundle up there in my bathrobe in January by going out front. That's *her* place, to be technical. I don't seem to have a place. It works out very well. The relationship was worth the difficulty. It has worked out so well that I'm glad it happened, although it was unpleasant while it was happening."

The male-female relationship is central to Parker's writing. "It's what the work is about really, in its most recent years, and it grounds the novels. The [late] president of the National League, A. Bartlett Giamatti, once said that I wrote about love better than anybody in the country, and he specified that he meant not just love for woman, but love of man for child, of woman for man, love of sweat, love of exercise, love of work. He told me that personally, when he was preparing for his position by being the president of Yale."

Is Spenser a simplified version of Robert B. Parker? "Yes and no. Certainly he doesn't think or know things that I can't think or know. He can't feel things that I can't feel. He is, in the sense of being a romantic hero, larger than life. He's braver than I am, he's taller than I am. But the connection between character and author is fascinating and inexplicable. No writer I know can deal with that."

And the detective as a figure of romance? "He's the evolution-ary descendant of the frontier hero, who is an evolutionary de-scendant of the chivalric hero. He's romantic in the Northrop Frye sense, in that he's superior to other humans but not to na-ture. He's braver than normal, and he's immune to temptation, whether it be money or sex, or the threat of death, and he does what we'd all like to do—that is, he's entirely autonomous. What makes him interesting is the struggle for his autonomy; for Spenser, it's a continuing struggle. Part of the reason he has to struggle is that he has allowed himself to be in love and to care. The struggle between care and commitment and autonomy lends tension to the form."

How people behave, the code by which they live and its suffi-ciency, or lack of it, are recurring themes in Parker's work. "That's what I'm interested in—is it sufficient? No. Nobody gets out of here alive, but it certainly is better than no code. If you know how you think you ought to behave, you may not always behave that way, but it's better than not knowing how you should behave. It helps you to be happier, I think, but is not a successful stay against confusion, finally, because the world is too compli-cated and too difficult for any single code to succeed, which is what various religions of the world, the zealots of all persuasions, have never fully understood.

"Machismo got a bad name starting with the feminist movement, where it was used to label male behavior that women found offensive. But if you called it a commitment to honorable behavior, it wouldn't sound half as awful. Machismo is committed to the idea that one's goodness is tested in physical success and some kind of violent circumstances. It's a perfectly coherent conception, but it seems to place an undue burden on young men growing up and is not as suitable an alternative as others. If you think of machismo as a variation on the chivalric code, which is what it really is—Lancelot was machismo—then it doesn't sound so bad. To act courageously and to refuse to be dishonored isn't a bad code. Its applications sometimes get out of hand. It's got the same place that the chivalric code had—not terribly useful, but a way to live."

The phone rings, and it's Parker's wife, who's been nursing a cold, calling from the upper reaches of the house. "Hello. How are we today?" Parker says. "Oh, that's very encouraging. How high? That's pretty good for grown-ups. How's the throat? Excellent. Pearl is now kissing [their dog] Miss Smith in the ear," Parker observes, and then negotiates: "I gotta go sign a few books at a bookstore, and you could come with me and make that less an odious task, and then I'll go to New Hampshire and pick up your drapes—how about a trade-off?"

Parker began his publishing career with Houghton Mifflin and then, after five books, shifted to Dell. The novel after *Crimson Joy* will be published by Putnam. "Houghton Mifflin thought they had something hot, then changed their minds and thought they had something stable. I switched to Dell and Delacorte—it was Seymour Lawrence who recruited me—and I changed agents. My first agent was fine, [but] he was just too busy, and I was low man on the totem pole. He had many writers who made him a lot more money than I did, and he allocated his time accordingly, which I would have done if I were he. But I wanted someone who would allocate time to me. I switched to Helen Brann, who seemed to feel from the very beginning that she could help me to become a brand-name author. And she has. She's a wonderful agent.

"Dell has done a wonderful job with me, [but] there were a series of incidents when Dell was in transition, when it was owned by Doubleday and half-managed by Doubleday and half-managed by the people who were supposed to be managing it, and we got caught in a crack. . . . We had the opportunity to sign with Putnam, without any option clauses, for more money than we had been offered by Dell. Then Bertelsmann took over, and I think if that had happened earlier, we wouldn't have left. Which is not to say I'm not quite happy to be at Putnam—I think Phyllis Grann is everything everyone says she is. If I were a writer starting out now, I'd seriously consider Dell again and might consider them again in the future. The Bertelsmann takeover and the Bantam fusion have made it an excellent place to publish.

"Being an originator of a reasonably successful television series makes everyone perceive you differently, and I think that was probably a big help. It convinced everybody in the publishing world that it would get me more readers. I suspect there's not as much overlap as everyone thinks. I have a feeling they may be two separate markets.

"One of the most irritating things about the publishing business is that people treat the author as if he were Leo Tolstoy— 'yes sir, no sir'—that no one ever pays any serious attention to you. They treat you like a precocious child, and they don't want you to have a tantrum. 'Oh, Bob, you're great, we love you, this is the greatest book that ever lived.' In the old days I used to say, 'If this is the greatest book ever written, how come you're only printin' up 15,000 copies?' " I appreciate their solicitousness, but it would be easier if we could all talk as if we were grownups. I'd love to have one publisher somewhere, someplace, say, 'The book may sell, but I didn't like it personally.' But nobody ever does. 'You look funny in your jacket photo, Bob'—that would be good."

Parker's work is popular beyond the U.S. shores. In Japan there's a guide to Spenser's Boston and a book of Spenser's recipes, as well as a line of men's cosmetics called "Spenser's Tactics." Forthcoming from Dell is a cookbook, done in collaboration with Kate Mattes of Kate's Mystery Books in Cambridge. Parker is "doodling" on five "movie-ish" projects, and he characterizes his life with Joan this way: "We work out, we eat out, we take some trips, we work on the projects, we work on the house, we visit our sons, they visit us. And we travel some, almost always on business. We went to England on a book tour last year, Denver, San Francisco, Carmel—it's tough, dirty work, but someone's got to do it.

"Being a celebrity writer is not so intrusive that you can't stand it. It's a minor irritation which results from a great deal of positive stuff—it's like getting a rash from drinking champagne. The hell with it, I'll drink the champagne."

AMANDA SMITH

RICHARD POWERS

Richard powers is a writer whose brillance has so far been matched by his anonymity. As far as standard author reference works are concerned, he doesn't exist. Literally nothing has been known about him—and he'd just as soon keep it that way. What little hard fact he wishes to reveal about himself can be told in one sentence—and that is in fact what appears on the jacket of the most recent of his three novels, *The Gold Bug Variations* (Morrow). No picture. No birthplace. No dates. No place of residence. Simply "Richard Powers is the author of *Prisoner's Dilemma* and *Three Farmers on Their Way to a Dance.*"

Even the bound galley of *Gold Bug* had a tad more information than that, reminding us that *Three Farmers* was a finalist for the National Book Award in 1985, informing us that Powers was the recipient of a MacArthur Foundation so-called "genius" grant, and recycling a few rave reviews.

In person Powers is no more forthcoming, though it is not an aloof personality he presents. Tall and rangy, with a penetrating, tender and humorous gaze, a flashing grin and a mind that seems as fully stocked as his books with knowledge, cross-references and sometimes arcane perceptions, he meets us in a suite at New York City's Plaza Hotel, where Morrow has seen fit to ensconce him. He is somewhat bemused by this, feeling that the kind of anonymity he craves would have been better served by a chain motel; at the same time there is a small boy's pleasure in the luxury and attentive service. He is ruefully resigned to the fact that he can no longer hide completely from the world: "All that is coming to a crashing end, unfortunately."

Still, old habits die hard, and when *PW* tries to start off with such staples as his age, place of birth and where he was brought up and educated, we are firmly but pleasantly put off. "I really don't see what connection all that has with the work," he explains patiently. "It's not what we should be looking at. All that sort of thing [author publicity] just creates confusion about the nature of the book, deflects attention from what you've done. That's what always seems to happen in this culture: you grab hold of a personality and ignore the work."

He has decided to break his anonymity sufficiently to do some interviews (his first in this country), partly to support *Gold Bug Variations*—"It's a long, tough book, and it can use all the help I can give it"—but also partly because "I feel more confident now about being able to handle it." Powers had broken the ice a few weeks previously by giving an interview to a Dutch magazine (he has been living in an obscure corner of southern Holland "off and on" for the past four or five years while working on *Gold Bug*), had even been photographed standing at a surviving stretch of the old Siegfried Line of German WW II defenses. It can be revealed here that Powers is 33 or 34 (he was born in 1957, as disclosed by the Library of Congress CIP data in his new novel), was born and brought up, by one or two references he let slip, somewhere in the Midwest. He probably went to school there too, though this is mere conjecture based on clues in his work.

One of the most impressive features of *Gold Bug* is the extraordinary range of detailed knowledge it displays, about subjects as various as genetic codes, the inner workings of Bach's *Goldberg Variations*, which gives the book its title and much of its exotic structure, 16-century Flemish painting and the manipulations possible in a giant computer database. A few more cracks let in light on the unknown. Yes, Powers was for a time a computer professional, also had "a quasi-preprofessional knowledge of music, as a studious cellist for many years." He had to study and read a great deal to write the novel, but "I don't know any of those subjects as well as a professional would know them; anything I learned would be available to anyone who wanted to know it. But the research doesn't compare with what you'd have to do for a nonfiction book, though I agree a novel doesn't usually get into that amount of material."

The intellectual pleasure, for Powers, lies in "the discovery of a resonance you don't entirely understand. For instance, I've long had a fascination with the Bach *Variations*, which is a work that doesn't yield itself up immediately, and also with the genetic code, and I began to see a relationship between these seemingly independent images, and could fuse them into three-dimensionality. Once you have all the pointers, anyone can master anything; it doesn't depend on vast reservoirs of previous knowledge."

What Powers doesn't say, of course, is that it does require uncommon intelligence, imagination and fluency to fuse together such disparate elements and at the same time create several touching love stories around them. He does say, earnestly, "I wanted to see if it was possible to write a novel that involves the whole person—including the intellectual side; to get those two inimicals, the head and the heart, going at the same time"; and, more playfully, "I thought I'd lure the reader in with a love story, though of course there's much more to it than that." There is indeed. The book, which interweaves early and late years in the life of Stuart Ressler, a brilliant genetic scientist who somehow lost his way, a young woman librarian who is searching for the key to existence, and a computer programmer with a passion for an obscure Flemish artist, is at once dazzling and challenging, as Powers is the first to admit: "There are those chunks of discursiveness unsupported by narrative."

Gold Bug is the latest, and most ambitious, in a trio of novels that have been, frankly and unabashedly, novels of ideas. Written within a seemingly limitless frame of reference, all concern, in one way or another, the mysteries of time, the problems of living in a confusing century and nothing less than making sense, at the profoundest level, of what human life is all about. Powers confesses himself overwhelmed at his sense of the rate at which molecules are disappearing, his "apocalyptic vision of the impossible challenge of the future we're building for ourselves." He thinks that although "we probably don't have the power to change anything, that doesn't exonerate us from the responsibility of at least making an effort."

In an enthusiastic blurb on the back cover of *Gold Bug*, Bob Shacochis asserts that "Powers equals Pynchon minus paranoia";

413

and in fact there is a kinship between these solitary souls in their brainpower, their sense of the density of life, their postmodernist fusion of history, politics and science—and, of course, their deliberate shunning of the limelight. And, like pretty well everything else, that comparison seems to have occurred to Powers too. "I used to think that Pynchon had the right idea, that his was the way to get on with your work. Now I think that in some way he has been defeated by the game, made captive by it, hasn't reaped the sort of freedom he had probably hoped for."

How did Powers's brief but already remarkable career begin? He talks of "the usual apprenticeship" before *Three Farmers* burst on the scene. While still at school he found that "shorter forms were easier to sustain," so he wrote stories. His first novel, he says, "sort of sprang full-blown" from his head. He was doing what he describes as "technical work," at the same time reading for pleasure several books, including a biography of Henry Ford and Barbara Tuchman's *The Guns of August,* when he saw, in an (unnamed) fine arts museum, a retrospective of the work of photographer August Sander, including the image of the Polish farmers dressed in their Sunday best on the eve of WW I. It became the inspiration for, and eventual cover illustration of, the novel.

Once the book had come together in his head, Powers quit his job, wrote the novel and began to look for an agent. Even that banal search gets the Powers touch: "I started looking in the middle of the agent listings in *LMP.* I thought a lot of people would begin at the beginning, and others at the end, so I went for the middle." The agent (unnamed, of course) sent it out, and "as far as I know Morrow was the first publisher that saw it." The viewer there was senior editor and Beech Tree Books head James Landis, who went on to publish the author's subsequent books and whose recent departure from the house was a blow to Powers. *PW* recalls the excitement with which Landis had called to ensure proper attention to *Three Farmers,* and Powers is somber: "Yes, he would do that, and I wonder who else will. I was deeply sorry to see him go."

This leads him to thoughts on the current state of publishing and writing in America. "It's so fatally easy for a writer to be distracted from his real purpose, to be sucked into a runaway condition of second-guessing. I can't be thinking all the time about whether Morrow will publish my next book or who'll read it there. Publishing may be a business, but writing is decidedly *not*—and who's going to buffer you from that? Ultimately it has to be me, and I don't want to do it. As a writer, I need the freedom to be out there without a safety net. Sam Shepard said something wonderful: 'I don't want a career, I just want to write the things I want to write.' That's just what I feel. Too many writers are looking for careers, and they get co-opted by the business; then you don't have a literature, you have just another aspect of the marketplace."

Powers has as pure a vision of the writer's role as we have heard. What he sees as success in his life is "whether I've contributed to the success of the writing animal in general—if I've made a contribution to what writing can achieve, and has achieved." He goes on, earnestly, but with such conviction that he doesn't sound pretentious: "The kind of life I'm trying to live is one where everything I read is valuable in some way, contributes to what I'm trying to do. The real glory of making a living as a writer is that there's no sickening divide, as there is for most people, between what you do and what you want to do." He's aware, of course, that his generous MacArthur grant, which has three more years to run, makes such a life easier for him: "I realize most people don't have that luxury."

Life in America, from which he exiled himself while he wrote about it, is a constant source of wonder to Powers. "It's hardly a culture, just an amazing mess—depressing, in a way, for a writer, because you know you'd just never be able to touch all the notes you'd like to. One of the great things about American fiction today is its outrageousness; you've only got to read certain writers to realize the country is wonderfully mad." He talks admiringly of Paul Auster and William Vollman, then stops, because he doesn't want to carelessly omit someone he admires.

Yes, he's working on another book, but he describes it as "very different—it doesn't require as much outside reading"—and in terms of style and range he's decided, he says with his infectious grin, to "reign in the gas a bit."

The ever-stimulating conversation voyages, like Power's novels, to the ultimate meaning of life itself. "What is the most successful strain of life?" Powers has his questing—and charming—librarian ask herself in *Gold Bug;* and has her answer, as he now tells *PW:* "A defective question. . . . Life is the sole strain,

415

perpetually becoming, a single, diversified proposition that succeeds altogether or not at all."

That's the dead serious side of Powers. The other is revealed when the Plaza waiter brings up a room service lunch and offers the bill to *PW* to sign. "You see!" he exclaims delightedly. "He automatically gave it to the guy in the suit."

JOHN F. BAKER

ANNE RICE

W RITERS WITH A large, avid following are not always noted for the literary quality of their creations. But Anne Rice, a novelist so prolific she needs two pseudonymns—Anne Rampling and A. N. Roquelaure—to distinguish the disparate voices in her books, has won both critical acclaim and a readership of cult proportions since she published *Interview with the Vampire*, the first of what is now celebrated as The Vampire Chronicles. On Halloween, or "All Hallow's Eve" as she terms it, Knopf officially published the third installment in the series, *The Queen of the Damned*.

Rather than awaiting the publication of her latest work in San Francisco, where she has lived for the past 28 years, Rice, her husband, poet and painter Stan Rice, and their 10-year-old son, Christopher, relocated in Rice's native New Orleans. Over coffee in the sunlit kitchen of their elegantly furnished 1859 townhouse, Rice—a pleasingly modulated California speech covering her Southern roots—says that the transition has been both happy and stimulating. Stan, who is on leave from his tenured position at San Francisco State University, has already finished four large paintings. Their new home is in the same neighborhood where Rice was raised: cousins are just around the corner in the house where her grandfather died, and from her upstairs bedroom Rice can see the side-by-side spires of St. Mary's Assumption Church, built in 1858 by German Catholics and now a National Historic Landmark, and St. Alphonsus Church, consecrated the same year for Irish Catholics, two blocks away. "Those were my ancestors," explains Rice, who is no longer a Catholic communicant. "I had a German great-grandmother. All the rest were Irish."

She finds New Orleans greatly changed since the time when her father was transferred to Dallas and moved his family of four daughters to suburban Richardson, Texas. "When I left, the city was out of touch; it was like a Caribbean outpost. Going from here to Texas was like stepping through TV to the world of America we had seen from afar. But that was a wonderful thing for me as a writer, to grow up in this foreign city and then discover America at age 15."

Now, New Orleans offers the best of both worlds—the old and the new—and has a vigorous arts community as well, according to Rice. "When I was a kid, people associated New Orleans with local-color writers, quaint writers. Now we know that Sherwood Anderson and Faulkner wrote here, but that wasn't talked about then." Her favorite reading included Victorian and Edwardian horror books she checked out from the old New Orleans Public Library on Lee Circle.

Only after she married Stan, her Texas high school sweetheart, and they moved to California to work and put themselves through San Francisco State, did she become acquainted with Louisiana history and such classic New Orleans writers as George Washington Cable and Grace King.

"I began to be haunted by the past," recalls Rice, who received an MA in creative writing in 1972. "I went to the University of California library at Berkeley and began reading everything I could find about Louisiana. Eventually much of that information went into *Interview with the Vampire* and *The Feast of All Saints*," the latter concerned with people of color in antebellum New Orleans. "I had found a wonderful description of these people, including the fact that quadroon men had started the first literary magazine published in Louisiana. And I had sort of fallen in love with them." But first she wrote *Interview with the Vampire*, "and that research was right at my fingertips—what kind of wallpaper there would be, when there were gas lamps, the architecture, all that sort of thing." Often research can be creative, Rice points out. "Sometimes when I read nonfiction, my mind is just popping with ideas for a novel." *The Queen of the*

Damned draws "quite a bit" on the history and archaeology books she favors.

The first vampire novel, however, actually began as one of a series of short stories Rice set out to write, working every night in the late '60s. One evening Rice sat down at her typewriter without any idea of what direction the story would take. " 'Do you want to hold the interview here?' asked the vampire," she began, a line she regrets omitting from the novel that later germinated. "It was just a brief thing originally," says Rice, "but over the years I would rewrite it, deepening it a little each time. Just after Michelle died [the Rices' first child, who succumbed to leukemia in 1972] I showed it to Stan and a good friend of ours, and both remarked that there was really something there."

Rice continued to work on the tale, expecting to include it in a collection she planned to enter in a short-story contest sponsored by the University of Iowa. But to her surprise, the story began to develop into something larger. "I got to the point where the vampire began describing his brother's death, and the whole thing just exploded! Suddenly, in the guise of Louis, a fantasy figure, I was able to touch the reality that was mine. It had something to do with growing up in New Orleans, this strange, decadent city full of antebellum houses. It had something to do with my old-guard Catholic background. It had something to do with the tragic loss of my daughter and with the death of my mother when I was 14. Through Louis's eyes, everything became accessible. But I didn't ask when I was writing what it meant; I only asked if it felt authentic. There was an intensity—an intensity that's still there when I write about those characters. As long as it is there, I will go on with them. In some way they are a perfect metaphor for me."

Captivated by the creative process of her story-turned-novel, Rice never did submit her stories to the Iowa contest. "I entered *Interview* in another contest," Rice says, "but I later discovered from an inside source that a reader had thrown it out before it even got to the judges." Later that year, in 1974, she took the novel to a writer's conference in California, where it was accepted by an agent (not Lynn Nesbit, who now represents her) who sold it to Knopf. Coincidentally, Vicki Wilson, the acquiring editor at

Knopf, was also at the conference, although Rice did not meet her there. Wilson remains her editor today.

When *Interview* was published in 1976, the reviews were sparse and rather cool. Gradually, however, a word-of-mouth readership developed, and pushed the novel into the realm of success. Was she surprised? "The gracious thing of course, is always for a writer to say 'Yes, I was surprised,'" Rice answers. "But I really was a person who was fueled by dreams of grandeur." She confesses that Socrates' formula for drama—plot, character, spectacle—used to hang above her typewriter. "I emphasized spectacle," she explains. Writing was a therapeutic outlet in those years. "I didn't have a career or a job. Stan was a successful poet and a respected college professor, and it was perfectly okay with him if I just wrote. So I had nothing to sustain me but my dreams. And I have to admit I dreamed of great success and recognition. I had thrown in my lot with the most bohemian kind of life, and if I was going to be redeemed it had to be by great success. So I don't know if 'surprised' is the right word. But I had the amazing thing happen: my dreams came true."

After *Interview*, Rice returned to her fascination with the New Orleans' *gens de couleur libre*. Her editor for *The Feast of All Saints* was John Dodds at Simon & Schuster, who later, at Arbor House, also edited the two Anne Rampling novels—books, she says, that are reserved for her "contemporary California voice." When Dodds died, just after the publication of her Rampling novel *Belinda*, Rice received the news in Philadelphia while touring to promote the Ballantine paperback edition of *The Vampire Lestat*, the second of The Vampire Chronicles. "I really loved John Dodds," says Rice, who includes him in her dedication to *The Queen of the Damned*. "He was a remarkable man. Not enough was said about him when he died, the experiences he had had and the writers he had worked with. If he had written the story of his life it would be quite amazing."

Bill Whitehead is another editor she remembers with admiration and affection. According to Rice, Whitehead was the only editor who would have taken the chance of publishing the erotica of A. N. Roquelaure (French for "cloak"). She wrote the three books to fill what she felt was a literary gap. "I had never found the erotica I wanted," she says in straightforward fashion. "So I just created what I thought was fun." Whitehead, she holds, "understood them perfectly," produced them tastefully at Dutton, and arranged for "wonderful distribution." *The Queen of the Damned* is also dedicated to the memory of Whitehead, whose passing, she says, was a devastating loss for her. In addition to being her editor and friend, he facilitated her meeting with John Preston, a gay writer who has become her best friend. "I never got a chance to tell Bill how grateful I am for putting me in contact with John," Rice says sadly.

Although the Roquelaure fantasies remain in print and readers still bring them to autograph parties for her other books, the pseudonym is a niche in her past. There is a third Rampling novel evolving in Rice's mind, however. And there is a work in progress—*The Witching Hour,* a novel about a family of witches set in contemporary New Orleans—that she abandoned to write *The Queen of the Damned.*

She had created in *The Vampire Lestat,* Rice says, a situation in which the protagonist was "trying to affect all the immortals." But she ended her narrative at the climactic point of rock star Lestat's heralded concert in San Francisco. She made Lestat a rock star because "I felt that was absolutely what he would do. Rock muscians are something new under the sun. . . . they are the epitome of the romantic artist in that they are expected to surprise and change and remain independent all at the same time. It's the perfect thing for Lestat to be, and the perfect way for him, in *The Queen of the Damned,* to send out a call to all the immortals he's lost contact with, all over the world."

In writing the third volume of the series, Rice says, "I wanted to broaden my canvas and see what it would be like when all those forces were brought together. I wanted to capture whole lives, the vision of an entire existence." And to do that she had to move away from the first-person narrative of the previous chronicles to a third-person narrator.

In executing the complex novel, Rice enjoyed a new, gratifying experience. With the previous books "there had been a sacrifice, always some way in which the finished thing fell short of the vision. *The Queen of the Damned,* for better or worse, is the first book in which the vision is all there. Early on I had a vision that involved the Twins [archetypal characters] and the dreams the immortals were having all over the world. My first reaction was

'You'll never get all that on paper. You'll get maybe half of it.' But this time I decided I was going to write the dream book in its totality. And I did. For me that was a tremendous leap forward, at least in terms of intention and accomplishment."

BOB SUMMER

HENRY ROTH

His FIRST AND only novel, published in 1934 when he was 28 years old, is considered a classic but, enigmatically, he pursued a nonliterary, anomalous career track that included stints as a teacher, a machinist, an attendant in a mental hospital and a waterfowl farmer. Some 50 years after Henry Roth's debut with *Call It Sleep,* the Jewish Publication Society recently released his second book. Compiled, edited and conceived of by Mario Materassi, who translated *Call It Sleep* into Italian, *Shifting Landscape: A Composite, 1925–1987* is a multifarious collection of short stories, essays and political statements that first appeared in magazines as diverse as the *New Yorker* and a trade journal on ducks and geese. They are accompanied by interviews with Roth and selections from his correspondence.

On a visit to Manhattan with Muriel, his wife of 48 years, the author holds court in his modest hotel suite. Roth, of course, is no stranger to this city; he grew up in the Jewish slums of the Lower East Side, where he set his autobiographical novel, and in Irish East Harlem. But a flannel shirt and lanyard tie bespeak this small, elderly man's adopted home of Albuquerque, N.M., where he has lived since 1968 in a trailer in relative anonymity. In fact, Roth is somewhat disoriented by the hullabaloo of New York and the attendant publicity, and alienated from his literary renown. "It's as though I were some kind of holy relic," he says. "There's such a gap between the temperament, the outlook and the whole psyche of the individual who wrote *Call It Sleep* and this old man here that it's as though he were a stranger."

According to Roth, an artistic commitment to the Communist Party credo of social realism and his rejection of Judaism combined to thwart his creative impulse and burgeoning career. Maxwell Perkins of Scribners bought the rights to Roth's second book, but this proletarian novel, with a German-American protagonist, was never finished.

Roth considered writing short stories commercially but found that this "business of trying to write according to someone else's standards" triggered creative paralysis. Writer's block began to plague him when he was writing a piece ironically entitled "Broker." "I had one of those walking nervous breakdowns where you're still in control but I developed a ferocious anxiety neurosis. One night I felt a strange presence, a dybbuk. It was so bad I had to get out of the rooming house. I must have walked 10 miles trying to run away from this obsessive thing. At about four in the morning, I came back and fell asleep, but it was there to meet me the next morning. From then on it was always there.

"Always I was looking for some kind of explanation. Why were these years going by and I wasn't producing anything when I seemed to have had a lot of initial talent?" Roth proffers what he describes as a Hegelian-Marxist prescription: "You have your thesis, your antithesis, and somehow there has to be a synthesis. My thesis was my Judaism as a child. Here was a one-time devout Jew who had been part of a very homogeneous society. The best work that I had done was rooted in Judaism, but at the same time I had tried to turn my back on Diaspora Judaism."

Roth says his plight was shared by many writers in the '30s, and compares his predicament to that of James Joyce: "Here I was living the New York intellectual life in the Village and spending my best creative efforts on writing about the Lower East Side, the other world that really had meaning for me, in the same way that Joyce was living on the European continent and doing nothing but writing about Ireland. Just like Joyce, I was not able to absorb the particular intellectual environment in which I was living. There's a sense of personal disintegration, the sense of becoming more and more at loose ends. You begin to lose faith in your own perceptions.

"Then you have to have a negation of your negation. However, here the final negation comes out in the form of embracing Israel, not in a return to Diaspora Judaism." With the 1967 Arab-

Israeli War, Roth broke with the Communist Party, which "dictated that I should aspire to the cause of the Arabs against this imperalist agent Israel."

Parallel to the vicissitudes of the author's political ideology and professional life, the course of *Call It Sleep*, too, never did run smooth. Roth attributes his novel's publication to a fortuitous ménage à trois. He wrote his masterpiece when he was living with his lover and patron, Eda Lou Walton, an NYU professor whose Greenwich Village apartment was a salon of sorts for writers. "She never could resist the temptation of indoctrinating or initiating young people," he reminisces. "It was really Eda Lou who insisted that the book was of a literary quality. After Knopf or somebody else turned it down, she was determined that David Mandel, who was also a lover of Eda Lou's, at the same time, get it published somehow. He was a lawyer, he had money, and he bought into Ballou and Co. As a part owner, he urged that *Call It Sleep* be published. [Robert O.] Ballou also thought it was a worthwhile book."

Roth's 81-year-old eyes loom large behind his glasses, his hands are misshapen by rheumatoid arthritis and his cane rests nearby, but his smile exudes a boyish charm as he combs his memory. "Eda Lou was about 11 years older than I was and David about 10 years older. I was in the role of a child prodigy. There was a maternal-paternal relationship toward me and it obviated jealousy."

For a first novel from a small publisher, *Call It Sleep*, issued by Ballou and Co. in 1934, did respectably well. It went into two printings, sold 4000 copies and garnered an impressive set of reviews. "It looked as if it would go places, but Ballou hadn't expected there would be that kind of demand. They sold out the first printing almost immediately. If they had a second printing on hand, *Call It Sleep* might have gained momentum and gone on. They were a little unprofessional and maybe they didn't have enough money behind them. The belated second printing went a little ways and then petered out." Soon after, Ballou went bankrupt—a not unusual episode in the grim Depression years.

Roth advances another hypothesis for *Call It Sleep*'s demise in the '30s. Although it depicts the squalor of slum life at the turn of the century, the work's focus is the inner world of an immigrant boy, David Schearl, and the classic Oedipus complex at the core of his agonizing family relationships. As psychological

425

rather than social fiction, the book "went against the stream. It was neither a novel of escape or romance that might appeal to the middle class in the depths of the Depression, nor was it socially significant in the sense that it fit in with the dictates of the Communist Party ideology, which promoted the proletarian novel and the class struggle."

In 1956, the *American Scholar* ran a symposium on "The Most Neglected Books of the Past 25 Years." "*Call It Sleep* happened to be the only book approved of twice [by Leslie A. Fiedler and Alfred Kazin] as worthy of being reprinted," notes Roth. A few years later, critic Harold Ribalow showed up at Roth's waterfowl farm in Maine to advise him that the copyright on *Call It Sleep* was due to expire and the book would be in the public domain. "He thought he could get it republished. At that time I was so divorced from the sense of being a writer that I simply said, 'Sure. Go ahead.'" Roth also signed over to the enterprising Ribalow a large portion of any subsequent profits. Ribalow did not have substantial publishing contacts, but he managed to get the book republished in 1960 by his friends Chip Chafetz and Sid Solomon, owners of the secondhand Cooper Square Bookstore in New York and of the now-defunct Pageant Press. This second hardcover edition didn't receive much attention from the critics or the buying public. But, serendipitously, in the late '50s, Peter Mayer, who is now publisher of Penguin but was then a taxi driver living near Roth's former home on the Lower East Side, was tipped off to the book by another cabbie, Edward Adler (who subsequently published *Notes from a Dark Street*). Mayer read *Sleep* in the public library because he couldn't find a copy in a bookstore. Five years later, now an editor at Avon, he acquired the book and, although it was a reprint, sent it to reviewers in bound galleys. Mayer's ingenuity paid off: *Call It Sleep* made the front page of the *New York Times Book Review*—a first for a paperback—and a surprised Avon had to rush a printing of 25,000 copies and hand-deliver books to the New York stores. Now, after 30 printings, there are 1,200,000 copies in print.

Roth had severed his relationship with Walton soon after the publication of *Call It Sleep*. In 1938, he met Muriel Parker, a composer and pianist and the daughter of a Baptist minister, at Yaddo, the artist's colony. "I needed someone else to give me an incentive to break this very, very comfortable existence of being supported by Eda Lou. Here was somebody I could cling to who would compel me to start growing up," he says. Roth recalls that his separation from Walton was particularly painful. Walton and Mandel would marry and divorce, and Walton began to drink heavily. "She was always confident that the book would gain a place. I'm sorry now and I always will be that she didn't live long enough to see her choice justified when *Call It Sleep* came out as a paperback."

The phenomenal success of the 1964 Avon edition undermined Roth's lifestyle ("I no longer could be a slaughterer of ducks and geese. It made me feel rather freakish") but stimulated his creative juices. Later, the appeal of Zionism and a literary correspondence with William Targ, former Putnam editor-in-chief and the husband of Roth's agent, Roslyn Targ, served to buoy his newfound resolve and to exorcise his old dybbuk.

The author did not choose JPS as his publisher. Rather, the small Philadelphia nonprofit company came to him. Associate editor Diane Levenberg (who has since left the firm to become an English professor) had included a section on Roth in her doctoral thesis on American Jewish literature. Convinced that Roth had a manuscript squirreled away, Levenberg visited him on his 80th birthday in 1986. Materassi was present as well with his concept for a collection of Roth's published writings. Levenberg closed the deal with a competitive advance, aided by Roth's enthusiasm for all things Jewish and the fact that a few years ago, agent Targ had come up against a brick wall when she tried to sell a collection of Roth's short stories to some of the major literary houses.

This morning, Dan Wolman, an Israeli filmmaker who has an option on *Call It Sleep* and is also making a documentary on the author, has taken Roth to the novel's locale on Ninth Street and Avenue D. "Unfortunately, the house has been razed," reports Roth, who laments the fact that the Lower East Side has lost its Jewish homogeneity. Roth is hard at work on his new novel, tentatively titled *Mercy of a Rude Stream*, which "will offend everybody. That's why it's going to be posthumous." Roth describes it as "an autobiographical study of a writer going through the creative phase and the blocked phase." He has advice for others on how to avoid the dreaded writer's block, cautioning novelists not to view their writing "in terms of your own preestablishment of some kind of unity within yourself, of some kind of necessary

427

estheticism. Write as a pro. I couldn't do it," Roth says with candor. "Secondly, you'd better go back to the environ, as Faulkner did, that provided you with your most stimulating material. If it exists."

PENNY KAGANOFF

428

PHILIP ROTH

W HEN *The Counterlife* won the National Book Critics Circle Award, Philip Roth, traveling in Israel, sent a taped acceptance speech to the NBCC awards ceremony. The book he had just completed was on his mind as he spoke of the relationship between fact and fiction:

"You begin with the raw material, the facts. . . . This can take days, it can take years. The mind conducts the examination at its own pace . . . and one day turns the facts over to the imagination. . . . The butcher, imagination, wastes no time with niceties: it clubs the facts over the head . . . slits its throat, and with its bare hands, it pulls forth the guts. . . . By the time the imagination is finished with a fact, believe me, it bears no resemblance to a fact. . . . Eventually, there's a novel. . . . "

With Farrar, Straus & Giroux's publication of his 17th book, *The Facts: A Novelist's Autobiography,* Roth returns to the raw material, the facts of his own life from which he has drawn many elements of his novels and stories. *The Facts* is an astonishing and original autobiographical narrative that can be read as a counterpunch to *The Counterlife*—a counterlife to the fictions.

Meeting with us in a book-lined conference room at FSG, Roth appears to be brimming with energy and vitality. He is a young 55, and has grown only a little more bald and gray than in his most recent book-jacket photos. There is no hint of his breakdown in spring 1987, when, following minor surgery, he suffered "a prolonged physical ordeal that led to an extreme depression," which carried him "right to the edge of emotional and mental dissolution," as he writes in *The Facts*.

Getting "bluer and bluer," unable to work at all, Roth says he finally began to write "three- or four-page bits" about his childhood and early memories. Those first sketches later evolved into the first section of *The Facts*, called "Safe at Home."

"I didn't conceive of it as a book at the time," says Roth. "I didn't *conceive* of it. I just began to *do* it, the way you do occupational therapy. It never entered my mind to write an autobiography."

When pressed further about his momentary turning away from fiction, Roth refers to the opening pages of *The Facts*, which begin with a letter from Roth to Nathan Zuckerman, his fictional counterpart. In the letter, Roth explains his reason for writing the book, saying that he appears "to have gone about writing . . . absolutely backward, taking what I had already imagined, and, as it were, dessicating it, so as to restore my experience to the original, pre-fictionalized factuality."

Roth describes his need to find himself after his illness as an "effort to repossess my life." In order to "transform myself into *myself*, I began rendering experience untransformed."

If Roth didn't know what he was about while he was writing the autobiographical narrative, he certainly knew what he had when he was finished. His letter to Zuckerman goes on to say, "This manuscript embodies my counterlife, the antidote and answer to all those fictions that culminated in the fiction of you. If in one way *The Counterlife* can be read as fiction about structure, then this is the bare bones, the structure of a life without fiction."

The letter ends with a question: "Is the book any good? Be candid." Awaiting readers at the other end of Roth's narrative is Zuckerman's letter back to Roth: "Don't publish," he says, and points out many flaws in the manuscript. He quotes his wife Maria at length (Roth comments to *PW*, "I like it when Maria says, 'Uh-oh, still on that Jewish stuff, isn't he?' "), and ends in a plea to Roth "to alter the imaginative course so long ago laid down for you."

Roth says he began to write the letter to Zuckerman somewhere at midpoint, when "I began writing about why I was writing the book." At one stage he considered having Zuckerman comment in the margins of the manuscript. At another point he considered an appearance from Alexander Portnoy, "but he doesn't exist today. I would have no access to such a character. It's been a hell of a long time. Zuckerman is very fresh. I'm close to the character. In some ways, you could say this is a sequel to *The Counterlife*."

Divided into five segments, the memoir takes the reader from the security of Roth's early childhood on through his college years, romances, marriage, and the publication of his first three books. *The Facts* leaves off with Roth on the eve of publication of *Portnoy's Complaint*, the novel that was to transform his public image and provoke even more accusations of "Jewish self-hatred" than had *Goodbye, Columbus, Letting Go* or *When She Was Good*. Zuckerman's circumstances in the closing pages of the book mirror Roth's: he and Maria are about to give birth, not metaphorically to a work of fiction, but fictionally, to a perhaps metaphoric baby.

While Roth is free to invent the facts for Zuckerman, can we trust him to have given us the straight goods about himself, as he says he does?

"These are the facts, your honor, as I remember them," replies Roth solemnly, and then he laughs, as he does frequently during the interview, a real "ha-ha-ha" laugh. "There is nowhere that I deliberately mislead anybody. There are omissions, yes. It's a very short book. It only takes us to age 36. It's about what it's about. It's not about what it's not about.

"There were other parts to the book that aren't there now. It went farther along in time. But that wasn't as interesting. I suppose, because a calm and orderly life is not as interesting as pressure and crisis. This is very much about finding a voice, isn't it? What happened after didn't matter to me in the same way."

Central to Roth's story is his marriage to a woman he calls Josie. Now dead, she was an alcoholic, an unstable shrew—as Roth portrays her—who lied and manipulated in incredible ways. She once went so far as to fake a pregnancy, purchasing urine for the test from a pregnant black woman in a park. This event found its way into *My Life as a Man*, only one of many episodes in Roth's life that he reveals as the basis for specific incidents in his fictions.

In his letter, Zuckerman carps at Roth for changing the names of most of the women in his life. Above all, Zuckerman says, "Josie is the real antagonist, the true counterself, and shouldn't be relegated like the other women to an allegorical role." Though he allowed Zuckerman to suggest that he give Josie her own name, Roth did not do so. "I didn't want to read those names in the reviews," he says, "and I wanted to protect the privacy of those people. I wrote the first draft with everybody's names, because that was helpful to me. David Rieff [Roth's editor at Farrar, Straus] read the manuscript with the real names."

Roth calls Rieff "a terrific reader, an excellent editor," one of several fine editors with whom he has worked. From his first book with George Starbuck at Houghton Mifflin to Joe Fox, Jason Epstein and Aaron Asher, Roth says, "I've had the best editors anyone could have at every publishing house I've been with."

Revealing that he works without a contract, he explains, "I don't want a contract or money until I'm done. *All* done. I want to be able to abandon a project at any point. I don't want the pressure to finish something because I have a check. The only book I ever took money in advance for was *Letting Go.*"

Represented by Candida Donadio until 1970, Roth has felt no need for an agent since then. "I don't mind doing business myself," he says. "I don't need someone to stand between me and my publisher and say the dirty word 'money.' I can say it."

Time and again, when *PW* raises points about the autobiography, instead of responding directly, Roth quotes criticism from Zuckerman or Maria in *The Facts.* Roth has lived with the actress Claire Bloom for more than a dozen years, for example, but she is never mentioned. "Yes, Zuckerman makes that point," agrees Roth. When the subject of psychoanalysis is raised—Roth was in analysis from 1962 to 1969, but omits mention of it—he responds, "Yes, Zuckerman calls me on that." He really has all the bases covered, then, doesn't he? Roth explodes with laughter, but points out, "Except the business of covering the bases isn't covered."

More seriously, he adds, "The Zuckerman letters have another function as well, as part of the novelist's autobiography. This is autobiography too—this is to give you some sense of what it is to be a writer. The letters are also what they appear to be: a genuine challenge to the book. Yet that challenge comes from me. We know, therefore, that this self-challenging aspect is a very strong ingredient in my life as a novelist. That's what I thought the inspiration was in the last section. So it really didn't have to do with covering the bases, but rather with establishing, as dramatically as I could, the whole notion of self-challenge."

Is Maria right when she observes that Roth is "not interested in happiness?"

"That's what she concludes," says Roth. "I'm not taking sides with Maria, or Zuckerman, or me. This is an interpretation, and it's there to allow the reader to enlarge his perception of the book."

Roth says he enjoyed writing Maria's part the most "because with the Zuckerman and Maria letters, I was working my way back into writing fiction."

The Facts leaves Zuckerman expressing fear that, like Roth, he'll have a breakdown. Psychoanalysis, while omitted from *The Facts*, has clearly been a significant factor for Roth. When asked to characterize his analysis, Roth is playfully evasive. Was this a traditional five-days-a-week analysis? "I think there were eight days a week." Asked to compare his writing of *The Facts* to the process of analysis, he responds, "In analysis you organize your life according to the perspective of psychoanalysis. You are a willing patient. This is not the work of a patient. The analysis isn't interested in the facts so much as the associations to the facts. . . .

"Writing leads to controlled investigation. The object of analysis is uncontrolled investigation. The goal was to write about things that strike me as tedious without being tedious."

Isn't that what a great writer does?

"There wasn't a great writer around. There was only me."

In *The Facts*, Roth says he is "worn out and tired of further fictionalizing." Is he still?

"For the time I was writing *The Facts*, I wasn't engaged in that laborious job, I was engaged in this laborious job. Like most writers my age, I'm tired of a lot of things, and this was a vacation, although not a pleasant vacation. I'm tired of sitting alone in a room. It's a nice prison."

Roth sits alone in rooms in northwestern Connecticut, where he has a studio next to his 18th-century house, and in London, where he has spent parts of most winters for the past several years. He plans now to spend less time in London and more time here, probably in New York.

433

He is currently at work again, but won't characterize it in any way. "I don't know what I'm writing," he says. "It's too amorphous to say." He concedes that it *might* be about Nathan Zuckerman. Perhaps he has taken Zuckerman's advice to heart. "The distortion called fidelity is *not* your métier—you are simply too real to outface full disclosures," writes Zuckerman in his letter at the end of *The Facts*. "It's through *dis*simulation that you find your freedom from the falsifying requisites of 'candor.' . . . Your medium for genuine self-confrontation is me."

KATHARINE WEBER

SUSAN FROMBERG
SCHAEFFER

Reading susan fromberg schaeffer's novels is rather like falling into a time warp and experiencing events through total immersion in the mind of the protagonist. So carefully does she build character, so meticulously does she convey details of time and place and social mores that one wonders with each new novel if the author is writing autobiography in the guise of fiction.

Readers of *Anya* were convinced Schaeffer was a survivor of the Holocaust; those of *Time in Its Flight* believed she was a born-and-bred New Englander; closest to the mark were those who guessed she was a third-generation descendant of a Russian-Jewish immigrant family resembling the characters in *Love*.

In *The Madness of a Seduced Woman*, Schaeffer not only faithfully communicates the quality of life in a small Vermont town in the early decades of this century, but writes so convincingly of the awakening of a young woman's sexual passion and its inexorable progression to tragedy that readers are sure to speculate about the origins of her material.

Schaeffer provides a clue with an intriguing authorial note accompanying advance galleys of the book, in which she reveals that the genesis of the narrative occurred a good 18 years ago when she was researching *Time in Its Flight*. In an old Vermont newspaper she came across accounts of a young woman's trial in Montpelier for murder. The defendant had shot the fiancée of the

435

man to whom she had believed herself engaged, had attempted suicide, but had survived both her gunshot wound and later brain surgery to remove the bullet. "I thought then: what an awful fate, that no matter what she did to herself she was destined to go on living," Schaeffer says. "And that led me to speculate about any usual person finding happiness in life, especially one with an obsessive determination to change the nature of reality. And the seductive possibility of being able to visualize a better world than the one you were given by birth or inheritance."

Feeling that she was then not old enough to understand the implications of her conception of the woman's character, Schaeffer put the clippings into a box and went on to write other books. Eventually she understood what it was that she wanted to write about, which was, she says, "the way in which fate and your own character get a hold of you, and what room you have to manipulate your own destiny between the pull of those two forces."

While the ideas for *Madness* had been germinating, Schaeffer had followed what is for her a typical pattern of research, which she characterizes as "very peculiar. I do an immense amount of reading that has no direct connection with what I am writing about." The complete standard edition of the works of Sigmund Freud, a history of the state of Vermont, a trove of old newspapers were some of the background material she assimilated. She also read a great many turn-of-the-century romantic novels, "most of which seemed to be written by a man named Charles Garvis, who must have been about 25 different women. They all invariably revolved around some sort of sexual betrayal."

A 15-year summer and holiday resident of Vermont, Schaeffer went twice to Montpelier (scene of the novel's main events) and "just wandered around the streets and listened to the bells and train whistles. There's a kind of glass bell over the state; except for the ski areas, very little has changed in the last 50 years," she notes. Her chance question about how one traveled from Montpelier to Barre afforded an illuminating reply from a native Vermonter: "These days you have to drive, but in the old days, you took the cars." Schaeffer was thus alerted to the existence of a trolley line that became integral to the novel's action.

When she came to the actual writing of *Madness*, Schaeffer hung an elegant black dress of the era on a bookcase in her study, directly in her line of sight. A child's purple dress was displayed nearby. "Objects themselves seem to have a storytelling ability to me," she notes. Under glass on her desk she placed four or five photos of people of the time who seemed to look like the characters she imagined, because, she says, photos have a galvanizing effect on her imagination.

In appearance and in the quality of old-fashioned decorum she projects, Schaeffer herself might have stepped out of one of those photos. Pale as a cameo portrait, her face is illuminated by expressive brown eyes and surrounded by black hair cascading in deep waves to her shoulders. Three silver rings adorn each hand. White collar and cuffs set off a burgundy dress that is demure rather than chic; it is clasped at one hip by a museum-piece reproduction: a cherub-shaped gold pin. Only an outsized digital wristwatch betrays Schaeffer's existence in the present decade.

Her writing methods are equally distinctive. "I don't start to write until I know what the book is about from beginning to end, scene by scene," she tells us. "When I actually begin writing, something strange happens. I become enveloped in a kind of conflagration, a burning to get the book out of my system. I write the book all the way through, stopping as little as possible. I sleep only two or three hours a night. All the energy I might release if I wrote a little at a time builds up and spills out almost beyond my control. I acquire a kind of immunity, but after each book is finished, I always get sick."

Once recovered, Schaeffer completely retypes the book, "from page one to the end." She is unable to make revisions with a pencil or a pen: only actually retyping the book allows the creative process to begin again, she says.

In this fashion Schaeffer has produced four books of poetry, one volume of short stories and five critically acclaimed novels, all in a little over a decade. Her productivity is all the more remarkable in view of the fact that she has been a teacher for 20 years at Brooklyn College (where her husband, Neil, is head of the English department) and is the mother of two children, nine and six years old. Balancing all her responsibilities is "torturous," Schaeffer says simply. "If a child gets sick, there's all the trouble that causes anybody who is a mother, and all the frustration that your writing is being interrupted, plus the guilt for even thinking that way. It's not a life I would choose if I felt I had a choice about it," she muses, implying, not for the first time, that writing is an addiction over which she has little control.

She expresses gratitude to her husband for accepting as "perfectly reasonable" her need to write and teach and have children. Writing at home does mitigate some of her guilt about depriving the children of her company. While she works behind a closed door, the children are allowed to interrupt her if the need arises. She plays the same music (usually Bach) over and over again as a "Pavlovian aid," and when the music changes, they know the book is finished. Schaeffer recalls with amusement a time she was bewildered at her small son's distress at bedtime. "It turned out that he was unhappy because he had stopped hearing the steady sound of my electric typewriter coming through the floor. I had to go upstairs to the study and run the typewriter for five or six minutes, and he went right to sleep."

During her own childhood, as the daughter of middle-class parents in Brooklyn and then on Long Island, Schaeffer was convinced that she would be a writer. When she was eight years old she sent a story to the *Ladies' Home Journal* (it was about wanting to be an orphan, she remembers), and she was not a bit dismayed to receive a printed rejection slip. "I thought it was the most elegant thing I had ever seen," she reminisces. "In some ways it was an excellent experience. It inoculated me against rejection slips for a long time." For three years at the University of Chicago, Schaeffer was in premed. Parents scarred by the Depression had "drummed it into my head that you needed a sure way to make a living. Besides, I had nothing to write about, nothing to say."

Schaeffer switched to an English major in her senior year and, in what she calls "one of the mysteries of my life," discovered six weeks after graduation that she was writing a poem mentally, composing it in her head. Although she thereafter succumbed to the irresistible impulse to write poetry, Schaeffer gave herself an arbitrary limit of producing 100 poems before she sent any out. Shocked that they were not rejected, she pursued the craft for another five years (while she was completing her master's and Ph.D. degrees) before she could work herself up to writing fiction. "I was afraid of what that commitment would involve—a kind of swallowing up—and I was right."

Schaeffer speaks of writing as though it is an obligation she cannot resist; she seems, possessed by a force working through her. Cynthia Ozick has called her "a natural writer," and she says that "writing comes more naturally to me than any other thing. When I write I am absolutely happy. Other writers may consider it torture, but for me it's an absolute pleasure to play with a sentence to see how it will come out. It seems to me a very childlike activity."

Yet Schaeffer feels she does not have the ideal personality for a writer. Negative reviews ("even from the man who reads the water meter") upset her, and the period following the completion of any book is not an enjoyable time. Inevitably, to get her mind off one book, she begins writing another. "It's like a snake eating its tail," she says in one of the vivid images that characterize her work and her speech.

A certain serenity has begun to comfort her now that she is 42, Schaeffer says. "I don't feel the pressure of time so much. I've done some of the things I wanted to do. On top of that, I know I can't work any faster than I do; I can't stuff any more hours into the day."

She is also cheered by the fact that she is not an autobiographical writer; in fact, she finds the idea of direct self-revelation "horrifying. It violates my own feeling of privacy. As subject matter I don't seem very interesting to myself. It's a good thing, too, because at least I don't have to wait to live a certain length of time before I have new material to write about."

Other people interest Schaeffer to an obsessive degree. "I don't know what it is about me that elicits stories from people," she muses. "It's as if there's some kind of protective membrane missing between me and the rest of the world that I compensate for by the kind of identification I have with my characters. At school I'm famous for managing the really difficult students no one else can handle. It's a peculiar psychic tie. I have no idea where it comes from or how it establishes itself."

Whatever the sources of her sensibility, the ability to draw her readers inside her characters' heads, Schaeffer hopes that she has broken new ground in *The Madness of a Seduced Woman*. "I tried to go deeper and closer to the bone than I did in either *Anya* or *Time in Its Flight*. I wanted to really get at the basic motives, the wellsprings of behavior, to explore the conflicting

439

impulses between a woman's esthetic and biological drives," she says.

Her hopes for *Madness* are augmented by its sale to the Jaffe-Lansing movie production team, a development she characterizes as "simply wonderful! After books, movies have been my consuming passion since I was tiny," she says. If she were doing the screenplay, she might be overprotective, she says, but basically she regards movies as "translations, not exact replications on celluloid of what is on a page. I'm very happy that the book will take on another incarnation, and of course I'm curious about what it will be."

In the meantime, Schaeffer is gratified that readers report being mesmerized by *The Madness of a Seduced Woman*, to the extent of being lured into all-night reading sessions. "Over the years people have told me that I'm responsible for burning a lot of dinners," she says, totally without pomposity or complacency. For Schaeffer, writing is a calling she observes with respect.

SYBIL S. STEINBERG

LYNNE SHARON
SCHWARTZ

"I ALWAYS THOUGHT of myself as a short story writer," says
Lynne Sharon Schwartz, nestled in an armchair in her Upper
West Side apartment, nibbling cherries. "I wrote novels because
people told me you have to in order to get published. Each time
I did a novel, Harper & Row would say, 'Wait. When you have a
reputation, we'll do your stories.' I really never thought they
would, but they did."

Harper & Row's sense of timing, as it happened, was acute.
Not only have various literary magazines declared a short story
"renaissance" in progress, but Schwartz herself has acquired a
substantial reputation as a major practitioner of the neglected art
of realistic short fiction. *Acquainted with the Night and Other
Stories* collects more than a decade's worth of short stories; it
demonstrates that Schwartz can juggle the minutiae of daily life
and serious philosophical themes as easily in a 15-page story as
she did in such novels as *Disturbances in the Field, Balancing
Acts* and her brilliant 1980 debut, *Rough Strife*.

In fact, *Rough Strife* was originally a series of short stories
about a couple named Caroline and Ivan and their turbulent marriage. Schwartz regards its metamorphosis into a novel as a turning point in her life. "It was important to me," she says, "because
it really changed what I would be, from a writer of short stories
into a novelist." Ted Solotaroff, then recently arrived at Harper &

Row from Bantam, liked the five stories Schwartz had written thus far and wondered if she could do more with Caroline and Ivan. "He said he would publish it," remembers the author. "I wasn't sure I believed him, but I was feeling very rejected—I literally *was* very rejected, couldn't sell anything for years—and depressed, and at least this guy said he would publish me.

"So I wrote a novella, maybe 120 pages. It overarched the stories; it was about their whole 20 years together, and the stories took place at various points. The way I always thought of it, the novella was like a road map, and then when you turn the map over they take individual cities and give you an enlargement in a little box. I thought it would make an interesting book; you don't get that often, a long story and five little ones.

"I gave it to Ted," says Schwartz, giving a characteristic low giggle as she recalls her editor's response, "and he said, 'Wonderful! Terrific!' for about five to 10 minutes. *Then* 'By the way'—he's a very diplomatic man—'by the way, do you think maybe you could stick the stories into the novella and make it a novel?' And I did; I actually cut them all up and pasted them into the novella, then edited a lot and wrote a lot of transitions, and it became a novel. Really a brilliant stroke on Ted's part, because I never intended to write a novel. Now I've written three, so I guess I'm a novelist."

The short-story-writer-turned-novelist is an attractive woman in her 40s with a mop of wild curls that spill out over her shoulders and seem to belie the somewhat cautious expression in her eyes and mouth. When discussing her work and personal feelings, she's candid and forthright; and if she doesn't want to talk about something—her novel-in-progress, for example—she says so without evasion. One feels she's an introspective person who's genuinely interested in self-analysis and not afraid of revealing her emotions to a stranger.

It's surprising to discover that Schwartz feels her real vocation was for short stories, since even the briefest ones in *Acquainted with the Night* display the depth of detail and breadth of scope one associates with a novelist, and not a contemporary novelist at that. "I'm a 19th-century writer," she says. "I'm unfashionable"—the thought clearly doesn't disturb her—"but I can't help it. I'm not spare—I mean, I *think* I'm spare; I cut out lots and lots of stuff, and whatever is left is what has to be there. This is the way I write."

Marcel Proust and Henry James are her literary idols, and among modern writers she admires Gabriel García Márquez and Nadine Gordimer. "Márquez is just a genius; he's like Proust," she says. "And Nadine Gordimer I love because I would love to be able to do what she does, to write wonderfully about the personal life and the public life and somehow make them merge. I would like to do it, but I don't see a way. I'm very concerned about issues, but when I write they don't come out. I think there are political and social issues in my work, especially in a story like 'The Middle Classes,' but I didn't sit down to write about race relations; I wanted to write about my piano teacher and my old block. I really mean to bring in the whole world, but it doesn't come in the form of political statements."

One of the most powerful examples of this indirect social commentary is in the first story in *Acquainted with the Night*, "The Age of Analysis," which suggests the emotional isolation of modern life in the story of a boy who can only break through his parents' shield of deadening psychiatric babble with acts of violence. "I don't feel negatively about analysis necessarily," comments Schwartz. "What I feel *very* negatively about is the way the values and methods and jargon of analysis have permeated people's lives so that they live according to this—well, it's like a religion, except it's such a mean-spirited one, there's so much less to it than most religions. Certain values—that self-fulfillment is the highest goal, that you can do anything you need for yourself, throw people by the wayside because you feel like it—I find repugnant. I keep thinking of Henry James—that was kind of sick, too; I don't believe in renouncing everything the way his characters did. But people can't even talk about their feelings now without using certain catch phrases—'I need space,' 'I'm not in touch with my feelings'—that make it unnecessary for them to really know what they're feeling.

"I had a thought about this," she continues, "and I'm going to use it in a story. There are words we use now, like 'parenting' and 'commitment'; they've become ugly words. I think they exist because when people cease to *do* or *have* something in their lives, then they find a word for it. When people brought up children,

443

as everybody has from time immemorial, there was no word 'parenting'; that's what you do, that's life. But now it's a *thing*"— she stresses the word with disgust. "People used to be lovers or friends or wives or families; now they're 'relationships.'

"I don't take these things lightly," Schwartz says. "When you care for a person, when you become intimate to a certain degree, you accept that this person is in your life, and for me that's it. It's not just marriage; I have women friends I feel this way about: like it or not, this person is a permanent part of me. I've been married to the same person for the duration, but I don't know that my marriage is any better or worse than others that have broken up. It's not the institution of marriage; it's the depth of feeling that you bring to your encounters with life. And that's what I miss. Everything now is so transient, I think people flit around in life; they don't settle in. I don't mean settle in and buy a house—I hate that—I mean have rooted feelings. It's very dangerous not to; life becomes trivialized, minimalized. Maybe I'm just a hanger-on; I don't like to drop people. You almost can't choose; oh, you choose a husband or a wife, you choose a friend, but there comes a point when it is no longer a matter of, I chose you, I can drop you. You *can't*.

"I really don't mean to sound stuffy," says Schwartz, but her tone is unapologetic; she cares as little about offending psychiatrists or people with transient emotions as she does about writing in an unfashionable style. The new book's title, she thinks, expresses that going-against-the-grain quality in her work: "*Acquainted with the Night*, acquainted with those subterranean feelings," she muses. "Beneath all the layers of dailiness, the commonplace that I write about, I really try to get at these things that nobody wants to look at, and that's why people don't love to read my work—well some do," she amends hastily, then laughs, "but not enough! Because there are a lot of things that I write about that make people uncomfortable, certain aspects of life they'd rather turn away from. And that's exactly what I'm interested in."

An example that immediately springs to mind is Schwartz's ability to write graphic sex scenes that are integral to her novels' plot and character development—and also very hard to read. "They're hard to write!" she says, laughing. "Some of these things are very embarrassing. I certainly wouldn't talk to people like this, and I'm not even grown-up enough to read some of them before an audience. But when you write you have to be totally shameless. I faced it years ago. I would be writing, and I would think: well, I can't put that down, I can't even look at those words; I mean, what would my mother say? And then I realized if you're going to write, you have to do it. Now I don't care anymore; I can write about almost anything—*almost* anything—I think."

Schwartz is remarkably calm and confident about her work; "I'm not too interested in anybody's criticism," she admits at one point. "I just have to figure it out for myself." One reason for this attitude—which is not arrogance, but rather a matter-of-fact acceptance of her strengths and limitations—may be the fact that there was a gap of many years between her initial desire to write and the time when she finally sat down and began her first novel. "When I was seven I thought I'd be a writer," she says, "and in college when I was taking all those writing courses I still thought so. But I got married very young, and—I don't know, I stopped thinking." Her voice, normally so strong and sure, falters, and her words come much more slowly now, as she considers behavior that is clearly still a mystery to her. "I followed my husband around, and wherever he got a job, I would get one of these odd jobs—I was an editor, translator, this and that. I didn't think. I must say, my brain was . . . mesmerized. I can't account for it. I mean, the social explanations are easy enough—being a woman and all that—but why me, why I did this . . . I don't know. I guess growing up in the '50s was just too powerful. I let myself drift and wait and do nothing—I don't know why. I was like lots of other women.

"Then I went to graduate school," she continues, "and I was just about to get a Ph.D. in comparative literature, which was about the last thing I wanted or needed, but I didn't know quite what else to do. I had babies, and graduate school is nice when you have babies. I was just about to write my thesis, in 1972, and I couldn't face it; every topic I thought of was no good, and every time I went down in the NYU stacks I'd just get sick. Then suddenly it dawned on me: I was a little over 30, and if I was going to write, I'd better write. I had thought it would *happen*—I would wake up one day and be a writer—but I didn't *do* it. That has a lot to do with the way women are brought up; you expect that things will happen to you, not that you should go and pursue them. So I dropped the Ph.D., went home, and I just wrote.

"Yes, I have regrets," she says. "Not over having my children, they're wonderful, but over not seeing earlier that life could be lived in a more original way. I was very conventional—*not* anymore, I'll tell you," she says firmly and proudly. "I stopped at about 32. It came to me when I dropped out of the Ph.D. program that I didn't have to live 'the way it was done.' I don't want to do *anything* anymore the way it's done. I don't want to be married the way it's done, I don't want to raise my children or do my writing that way. I've got to find another way, or else I can't do it. And when I saw that, then I was fine."

WENDY SMITH

CAROLYN SEE

IF CALIFORNIA IS a state of mind, Carolyn See is its literary exemplar. A native Californian and proud of it, See grew up in Pasadena in an "obscure family with little money and less culture," and lived in near-squalor in a seedy apartment house she and her first husband managed while pursuing graduate degrees at UCLA. Now she enjoys the good life in tranquil Topanga Canyon, with her longtime companion, distinguished professor and writer John Espey. "What we've got in California is essentially paradise, especially as compared to a lot of other places," See says, her smile conveying irony as well as humor.

"At a cocktail party in Manhattan some quintessential dimwit once said to me: 'Here in New York we think we are the brain of America. We're pretty sure that California is the genital area.' I was irritated but smiled politely, but later I thought: Where would you rather be in the long run? Where are they having more fun? The truth is that in certain parts of California, life, on the surface at least, is free of agony."

In five novels set in her home state, including *Making History* (Houghton Mifflin), See implicitly asks a question about this Edenic union of ideal climate and sybaritic lifestyle. As she expresses it to *PW*: "Are we going to throw away our paradise, or are we going to keep it?" The answers her books provide illuminate human volatility—as refracted through a special sensibility that comes from living on the Pacific Rim. "The whole country looks west to us. When we look west we see Australia, China,

New Guinea. We see the Old World in a new way. It's the West Coast vision of utopia."

Typically in See's novels, the serenity of nature mocks the confused, questing or desperate lives of her characters. Divorce is endemic. People self-destruct. Accidents happen. The nuclear apocalypse sears the landscape and turns the desert to glass. Yet characters come to terms with their lives, reinforced by sardonic humor and wry optimism.

Despite her demure, deceptively mild demeanor, See is the possessor of a subversive sense of humor coupled with a Zen-like view of existence. In her conversation—and her prose—a singing phrase or a knockout metaphor are juxtaposed with the zesty immediacy of street vernacular. She is a lady who knows how to have fun, hoist a beer, dance all night—and confront the unthinkable.

In *The Rest Is Done with Mirrors, Mothers, Daughters* and *Rhine Maidens*, the unthinkable for her women protagonists is divorce; *Golden Days* takes a quantum leap and dares to imagine life in California after a nuclear explosion. In *Making History*, See again takes risks. Here the focus is on an affluent, loving family with (a departure for See) a strong, caring husband and father who provides the ballast of good moral values. Random fate strikes them twice, in unrelated accidents. The grief-stricken survivors find the strength to go on.

What these novels have in common are incidents in See's own life that she has transmuted into art. *Making History* germinated during the time that Clara, the younger of See's two daughters, was recovering from a serious auto accident. While still recuperating, Clara was again badly injured when her car was demolished by a galloping runaway horse. "She burst into the bedroom covered with bloody gashes," See recalls, shuddering. After Clara's second accident See found herself "preoccupied with safety. It's part of a general California feeling. Things are so good that people are terrified that it's all going to be taken away. Because, of course life is never safe; that's just a mirage."

But if tragedy can strike anywhere, anytime, serendipitous events can also occur. See believes that things happen when one wishes for them—albeit in unexpected ways. When she applied for a Guggenheim to write *Making History*, she asked for "a whole bunch of money to go to New Guinea," one of the places where the novel's protagonist travels. "They laughed, of course," she says, amused at her own chutzpah. The information she needed came from an unexpected source—a photographer who took her picture in connection with an article about Australian literature (which See teaches at UCLA). "He just opened his mouth and asked: 'Have you ever sailed along the Indonesian archipelago? Have you ever been to Papua, New Guinea?' I nearly fainted. He spent two hours on a raving tear telling me about Komodo."

What she calls "the mystic element of needing and getting" was at work here, See believes. "It's more like the law of particle physics. It's like listening to AM and FM. We live on AM most of the time. Once in a while we get tuned in to a higher frequency."

The man who inspired See's mystical belief appears in *Rhine Maidens* as the leader of a positive thinking seminar, and as a charismatic guru in *Golden Days*. "He was very important in our lives," See says of the visionary she calls Leo. Assigned by *Money* magazine in 1977 "to debunk his crack-brained seminar," See hardly expected a mind-bending experience. But she and John Espey found themselves "blissed out" and persuaded by his philosophy—"a blend of early Christian doctrine and Eastern religions and the laws of chance and particle physics. Moral goodness was not part of his equation. It was about living creatively—and about finding parking spaces," she wisecracks. "It's as simple as putting a quarter in a telephone box to give someone else a free call. It encompasses everything from tithing to believing in *wu-wei*, a sophisticated Eastern idea that struggle gets you nowhere: the harder you swim, the more likely you are to sink."

Admitting that she's somewhat uncomfortable confessing this unorthodox vision of the world, See observes: "It's California-flaky but at the same time it's totally true. The universe has intelligence. There must be a spirit world. There is a whole lot of destruction going on, but it's not necessarily a bad thing."

Walking a conventional path has never been See's method of perambulation. In 1954, she married fellow graduate student Richard See—his grandfather was Chinese, his father was Eurasian—and became "the third generation of penniless Irish girls that they brought into this highly structured, ambitious family." (Her elder daughter, Lisa See, is writing a book about her father's fascinating clan.) Six years later See left him for another graduate student, Tom Sturak, Clara's father. She scoffs at the suggestion that she is an inveterate risk-taker. "What could I lose? My reputation, my standing in the community? I didn't have any of that."

She claims she remembers the exact moment when—in the slum apartment "with the roaches flying around"—she sat down to write her first (unpublished) novel. "We had some very tough times there, but I had a feeling of serenity and enthusiasm. If I wrote my thousand words a day, I felt that nobody could touch me. I must have been a real pain in the butt. I was very smug."

Her next book, *The Rest Is Done with Mirrors*, was bought by Little, Brown in 1970, and edited by Harry Sions, a "wonderful guy." It received "a blistering bad review" from the *New York Times*'s critic, who claimed that See's depiction of how the Rand Corporation and the defense industry worked (information she gleaned from classified documents brought home by Sturak, who worked at Rand) "was outrageous and made up and way out of my depth. He said the parts about living in vets' housing were accurate. But I had never set foot in vets' housing. They just weren't prepared to believe this scary stuff from an unknown dumb girl. I was mad as hell."

Her next book, the nonfiction *Blue Money* (1973), grew out of See's Ph.D. dissertation on the Hollywood novel. Among her resource materials were 125 so-called "night table" books, i.e. soft-corn porn. About to be divorced again and "poor as stones," See supported herself for two years as an expert witness in pornography trials. Meanwhile, her father, a former journalist and advertising man—"desperately funny, a real sport," and a much-married charmer—read his way through See's stack of books and determined he could do better. At the age of 69 he started writing hard-core pornography, producing 73 books before he died.

In an essay in *Esquire*, See wrote about her father's late-blooming career. "Somebody said, This looks like a book. Ken Rawson [then at McKay] liked the idea. *Blue Money* was easy to write because the research had already been done. I was in a position that almost no one else in the country was in at that time," See says with equanimity.

What some might call another manifestation of the laws of particle physics brought See, her agent Elaine Markson and her editor Joseph Kanon into the same orbit. Kanon bought See's second novel, *Mothers, Daughters*, "the very first day he went to work for Coward, McCann in 1976. That was pretty gutsy, since I was totally unknown: the wrong coast, the wrong sex, the wrong time. It was an extremely stylish thing for him to do."

Kanon also edited *Rhine Maidens* for Coward, McCann. He was editor-in-chief at Dutton—but about to leave—when he read *Golden Days*. "He couldn't buy it, but his faith in it meant a good deal to me,' See says. "When he bought *Making History*, he said: 'What goes around, comes around.' "

See calls Kanon "a brilliant line editor. He'll never tell you what's wrong, but you find that you've come to a stop. You look at the line and you see he's giving you this big smile. You start fixing the line. He doesn't push you. It's very oriental."

Seemingly endowed with indefatigable energy, See finds writing projects everywhere. With daughter Lisa and John Espey she has written two atmospheric sagas under the pseudonym of Monica Highland. Earlier this year John Daniel issued *Two Schools of Thought*, a collaborative memoir of Espey's experiences as a Rhodes Scholar at Oxford and See's as a graduate student at UCLA. The book was harder to write than they had expected. "I wanted to be careful about my ex-husbands, who are both nice guys. On the other hand, you don't want to take the blame for stuff you haven't done," she jokes.

Of the elegant, courtly Espey, her companion for 18 years (he had chaired her dissertation, and, a decade later, called her exactly a year and a day after his wife died), she says, "His kindness is off the graph. He has good manners and decency to burn. He has been a great education for me."

See also is a freelance book critic, regularly reviewing for the L.A. *Times* and *Newsday*, and contributing to the *Washington Post*, the *Chicago Tribune* and the *San Jose* [Calif.] *Mercury-News*. She is an adjunct professor of English at UCLA, is serving her second term as president of PEN Center USA West and also sits on the board of the NBCC.

She is unfazed by the prospect of working on her next book during the author tour for *Making History*. "No sweat, I'll just write my thousand words a day," she says serenely. A nonfiction account of her family history from the Depression to the '90s, it will focus on See's half-sister, who became a heroin addict at 19. "My sister is funny, she's goofy, she's a total outlaw. The book is me, it's John, it's the folks. It's how you get through the day."

How See gets through the day often requires a leap of faith. "There are so many suicides in my family, and both my parents were prey to extreme depression. They would insist that the nature of the universe is hostile and that mankind doesn't have a chance. I can't let myself believe that. So"—a grin, a brief expressive shrug—"I'm taking the other side."

SYBIL S. STEINBERG

MARY LEE SETTLE

MARY LEE SETTLE's novel *Celebration* (Farrar, Straus & Giroux) marks a new chapter in the career of a remarkable woman who has refused all her life to be bound by other people's expectations, whether they were the narrow limits of respectable feminine behavior laid down by the genteel, well-to-do Southern society in which she was raised or the restrictions imposed by literary critics who felt a writer must have an easily defined subject matter and style.

After nearly 30 years of work, her magisterial Beulah Quintet, a series of novels examining the American democratic experience from its roots in England's Civil War to the history of three West Virginia families over the course of three centuries, was completed in 1982 with the publication of *The Killing Ground*. She turned immediately to *Celebration*, a joyful and serene novel about a group of expatriates in London who have "crossed the river Styx" of death and despair to build a community of friendship and love radically different in mood from the often somber atmosphere of the Quintet.

At the same time, Scribners' program of reissuing Settle's earlier work in Signature Edition paperbacks—her National Book Award winner, *Blood Tie;* two early novels, *The Love Eaters* and *Kiss of Kin; The Clam Shell* and the Quintet—represents a growing recognition of Settle's entire body of work, which has examined with power and perception both the specific historical forces that shaped America and the larger moral issues that face all human beings.

After decades of adventurous living all over the world, Settle has returned home to the South. She and her husband, columnist and historian William Tazewell, recently purchased a house in Charlottesville, Va.—near her roots in West Virginia and his in the Tidewater city of Norfolk. She has written of feeling newly reconciled with her past, but there are still traces of the insurgent young woman who horrified her family by leaving college in 1938 to become a model and actress in New York. She's livened up the tasteful gray color scheme created by the previous owners of her "stone castle" with splashes of brightness: a red dining room, purple porch furniture and a bedroom of a bright orange that prompted her friend Ann Beattie to exclaim she hadn't seen such a wild shade since Janis Joplin died. And when a 68-year-old author pulls up at the airport in a black Mazda sports car, you know that she's still a rebel at heart.

Settle's brand of Southern hospitality combines the good breeding typical of her generation and class with a down-to-earth warmth and open-heartedness that go much deeper than manners. She invites *PW* up to her third-floor study, where the professional atmosphere created by the presence of a word processor and enormous metal filing cabinets is offset by a yellow carpet, red table and chair, and the small daybed, complete with large pillows and a quilt, on which she reclines as she talks about her work.

The gaiety that early reviewers have noticed in *Celebration,* she thinks, comes partly from her relief over the completion of the Beulah Quintet. "I can't tell you how glad I am to get away from the Beulah books," says Settle. "They're completely finished, they've finally formed the circle I intended in the first place—so now I can celebrate!"

The personal preoccupations that prompted *Celebration* are explained in the introduction to the book's Franklin Library first edition, from which she reads with the ease of someone more comfortable with written than spoken words: "I had had cancer, and I wanted to explore survival and getting on with life. . . . The first vision came in the middle of dinner with Ann Beattie in the fall of 1982. She says that I told her I had to leave because I was going to write a novel. I do remember borrowing paper from her and sitting in my car and writing down glimpses of a woman alone making a list. That was all. The next image was of a small group of people gathered in London and celebrating the death of Charles the First. Between those two visions was *Celebration.*"

All of Settle's books have arisen out of such flashes of vivid imagery. "I don't seek these images—if you seek, you'll never find them—but I find myself waiting for them. And you need solitude and silence to wait, because if there's all that noise, how are you going to listen?"

She gives two examples of the mysterious process by which a writer stumbles upon inspiration. "The hardest time I ever had getting an image was with *Know Nothing* [Beulah Quintet's middle volume]. I knew *why* I was writing—I was writing about the causes of the Civil War in terms of a family—but I could not get an image. Finally, my son and an old friend and I went fishing one day. I walked away from where they were fishing, put the line in the creek, lay down on a rock and fell about half asleep, and—boom!—I got it. There was little Johnny Catlett being thrown into the river, and that was my first image for the book.

"Often the images I get initially aren't at the beginning of a book," she continues. "The image that first came to me for *Blood Tie* was of a lipstick. I was diving near a large undersea hole where an earthquake had dropped the sea floor down; at the bottom of the hole I saw a lipstick—and that was the image." It appeared in the novel's final pages, a memento of a drowned girl transmuted into a metaphor for the waste and careless destruction that permeate *Blood Tie.*

Important as the images are, they always grow out of ideas that interest Settle, whose work—especially the Beulah Quintet—is firmly grounded in painstaking research and a consuming passion to discover the roots of the American character in our nation's past. "I always have a concept of what I want to write about," she says. "At the beginning of *Prisons* [the first volume in the Quintet's chronology, though it was written after *O Beulah Land* and *Know Nothing*] I realized that, in what was then still a trilogy, I had not yet found our language. I'd found land hunger, I'd found decadence, but our language of democracy was still missing, and I decided to search for it. I had read Trotsky's anti-Stalinist remark about the time of Thermidor, when the revolution turns right and a dictator takes over, and I wondered if this had ever happened in our Anglo-American history. Indeed it did; it happened at Burford in 1649."

Settle is referring to a little-known incident during the English Civil War, when radicals within Oliver Cromwell's army, who had expressed for the first time in world history the ideals of political representation and economic equality for all, were executed as rebels. The author came across her first bits of information on the roots of the democratic ideal in which she believes so strongly while researching a nonfiction book on the famous Scopes "Monkey Trial" of 1925. "The American Civil Liberties Union, which was involved in the Scopes trial, has a motto drawn from the words of John Lilburne (one of the 17th-century radicals)," she explains. "I was ashamed that I didn't know who Freeborn Jack Lilburne was, and I started thinking that maybe something in his world would give me my answers. I was in England, and I went to Burford."

Her discovery there led her not only to the seedbed of American democracy, but to the hero of *Prisons* and a renewed sense of commitment to the Beulah series, which she considered a failure after the unsuccessful publication in 1964 of an abortive early version of *The Killing Ground*. "I walked into the Burford churchyard," she remembers, "I turned left, walked straight up to the wall, climbed up on a low tombstone and—boom! like that—put my fingers in bullet holes in the walls of Burford churchyard.

"In one second, I noticed there were two rows of bullet holes, and I thought, My God, someone was shot here by a firing squad that didn't want to shoot him. I asked the vicar who had been executed, and he said, in dulcet Christian tones, 'Damn rebels, damn rebels! Should have been shot!' And it was Johnny"— Johnny Church, the executed radical whose story is told in fictional terms in *Prisons* and whose descendants are the West Virginians who grapple with the ramifications of his "democratical" dream over three centuries in Beulah Land.

"To me, my most autobiographical character is Johnny Church," says his creator. "His dilemma, and I think it's the same one Proust's Marcel had in *Swann's Way* and *The Guermantes Way*, is the two roads you can take. He's a Puritan in a Cavalier world, and that dichotomy—between slave owner and rebel— goes through all the Beulah books. The names change, but that basic split is the American split. Brother Johnny, the young freedom fighter, and Uncle Sam, the authority figure, were the two

456

new American metaphors, and Uncle Sam won out—except in my mind! Actually, I think it's a very healthy dichotomy, and it's reflected in the way our government is set up, with checks and balances."

She may recognize the need for balance, but her sympathies are always with the rebels. "I love the real sense of that damn tough, human, individual responsibility that is very American, coming out of the English Revolution," she says. "It's saying 'no,' a choice not to go along with something wrong. You say, 'No, stop,' and then find your own path. In a way, *Celebration* is about the yes that comes after the no. Teresa says yes to love and to the world because she's lost everything, including almost losing her life; Pius (an African Jesuit priest) says no to his Dinka grandfather and walks 400 miles to find his own yes."

Settle's own journey from saying no to saying yes is delineated by her evolution from a young rebel who violently rejected the Southern myths about the past she refers to as "The Night the Old Nostalgia Burned Down" (after a Perelman story) to a mature author who thoughtfully reexamined those dreams to find the true meaning of American history. She may reject the Old South's fantasies about noble plantation owners and happy slaves, but she is equally out of sympathy with the ahistorical quality of much American fiction. "We're not tumbleweeds," she says. "This business of being rootless is an American myth. I'm so tired of American fiction's non-recognition of its past I could spit nails. I just don't care whether someone in some bleak suburb is unhappy or not: it's whiny and pastless and boring! After all, the great novel about this is *The Great Gatsby*, the man who had no past. And how does it end? 'Boats against the current, borne back ceaselessly into the past.' Where does Jay Gatz come from? The world of Huckleberry Finn. Jay Gatz goes down on his own raft and makes his dream come true."

What knowledge does she hope her readers can draw from her own lengthy consideration of the American dream? Settle refuses to be drawn into an easy answer, and this deeply literary woman rummages once again through her bookshelves in search of the perfect written expression of her beliefs about a writer's task. She finds it in Joseph Conrad's preface to *The Nigger of the Narcissus*—"it's my credo"—and her low, husky voice rings with fervor as

457

she reads the famous lines she has lived by: " 'My task . . . is, by the power of the written word, to make you hear, to make you feel—it is, before all, to make you *see*. That—and no more, and it is everything.' "

WENDY SMITH

KATE SIMON

To the cognoscenti, Kate Simon's travel books are in a class by themselves, distinctly personal guides of rare good taste and discernment, expressed in an urbane and witty style.

Few who read these books (*New York: Places and Pleasures,* etc.) are aware that their cultivated voice belongs to a woman who arrived on these shores as the four-year-old offspring of immigrant parents fleeing the poverty of the Warsaw ghetto after World War I. Simon writes about her early years in the autobiographical *Bronx Primitive: Portraits in a Childhood* (Viking), a richly evocative memoir of life in a teeming multiethnic neighborhood.

"Mine is a very exotic voyage; it's as if I've lived thousands of years, in a sense . . . traversed a great many periods of civilization," she tells us, speaking of the chasm separating the world of her ancestors in Poland from that of dingy Lafontaine Street in the South Bronx, from her travels in many countries and from her literary career. "My mother still sits on my shoulder, making wry comments when I deliver a little speech at the Plaza," she says. "Everything about my life is a long way from Lafontaine Street."

Simon's decision to re-create the Bronx of her childhood came about in what she calls "a very casual way. I'd been telling stories about my family and our neighbors for years, and people kept saying, 'When are you going to write them down?' But somehow the opportunity never occurred." She was immersed in a book about the Renaissance duchy of Mantua when she happened to relate to Barbara Burn, her editor at Viking, her memories of

459

trekking out to Orchard Beach in the summer when she was a girl. Burn, intrigued by this glimpse of a vanished era, suggested that Simon take a year off from the Mantua book to try to recapture the ambience of a more recent though perhaps equally fascinating period. What Simon refers to as "the ticker-tape in my head, always busy soaking up observations," immediately issued forth colorful and intense memories.

Simon is gifted with almost cinematic visual recall; images appear in her mind "like snapshots: they are extraordinarily vivid to me, and they always have been." Details of place and atmosphere, of appearance and character, are augmented by an ability to recall smells, tactile sensations and weather. "I remember the aroma of chicken soup and lemon oil furniture polish in a Jewish home that observed the Sabbath more strictly than we did. I remember the feel of a snowfall, the subtle change in the air before it began," she observes. "I can see, feel, smell it as if it were yesterday."

Today she is still surrounded by images. Mementos of her travels adorn Simon's apartment walls. One charming surreal floral composition is by a Haitian artist whose work was later bought by the Museum of Modern Art; he asked Simon for $8 for it, and she gave him ten. "I'd have to be down to starvation to sell it," she says. Simon herself is an accomplished painter; her work more than holds its own among the other art in her collection, revealing the same sharp eye for detail and feeling for the subtleties of atmosphere that serve to distinguish all of her books.

Reminiscing about what it was like growing up in an impoverished melting-pot neighborhood, Simon thinks one of its great contributions was that "no one ever promised us that we'd be happy. We had no expectations of anyone giving us anything; we were never entertained. We had the powerful statehood of the streets—with its loyalties, its laws, its politics—or we sat quietly and we read or we *thought*. We had the time to wonder about things. Kids today have no endurance, no patience, no sense of mystery. Ours was a hard life, but it prepared us well."

Speaking of her four-year-old self in *Bronx Primitive*, Simon writes of "the wariness that was already as much a part of me as blue eyes and wild blond hair." The hair is now a chic, coiffed gray, and the blue of her eyes is soft rather than arresting. The wariness remains, however, masked by an elegance of speech and manner and a gracious smile. It comes through in a diversionary pause to light a cigarette or a measured hesitation in her well-modulated voice as she recalls the dynamics of a difficult family.

Certainly the demands of a harsh, manipulative father nurtured Simon's unsentimental view of the world, and also her need for independence and her ambition to transcend the conditions of her early existence. The path to a literary career was an arduous and circuitous one. *Bronx Primitive* ends with Simon on the verge of her teenage years, and her life for more than a decade after that seems like a Baedeker of assorted skills and experiences.

"I started my business career at age 13 as a mother's helper, taking care of two little children at an anarchists' colony in Peekskill, where their parents were vacationing. It was a great learning process," she says with ironic understatement. Determined to attend high school despite her father's disapproval and without his support, Simon worked her way through "by tutoring foreign ladies in English and teaching piano playing to little kids at 50¢ a lesson," she recalls. For a time she modeled. The experience she looks back on most fondly was her stint as a "grandma sitter" in the home of one of her teachers, who deflected Simon's chronic truancy (she was spending schooldays at the New York Public Library, reading voraciously), and provided her with room and board, in return for which Simon was companion to the "utterly charming" older woman, who filled a void in her life.

When she had accumulated enough money to enroll at Hunter College, Simon found that pursuing a major in English in the depths of the Depression was "like going in search of the Holy Grail." English teacher exams had been suspended to reduce a glutted market, and colleges were winnowing out candidates by demanding near-perfect grades and courses in Anglo-Saxon and Middle English as prerequisites. She has never regretted that strenuous immersion in English language and literature. It came in handy after graduation, when, to qualify for a Christmas job as a bookseller in Macy's, she had to pass a test ascertaining her knowledge of literary classics.

Later Simon worked as a special correspondent (read: imaginative secretary) for the Book-of-the-Month Club. ("I answered letters from people who assumed the BOMC *was* a club, and wrote to request that it set up picnics in Central Park for members, and so on"); was a "female Figaro" for an in-house magazine at a printing company, and even toiled at *PW* for a short time ("It was a strictly nonliterary job, and *very* boring").

Moving up in the world a bit, she wrote book reviews for *PM*, the *New Republic* and the *Nation*. "One day I got a book to review that was worthless . . . not well-planned or well-spoken or well-thought or well-anything," she recalls. "Now, it had always seemed to me that there is nothing a man can do that is as innocent as writing a book. He's away from the world; he's not even bothering his family. It is entirely without harm, except, of course, if the book is *Mein Kampf*. But this book was so bad, and I was flooded with sympathy for the poor soul who probably had spent years of his life writing it." Simon found she could not review the book at all, and quit literary criticism forthwith.

Into this brief crisis in her life came a serendipitous conversation with a friend who was a publisher. He had brought back from England a guidebook exclusively devoted to very chic and expensive London restaurants and snobby social spots. "He knew how I loved to prowl around New York, and he suggested that I do a similar book," Simon remembers. "But I had a brainstorm. I said to him, 'Why not reverse it? Anybody can have a $34 lunch; why not write a book that tells where to get a 34¢ lunch?' " Guidebooks about New York at that time were, according to Simon, "as stimulating and selective as a telephone directory."

New York: Places and Pleasures, published by Harper & Row in 1959, changed all that. "It was, in a small way, a knockout," Simon observes. "It was first on the paperback bestseller list for a long time, and I will soon be revising it for a fifth edition. That began a lovely time for me. From then on publishers asked: 'Where do you want to go?' and I went."

Mexico was Simon's next choice, where she produced *Mexico: Places and Pleasures* (T. Y. Crowell), one of her two favorites among the eight classic guidebooks to her credit. She takes great pride in the fact that *Mexico* is used as a sociology text in the department of Latin American studies at a Texas university. Her other favorite, *Italy: Places in Between*, is now out of print, but it led to her becoming "enamoured" of the small cities of Italy, and eventually to her work in progress, whose tentative title is *The World of the Gonzaga of Mantua*.

462

Talking about it, Simon's voice goes vibrant with enthusiasm: "That small court had everything: music, theater, art. It was a fabulous, ambitious court, which lasted—because they were tricky, and they were lucky. They knew how to marry their girls to what powers, and they were like acrobats, jumping off one wire onto another."

Simon's own life, of course, has had a share of luck. It's been full of movement and color, and as she awaits publication of *Bronx Primitive*, she remarks that her two dozen years of traveling with one manuscript or another and a couple of dresses "were marvelously exciting. It's the way everybody should lead the middle years of their lives."

SYBIL S. STEINBERG

ISAAC BASHEVIS SINGER

A SOFT YIDDISH-ACCENTED "Coming!," a slight movement at the peephole and Isaac Bashevis Singer opens the door to his spacious upper West Side apartment in New York. We walk down the Persian-carpeted hallway, with its walls lined with books and magazines on Judaism, mysticism, the Cabbalah, the occult, into a white-walled living room.

It's eight o'clock on the eve of Singer's annual winter departure for Florida, which has suddenly been pushed forward a fortnight, meaning a last-minute rush of preparations. Alma, his wife, greets us and then leaves, reappearing briefly with glasses of freshly squeezed orange juice. Singer, born in Poland, and Alma, German-born, who understands but doesn't speak Yiddish, communicate in English "in our own way."

We are here to speak with Isaac Singer as a writer for children. The 77-year-old Nobel laureate is cordial but seems tired. Still, as the hour wears on, he grows more animated and answers our questions eloquently. The 1978 Nobel citation to Singer referred to his "impassioned narrative art," the ability to tell a story unlike anyone else, and this spills over into his conversation.

Zlateh the Goat (1966), a kind of love story between boy and beast, was Isaac Bashevis Singer's first story for children. He was past 60 at the time, and the book was written in response to a request for a story about Chanukah from his friend Elizabeth Shub, then editing children's books. It won Singer his first Newbery Honor.

Since then he has continued writing for children, mostly short story collections or picture books that have been illustrated by such people as Maurice Sendak, Uri Shulevitz (who did Singer's latest, *The Golem*, from Farrar, Straus & Giroux), Margot Zemach, Nonny Hogrogian and Eric Carle. All are written originally in Yiddish, translated into English and eventually into other languages: Hebrew, French, Spanish, Italian, Swedish, Japanese, etc. Among these books are a National Book Award winner, *A Day of Pleasure* (1970), two additional Newbery Honor books, *The Fearsome Inn* (1967) and *When Schlemiel Went to Warsaw* (1968), and a number of books named ALA Notables: *Mazel and Shlimazel* (1967), *When Shlemiel Went to Warsaw, The Wicked City* (1972), *Naftali the Storyteller and His Horse Sus* (1976) are four examples of these.

Did Singer's immediate success in children's books surprise him? Not so much. "I read the story myself, and I liked it, and my editor liked it, so if I got a prize, I thought, so maybe the committee also liked it. And this was the end of the surprise."

What *does* surprise him is the range of languages his books appear in. Many are translated into Japanese, for instance. "What do Japanese children know about Poland? But then, it's not really such a surprise. When I read Andersen's stories or the Grimm stories as a little boy, it was also an environment far from me. And I loved them. Everything which is good is international—a good picture, a good story, good philosophy, good science. What I'm surprised at is that people *don't* understand each other to such a high degree—or maybe I should say to such a low degree."

The fact that children like his stories is a source of great satisfaction to Singer, who finds children wonderful readers, more independent than adults. In the statement "Why I Write for Children"—a list of 10 reasons prepared for his National Book Award acceptance speech, read in Stockholm and published with his Nobel lecture—he wrote, "Children read books, not reviews."

He repeats that now, adding, "A child will accept or reject a book only because of his real taste, what he likes and what he doesn't like. If you tell him that Freud or Moses praised this story, he will be unimpressed."

What makes a good children's story? The same qualities that make a good adult story: "It must be a real story with a beginning, a middle and an end. There must be suspense in it—the child must not know when beginning the book what the end will be."

Although Singer's stories for young and older readers come "from the same source, the same mind," he says that when writing for the young, "I will not write a love story with sex. I have lately seen people who really have sex in children's stories, but I don't believe in this. I don't think children would appreciate it." Love is a different matter. "Oh, yes, love, love. Absolutely!"

The picture book titled *Why Noah Chose the Dove* ends with the words, "The truth is that there are in the world more doves than there are tigers, leopards, wolves, vultures and other ferocious beasts. The dove lives happily without fighting. It is the bird of peace."

Does he, then, believe in morals or happy endings? Not on principle. "If my publisher would tell me, 'Write a moralizing story,' I couldn't do it. But if I sit down to write a story by myself, and if I feel there is some moral in it, it will be there. The main thing is that a writer should not be pushed by anybody.

"This is the reason, I think, why in Russia and in other such countries the writers are terribly confused. They get orders: you have to write so that the Revolution should come out beautiful and useful and necessary and so on. Once a writer gets these orders he is in a bad way. I would say writing is like sex. If a man is told, 'You have to satisfy me; you have to give me six orgasms,' he is *kaput*. If people are relaxed, and they love one another, there will be success."

What about children? Must a children's writer know children? Singer was separated from his own son, at five an emigré with his mother from Poland to the Soviet Union, until the young man was in his 20s.

Singer's four grandchildren live in Israel, and he doesn't see them often. Also, they speak Hebrew and, although Singer reads Hebrew, he has trouble pronouncing it. So communication with them is less frequent or full than he likes, and they probably know him best through the Hebrew-language editions of his books.

Singer does have contacts with other children—at readings. "I look at these children when I read the story to them, and I have the feeling they don't care. They don't listen. It's just a burden to them. And suddenly they begin to ask questions, and I realize they heard every word, they understood every sentence. These little children are something remarkable."

Singer's own childhood, and the child within him, remain vividly alive to him. One early memory, about which he has written much, is of the *cheder* (school) to which "they carried me the first time" at the age of three. There he learned the Hebrew letters used both in Hebrew and Yiddish.

Isaac Singer had only a few toys but he played with books before he could read, pretending to be a scholar like his father or a writer like his brother Joshua, 10 years his senior.

He listened to folk tales told by his father and mother, many of which form the basis of his own stories today, or he listened to stories from the Bible. "My children's books were the Bible. The Book of Genesis is full of beautiful stories—the Joseph story is a sublime story, the Book of Samuel, the Book of Kings."

At age eight or nine, Singer discovered Sherlock Holmes, who inspired his first literary effort—an imitation that lasted for a page or two. The Holmes stories, read in Yiddish, had "all the qualities for which I looked—adventure, suspense."

Understanding "one sentence in six or so," he read *Crime and Punishment* in Yiddish while barely in his teens. "But I understood that he was a great writer." The novel "kind of lifted up my spirit. I felt terribly sad, yet very happy that I could read something like this."

Not long after, he was also reading German; the language in which he read was a matter of what books he could borrow from friends. "Who could buy a book in those days?" In Hebrew, he read *The Picture of Dorian Gray*, which he found very beautiful, and *The Pickwick Papers*, and in Polish the stories of Edgar Allan Poe ("he was as marvellous as he is in English"). Today it is Poe, along with such other 19th-century writers he first read during that period—Tolstoy, Dostoyevsky, Gogol, Pushkin, Flaubert— whom Singer admires most.

Eventually, after a spell in a seminary, he moved to Warsaw, and there, under his brother Joshua's tutelage, he became part of the Jewish literary scene, working one or two days a week as a proofreader for a journal Joshua co-edited.

Singer attended a club called the *Literatenferein*, the Union of Writers, with a guest card from Joshua, a member. When Isaac had published some dozen stories, he was presented with a card of his own: "A great day in my life."

In those early, pre-America days, when he was struggling as a young writer, one of the things Isaac Singer sought most was his brother's approval. Now, however, no one tells him how to write.

"Sometimes when an editor tells me that there's some mistake, in grammar or something, of course I tell him, 'correct it by all means.' But they never really try to teach me how to write. It's too late for teaching."

Nor does he worry overly much about critics, although he does look at reviews. "If the reviewer would try very hard, he could manage to hurt me," he says. But, "I'm not easily hurt. All I say to myself, there are different tastes, different readers, different opinions. You have to make peace with it that you cannot please everybody. But, as a rule, I've no complaints."

MIRIAM BERKLEY

JANE SMILEY

J ANE SMILEY MEETS *PW* in the Thoroughbred Lounge at one of the grand old hotels of downtown Louisville, having flown in that morning from her home in Ames, Iowa, where she teaches at the state university. Very tall, moving with a lean and rangy grace, Smiley has got her black wool shirt tucked into narrow gray stone-washed jeans, thick socks folded over scuffed pink high-top sneakers. She eases down her shoulder tote, in which there is a pristine advance copy of *The Greenlanders*.

Should we be surprised that Smiley has written this hefty Scandinavian saga of the 14th century, after having produced three novels about contemporary life? Between 1980 and 1984, she published *Barn Blind* (Harper & Row), *At Paradise Gate* (Simon & Schuster) and *Duplicate Keys* (Knopf). Her stories have appeared in *Playgirl*, *Mademoiselle*, the *Atlantic* and *TriQuarterly*. Her outstanding short story collection, *The Age of Grief*, was nominated for the 1987 National Book Critics Circle Award in fiction.

Explaining the genesis of *The Greenlanders*, Smiley says that after she got her B.A. in English lit from Vassar in 1971, she went to Europe for a year and worked on a medieval archaeological dig at Winchester. She and her first husband then headed for Iowa City, where he began graduate school and she went to work in "the local teddy bear factory." She laughs at this—a warm, contagious laugh. Her accent is Midwestern; she grew up in St. Louis. At a party at the university, she met John McGalliard, a scholar in Old Norse. "I talked my way into his class, and I talked my way into the Ph.D. program," she says. "I found the sagas fascinating as examples of absolutely pared-down narrative. I decided that they were really about cause and effect more than anything else, because some little tiny cause would always lead to cataclysmic effects, and the saga would map out these effects, both geographically and historically."

When she was 27, Smiley won a Fulbright to Iceland. There she became intrigued by tales of the Norse settlement in Greenland, colonized in the 10th century by Eric the Red, and dying out by 1500. "I knew even then that I was going to write this book. I also knew I couldn't write it as my first book." Smiley claims she wrote her contemporary novels to get the necessary "practice and technical skill" for *The Greenlanders.* Writing novels was something her mother had tried to do. Frances Nuelle— today a journalist for the *Island Reporter* in Sanibel, Fla.— wanted Smiley to succeed. "I sort of imbibed that," she says.

With her early novels, Smiley kept switching publishers. She followed Barbara Grossman, her first editor at Harper & Row, to Simon & Schuster, where her second novel was issued. "Right before that was published, Barbara went to Crown, and Crown was not interested in *Duplicate Keys.* So I just found Knopf then." Smiley's first agent was Elaine Markson, whom she met at Bread Loaf, where she had a scholarship in 1977. It was her present agent, Molly Friedrich, who sold *The Greenlanders* to Knopf, where her editor is Bobby Bristol. "Sonny Mehta made a commitment to the book. I think he liked it a lot."

The characters in *The Greenlanders* exhibit the same traits found in the medieval family sagas. There's a laconic tone, a grim sense of loneliness, of life draining away, of fatalism. Smiley thinks of Gunnar Asgeirsson as the chief character, but readers will be equally interested in his sister Margret. Of Margret, Smiley says, "I wanted her to have a terrible life full of suffering. I think there are people in the world, who, the more they want to love somebody, the more tightly they protect themselves, so that their passion just generates and regenerates, and they have no release for it." Smiley says she "loves" Gunnar, but as for Margret, "she's not one of the characters in the book that I love. I respect her a lot."

The somber sense of life arises in part from Smiley's study of such sagas as the *Njals Saga, Groenledninga Saga* and *Gisla Saga.* "Reading Icelandic and having to translate every sentence,

470

somehow the sagas just were *engraved* on my consciousness, and that view of life as tending toward disaster seemed extremely pertinent to me." She also acknowledges as inspirational a minor work by the Iceland Nobel author Halldor Laxness called *The Happy Warriors,* based on *Fostbroethra Saga.*

Some of the people in *The Greenlanders* did exist, and Smiley invests them with lifeblood. "Because a lot of the characters were historically attested, they really seemed to come to me as living things outside of myself. I felt as though I were bringing to light the story of a lost people, as if I'd known those people and was finally telling their tale to the world in the ways that they deserved to have it told."

A ship of Icelanders, prophesied in the novel by the madman Larus, actually sailed into Greenland in 1406 after being blown off course. The visitors stayed a few years before going back to Iceland with Sigrid Bjornsdottir, one of the women Smiley puts in her novel. An entry in the Icelandic Annals provided Smiley with a glorious tidbit that she expands into a climactic event. "It just gives the facts in that Icelandic way," she says, referring to the terse saga style. "It says: 'Steinunn was seduced through witchcraft by a Greenlandic man and he was burned at the stake and Steinunn went crazy from the grief.' That seemed, for a novelist, like an absolute gift. I glommed onto it in a hurry. This woman's life just really spoke to me from 500 years away."

She wonders if it's "arrogant" to claim to know her Greenlanders so intimately. "And yet I really did feel a responsibility to make their way of life and their agonies and passions known, these people that fell through a hole in history and disappeared." She takes pains in the novel to show the decline of the Greenland settlement by imperceptible degrees.

In one of the farmsteads where modern Danish archaeologists have dug, they found one man "face down in a passageway with a little knife in his hand. The knife had a crescent-shaped blade, which meant that it had been sharpened so much that it had worn away. I found that a very poignant image," Smiley says.

It was no easy matter for her to gather material and funnel it into the book in a way that would bring to life a world that might seem—as she puts it—"dense and alien" to modern readers. She scanned archaeological evidence. She talked often with Tom McGovern of the anthropology department at Hunter College in

New York. She used the findings of Danish medical archaeologists who discovered the thighbones of corpses to be "slightly bent, slightly curved, and very deeply striated. The thighs were so pulled by the strength of their muscles that it would cause the bones to curve. They also had little ridges on the bony tissue of their jaws around their gums, called torus ridges. These are from chewing very tough food."

In the Danish National Museum, Smiley examined clothing—gowns sewn with gored skirts, for instance. "At the beginning of the 15th century the permafrost level suddenly rose and so the clothing, in a kind of two-by-two twill weave, was almost perfectly preserved by the ice. You can get down on your hands and knees and see the little hemstitches." Smiley marvels at the Greenlanders' infatuation with things European, notably in fashion. "Here are these people, you know, they're all about to croak, and they're looking to Paris for stylistic inspiration!" She thinks cultural rigidity prevented them from adapting completely and choosing to dress like the Eskimos and live in tents. This could account in part for their downfall, she speculates. She researched, guessed at, or extrapolated in precise details the Greenlanders' life-sustaining arts, from weaving to the great communal seal hunts.

In 1984, after she had written about 200 pages, Smiley went to Greenland. "That was a real rush, because when I got there I realized that I hadn't misimagined the place. The weather was very inspiring, too, and the icebergs and the fjords. Everything about it really gave me a wallop." When she returned home, the work raced ahead.

"I couldn't get it out fast enough. I ran to my word processor; I adored writing it. At the end it was coming out 12 to 20 pages a day. It was that classic experience where it seems that others are speaking to you, you're not really creating them. And I don't know where it came from."

We talk too about *The Age of Grief*, whose title story, a novella, deals with a pair of dentists and their three small daughters. The marriage is foundering; the wife has a lover. Told from the husband's viewpoint, the novella gets inside modern family life with exquisite sensitivity. The husband senses that he has arrived at a grief which is "the same cup of pain that every mortal drinks from."

Smiley says she was incredulous when *The Age of Grief* was nominated as a finalist for the NBCC Award. "I think if they had actually chosen me I would have been appalled, but it was great, it was totally unlooked for, so it was like this completely positive and totally abstract experience." Even the splendid reviews took Smiley by surprise. "I was unprepared for the personal way that a lot of people took it. I received letters that in some ways were more astonishing than the reviews. Tons of men wrote me saying that [the title story] was very convincing. It seemed like a phenomenon, as if I had tapped into some deep nerve without expecting to."

She finds she has no difficulty writing from a male viewpoint. "I think partly because I'm 6'2". I think being tall makes my femininity less of a disadvantage. In a big city I notice that I never get accosted or even spoken to. And I think I live in a slightly different world from most women because of my intimidating height."

Whether she is writing from a man's or a woman's perspective, in a medieval or a modern setting, the topic of family life preoccupies Smiley. Living with her third husband, screenwriter Stephen Mortensen, and young daughters Phoebe and Lucy, Smiley finds that parenthood has had a powerful effect on her creativity. "The day my first child was born was a day in which my imagination became fully engaged. Now I'm interested in questions like: How do mothers grow to love their children, and what does that mean? I love books on theories of child-raising."

Her next "big novel," she says, will be set in Wyoming in 1900. It centers on an immigrant woman, referred to in *At Paradise Gate* as Anna Robison's mother and patterned on Smiley's Norwegian great-grandmother.

Besides entertainment, Smiley wants to give the reader something to think about. Of *The Greenlanders*, she says: "The whole time I was writing it, I felt very socially responsible. One of the first things that intrigued me about it was that it was the only attested case of an *established* European civilization or culture falling apart and vanishing. There's the sense that if we in our time knew how they in their time somehow managed to let go, somehow managed to lose control, then it would help keep us from losing control of our own situation."

MARCELLE THIÉBAUX

ELIZABETH SPENCER

Elizabeth spencer is part of the grand tradition of Southern writers. The distinguished novelist and short-story writer, author of such works as *The Light in the Piazza* and *The Voice at the Back Door*, Spencer recently published a crucial work in her 40-year career, a masterly collection of short stories, *Jack of Diamonds* (Algonquin).

Spencer lives now in the South, after being away from the area physically if not spiritually for more than 30 years. She and her husband make their home in Chapel Hill, where two years ago Spencer came to teach creative writing at the University of North Carolina. They live in a pleasant suburban house graced by tall pines that drop cones on the front yard. Elegant and beguilingly gifted with a combination of strength and delicacy, Spencer talks to us in a gentle, soft-voiced southern drawl.

Spencer's southern roots have been the central influence on her fiction. Her work has just been recognized by the awarding of a Senior Fellowship in Literature Grant from The National Endowment for the Arts—she is the only fiction writer so honored this year. Many of her subtle, luminous stories that explore the mysteries of the human heart are placed in the South, and even those set elsewhere have Southern overtones.

Spencer was born the daughter of a businessman in 1921 in the town of Carrollton, Miss., population 500. "We were very family- and land-oriented," she says. "The outside world was almost a total mystery. Both sides of my family had been in that country since the Indians. My husband always said he'd never want to

474

live in Mississippi 'cause I'm kin to the whole state, and that's pretty much true.

"I was fragile when I was a child, and my mother used to pass the time reading to me, mostly fairy stories and myths. The summers were interminable, long and hot." Though she wasn't allowed to join her brothers in their sport of frog-gigging, Spencer accompanied her father when he hunted deer, squirrels and doves on "a wonderful island they bought in the middle of the Mississippi. It's a great saving thing to the health of your spirit to get close to natural things. During the Depression, I could never make anybody believe that we had quail so often for breakfast— but everything we ate had birdshot in it."

Spencer's mother's family owned a large plantation. "They've never been out of debt from the time of the Civil War, but it was still carried on anyway by my uncle. I used to spend long summers down there, but I was just too young or too gullible or too much a part of the society to evaluate it as being a system of exploitation. Yet is was also kindly and generous-hearted in many, many respects. One didn't feel . . . any cruelty at all.

"It was not an ignorant society. My uncle was a great person for *demanding* that his niece read certain books that he valued. One of 'em was *Les Miserables;* I read it much too young, because he was standin' right over me practically the whole time. He felt I would learn the whole scale of human misery and all the things that went into making Jean Valjean a real man. My uncle thought the love story of Marius and Valjean's adopted daughter was a very fine treatment of love. It's odd, isn't it, a Mississippi plantation owner thinkin' this French experience was so real and had to be understood? At home, they were reading and discussing Dickens. The curious thing is that the Southern Renaissance, so called, in literature was going on, but it was judged that the books William Faulkner and Erskine Caldwell were writing did not reflect the South in best light, and therefore were to be ignored. To my family, William Faulkner was somebody up the road who was writing to make money, and they didn't see the scope of his work at all. I didn't read Faulkner 'til I was in graduate school."

After high school Spencer went to Belhaven College, a small girls' finishing school in Jackson. "It was right across the street from where Eudora Welty lived, and she had begun to publish when I was a student there. Some of us in a writing group called up and asked if she would come over for an evening, and she consented. She spent a good deal of time on that first occasion talking to me and being interested in some little thing I had written. We've been friends ever since."

Spencer got a scholarship to Vanderbilt and went off to Nashville, remaining there to teach after graduate school. Her publishing career began when an editor from Dodd, Mead came through Nashville, saw the manuscript for *Fire in the Morning*, her first novel, and sent her a contract before she'd finished the book. "Southern literature was in the ascendancy, and people were looking for new southern writers as a matter of course, so I seemed to fill that need," she says modestly.

Dodd, Mead also published her second book, *This Crooked Way*. Spencer later went to McGraw-Hill, then to Doubleday for a large collection of short stories, and subsequently to Viking for the current volume. On the basis of the first two works she won an award from the American Academy of Arts and Letters in 1952, and lived in New York on its proceeds. "I had a number of boyfriends who would take me out, and the $1000 lasted me all summer," Spencer laughs gently.

A Guggenheim sent Spencer to Italy, where she intended to stay for a year. She met her husband, Englishman John Rusher, there, and remained for the better part of five years. Italy has infused her imagination and her fiction ever since. There she wrote most of *The Voice at the Back Door*, about a racial situation that has its roots in the post–Civil War era. "That book depends so much on voice because it's totally about a small county in Mississippi. There are so many levels of speech that became very clear to me when I was in Italy because I was in a foreign atmosphere. If I'd been at home hearing them all the time, there would have been things that were merging and becoming vague." One reason for the book's "phenomenal success," Spencer thinks, was its coincidental timing with civil rights activism in the States.

"I began to get fascinated with Italy, and it began to seem like a possible second country. I still feel that way to a large extent. We would have stayed on, but it's hard for outsiders to make a living in Italy. It seemed too far from other bases where we might do better financially."

Eventually Spencer's husband took a job in Montreal, where they lived for 28 years, although Spencer says, "There hasn't been a year in my life that I haven't come back to Mississippi or the South at least two or three times. With experience first in Italy and then marrying an Englishman, I began to see that my existence wasn't just one straight line; it was being broken up into different packages, and I began to try to adapt, write stories on that basis. Though many of those stories I wrote in Canada must have been motivated a bit by homesickness because a lot of 'em are about memories of the South.

"Italy had a lot to do with changing the focus of my work over the years. Before I went to Italy I thought I would always be encased in the southern social patterns and lineage and tradition, and if the South changed, then I wanted to be part of that change. I didn't see myself as separate from it. Then, especially after I married, I had to come to terms with a life that was going to be quite separate from that. I got to thinking that the southerner has a certain mentality, especially southern women—you can no more change a southern woman than you can a French woman; they're always going to be French no matter what you do. So I thought that really nothing was going to happen to me as far as my essential personality was concerned, that it could broaden and include more scope and maybe get richer. I looked at that from the standpoint of my characters, that the southern approach was going to be valued no matter where they found themselves. It seemed to me that there wasn't any need in sitting at home in the cottonfield just to be southern, that you could be southern elsewhere, in Florence, or Paris, or anywhere you found yourself."

We go off to lunch at the local favorite, the Pyewacket, later pay a visit to the small ranch house where Algonquin Books is located and meet publisher Louis Rubin, to whom, along with his wife and Max Steele, *Jack of Diamonds* is dedicated. We stop, too, for coffee, at the delightful Hardback Cafe and Bookstore, whose owner, Grant Kornberg, will shortly publish a single Spencer story in a limited edition.

"The part of the States that is still *incredibly* attractive to me," Spencer continues, "is the coastal regions of the South. I've written a lot of stories in the past about the Gulf Coast. Mobile isn't

477

far from the area I wrote about in *The Salt Line* [her novel about rivalries that reemerge in the wake of a hurricane's devastation], and they have bumper stickers that say, 'Thank God I live south of the Salt Line.' " Indeed, Spencer has one in her writing room upstairs. "Somebody in Montreal said, 'Of course you took that from the common vernacular, but it made a good title.' I made it up!"

Spencer tells us that the stories in the current collection "simmered around with me since the last novel came out and before that." She was invited to the Villa Serbelloni in Bellagio, Italy, where she wrote "The Cousins," her exquisite story about five young southerners who go abroad together. "Writing that story was a sheer joy to me from beginning to end. I wrote to Walker Percy the other day and was going on about my new novel and said it took me a while to get to know the characters, and then I said, 'Writers are crazy. I made all these people up, and then I think I've got to spend time getting to *know* them. You ought to lock me up.' I get frustrated when I think of people like Eric and Ben [the two cousins that the protagonist, a woman, is enamored of], that I'll never meet them. I knew a lot of people similar to them, rather dashing and terribly well-read young men. When I was at the age to fall for somebody like that, they were all in the war. It was a long hiatus out of my life. I still admire that kind of guy very much, but I think they have their faults and weaknesses, too. The story brings out some of that."

Regarding the complex relationship at the heart of "The Cousins," Spencer says, "It seems to me that real relationships don't ever perish. My object is to bring people to a certain point— usually a spiritual point, an awareness of all the elements involved. It's like focussing a camera. In *The Salt Line* what I was trying to say was that the life force is hanging on and has to be reckoned with."

Spencer's stories are full of mystery about their characters. "If you got to the point where they cleared it all up, that story would vanish and another one would come on." Her friend, novelist Lee Smith, pointed out to her that in every story in her current collection people hide something from each other. Spencer's response: "There's a certain mystery at the heart of relationships that is difficult to penetrate.

"My idea of a story is that it's something that should go on living in your mind. I judge books and novels and stories like that, that there's something I can feel I'm living in, and after I finish that I can meditate on its various angles. I try to aim for that effect, because it's what I like to read. I have this optimism that the good things do have the tendency to last."

AMANDA SMITH

WALLACE STEGNER

WALLACE STEGNER IS 78 years old, and publication of his novel, *Crossing to Safety*, is designed to coincide with the 50th anniversary of his debut as a writer. His first novel won a $2500 prize, and on the strength of it (in 1937) he quit teaching and bicycled around England and France for a summer. Since then his copious flow of novels, stories, histories and memoirs have won many other prizes, including several O. Henry Awards, a Pulitzer (for *Angle of Repose*, 1972) and a National Book Award (for *The Spectator Bird*, 1977).

It has been a long, productive and honorable career, as both admired author and teacher (at Stanford and Harvard) of a generation of younger writers; and Stegner is in a reflective, almost elegiac mood as he talks about it to *PW* one recent summer afternoon. The scene is the remote Vermont country hideaway where Stegner and his wife Mary retreat for a few weeks every summer. Home the rest of the year is a handsome house in the hills above Los Altos, south of San Francisco, not far from the campus where he taught creative writing for several postwar decades.

Since Stegner has always been thought of as a writer predominantly of the American West and its history (his award-winning books and *The Big Rock Candy Mountain*, his biggest commercial success, are all set there), the conversation turns initially to what sometimes seems like a cultural conflict between East and West. "Don't you believe it," says Stegner. "It's like the talk of war between the cattle and sheep men. It doesn't really exist."

He ponders his replies only briefly and then makes them crisply in well-formed sentences, spoken in a quietly resonant voice quite without regional inflection. "I've taught at Harvard, and been coming up here for 50 years. What I like about this part of the Northeast is that it's been a summer home for generations of families. It has a sort of continuity no Westerner could comprehend without actually coming here. It's a sort of stable world with which unstable people can identify. And a lot of the Westerners I know seem rather uprooted these days, somewhat like orphans. But this place has a frontier look, wild and undeveloped. In fact, it's more like the notion of the West than most of the West is now."

That part of Vermont is, in fact, important in *Crossing to Safety*, which is a study, ripe with the wisdom and regrets of age, of the sometimes troubled friendship of two young college instructors and their wives over the years. There is a summer gathering place in the book that seems not unlike Stegner's Caspian Lake, though he swears there is little resemblance. And its narrator is a westerner who feels not a little out of place in the East, envious of its rootedness and easy authority. Stegner sounds faintly rueful when he is reminded of this: "It's a mistake to project myself too much into a book. Sometimes I just don't realize how much I'm doing it. But, you know, I *am* a westerner. I was never east of Cheyenne before I was 21."

The novel also displays expert knowledge of the ways of academe, and how the fight for tenure can warp a person. But Stegner was not, he says, sniping at the scholarly community, and he has had no cause to be bitter. "I've quit a couple of times, but never been fired. I took a chance on the academic business and I can't complain, though I know a lot of people have no sympathy with that insulated world—and it's true, it does get narrow and develops some pretty stuffy characters."

He never expected to be a teacher—or in fact even a writer. "I didn't know what I wanted to be—maybe make a living selling linoleum. I'd never met a living writer until after graduate school. We didn't get many of them out in Salt Lake City. I can't claim I ever had a dedication to the arts. I guess I've been a kind of weathervane, taking the line of least resistance, going wherever friends who knew better kept pushing me."

Where they pushed him eventually was into journalism and teaching, thence into writing. His first novel, *Remembering Laughter*, won that 1937 prize (from Little, Brown) and launched his writing career. But he still had to eat and, when the prize money was spent, took the first job that offered; an instructorship at the University of Wisconsin (once again, as in *Crossing*). The next move was to teaching composition at Harvard for six years, during which his reputation slowly grew. There were *On a Darkling Plain, Mormon Country, Fire and Ice*, then, in 1943, the novel that really made his name: *The Big Rock Candy Mountain*.

The book had a difficult birth. Stegner had left Little, Brown, since "they didn't like my second book. They were right and I was wrong." He ended up with a new publishing house that had just been set up by Charles Duell, Sam Sloan and Charles Pearce. "I heard *The Big Rock Candy Mountain* might win the Harper Prize if I took it to Harper, but I thought it would be dirty pool. Then Sam Sloan fell on the sidewalk and died and things were rough for a while. It was wartime, and they couldn't get enough paper, and *Mountain* was a very long book, so they had to print it small, and right up to the edge of the paper. It was a terrible-looking book." It was a bestseller, however, selling about 40,000 copies in hardcover. Pocket Books later brought out a paperback, which has been in print ever since.

His next publishing move came out of an anomalous project in his career: a group of writers for *Look* magazine were to examine the condition of racial minorities in the U.S. as the war neared its end, the results eventually to be a Houghton Mifflin book, *One Nation* (1945). Stegner wrote one of the major essays, then found "the magazine had gone chicken and simply wanted to make it one long, innocuous article. The country was still very racially divided at that time, and I remember that when *Ladies' Home Journal* did an article about a black Army major, they had 50,000 canceled subscriptions, just like that. So I got disgusted, and took over the book myself." He stayed with Houghton Mifflin for a decade, even served as its West Coast editor for several postwar years while he taught at Stanford. "I brought in some writers, scouting among my own students. Tom Heggen, with *Mister Roberts*, was one."

In the end, however, Stegner felt it awkward to be working for his own publisher, and the combined burden of writing, teaching and scouting proved too time-consuming, so he quit. His next books, *A Shooting Star* ("not a book I'm fond of now; it came dangerously close to being a soap opera") and *Wolf Willow* ("a book I do continue to respect, though it's a librarian's nightmare; they never know how to classify it"), were published by Viking.

In the '60s, Stegner tired of teaching, decided he wanted to devote himself only to writing and shopped around for a publisher who would give him a multi-book contract. Doubleday complied, and from *Angle of Repose* on, all his fiction and much of his non-fiction—including his biography and collected papers of Bernard De Voto—came from that house. "I'd been happy there with Ken McCormick and Sam Vaughan, but when Sam left, and this 50th anniversary was approaching, I felt I had to do something with my next book—fish or cut bait. I asked around, then wound up going with Sam to Random House." He muses a moment. "It seems right somehow. I was a good friend of Alfred Knopf for many years, and I don't know why he never published me."

Today's publishing scene worries him. "I don't like this tendency to try to sell more and more of fewer and fewer titles. It means the springs are pinched off, that good young writers get crowded out." He grins. "Even older ones like myself who don't sell enough get overlooked."

In an early book Stegner used as an epigraph a quote from Archibald MacLeish: "Men are brothers by life lived and are hurt for it." And it has seemed to a number of critics that one of the obsessions in his fiction is how a man can live a good life. What is the philosophy that governs his thoughtful novels? Stegner laughs a little at the quote. "I was very young and pompous to use that," he says, then adds: "I guess I'm a pessimist. There's enough black Norwegian in me to make me a bit of a Gloomy Gus on occasion. I might be a pessimistic meliorist—hoping something can be done to improve our lot, but not at all sure it can."

One of the movements Stegner has felt able to embrace is the environmentalist one: "Natural things soothe my soul, and I like to help preserve them if possible." To this end he has written tirelessly on environmental issues, has been active in the Sierra Club and Wilderness Society and was once for a short time an assistant to then–Secretary of the Interior Stewart Udall.

It has been noted of his best books (including his latest one) that they all contain strong and sympathetically observed women, whose lives are often made difficult by the blindly aggressive, unthinking actions of their men. "Yes, I've been told there's a feminine sensibility in some of my books. Maybe it comes from being a mother's boy when I was a kid. *Big Rock Candy Mountain* is really all about a woman being dragged around when all she wants to do is nest. And *Angle of Repose* is a different version of the same thing. Maybe it's true that everyone has only one book in them, and that was mine!"

Stegner's legacy as a teacher of writing is remarkable. Mention of the current success by Scott Turow reminds him that Turow was once a student—along with a roster of other notables, including writers as various as Larry McMurtry, Thomas McGuane, Ken Kesey, Tillie Olsen and Robert Stone. Still, he sees today as "not a particularly rich time in fiction," and finds that most of his very favorite novelists "turn out to be Russian or Polish." For pleasure he reads "nature stuff of a Thoreauvian kind" and mentions with admiration the work of Annie Dillard and Barry Lopez.

Who were his own models as a writer? "I learned a great deal from my students, many of them very technically adept. And I never stop learning. *Big Rock Candy Mountain* was basically a 19th-century chronological novel, and it was a long time before I had the skill to do something as difficult as *Angle of Repose*, with its changing time frames. You know, you catch up slow when you come from the frontier as I do. It took me until I was 60 or so to learn how a novel should be written. Short stories I have theories about, but novels elude any theory."

Looking back on his own books over a half-century, Stegner is somberly self-critical. "Some I wince at a little bit, some I wince at a lot. When you write books you get your education in public, especially when your enthusiasm outruns your experience—and mine did." He has, he says, "a good deal of faith" in his latest book. "But would I want to go to heaven on it?"

Which leads, clearly, to a question about future plans.

"Maybe at my age I should hang out the 'Closed' sign. But somehow I've always had something in mind for the next book ever since 1937. I came up here expecting just to sit in the sun, but after a week I found I was picking at some essays. So I guess I'll just keep at it till I die."

JOHN F. BAKER

ROBERT STONE

THERE ARE MANY authors whose lives boil down to: ". . . and then I wrote." Not so Robert Stone. While each of his novels has been a literary milestone, they have also been refractions of events in his own life that represent some of the distinguishing hallmarks of our age: experiences with drugs, addiction to alcohol, firsthand awareness of the violence in Vietnam and of the conditions for upheaval in Central America. Stone's *Children of Light* further raised his reputation as a writer with brilliant insight into the American psyche. Here he has used observations gathered during several stints as a screenwriter to portray the sickness of soul lurking below Hollywood's glittering myth of happy-ever-after.

Stone has, as they say, been around. He is now 47; the blond hairs in his beard have been overwhelmed by grey; in casual sweater, corduroys and sneakers, his figure is burly and beginning to thicken. As he welcomes us to his cozy house on the Connecticut shore, he seems at first the picture of a contented writer in his safe retreat. On closer inspection, however, his eyes are guarded and wary, and his face wears a weary look, betraying the ravages of a peripatetic, emotionally and intellectually engaged life on the edge. He is a man whose maturing years were difficult, and who ever since has deliberately confronted risk and challenge.

Born in Brooklyn in 1937, Stone never knew his father. He and his mother, a teacher who was increasingly incapacitated by severe emotional problems, moved to Manhattan when he was young. After his mother was institutionalized, he lived for four years in a Catholic school that was "the last vestige of the old-fashioned orphanage," continuing to attend as a day student when his mother was released. Despite its strong undercurrent of anti-intellectualism, Stone credits the school for deepening his respect for literature, initially instilled by his mother, and for providing him with a solid grounding in the English language. By the time he left high school at 17, Stone was reading Ovid ("in the expurgated version, of course"), but an adolescent resistance to authority compounded by some serious drinking had resulted in academic failure. Stone joined the Navy, spending the next three years on an expedition to the Antarctic.

Returning to New York, Stone attended NYU by day and worked at night as a copyboy at the *Daily News*, a schedule that proved onerous. Though he left college after a year, two significant events had already occurred: Stone met Janice, now his wife of almost 30 years, and he took a writing workshop with M. L. Rosenthal, whose encouragement Stone credits with determining his career.

First, however, Stone and Janice decided to see the country. They got as far as New Orleans, where they both worked at a variety of menial jobs that never lifted them above the poverty level. Their daughter was born in a charity hospital there, and it was not until Stone got his seaman's papers and respectable paychecks that they were able to accumulate enough money to get back to New York.

In short order, they joined the burgeoning beatnik scene, mixing with Jack Kerouac and his disciples, while Stone worked on what would become his first novel, *A Hall of Mirrors*, its setting New Orleans. On the strength of the first chapter, Stone won a Stegner Fellowship to Stanford, an event that he claims changed his life. California was "the place to be in the '60s, even if it was not the best place to work," he says.

The Stones joined a coterie of people who "seemed to be just a bunch of Stanford graduate students, but actually turned out to be the future of mankind." Falling in with Ken Kesey and his Merry Pranksters, they lived in an off-campus enclave called Perry Lane, a place later celebrated by Tom Wolfe and others. Some hospitals in the area were conducting experiments with psychological drugs, calling for volunteers. Psychedelic drugs became standard fare at parties, and an atmosphere developed that had profound repercussions on the state of American society. "Life in California was in a way the affluent American experience at its peak," Stone says, "but at the same time there were other strong forces at work: civil rights activism, the rebellion against the '50s, a new sense of freedom, even a spirit of anarchy; the refusal to buckle down to arbitrary norms. All of these things collided in one enormous explosion."

It was very exciting to be part of that scene, Stone recalls, "although looking back it is easy to see that we were doing something that was dangerous. For all the good times and insights that we experienced through drugs, an age was coming into being in which it was going to be very difficult to bring up children. But of course we didn't forsee any of that. We were mainly optimistic."

Yet Stone himself felt a vestigial strain of Catholic guilt at the core of his partying. "I always thought: nothing is free. And nothing was free. A lot of people paid a very high price for it later."

During what he calls "those anarchic and fertile years," the novel that was to become *A Hall of Mirrors* was giving Stone trouble. "I was changing, the country was changing and the book was changing in my hands." Although he began by writing a conventional novel, Stone found himself veering away from the realistic mode. "I came to believe that when George Eliot said, 'I will write things just the way they are,' she was deluding herself. You can't write things just the way they are. Being and writing are not the same things. Language is language and things are things."

When Stone realized that he would never finish the book in California, the family came East again in 1965. He worked for a now-defunct tabloid until *A Hall of Mirrors* was published by Houghton Mifflin. The book won the Faulkner Award for the best first novel of 1967 and a Guggenheim for its author. For the next few years, the Stones (they now had a second child, a son) bounced back and forth between London, with Stone trying to make progress on a second novel, and L.A., where he periodically had movie jobs, writing the film script of *A Hall of Mirrors*, which became "a dreadful film called *WUSA*," and a couple of other projects that never got made. "By now I was a frustrated one-novel novelist," Stone says, giving a clue to the dark thoughts of the character Dongan Lowndes in *Children of Light*.

487

In 1971 Stone wangled an assignment to Vietnam from a London magazine called *INK*. It was the period of so-called Vietnamization, when American troops were being kept back out of the line, "not the most dangerous or tense part of the war. But I did get to know far more than I wanted to know about the Saigon underworld. I found that scene thoroughly scary—so scary that sometimes I felt safer when I went out toward the line than I did in Saigon."

Back in London, Stone immediately started *Dog Soldiers*, again published by Houghton Mifflin. The novel won rave reviews, a movie adaptation (Stone wrote that one too; the movie was titled *Who'll Stop the Rain?*) and the National Book Award in 1975. By that time Stone had become a member of academia, teaching for a year at Princeton, then moving on to Amherst, then Harvard, all the while working on a book that he says gave him "endless trouble." He was restless, and when a reading at the University of Alabama put $1000 in his pocket, Stone took off for Central America to do some snorkeling. He became fascinated by the political upheaval simmering there, extending his stay and eventually making two later trips encompassing visits to Honduras, Nicaragua and Costa Rica. "By then I had met enough people, and listened to enough conversations, and seen enough things, that I knew I wanted to write about Central America," he says. Stone took *A Flag for Sunrise* to Knopf because he knew editor Bob Gottlieb "has so high a quality of intelligence that I could not put anything past him." *Flag* was nominated for the 1981 American Book Award and made Stone seem prophetic for anticipating history. "Because I'm a slow writer, I was overtaken by events," he says, "but you didn't have to be prescient to see what was going to happen there."

Ever in search of new experiences, Stone next taught at the University of Hawaii and at two campuses of the University of California. "And then I came here and began working on *Children of Light*," Stone says, summoning us into the present.

"Here" is a shingled, narrow, three-story house on an inlet of Long Island Sound. Floor-to-ceiling windows give directly to the beach, where a family of swans makes its home on a nearby island and dozens of resident mallards sometimes honk up such a racket that Stone has to shoo them away. Comfortably furnished, with an electric heater in the fireplace giving off warmth and a glow,

488

the home could typify the bourgeois lifestyle Stone claims to have adopted as his own. But he admits that the counterculture adventurer still lives inside the homeowner and successful author.

The years of the counterculture, Stone says, are now part of the American social fabric. "There's a sense in which America's high bourgeois age has been over for a long time. So many of us who constitute the American middle class now carry within us the experiences of the edge. It gives American society its distinctiveness."

He could not have written *Children of Light*, for example, had he not participated in the drug culture of the '60s. Here again he is describing addicted personalities; his characters are dependent on alcohol and cocaine. But in a larger sense, drugs played an important part in transforming Stone's view of the meaning of human existence. "I think that my experiences with drugs enhanced my sense of the numinous," he says. "I became less ashamed of confronting religious impulses than I would have been if I hadn't been exposed to drugs. One of the reasons for the prevalence of drugs in our society is the aspiration for something transcendent, something above the daily life, something more meaningful than ourselves.

"All of my characters are looking for transcendence, whether they know it or not," Stone continues. "The reason that they don't find it, and the *only* reason that they don't find it, is that *I* can't. The moment I find it, I will have a character who finds it. It's on my mind a lot."

Despair is a pervasive word in the new novel, as it has been in Stone's previous books. He claims, however, that this bleak vision is not his message. "I don't *believe* in despair. I say that we have to get on with living, even if we have to begin, in a sense, in despair. Heidegger spoke of 'the dynamics of an absent God.' That means that God is absent, not available, but it does not mean that He does not exist. This is the condition at which one starts living, at which one starts dealing with other people and chooses to deal with them decently, at which one makes all one's moral decisions. This is despair of a special and dynamic kind."

He is modest about his influence as one of the few "popular" writers who has a political conscience. "I feel that a writer has a moral responsibility to speak out, to bring one's weight to bear on the side of human rights and other moral issues. I think, however, that this is much more difficult to do effectively than many readers

489

realize. Governments are extremely skillful at using writers and artists and people of ideals—intellectuals—for their own purposes. It's necessary to be very wary lest one become an accomplice for something that one would not have wanted to support."

Stone's voice has not lost its mild, even tone, but his strong feeling is evident. As he speaks of matters of the spirit and of conscience, he closes his eyes as though groping for an image, makes an enveloping gesture with his arm as though calling ideas out of the air. The room has darkened along with our conversation. Outside, the water has turned opaque and murky; the mallards have found safe harbor; the beach is deserted of strollers and dogs. In the snug warmth of Stone's home, however, one hopes the dark night of the soul will be kept at bay.

SYBIL S. STEINBERG

PETER TAYLOR

THE SOUTH HAS traditionally been one of America's more gothic literary landscapes: suffering and violence grow in abundance there, at least in writers' imaginations, and southern writers' prose is usually as luxuriant as the foliage. For more than 40 years, however, Peter Taylor has cast a cool, classical eye on his native territory, delineating changes in its socioeconomic structure and dissecting its inhabitants' passions in elegant, measured language more reminiscent of Henry James than William Faulkner.

Yet Taylor's work is as distinctively southern as he is. *The Old Forest and Other Stories* (Dial/Doubleday) collects 12 previously published and two recently written short stories delving into the lives of the people among whom Taylor grew up: wealthy, aristocratic Southerners whose families picked themselves up after the debacle of the Civil War, left the plantations and moved into the South's growing cities to become lawyers, doctors, cotton brokers—a new professional class whose code of behavior was still firmly rooted in antebellum moral values.

It's the effect of this external reality on the private concerns of his characters that interests Taylor, whose own life has been at once deeply rooted in the South and also detached from it by the exigencies of first his father's and then his own career. Growing up all over the South and Midwest, spending every summer in the Tennessee mountains, he now lives in Charlottesville, Va., near the university where he taught for many years. The Taylors' handsome gray clapboard house is in the colonial style, not an

491

antebellum mansion by any means, but southern in mood nonetheless. The library in which he chats with *PW* contains an almost Victorian profusion of furniture (including a red settee that
was a gift from the writer Jean Stafford, a lifelong friend) and
books (complete sets of Henry James and Anthony Trollope jostle
short story collections by Tolstoy and Chekhov, with the works of
Faulkner and other southern writers also prominent).

The library also displays several paintings, one of which is a full-
size portrait of Taylor's great-grandfather. Its companion, a painting of the author's great-grandmother and her children, hangs in
the adjoining room. "Very Tennessee, don't you think?" remarks
their descendant, whose attitude is affectionate but hardly respectful and whose own accent is also "very Tennessee." A handsome man in his late 60s, with a strongly lined face framed by a
shock of white hair, Taylor wears both his age and his aristocratic
heritage lightly. Unlike many modern writers, he remains deeply
connected to his family and its history, but he views both with an
amused detachment that suggests a man at peace with his past.

Taylor's wife, the poet Eleanor Ross Taylor, is at home working
today, but although her husband speaks with her briefly in another room, she does not appear to greet his visitor. "She's in her
bathrobe," Taylor explains. "We both love to work in our pajamas!
We write in the morning and try not to see each other before
lunch at 2 o'clock, because if we do, if we meet and start talking,
then before we know it, the day's already gone. She works upstairs, and I work just underneath this room—we have a basement that opens out on the garden—so that we can't hear each
other's typewriters. I find it depressing to hear somebody else's
when mine won't go!"

Although Taylor is essentially a short story writer, most of his
work begins as verse. "I write nearly everything that way," he
says. "I like it because you get more emphasis on the groups of
words and the language and the rhythms. I can't sustain it very
long, but I try to finish a story in verse, then go back and put it
into prose. I began writing that way as an effort to compress; in a
story you have very limited space, so every sentence has to do
more. I have a theory that a story ought to do as much as a novel,
and a poem ought to do as much as a story—in fact, if a poem
doesn't do a great deal more with its language, with the form,
then it's not as good as a story."

His method is certainly unusual, but given his history it's not surprising that Taylor should work in verse. Not only is he married to a poet, but at Vanderbilt University and Kenyon College in the late 1930s he studied with the influential Southern poets Allen Tate and John Crowe Ransom. In that same period, he also met two contemporaries who would become his lifelong friends: poets Robert Lowell and Randall Jarrell. "It was wonderful, and it certainly had a great deal to do with my going on in writing," says Taylor. "To come at that age into a group of people who were very highbrow, very serious and articulate about writing. You learn so much from your peers; I always tell my students that. I learned a lot from Tate and Ransom, but more from Lowell and Jarrell."

Jarrell, who was four years older than Taylor, was a formidable critic. "Kenyon was his first teaching job, I think," says Taylor, "and we were all sort of scared of him. If he didn't like what you wrote, he would get furious at you. One time, when he and I were both living in a little town in Italy, I passed him on the street, and he wouldn't speak to me. I saw his wife later and said, 'Well, what in the world?' and she answered, 'Well, he doesn't like that new story of yours.' He would do the same thing to Lowell. The thing was, you were his friend, but there was this *other* you that had done this awful thing! But he'd get over it, and later he might even come to like the piece. This is often true of your friends: if you change and begin writing something rather different from what you'd done before, they don't always want you to, because they liked what you'd been doing. I know when Lowell broke from his formal verse and began to write more freely, I was very critical—but I was wrong. He needed to break out and deal with his experience more directly."

Taylor was Lowell's close friend for nearly 40 years (the poet died in 1977), and when he speaks of their relationship his tone is warm. "We never had any real quarrel," he says. "He was a wonderful friend; he could make you feel good about anything. One of the problems with Ian Hamilton's biography, although I thought it was good in many ways, was that it didn't give any impression of the other side of him. He had the most marvelous sense of humor; he was the gentlest person and the most loyal of friends. He was lots of fun to be with, just to talk to; he would call, and we would talk on the telephone for hours. Our wives

493

used to say that we liked each other's jokes so much that we would sit up telling stories we'd heard a dozen times before, and we would just roar with laughter!

"Lowell had a tremendous influence on me when I was beginning to write," Taylor continues. "For example, all through college I took Latin and had a great respect for classical literature—not a profound knowledge, but respect and an acquaintance with it. I had always wanted to be a fiction writer, but I just wrote stories wildly without much form or much reference to the formal history of literature. His concern with poetry from Homer to William Carlos Williams, his need to have it all in place, to understand it and incorporate what he needed in his own work, made me try to read fiction more with a view to its form than I would have otherwise. Of course, poets are often more articulate about things and more concerned with tradition. He made me more scholarly than I would have been otherwise; I might just have read contemporary material, as most young writers do."

The deep seriousness and reverence for tradition that Lowell imparted to him are reflected in Taylor's fairly classical beliefs about what fiction should do. "My feeling is that stories ought to be about something that's over and done with, so you can judge it properly," he says. "You can't really trust what writers say about their work, but it seems to me that what I'm trying to do in my stories is to look at the characters from several points of view, to make sure that I'm at a distance so that I can discover what this character's like and how to look at it. And so I felt that during integration, for example, I couldn't really write about it." (Taylor's stories, in fact, are virtually all set before 1954.)

This doesn't mean that Taylor's fiction won't engage issues or make moral judgments. "I think writing fiction is a cognitive instrument," he says. "You learn what you really think from what you write. My parents were great storytellers, and so were our [black] servants; they were all part of that southern oral tradition. As a young writer aspiring to be an artist, I just had to do something with those stories—they were so marvelous. My parents didn't have any idea of moral or intellectual judgment; a story was just a funny story or a sad story to them. But as I put them down on paper, I began to see that in all these fine old southern stories blacks were getting the short end from women, who were getting the short end from men. I didn't know what they meant until I wrote them."

Taylor's parents weren't always happy about his use of old family tales in his fiction. "My father once even threatened me physically because of a story that came out in the *New Yorker* about my great-aunt," he remembers. "It wasn't really about her, but it used an incident from her life. People don't understand that in fiction you're just using them for character and detail; they're not concerned with the basic ideas of the story. You have to use the details, just as you use colors in a painting, but what's important is the interplay, the contrast of people's lives with the decline of society, or the deterioration of the family. The real poetry emerges in the coincidence between the context and the character, as in Chekhov's stories: the estate is going to pieces, the whole order is falling apart, and the characters are the same—there's no satisfaction, nothing's working, and that all makes sense. In Ibsen too: the gloom of Scandinavia and the characters' gloom do something to each other; they interpret each other, make you believe in them, like rhyme and meter in poetry."

In Taylor's own stories, the characters' personal preoccupations and behavior do indeed reflect the larger nature of the South, but in a subtle, unmythical way that may account for his curious lack of fame; America seems to prefer its southern writers to be more flamboyant. "It's partly temperament," says Taylor of his restrained approach. "Also, although I admire all these mythical writers about the South tremendously—I'm just a slave to Faulkner, I think he's wonderful, and Eudora Welty and Katherine Anne Porter—I thought it was time to try something else." As for his admirers' loudly expressed belief that he deserves to be better known—"I don't write for that," he says simply. "I've always had a lot of appreciative literary friends, and maybe that meant more to me than it should have, but it's all chance whether or not you become well known in your generation. My concern is with how good what I write is and with the opinion of my peers."

Taylor has let the outside world influence him to the extent of writing his third novel recently. (His first, *A Woman of Means*, was published in 1954 and reissued in 1984 by Frederic C. Beil; a second was destroyed by Taylor in the 1960s when he decided it was unsatisfactory.) "It used to infuriate me, the attitude that you wrote stories until you were good enough to write a novel," he says. "I much prefer reading stories: I like James's stories better than his novels, and Faulkner's, and I think D. H. Lawrence's stories are *much* better than his novels. But people always pressure you, and it does seem like a challenge—the scope of it. So I've just completed a second draft, and it needs about one more. It may not be any good, but I have written it, by George. I wanted to see if I could write a novel."

Work seems to get done faster now that he's no longer teaching full time, Taylor finds. "I guess it kept me from writing more than I realized," he says, "but it taught me a great deal too. I think teaching's been good for me: I'm a very gregarious person, I like to be with people, and it's also made me more articulate. I wanted to do something to support my family and not feel they were interfering with my writing. So many writers have to just turn it out, and it shouldn't be that sort of thing. The writers I knew—and that's how I feel too—thought that you write out of compulsion, because there's a need to tell a story or to write a poem; you don't write because you've got to have another book out this year. Professionalism gets very near commercialism. Now, some writers, like F. Scott Fitzgerald, just have to be in the mainstream, and that's right for them, so I wouldn't want to make rules about it. But I think, generally speaking, people do better if they have another profession and don't depend on their writing to make a living. Because if you do, you've got to please the public: you try to fit your writing to their taste instead of forming the taste. Most good writers—and by good writers, I mean really good ones, like Proust or Lowell—didn't answer the demands of an audience, they created a whole new one. And that's what you should aspire to."

WENDY SMITH

WILLIAM TREVOR

Wɪʟʟɪᴀᴍ ᴛʀᴇᴠᴏʀ ᴄᴏx is proof that one art's loss is another's
gain. Trevor Cox had been a sculptor for some 16 years before he
abandoned the métier in favor of writing. Almost a quarter of a
century later, as William Trevor, he is regarded as one of the British Isles' finest writers, increasingly popular in this country as
well. His 10th novel, *Fools of Fortune,* is a romance set against
the last half-century of Irish conflict. In tandem, *The Stories of
William Trevor* (Viking) is an omnibus collection of Trevor's masterly short stories, his graceful glimpses into ordinary lives that
often turn out to be not so ordinary after all.

The author who meets us at the British Rail station in Exeter is
a trim man of 55, gentlemanly, affable, a little guarded. Later, he
admits to disliking interviews: "I always say each one is going to
be my last." Nevertheless, he drives us off in his large green
Volkswagen-cum-Land Rover. Some 15 minutes down the road—
much of it single-laned and lined by tall hedges—deep in the
Devon countryside sits the 200-year-old farmhouse, which is tit-
ularly Trevor's home but which he is, in fact, visiting for only a
month "to catch up on things" before returning to Italy, where, at
least for now, he prefers to do his writing. As we sit on the lawn
and chat, swallows wheel overhead, occasionally landing on the
half-thatched roof of the Trevor farmhouse. In a field above us,
Trevor's wife, Jane, runs the family's Irish setter.

Born in Ireland, the son of a bank manager, Trevor spent his
boyhood moving from town to town, some 13 of them. He counts
his peripatetic childhood as an advantage; much of what he now

writes is of the provincial Ireland of his youth. Trevor read history at Trinity College, Dublin, and then began his artistic life as a sculptor, exhibiting in Dublin, Bath and London. Two of his pieces still hang in the entry foyer of his Devon farmhouse: rectangular planes of highly polished, warm wood, inset with smaller rectangles of black and white. There were years of teaching and a stint as a church sculptor in Somerset, but the arrival of the first of his two sons led him to a job in a London advertising firm.

Trevor explains his unlikely start as a writer: "I found myself in an office with a typewriter and a *great* deal of spare time. They tend to give you an awful lot of time to write four lines about paint or socks, because they think they're very important. I found I just couldn't do that, so I began to write short stories."

Meanwhile, his sculpture had become increasingly abstract until, he explains, "I just stopped altogether. It was quite a big break. I think the humanity that isn't in abstract art began to go into the short stories. The absence of people, I think, was upsetting me. I still don't like pictures without people in them."

And the name change? "In Ireland in particular, I was known as a sculptor, and it just seemed quite wrong—sort of untidy—to write under the same name, a completely different kind of thing. So I just used my first two names."

But still he finds the sculpting and writing are connected. "Being a sculptor does help you to form things. There's a way in which you think as a sculptor. You see things in the round very much. You have to have an extra something; you have to go see around the back of somebody's head, as it were. And I've found that I still think like that when I'm writing. I'm still obsessed by form and pattern—the actual shape of things, the shape of a novel or the shape of a short story.

"I always tend to say, just to annoy everyone, that I'm a short story writer who writes novels, because most novelists are novelists who write short stories," Trevor observes, and it is the short story which remains his preferred form. His move into the genre was almost inadvertent. Some two decades ago, the Bodley Head—still Trevor's English publishers—"said they would publish a collection of short stories, but wouldn't I write a novel, which is what publishers always say. They said, cleverly, we'll give you £50 to write a novel, and that was a great deal of money as far as I was concerned, and I said yes." Thus, *The Old Boys*,

Trevor's novel of the conundrums and connivings of the geriatric set, was published and subsequently given the Hawthornden Prize. Trevor is, in fact, much prized: in the intervening years he has won many literary awards, been made a member of the Irish Academy of Letters, and honored with a C.B.E.

Both Trevor's short stories and his novels are distinguished by his quiet concern for humanity, but the novels are sometimes delicately surreal. Trevor writes often of chaos—the chaos a sadly malicious adolescent causes in a seaside town in *The Children of Dynmouth,* the chaos a repressed homosexual produces in *Other People's Worlds.* In *Fools of Fortune,* the chaos is historical, violent: the lives and love of two cousins are cruelly interrupted by the political conflicts about them.

"I don't really have any heroes or heroines. I don't seem to go in for them. I think I am interested in people who are not necessarily the victims of other people, but simply the victims of circumstances, as they are in *Fools of Fortune.* I'm very interested in the sadness of fate, the things that just happen to people."

Trevor prefers writing about women to men. "There are far more women in what I write about than there are men. I don't know why, except I think it has to do with the business of being curious about something which I don't know about. I wrote about old people long before I was anything like as old as that because I didn't know about them, and when I had done that, I began to write about women . . . and I suppose I still write out of an enormous sense of curiosity about them. And as I get older, I write more about children, because I've forgotten what it's like to be a child.

"Your surroundings impinge on you, and you remember things, and if you remember things vividly from several years back—I mean useless things like the color of the Aga cooker, when you should be remembering your income tax figures—if you remember all those silly things, it seems that you are remembering them for a very good reason. So you put them in. That is the way in which I am an autobiographical writer. I don't tell anything about myself. I do use these little backdrops.

"What interests me most of all about writing is the relationship between you and the unknown reader and the sort of link you have with that person, the way in which that person actually picks up something which isn't in the story, as though you sort of nudge them. Some people will pick it up; other people don't get it at all. It's like looking at a picture which you don't like. Somebody else comes along and adores it. There's that odd, peculiar relationship. I think, between writer and reader. It's not in any way a personal one. It's purely people on the same sort of wavelength."

As for what he reads himself, Trevor says, "When I think of English fiction, I always think of the 19th century. I'm very fond of Dickens and George Eliot and Jane Austen." The list of American writers he admires—McCullers, Faulkner, Purdy, McCarthy, Updike, Thurber, Tennessee Williams—is interrupted by his wife's bringing us tea, a tray perched on an upended garden bucket. "Thank you, Jane," Trevor says to her appreciatively. "That's very clever."

Trevor laments the fact that in Britain, nonfiction receives more coverage than fiction. "I think fiction is probably a little bit more highly regarded in America than it is in Britain. If you write a nonfiction book here, even though it's the most trivial book, it gets far more space. It seems the wrong way round. It's not exactly fashion—it's a habit, I think. It's just the way it's done. It's a very conservative country." So he anticipates that, ironically, his upcoming *A Writer's Ireland*—a study of landscape and literature, along the same lines as Margaret Drabble's *A Writer's Britain* and due, appropriately, on St. Patrick's Day from Thames and Hudson in England and Viking here—will get more coverage in the British Isles than does his fiction.

But why does an Irish writer who's also strongly associated with England live in Italy? William Trevor Cox is permanently in transit, it seems, permanently peripatetic.

"You see Ireland much more clearly from England. I began to write about England because England was a strange country to me. I knew just enough about it to be fascinated. And then a long time went by, and Ireland had become distant because I had been living here, and then I began to write stories about Ireland. It was much clearer, much, much easier to see. It's very difficult to write about either Ireland or England because I go to Ireland a lot and I'm in England a lot.

So the same thing really has happened all over again, which is why I go such an awful lot to Italy. I write in Italy now, well away from the English language, well away from the things which interest me. You get that nice perspective which you're looking for all the time. It's a nuisance, but it's true.

"I feel more at home in Italy, I think, than I feel anywhere else. I don't speak Italian, which helps. It's very nice, actually, *not* to know what people are saying all the time because you relax more. If you do know what they're saying—in public places, on trains—you tend to listen, because writers are great eavesdroppers, and there's tremendous relaxation just to have this very, very pretty language go on all around you and you only understand bits of it here and there and never really take part in a sort of reasonable conversation, but just manage to get along in restaurants and shops and things like that. And that's the way I like to keep it."

Where do stories start for Trevor? A face glimpsed on a train, perhaps, or "something that somebody says. Or something that you remember from a long time ago, from childhood, or from some experience, or from some person. Or it starts when one is just wondering about things, mainly curiosity, mainly that kind of irritation at not knowing something and wanting to know. You write to find out. Speculation, wondering if you've got it right— that sort of thing. But always with people. Never just with plot, with just a story. People do come first. It's the people who interest me."

AMANDA SMITH

BARBARA TUCHMAN

BARBARA TUCHMAN HAS spent the past 26 years making history as enthralling for the general reader as it has always been for her. Captivated from age six on by historical novels—first the Twin series for children by Lucy Fitch Perkins, then the swashbuckling novels of Alexandre Dumas and Arthur Conan Doyle—she grew up to feel that "real events and facts make a more interesting, authentic story than any pattern you could impose." Not until she was in her mid-40s and had raised three daughters did Tuchman have a chance to test her theory in *The Zimmermann Telegram;* the 1958 publication of that account of the origins of World War I made her a bestselling author and America's foremost popular historian, and she continues in both roles to this day.

Whatever her subject, Tuchman brings to it a flair for the dramatic, a striking ability to combine narrative sweep with individual character analysis, and a vividly entertaining prose style. Other historians have won Pulitzer Prizes (Tuchman has two, for *The Guns of August* and *Stilwell and the American Experience in China*), but who else could have written a book about the 14th century (*A Distant Mirror*) that sold more than 700,000 copies?

If there is a theme running through Tuchman's heterogeneous work, it is the persistence of human folly, the insistence of both individuals and governments on doing things that are obviously self-destructive. The atmosphere of fear and suspicion that led to the outbreak of World War I, a conflict no one wanted, is an example she has treated in several books. "The calamitous 14th century," as she has called it, with its routine violence and pointless territorial squabbles, is another. Her book *The March of Folly: From Troy to Vietnam* (Knopf) treats this subject directly, analyzing four historical episodes that demonstrate folly in full bloom.

Both in structure and in content, *The March of Folly* is something of a departure for Tuchman. "I've done what I always said I would never do," she remarks, "and that is to take a theory before I wrote a book. My other books were narrative, and I tried not to adopt a thesis except what emerged from the material. It's what I don't believe in when writing history, actually."

Tuchman speaks with *PW* in her New York apartment, a pied-à-terre she and her husband use when a late night in the city makes it difficult to drive back to their house in Connecticut. She is quieter than one might expect from her forceful prose, and although she is never less than gracious, one suspects that giving interviews is not her favorite pastime. Nonetheless, perched nervously on the edge of a chair, she devotes more than an hour to discussing *The March of Folly* and its disturbing implications.

"It started from a speech I gave," she says. "I was invited to speak to the CIA, of all the funny things—they used to invite outsiders to come down to that place of theirs outside Washington and cheer them up a bit—and in thinking about subjects, I came up with this. It had puzzled me frequently when I studied history to find governments making so many errors, walking into obvious traps, these quicksands that were going to defeat them. So I did a speech on that, gave it up at West Point, too, and then when I was looking for another book topic, it occurred to me that I might enlarge it."

Tuchman examines four instances of folly in government: the fall of Troy, a direct result of the Trojans taking within their walls the wooden horse left by the Greeks, despite clear warnings that to do so was to invite disaster; the Protestant secession, provoked by the corruption and avarice of the Renaissance popes; the American Revolution, which Tuchman argues could have been avoided had the British been more willing to compromise; and the disastrous American involvement in Vietnam, a product of anti-Communist hysteria and the inability to recognize that determined nationalism could not be defeated. "I chose Troy because it struck me as the prototype of the subject, a crystal-clear example of doing the self-defeating thing," she says. "The other three were episodes that had enough scope, covered enough time and

503

had enough people involved to allow for narrative; they gave you room enough to tell a story, and I cannot write except in that form.

"I think that history *is* storytelling," says Tuchman. "At least, that's why it appeals to me. I once had an idea for a book—believe it or not, it was a history of cookery: how cooking methods had been developed, who was the first person to beat an egg, that sort of thing. I did a lot of research, but I never did anything with it, because I couldn't get a story into it. Details about how people live and so on interest me very much, but I try to insert them without letting the reader know. I like to tell a story that carries the reader, and to let all this texture of life find its way into the text sort of quietly, without signs on it."

The March of Folly has a more theoretical structure than her previous books, but Tuchman's storytelling ability is still very much in evidence, though it was a bit more difficult with four distinct topics. "You don't build up the familiarity that you do in a book on one subject," she says. "Normally, with the general reading, you start to know who's who and where to look for more information, but in this case I had to start fresh with every chapter, and that was very hard. I knew nothing whatever about the Renaissance papacy, and next to nothing about the American Revolution, and Vietnam was the worst of all, because it was so distressing—such a negative experience, and so wrongheaded."

Wrongheadedness—or "woodenheadedness," as Tuchman usually calls it—seems to be the principal ingredient of all governmental folly. Tuchman describes this trait at some length in *The March of Folly*, but it can summed up briefly as a "don't confuse me with the facts" attitude, a refusal to heed any evidence that runs counter to one's preconceived notions. "It's so clear even with the Trojan Horse," says Tuchman. "When Laocoön throws his spear at the horse, it sets off this vibration of the weapons inside, which is heard—but they ignore it! The Renaissance popes simply ignore the real desire for reform among their constituency because they're absolutely fixed in the idea that any reform would undercut their own power, dilute their authority. The British ministers in the 18th century ignore the criticism of their fellow members of Parliament, who were telling them that going to war with America over taxes was a terrible mistake, because they were obsessed with the idea that they must establish their right to tax, because it was their right to rule."

But wasn't the American Revolution inevitable? *PW* wonders. One of Tuchman's stated criteria for judging a government policy as folly is that "a feasible alternative course of action must have been available." Could the British ministers, or the Renaissance popes, really have averted the Revolution or the Reformation? "Well, I think the Protestant secession possibly could have been averted if there had been a Church hierarchy truly aware of its spiritual mission," she says. "But none of the prelates could really allow himself to recognize the need for reform, because it would have undercut his own power and financial base. As for the American Revolution, perhaps the alternative—letting Americans tax themselves—wasn't psychologically feasible, even if it was theoretically feasible.

"Certainly in Vietnam, though, the alternative of staying out and letting this conflict resolve itself was perfectly feasible. America should have recognized the strength of the North and the desire for independence, which was clear enough right from the beginning, when the French were fighting the war. We always seem to be lining up with the *ancien régime*, with the old gang, in these situations," she says regretfully. "And then when there is criticism, the government begins to distrust and separate itself from the people. Certainly Nixon did that: he regarded everyone protesting the war as an enemy, a thug. His administration saw the protest movement as inimical; it never occurred to them that the protest movement was trying to tell them something about American feelings!"

Tuchman doesn't think much of America's current foreign policy, either. "And here we go again with President Reagan," she says. "Why are we establishing our credibility by going into Lebanon and getting ourselves all shot up and accomplishing nothing? What did he suppose Marines, alien soldiers with no education about, and no familiarity with, these people or their problems, were going to do when they got there to establish peace? That's what makes me so infuriated: what was the *idea* behind this mission? It's quite frightening the way history repeats itself," she says. "That's one reason why I wanted to write this book."

The closing chapter of *The March of Folly* calls for "moral courage" from the world's leaders in order to avoid the mistakes of the past, but Tuchman acknowledges that it's doubtful whether voters would recognize this quality, even in the event that one of the candidates possessed it. "People used to have faith that if you educated the public they would give themselves better government—they would demand it—but I don't know," she says. "That's the crucial question: why does the electorate allow itself to be swayed by demagogues and extraneous characteristics?

"I'm something of a pessimist about human nature," she says, a comment that is no surprise to anyone who has read her books, "but I'm not so much of a pessimist about war and nuclear destruction. People are always asking me, 'Will we survive?' and perhaps I'm an optimist in believing, in spite of everything I say in this book"—she laughs, somewhat grimly—"that neither superpower would really wish to start a nuclear war or even do it carelessly by mistake. I don't think it's going to happen accidentally—you know, some mad general pushing the button—and I don't think it's going to happen deliberately, either. Here I may be too naive or too optimistic, but I can't believe it, because there's no visible gain that could be achieved by nuclear war."

But she's just written a book that demonstrates rather conclusively that people seldom act in their own best interest, *PW* points out. "That's right," she replies. "People aren't guided by reason much—that's what scares me."

WENDY SMITH

SCOTT TUROW

"THE TIE BETWEEN being a lawyer and a writer is knowing how these things really could happen. And being able to layer back through events, I had an advantage over most people who would write courtroom procedurals."

Scott Turow speaks judiciously, and allusively, as perhaps a good lawyer must, but he is guilty of understatement. *Presumed Innocent* is everywhere—most happily, comfortably and immediately—on bestseller lists across the country.

Success as a novelist may be new to Turow, but he is no stranger to readers of nonfiction. *One L*, his chronicle of his first year at Harvard Law School, was published by Putnam in 1977 and remains in print from Penguin. And Turow is no stranger to the citizens of Chicago, where for several years he was involved as a prosecuting attorney in "Operation Greylord," a highly publicized series of trials in which vast judicial corruption was exposed.

"I was just a lawyer in the vineyards," Turow remembers. "And through a weird series of happenstances, I ended up with what I think was the most publicized of the Greylord cases. It went on and on and on, and I had all these lawyers to put on the witness stand who said, 'I gave the judge $10,000,' 'I gave him $5000.' As the trial progressed and we kept getting the witnesses telling the same goddamn story, the case became extremely well known."

In the publishing world and in the world of movies, Turow, who left the prosecutor's office for the legal firm of Sonnenschein Carlin Nath and Rosenthal, has become extremely well known himself. *Presumed Innocent* was sold to the movies for $1 million;

there is a six-figure floor for the paperback rights; and Farrar, Straus & Giroux paid Turow a $200,000 advance, larger than any the company has paid for a first novel in its history.

Presumed Innocent is the story of Rusty Sabich, a deputy prosecuting attorney in an unnamed major city like Chicago, who is charged with the murder of a female colleague with whom Rusty had been having an affair. Is *Presumed Innocent* a modern-day *Murder of Roger Ackroyd?* Did the narrator do it? Or, as the defense charges, has Rusty been framed? And, if so, who framed him? These are the questions the reader must ponder. But they are the plot twists invented by Turow to reveal his deeper aims.

The book is partly "meant to be a comment on the different kinds of truth we recognize. If the criminal justice system is supposed to be a truth-finding device," Turow says, "it's an awkward one at best. There are all kinds of playing around in the book that illuminate that, and yet by the same token, the results in the end are just. And that's not accidental. . . . Absolutely everybody in the novel is guilty of something. That's a truth of life that I learned as a prosecutor.

"We all do things we wish we hadn't done and that we're not necessarily proud of," says Turow, recalling a conversation with an attorney friend. "As I was looking for a job [last year], I talked to one lawyer about the possibility of going to work for him. We were talking about caring about professional standards, and one of the things he said to me that made me *know* he was an incredibly honest guy was, 'You think I'm telling you that as a lawyer I haven't done things that I'm ashamed of? I have! I've done some things I hope to God no one finds out about.' That's true of all of us."

Despite the fact that both Turow and his protagonist worked in the prosecutor's office, the novel is not based on Turow's own experiences as a lawyer—even though judicial corruption does play a part in *Presumed Innocent*. "The bribery thing had introduced itself at the end of chapter five in my way of thinking—I don't know what chapter it is now," Turow says. "That was the last major element of the plot that I figured out, and I didn't have it in my mind until last summer. I didn't know *who* got paid off. And then when it came to me [who it was], it fit in with the rest of my ideas."

508

Turow admits, "I was very self-conscious about that aspect of the plot because I didn't want to write about situations I was involved in," although he had tried a case in which the physical setting of the North Branch that's described in the novel was obviously the physical setting of one of the Greylord cases he worked on. "But I think if I take being a lawyer seriously, which of course I do, then I've got to respect clients' confidences and their privacy and not have investigational results trotted out all over the country. I just don't want to be writing about the confidences that come to me.

"I offered, frankly, to let the U.S. Attorney's office read the book when it was accepted for publication because I didn't want anyone to think that I had engaged in a kind of kiss and tell. . . . And nobody, I'm very pleased, nobody who's familiar with my past employment has even raised a hint of it."

Turow "spent about two years thinking about *Presumed Innocent*, not writing it, but writing other things," including a novella that Turow says was the first thing that interested Jonathan Galassi in his writing. (Galassi, FSG executive editor, acquired *Presumed Innocent*.) "During that time I just thought out the book," Turow explains. "I can remember gardening on the weekends and figuring out what the plot was going to be, figuring out who committed the murder. I knew that early on, I suppose. As far as I was concerned, there were only two people who could have done it. It seemed to me that the story wouldn't be meaningful unless it was one of the two of them. I didn't think it through that intellectually, as much as I knew it emotionally," Turow says. "I spent a long time pondering which character it could have been." Those who have read *Presumed Innocent* will understand Turow's dilemma.

Turow is "telescoping the deliberations, of course," but says constructing the plot was "like a puzzle. I laid out all these things, and then I had all these elements, all these characters. *Then* I figured out what they were going to do. As I said, that took a couple of years. . . . Then the fine tuning went on for quite some time, too."

He worked out the plot "based on my thinking, If *this* happened, what would happen next? And what would happen in the real world? If you have the chief deputy prosecutor accused of murder, it's not going to be a small matter, it's going to be an enormous matter, going to get national attention. Think of the discredit on his office, especially in the way the case as I saw it unfolded. What would happen to him next?"

Enormous attention indeed. *Presumed Innocent*'s prepublication success has made Turow somewhat nervous. "Making money was not my intention," he says. "I wrote out of the same impulses that everyone else writes out of—I wrote because there were parts of my experience that I could best deal with that way. Obviously," he laughs, "it was enormously fulfilling." But the book is not completely behind him, he senses, admitting that if it does not succeed, "I would feel that I had let people down. I wrote it for myself, but now the stakes are even higher."

Turow awaited the first reviews with trepidation. "George Higgins gave it a good review in the *Chicago Tribune*, and I was interested in my own reaction. I have enormous respect for George Higgins as a writer, so I really appreciated the fact that he liked the book and that he liked it as much as he did. But my feeling as I read it was, Gee, what a relief! Afterwards, I thought, Hey, that's terrible. To be in a position where it's, 'Wow, what a relief,' instead of 'That's terrific, that's great, I'm euphoric.' "

Fear of "letting people down" made Turow realize he had become an author with investors. "I'm like a Broadway musical, I've got my backers: somebody holds the paperback floor; United Artists and Sidney Pollack spent a bundle of cash for the movie rights; 14 foreign publishers are going to publish the book; to say nothing of Farrar, Straus & Giroux. There are literally 17 or 18 interested parties, and if this thing flops, God, did I let those people down. All the money in the world doesn't guarantee anything."

The writing of *Presumed Innocent* was, of course, accomplished while Turow was working full-time as a lawyer (he is also married and the father of three young children, including a newborn). Being both a lawyer and writer, Turow says, is in one way "probably just a coincidence of my personality. But in another way entirely, it's probably no coincidence at all that I'm interested in the law. I find the law to be an enormously provocative subject . . . it is about the moral choices we all make. And I really am a lawyer. . . . I say to myself, I'm hopeless. I see the world the way the law sees the world." But he never stopped wanting to write, Turow says.

"As a lawyer, I never decided I didn't want to be a writer. I decided it would have to be a private passion, rather than something I could use. The fact that I have made all this money *as a writer* is unexpected—there aren't words in any language to talk about my expectations. My idea was to stay *alive* as a writer, just to continue to nurture that part of my soul. I thought it would be a great goal to write one decent short story a year when I went to law school. And I was extremely proud of myself when I sent my book to New York, just for having done it," Turow says. "I did think it was a good book and I thought it would be unjust if it wasn't published—not that I didn't think that wasn't possible—but I was just proud that I had had the self-discipline to write it. . . .

"The other thing I've got to to tell you I had *besides* self-discipline was unbelievable support from my wife, Annette, who [last summer] said, 'Don't work. Forget it, blow it off, burn savings,' which was a substantial financial sacrifice. We could have taken the money and gone to Europe. She said, 'Forget that, you'll never have this chance again, go ahead and do it.' " Turow finished the writing of *Presumed Innocent* in August 1986. He began his new career as a defense attorney in September, major work on his novel concluded. He jokes, "Now I can [afford to] go around the world if I want to. . . . But I just can't get the vacation time."

WILLIAM GOLDSTEIN

GORE VIDAL

"TALKING ABOUT BOOKS is the last thing I would think to do in real life," Gore Vidal announces near the end of a visit with *PW* at New York's Plaza Hotel, though he has already offered his opinions about books—his own, including his novel *Lincoln* (Random House), and others. "That's one of the reasons I don't see many writers," he adds. "They bore me.

"I don't like talking about myself, either," he continues. "I'd rather talk about, well, anything, from Ronald Reagan to the economy, to gossip about friends. The usual subjects interest me. After all, I don't write about myself, either. Which sets me apart from most of my contemporaries, even the very good ones. Like Saul Bellow. It's extraordinary how close things are in his books to his real life."

Vidal leans back into the flowered print of the couch in his sitting room at the Plaza, straightening his tie and pulling a navy blazer closed over a pink shirt with white stripes. He hastily arranges the seat cushions, which have slid out past the edge of the couch, bending beneath his knees. We've been talking for an hour; earlier, Barbara Howar of *Entertainment Tonight* had his attention for more than a half hour. We met precisely at 9:30 A.M.; there is no break between interviews for the author, who lives most of the year in Italy and is not available to the press very frequently. The blue-carpeted room is brightly lit, the chandelier glistening in the mirror above a false fireplace, the curtains closed against the gray rain outside on Central Park South.

A copy of *Lincoln* rests atop the mantle, as does an issue of the *New York Times Book Review* folded open to a full-page advertisement for the new book. Clipped reviews are collected on a side table between the windows, next to a biography of John Maynard Keynes. Vidal is now on the phone, arranging to meet a friend in Washington. "It was an old friend of mine," he explains, "a relative of Teddy Roosevelt. Well, once I told him, 'I don't like TR,' and he said to me, 'Well, Gore, old boy [Vidal imitates his English accent well], Uncle Teddy wouldn't have liked you very much either!'"

For nearly 40 years ("I begin to think I'm *eternal*") Vidal has kept us entertained. From *Williwaw* in 1946 (published when he was 20) through *The City and the Pillar, Julian, Washington, D.C., Myra Breckinridge, Burr, 1876* to *Lincoln*, Vidal has created a body of work unparalleled in its variety: screenplays, short stories, pseudonymous mysteries, prizewinning criticism. "Many are puzzled," he acknowledges, "about how the author of *Myra Breckinridge* can also be the author of *Julian*. They don't see how it works." He is silent for a moment. "I do, but I'm not telling." Reticence is probably the only thing Gore Vidal is not known for.

"I'm a natural writer. There are not many of those. Most people, it strikes me, write either out of vanity, as a means of therapy or simply out of ambition. I never wanted to be a writer. It is the last thing on earth I wanted to do. I was born one," he explains. "When I *read* my first book, I started writing my first book. I have never not been writing. And there's nothing you can do about that." He pauses. "I might not publish it, which might be an interesting form of *discipline*. But I was not interested in writing about myself," he resumes, pooh-poohing diaries. "I was interested in writing about other people. And invention. Being a natural novelist. When I hear about writer's block, this one and that one! F**k off! Stop writing, for Christ's sake: you're not meant to be doing this. Plenty more where you came from."

Vidal has no problem with writing. "If I had any problem with it, I wouldn't do it. You do what you do. It's like saying to a singer, 'Admittedly, you can't do high C, and you don't have any lower register, your middle register's pretty bad, and your higher register's impossible, but yes, you should sing *Tosca*.' This is the

American attitude. Anybody can bull thorough it, or fake it. Faking it is our great national pastime.

"The authentic people are kind of, I think, disliked." Vidal begins to talk about himself. "They always think that if you write well you're somehow cheating, you're not being democratic by writing as badly as everybody else does. That was in the days," he corrects himself, "when people knew the difference [between good writing and bad]. Now, as I say, they don't quite know what a good sentence or a bad sentence is."

The difference between good writing and bad writing interests Vidal; though criticism of *Lincoln* does not bother him, it offers an opportunity to criticize the critics.

"Anyone is naive who thinks if you write a good book you get a good review, if you write a bad book, you get a bad review. This might be true of unknown writers, although even then I wouldn't count on it, because few people even know what a good book is." Reviewers, he finds, all have personal axes to grind. He savages a few in particular. "The new trick now is to take two or three sentences from a book and say, 'Look at what bad writing this is,' sentences that glitter like diamonds in their prose. They don't know why it's bad. And it's always from the first 12 pages, because that's as far as they get.

"But in the case of somebody like *me*," Vidal exclaims, "they don't even have to have the book in hand before they know what they're going to write. It's all very personal," he believes. "I am one of the national villains, so I have to be treated that way." He is proud and compassionate. "I quite understand." If you want to know why he is a villain, "Ask them," he says. "It's for them to answer."

Intrepidly, Vidal hypothesizes: "I belong to the old America. I don't tell lies, which makes me very different from the average New York 'book chat' person." Vidal digresses. "I've never known such a city for liars as this place," he swears. "Everyone reinvents himself every day. And I think *I* represent oh, certain, *puritan* virtues they find *reprehensible*. And I make them nervous. I think they're very funny, and they don't like to be thought funny."

On the other hand, "I think I'm always kind of funny," Vidal says, explaining that his histories are not so different from his satires. "I do see comic aspects of our history. There's not much reverence in my view of these characters, including Lincoln. I

514

don't think *Lincoln* is reverential at all. Most of the people through whose eyes I see Lincoln don't like him." Vidal responds to his critics again. "It's a detached view, and you have to make up your own mind about Lincoln. It's an uncolored prose, which is the most difficult to write," he continues, "but you keep the subject in view and let the narrative unfold. It's for the *reader* to perceive what's at the center.

"I'm more wary of Lincoln [as a historical figure] because there are certain mysteries there that I haven't worked out. I think I understand them," he qualifies, "but I set it up so that the reader, if he's attentive, will begin to understand them." He hints at nothing. "They're in the book."

But is Vidal hoping for too much? An attentive reader? The contemporary America he speaks of is likely to have few. "People don't read books. Writing has very little influence on people at large. Very little influence on the ruling class. They don't read anything, either. However, half an hour with Johnny Carson and you can scare the s**t out of them." Vidal wonders "when the great cretinism began in the United States. When people really got dumb." It is a question he expects he must wrestle with in the next installment of his American Saga, *The Golden Age*, a look at America in the Age of Roosevelt and Wilson, 1907–1919, "sort of our high noon.

"I really dislike Theodore Roosevelt. I was brought up not to like Wilson. My grandfather [Senator Gore of Oklahoma] ran his first campaign, but couldn't bear him." Despite animosity, Vidal believes "the intellectual level of those two men is far higher than, let us say, any two heads of English or history departments at universities in the United States today, much less any politicians. The ignorance of our politicians," Vidal expounds, "is just dazzling. They don't know anything, any history. Both Roosevelt and Wilson were writers. Quite good ones, not great ones, constant readers, obsessed with history."

The American Saga, Vidal explains, is his attempt to "reach a Whitmanesque synthesis of the whole American experience. I'm telling the story of the country, through, as it were, one family, which is partly fictional and partly my own. If I survive," he adds, promising future volumes beyond *The Golden Age*, "I'll bring all the threads together at the end." He is, he says, "redreaming and recreating the republic, and my own family and, finally, myself." Vidal comments that when he writes about himself and his generation, as he has in *Washington, D.C.*, *he* will not be self-indulgent where other writers might be.

Vidal turns back to Lincoln to bring the conversation round to the future: "Lincoln took one big thing he believed in, which was the Union, that it could not be dissolved. He built his own life around this one controlling idea. Perhaps a dangerous, maybe wrong thing to do. But it defined him and made him the greatest of our presidents. He redesigned the United States in his own image, a task both fundamental and astounding, to use adjectives from his second Inaugural.

"He did what he thought was best at the time," Vidal says. "Times change. If I had been the president then, I would have let the South go. But he didn't. And he created a new nation, more horrible, more formidable than anything run up by Washington, Madison and Jefferson. Now we're ready for something else." Vidal foresees a global turning away from the nation-state organization he detests. "I suppose it's going to be a world confederation of states," he says. "Less centralized in some ways, more centralized in others. More regionalism, I should think.

"Anyway," he stops himself from speculating, "the 21st century is going to belong to Japan and China, so it's pretty irrelevant what we do. They've already taken over industrially. They have the numbers, they have the skills. What they lack in raw materials they'll buy from us. The Western hemisphere? I see us as eventually being happy peasants, providing the East with wood and apples. They'll take pictures of us in our bars. A kind of Disneyland for the Yellow People."

He deplores the state of literature. "Isn't 90% of what is written now about schoolteachers on sabbatical, committing adultery? I love Mary McCarthy's long list of what you now cannot write about in a novel: there are no sunsets, no revolutions, no murders, no kings, no intrigues. It's getting more and more focused on the sensibility of middle-class, middle-brow schoolteachers," Vidal repeats. "Since those are the writers, presumably those are the readers." That excludes an awful lot of people, Vidal believes, himself included. "It leaves to the junk writers," he says, "all the great themes, a funny thing nowadays. All the Tolstoyan themes are being written by" (he pauses for an author's name) "Mr. Frederick Forsyth. The serious writers are writing little books that tell of their sad lives, of their capacities as victims.

"Most writing today is about victims. Which is why I think it's interesting to write about the victimizers. If all literature is by victims, for victims, about victims, you're not going to change anything." Vidal quotes Sartre, who complained that he could write the darkest criticism of bourgeois society for the theater, and it would be accepted, though not necessarily liked. "Suggest any change in society, however, and your play goes off."

Vidal writes for himself ("What has eternity done for me lately?" he asks), and he writes of what interests him at the moment. "They impose themselves on you," he says of his "reflections," such as *Lincoln* or *Burr*, and his "inventions," *Myra Breckinridge* and *Duluth*. ("One of the funniest books ever written," says Vidal and, by far, he says, his favorite Vidal book.)

He surveys his position. "Happily, my reviews are the reviews of a very young writer. I'm attacked as if I were the youngest, most dangerous kid in town, with a switchblade, you know, 'Get Him.'" Vidal is contentious and satisfied, delighted to stab back. "Most writers my age are treated with veneration," he says, "regarded as wonderful old things, like what's his name, Wright Morris, the *correct* writer. Or Walker Percy, just benign, treated with great reverence.

"Not me." He is glad. " 'Here comes trouble,' they say when I appear. Yes, let me say, I would prefer that to getting literary degrees from Tufts every June."

WILLIAM GOLDSTEIN

KURT VONNEGUT

I T'S LIKE A scene from—well, from a book by Kurt Vonnegut. On a warm September day in New York City, *PW* is sitting at the kitchen table in an East Side townhouse the novelist shares with his wife, author/photographer Jill Krementz. We are careful not to sit too close, as he has a bad cold he's trying not to give anyone. Despite the cold, Vonnegut is chain-smoking Pall Malls, flicking the ashes into a nearby garbage pail. Suddenly, a plume of smoke is observed ascending from the aforesaid garbage. Unconcerned, the author rises casually, picks up the pail and carries it to the sink, where he calmly dumps a few cups of water into the plastic lining until the flames are extinguished. That accomplished, he replaces the pail on the floor, returns to his chair and resumes the conversation, as if the fire doesn't deserve any further acknowledgment. He does, however, start using a half-empty Tab can as an ashtray.

This determined nonchalance in the face of an unpredictable universe is an attitude familiar to readers of Vonnegut's work. His novel *Galápagos* (Delacorte/Seymour Lawrence) is equally cognizant of life's uncertainties, though it takes a somewhat longer view of the issues as it covers the evolution of humanity over a million years in a narration by the ghost of Vietnam veteran Leon Trout. "One reason the book took so long to write," says the author, "was that I had to figure out who the viewpoint character was going to be, since nothing lives a million years. In other books I've planted the beginnings of little stories, and in one book I'd mentioned that Kilgore Trout's son had deserted from

518

the Marines. [Trout is a Vonnegut alter ego who pops up in several novels. So I picked up that small clue. Actually, there are threads connecting all my books, which makes a hell of a lot of trouble every time we make a movie sale, because when a movie company buys a book they buy all the characters. I had to buy Kilgore Trout back from Universal Pictures [which produced the film version of *Slaughterhouse Five*]. It may be a fun thing to connect all the books, but it makes legal trouble."

The million-year time span was necessary in order to show human beings evolving, in the aftermath of a nuclear war, from destructive "big brains" into furry, flippered fisher-folk who can successfully survive in the hostile environment of the Galápagos Islands. Does he really feel this is a better way of life? "Well, it's better for the rest of the planet," he replies. "We are certainly destroyers of the planet's harmony. Right now we're on the verge of killing everything, and we wouldn't be able to do it if it weren't for our great big brains. Elephants have somewhat the same problem: as their grazing lands shrink, these big animals destroy a whole township every morning; they knock everything down in order to eat." His laugh is clogged with phlegm and cigarettes. "Being as big as they are and as strong as they are once seemed like a pretty bright idea, but it's no longer a good survival skill. And humans—every morning just here in New York City, eight million people get out of bed and go raging around for eight hours. My God, the amount of damage they can do in that time!"

Philosophical questions addressed in a light tone and from a scientific point of view are a trademark of Vonnegut's work, which has always been closer in spirit to science fiction than to most mainstream novels. "My education is technical," he says in explanation. "I started out to be a biochemist, then, after World War II, I took a degree in anthropology. Why wouldn't I be interested in technology? There is this prejudice on the part of critics, who customarily are English majors, that anybody who understands how a refrigerator works couldn't possibly be an artist." Vonnegut's tone is both irritated and amused, as it often is when discussing the world's foibles. "In the typical *New Yorker* story of a few years ago, people were characterized as somehow being wonderful if they had never looked under the hood of a car, or couldn't change a lightbulb; these people were presumably free to think more about God, or I don't know what. People with technological insights are regarded as coarse, a little blue-collar, and that's got to stop. During the Victorian era, which was a period of magnificent variety, the one subject they didn't cover was sex, and by leaving it out they grotesquely misrepresented life. Now technology is enormously important in our lives, and yet we still have people who insist on ignoring it entirely; they have misrepresented life as grotesquely as the Victorians did."

What led him from biochemistry and anthropology to fiction? "It was always easy for me to write," he says. "It was just something I took pleasure in doing." Work on the Cornell *Sun*—"I used to spend more time there than I did in class"—led to a post-college job with the Chicago City News Bureau, training ground for many Midwest journalists. "I would have liked to have been a Chicago newsman," remarks Vonnegut. "If I had become that, I'd be a very happy, satisfied man today. But it just wasn't possible; the jobs weren't there. This was right after the war, when many reporting positions had been filled by women, who had done very good work. Now they were expected, like Rosie the Riveter, to quit the job and go back and have babies. Well, they were damned if they would, and they were right. But the whole system clogged; there was no way to move up, and the pay was very nominal at the News Bureau. I had a wife and child, so I simply couldn't afford to hang on there anymore; I took a job as a public relations man for General Electric and moved to Schenectady."

His entrance into fiction came about for a reason that seems incredible today—"I needed money," Vonnegut remembers. "The one opportunity that existed was fiction, because magazines paid extremely well for short stories. They probably pay less now—well, certainly no more—than they did when I started out 40 years ago. Very quickly, I was making more money from my short stories than I was from General Electric, so I quit."

The publication of *Player Piano* in 1952 marked the beginning of a long-term relationship with Dell, which has issued all of Vonnegut's paperbacks for more than 30 years. Since 1969, the company has also been his hardcover outlet through its subsidiary Delacorte Press, which now controls rights to his earlier books as well. "This is the last of a five-book contract, so I became a free agent," says Vonnegut, "but I decided to stay with Dell, because I like the people working over there. They've had a hard time and they've pulled themselves together."

His previous book, *Deadeye Dick*, was published in paperback in 1983, just as Dell's parent company, Doubleday, was taking drastic steps to trim costs and staff. "They fired the sales staff the day the book came out!" he remembers. "They turned it over to Doubleday, which had never handled Dell books before, so it was a mess; I was furious. That was the bottom for Dell; in fact, it ceased to exist for a while, it was just a piece of junk. But the employees pulled out of it, and it's a real class operation now; they happen to have good employees."

In conjunction with the release of *Galápagos*, Dell will issue Delta trade paperback editions of five well-known titles: *The Sirens of Titan; Slaughterhouse Five; Welcome to the Monkey House; Happy Birthday, Wanda June;* and *Wampeters, Foma & Granfalloons.* "They're very handsome books, and I'm pleased with them," comments the author. They *are* handsome, but anyone who grew up in the 1960s must suppress a pang at the thought of these editions replacing the familiar mass market volumes that seemed to be in the hands of every high school student during those years. In fact, their popularity with students and subsequent presence on school library shelves made Vonnegut's books the target of many attacks by would-be censors. The most notorious instance was in 1975, when the Island Trees, Long Island, school board removed *Slaughterhouse Five* and eight other books from the libraries under its jurisdiction. A group of students sued, claiming violations of their First Amendment rights, and the case went all the way to the Supreme Court before the books were restored to the shelves.

Vonnegut, an ardent free-speech advocate, takes a surprisingly optimistic view of recent struggles against censorship. "There are a lot of diseases that people are talking about now that simply weren't identified before, so they look like sudden plagues," he says. "They've been with us a long time. What I think is happening is that people are fighting censors for the first time. I think that for 200 years, members of school committees or concerned parents, or whatever, just came down to the school library and threw anything they wanted into the garbage can, or told the teacher to stop teaching a subject, and got away with it. So this disease is being treated for the first time; I would say that this is good."

The fight against censorship is one of the few areas of modern life about which Vonnegut feels some measure of optimism. "I hate this Harvard Business School attitude of 'Let's just get through this quarter,' " he comments. "I grew up during the Depression; everything in the country had stopped; there was no work, the factories were cold and empty. People daydreamed about what this country was going to be like when it got going again—the kind of houses people would live in, the kind of cars they would drive, the kind of vacations they'd take, the kind of clothes they'd wear, and all that—and it was a dream for their descendants. I don't find anybody now who gives a damn about what kind of world their grandchildren are going to inherit.

"I think it's because they've been encouraged to just take care of themselves," he continues. His voice grows bitter as he describes the "consumership" he sees all around him. "All the ads tell you that your own life is short, enjoy it while you can: buy this right now, start drinking really good wines, just take a really swell vacation, drive a really fast car, do it right now. I think it's much more absorbing to plan a world for our grandchildren, but there are no ads that invite you to do that. In a way, the threat of the Bomb may be a boon to wine merchants, restaurateurs, manufacturers of fancy automobiles, salesmen of condos in Aspen. It's all going to blow up—that's part of the sales message."

Vonnegut can be an irascible man. The stupidities of his fellow humans prompt rage as well as laughter, and his litany of advertising's poisoned blandishments has dripped with venomous sarcasm. His voice softens, however, when a small blonde girl rushes into the room calling eagerly, "Hi, daddy!"

"Hi, darling," he responds.

"I'm gonna wash Snoopy, okay?"

"All right. I'm gonna sneeze, okay?"

Actually, it's not okay. Lily, who will be three in December, would like her father to take her for a walk, and she clambers up in his lap to tell him so more forcefully. He promises he will, "as soon as I finish talking with this lady." Satisfied, she retreats downstairs to her mother's studio, and Vonnegut resumes the conversation on a gentler note, explaining that, although he has strong social beliefs, he doesn't feel fiction is the place to express them.

"A book is a work of art; it exists for its own sake," he says. "The purpose of art is to make a gift that someone else finds of value. Most beginning writers simply want to tell people off, to present their program for how to save the universe. If you teach

522

creative writing, part of the process is to teach them how to be more sociable, to care about other people and not just to dump on them.

"I wrote *Galápagos* for the sake of the book, just the way you paint a picture for the sake of the picture," he continues. "The book was a technical problem, and I had a hell of a time making it work. It's all creative lying, like perjuring yourself on the witness stand; it all has to hold together. Technically, a novel is a very tough thing to make work, if it's as tightly reasoned as this one is. My books tend to be tightly structured, which makes them short. I was a journalist: you never go for length, you don't tell anything that doesn't belong in the story, and you tell as much as you can up front. The basic principle I have of storytelling is that you don't withhold anything from the reader. If the author should die while writing the story, the reader should have enough information by then to finish the tale."

And he goes off to take Lily for a walk, leaving his interviewer to finish this particular tale without the author's help.

WENDY SMITH

FAY WELDON

Fay WELDON RUSHES into the lobby of the Algonquin Hotel in a flurry of agitation. She is a few minutes late for our interview, having belatedly discovered, to her dismay, that banks in the U.S. close at 3 P.M., and having encountered the usual delays—usual in England, too, she assures us—in completing a simple transaction.

She is in this country for a short time to give a reading at Queens College. By coincidence, her agent is here, too, "so we have taken the opportunity to wheel and deal a little.

"Of course," she goes on, "I sometimes think you may do much better if you never appear in person; you're so much more mysterious that way. Just as you do much better as a writer if no one actually reads what you write." Delivered with a wry, mocking smile and a saucy gleam in her blue eyes, the statement is typical of Weldon's propensity for saying outrageous things with an air of bland innocence.

Weldon's novel *The Life and Loves of a She-Devil* is a case in point. Part parable, part fantasy, the book is a funny, biting satire of the war between the sexes, indicating not only the male establishment's standards of beauty and feminine worthiness, but also women's own willingness (perhaps eagerness) to subscribe to these standards, sometimes at great sacrifice, discomfort and even pain. The book, a bestseller in England, ends with a crashing irony: the woefully unattractive protagonist, having achieved money and power, ruined her unfaithful husband and vanquished her beautiful rival, willingly undergoes agonizing surgery to transform herself into the very epitome of a romantic heroine. This provocative flouting of the feminists' creed is sure to inspire heated reactions.

Weldon's reputation for outspoken opinions is well known in England, where her novels notoriously tend to *épater les bourgeoisie*. Even so, when as chairperson of the judges' panel for the 1983 Booker Prize, she delivered a scathing attack on British publishers at the awards banquet, she caused a storm of controversy. Accusing publishers of exploiting writers at the worst and not helping them to gain just benefits and protections at the best, Weldon recited a stirring litany of grievances that would, she warned, lead writers to organize against their oppressors.

Weldon expresses surprise at the British publishing community's reaction to her speech. "They were very cross indeed. I was quite astonished, in fact. I hadn't quite envisioned their anger. I didn't remember how middle-class, middle-aged men, after dinner, do not like to be made to *think*. I believe it was what they saw as my bad manners—speaking out at that time and place—that upset them. The whole bookselling world set up a storm. But the newspapers do have to have something to fill up their column inches, and in all it wasn't a bad idea.

"My own publishers, naturally, felt rather aggrieved. They felt I should have excepted them from the general condemnation. But I couldn't, of course. They're no better and no worse than the others."

Iconoclast that she is, Weldon apparently sees nothing unusual in her outburst. "I was obliged to make a speech. I see no point in making one in which you say nothing. A word about literature you can get over in two paragraphs. And then you must say something of some significance. And since all the publishers were gathered together for this august occasion, and we were judging *writers*, it seemed the perfect time and place. All of this razzamatazz has more to do with making money than literature, of course. So I felt the time had come to present the writer's point of view, since he is generally on the short end of that financial process."

We ask Weldon if, in view of the reaction she engendered, she thinks the Booker Prize committee will choose a female chairperson again soon. (She was the first woman to hold that honor in the group's 15-year history.) "I don't think they'll discriminate against women," she says. "I don't think they're going to get a *writer* for a long time, though. They'll probably go back to safer people—academics, mostly. Writers are always a great nuisance to publishers. If they could do without them, they would."

She is pragmatic about the furor surrounding her speech. "It's good for the Booker Prize, actually, if there's a hint of scandal every year. The judging is done with great solemnity and integrity, don't mistake me. But a little publicity gets people aware of the awards; it creates an attitude of some suspense. What readers want more than anything is to be enthused about books, or to be guided toward books. So the Booker Prize is good in two ways; it sets a worthwhile literary standard, and yet it's also fashionable at a high level; it's an event of some importance."

Weldon seems quite taken aback when asked whether she enjoys breaking eggs, in print or in person. "No, no, not really. If the occasion arises, I say what I think. I don't go out of my way to offer my opinions, unless people ask. One of the fortunate things about being a writer is that your value in the world is the written word. It's what you make up that counts. So you get out of the habit of making your views known ex cathedra."

Even so, Weldon seems to relish controversy, judging by the sangfroid with which she discusses the response of feminists when *The Life and Loves of a She-Devil* was published in England. "I think the feminists are always jumping up and down about one thing or another. I don't think they read me, actually. I confuse them. In fact, any serious feminist spits when I go by—and well she should.

"Actually, the first half of the book is an exercise in feminist thought. As Ruth Patchett [the heroine] finds, in order to be happy you must give away your children, burn the house down, acquire money and be absolutely ruthless in gaining your own way. It's the feminist manifesto, really: a woman must be free, independent and rich. But I found myself asking, what then? What is the point of doing it all if you can't share your life with someone? I think women are discovering that liberation isn't enough. The companionship of women is not enough. The other side of their nature remains unfulfilled."

According to Weldon, her novel finally expresses a well-known but rarely articulated fact: the envy of unattractive women of their attractive sisters. "All the in-between things ugly women do, all of their successes of one kind or another, are only compen-

526

sations for the admiration of men," she claims. "And since age equalizes all things, since one old lady is like another old lady, by then you'd better have all the money you need, because you'll be expected to take care of yourself. But what you still want is this odd thing, which is men looking at you in the street," she concludes.

Weldon seems conflicted about how women should react to this unequal distribution of beauty and sexual charisma. "It's not easy to believe in yourself as a person and not as something defined by men. It's an absurdity. The ability to be a sexual turn-on is the only thing of value in this culture. It is a pathetic culture, but we're stuck with it."

The author herself is a paradox if one uses what she says are conventional standards of feminine beauty. If her figure is more Miloesque than is currently fashionable and her blond hair hangs rather limply around her round, expressive face, she nonetheless exudes a definite magnetism that makes her attractive indeed. When she speaks to a caller on the telephone, her well-modulated voice takes on dulcet tones; one can imagine her charming a roomful of people—of both sexes—if she is so disposed. On the other hand, it is obvious that in a feisty mood, she is someone to reckon with.

She never set out to have a career as a writer, Weldon confesses. "Survival," she says, was her only goal when, at a young age and with a baby to support, she took a job in an advertising firm. "I had a degree in psychology and economics, but that didn't fit me for anything. I was very clever, though, you see; no, maybe not clever—I was very good at passing exams, and soon I discovered that I was very good at advertising, too. Or perhaps it was that other people were so bad. At any rate, I earned enough to keep the wolf from the door and the baby in nappies. And then eventually I got married and had another baby. He [the baby] was late in arriving, I was enormous, and I had to do *something*, so I sat down and did a script for TV. It was at a time when women didn't write for television; TV was seen as something technical and beyond women's capabilities. But since I'd written TV commercials, I wasn't intimidated and just sailed right in."

The Fat Woman's Joke, Weldon's first novella, started out as a TV script but was cut considerably, so that she finally withdrew it and transformed it into story form. "So I discovered I could do a

527

variety of things, and one thing led to another, and since then I have been commissioned to do things—other than what I want to do—at such a rate that I don't even remember what it is I *do* want to do," she says, looking not at all unhappy about the situation.

Today Weldon has four children—all boys: they are 28, 20, 13 and five years old. She has left the younger ones in her husband's care for this brief transatlantic jaunt, and she expresses amazement at the change in her mothering role. "I'm much bolder about leaving the little one at home for a week like this. I would never have left the older ones, I'm sure."

A question about her husband's means of livelihood turns her playful and evasive. "I don't know quite what he does now. He was an antique dealer. But he's rather retired from that, and now he plays the jazz trumpet. He's a painter, too; really, he does all kinds of things. We have six sheep, and they've had eight lambs, so you could say he's a sheep breeder."

She is more serious in describing her husband's reactions to the marital discord that reigns in her novels. Asked how he feels about her unsparing depictions, she answers, "Badly—in a word. It's all right now, actually, but it was hard at first. My work is all so obviously fictional, and he has come to accept that. But friends and acquaintances don't, I'm afraid."

Managing two households, in London and Somerset, does not disrupt Weldon's writing routine, she claims. "I write by hand, and if you do that, you can take it with you wherever you are. All you need is concentration." She started writing better when she stopped using a typewriter, Weldon swears. "It has something to do with the pace at which you move along and the ways you fill the space on the page. You use more adjectives when you type; it's just not as clean. Besides, typing is not a natural thing to do, whereas operating a pencil just seems to be. So I write by hand, and I can write nearly anywhere."

Her one rule as a writer is succinct: never show anything to anybody while in the process. There can be nothing worse than input from well-meaning family or friends, she feels. She has gone one step further and forbidden her children and her mother to read her books. "If they do read them, they don't discuss them with me, so we all get along very well."

Her novels have wide appeal—they have been translated into 11 languages—and Weldon is not surprised. "The predicaments of women seem to be universal, in every culture where you have an enormous, aspiring middle class. A mother of three is the same anywhere. The geography of *The Life and Loves of a She-Devil* is actually the western suburbs of Sydney, Australia, but in Scandinavia, where the book is selling very well, it's assumed to be set there. American readers may assume it's set in America. And that's very good, that's what I want, really, to illuminate woman's lot. Women must ask themselves: What is it that will give me fulfillment? That's the serious question I'm attempting to answer."

SYBIL S. STEINBERG

JOHN EDGAR WIDEMAN

JOHN EDGAR WIDEMAN is a man who disdains labels, who refuses to allow either his life or art to be boxed in or dismissed by descriptive terms like "black writer." The problem, he says, "is that it can be a kind of back-handed compliment. Are you being ghettoized at the same time as you are being praised?"

His writing, too, refuses to be pigeonholed. He has written one work of nonfiction, *Brothers and Keepers*, which was nominated for the National Book Award; three novels, including the PEN/Faulkner Award–winning *Sent for You Yesterday*; and two collections of stories. In addition, he is a professor of English at the University of Massachusetts, Amherst, where he has taught for the past three years.

But Wideman the writer/professor is inextricable from Wideman the man dogged by tragic past, which is ever present in his work. In *Brothers and Keepers, Hiding Place* and *Damballah* especially, he has tried to better understand the twists of fate that have made him what he is, while his brother, Robby, is serving a lifetime prison sentence.

On this beautiful fall afternoon, we have come to Wideman's newly built house on the outskirts of Amherst not to dwell on the "time capsules of his past" but to speak of his life as a writer and the publication of his book *Fever* (Holt), a breathtaking collection of 12 stories written primarily over the past few years.

A tall, handsome man in his late 40s, Wideman retains the physique of the basketball star he once was. (During his undergraduate days at the University of Pennsylvania, he not only played all-Ivy basketball but also ran track.) The basketball hoop is still very much with him; materially, at the edge of the driveway of his home in western Massachusetts; metaphysically, in his stories, which frequently feature a hoop and the male camaraderie associated with team sports.

We sit in Wideman's book-lined study overlooking the woods as he talks about *Fever*, which he regards as "his first collection per se." For him, the earlier *Damballah*—reissued by Vintage last fall along with the other two volumes in the Homewood trilogy, *Sent for You Yesterday* and *Hiding Place*—is closer to a novel with its discernible beginning, middle and end.

"These stories are more miscellaneous," he explains. "The key story, the pivotal story, is 'Fever.' I see the others as refractions of the material gathered there. All the stories are about a kind of illness or trouble in the air. People aren't talking to one another or are having a difficult time talking to one another. There's misunderstanding, not only on an individual level but on a cultural level. These stories are also about ways of combating that malaise through love, through talk, through rituals that families create."

The malaise of which Wideman speaks cuts backwards and forwards into the past, into the present, because of the very ambiguity of time, of history, of fact. ("I never know if I'm writing fiction or nonfiction," he remarks several times throughout the interview when speaking of his stories and books.) And that very ambiguity accounts for much of the bite in "Fever," which serves as a bridge to his forthcoming novel, *Philadelphia Fire*, due out from Holt in the fall of 1990.

On one hand the plague described in "Fever" is a historical fact of colonial Philadelphia; on the other hand it provides a powerful fictional prelude to the MOVE bombing that destroyed an entire city block in 1985.

That the story should float so freely from one period to another is, for Wideman, what makes it work: "It shouldn't be tied to any historical period, because it starts in this very room. I was looking out there, out this window, when I saw the snow, and that's where the story starts."

It is no coincidence, then, that this and other stories in the collection achieve a certain timelessness. "Stories are a way of keeping people alive," says the author, "not only the ones who tell the story, but the ones who lived before. You talk about authors being immortal, but there's not only the story, there are the people inside the story who are kept alive."

Wideman thrives on the potential for experimentation in storytelling. "How does one person tell a story that is quite meaningful to that person but is really someone else's story? What does it mean for people to carry around stories in their heads, little time capsules from the past? Yet if I'm telling it to you, it's present."

Elsewhere, in *Brothers and Keepers,* he writes about the pointlessness of telling stories in strict chronological sequence, as "one thing happening first and opening the way for another and another. . . . You never know exactly when something begins. The more you delve and backtrack and think, the clearer it becomes that nothing has a discrete, independent history; people and events take shape not in orderly, chronological sequence but in relation to other forces and events, tangled skeins of necessity and interdependence and chance that after all could have produced only one result: what is."

As the interview goes on it becomes obvious that time, like race, is one of the many barriers that Wideman seeks to overcome with his art. "Stories break down our ordinary ways of conceptualizing reality. Because when we talk about what's alive and what's dead, what's past and what's future, male/female, all these dichotomies that we need in order to talk, they're not really very accurate or descriptive.

"On one level of language we do that kind of crude conceptualizing, labeling, and it's necessary. But language can break down these categories, free us. So that we suddenly realize that past and future are not different. That living and dead are kind of arbitrary categories." Switching gears, he adds with a smile, "Why can't a blind man play basketball?" referring to the central image of "Doc's Story," the first offering in *Fever.*

With this deceptively simple query, he opens a Pandora's box of questions about some of our most basic assumptions about what people can and cannot be, do or say. Wideman himself has consciously attempted to break stereotypes. "If somebody told me I couldn't do something, that was often a good reason to go ahead and try to do it. And I got satisfaction out of that. On the other hand, as I get older I think I do things less because I'm oriented toward the outside, toward what somebody's thinking, than because I have some inner drive. But it often works out to the same kind of iconoclasm. Because if my goals are unusual and I accomplish them, then they'll be noticeable and will have the same effect as consciously trying to break a mold."

It's only natural that Wideman challenges the boundaries of writing. In "Fever" the narration passes back and forth from white to black, male to female, young to old. The rhythms beneath the prose also evoke a sense of flexibility, infused with lyrical sounds ranging from gospel singing to Rachmaninoff.

His home is filled with music as well as books. For him, "music breaks down the racial criteria by which we judge so much that goes on in our culture."

Wideman's prose seems to sing with cadences, too, especially those more typically found in oral storytelling traditions, a fact that he explains by describing his writing process. First come the many hours of thinking. ("I give myself space to imagine. I work really hard to get childlike, to get innocent.") Next he writes everything out longhand with his trusty Bic pen, then reads it aloud to Judy, his wife of 24 years, who not only types his work (the computer is kept in her study upstairs) but acts as his editor. "There's almost an umbilical relationship between Judy and me. She's always typed what I write and put it in an objective form. I'm very dependent on her willingness to go through that process with me. It's a real luxury to have that kind of closeness."

But a literary confidante is not his only luxury. Some would say that his career has been charmed. Unlike most would-be authors, he earned the attention of a distinguished editor, Hiram Haydn, before he even penned the first word of his first book. This happened in 1963, when he and another college graduate on the West Coast became the first blacks in 50 years to be awarded Rhodes scholarships. In newspaper interviews, Wideman was asked what he wanted to do with his life and responded: to be a writer.

Haydn's son spotted one of those news stories and said to his father, who was then editor of the *American Scholar* and an editor at Random House, " 'You always say that you want to help young writers. Why don't you help him?' So he sent me a letter," Wideman recalls, "The first time I had 30 pages, I sent something off to him." From those pages came Wideman's first book, *A Glance Away*, which was published in 1967, when he was just 26 years old. *Hurry Home* and *The Lynchers* followed soon afterward.

Wideman believes that such fortune is unlikely to strike today. "Now it's real tough to get published and to publish well. We're in a superstar syndrome just like in the movies. A book is either a big book or no book at all."

In Wideman's case it took an eight-year hiatus and the release of *Brothers and Keepers* (his first book with Holt) for him to achieve the type of media attention that sells books in a big way. Although that book was featured on *60 Minutes*, the three novels that he wrote in the early 1980s following Robby's arrest, and which later became the Homewood trilogy, were published to little fanfare. To some extent, the disappointing reception might be attributed, he believes, to the tendency of nonfiction to outsell fiction. More importantly, however, Wideman attempted to put some publishing stereotypes to rest by insisting that Avon issue the three novels as paperback originals.

"I realize that they were set in Homewood [a black ghetto of Pittsburgh, which remains his spiritual home] and that they are about black families—books nobody I knew could afford to buy. So I thought, why not go paperback? Paperback because it's cheaper, and because I had experienced the pointlessness of doing hardback novels without huge advances and just a few small printings in the beginning. Those just disappear."

Looking back, Wideman acknowledges his naïveté, yet he is also proud that those books were among the first, possibly *the* first, paperback fiction originals to be reviewed extensively in the *New York Times*. The author has nothing but praise for his agent, Andrew Wylie, who numbers Beckett and Rushdie among his clients, and who has helped steer Wideman's career over the past 10 years. Wideman considers him an editor in the Maxwell Perkins tradition, and applauds his determination to get "decent money for good writing . . . not just a polite smile."

Nonetheless, as a writer, Wideman is not content with what he perceives as business as usual. "Each book is treated as a commodity. This is particularly a problem for minority writers." He would like to see a new approach to book marketing that would look at who in the black community buys books, rather than ignoring that audience because conventional wisdom dictates that black people don't buy books.

But despite the statistics and the odds against minority writers—or perhaps because of them—Wideman, a man who likes to compete, has managed to make his writing stand out by turning the tragic and joyful sides of life into enduring works of art.

JUDITH ROSEN

CONTRIBUTORS

JOHN F. BAKER was editor-in-chief of *Publishers Weekly* for 12 years. He is now editorial director.

MIRIAM BERKLEY's literary journalism was published widely before she shifted her focus to photography in the late 1980s. She travels internationally photographing writers. An exhibit of her author portraits was held at the Frankfurt Book Fair in 1991.

The late ROY BONGARTZ was a widely published magazine writer (including *Esquire* and the *New Yorker*) and the author of *Twelve Chases on West 99th Street,* a Houghton Mifflin book from the early 1960s that was widely translated.

CATHERINE BRESLIN is the author of two novels, *Unholy Child* (Dial) and *First Ladies* (McGraw-Hill). As a magazine freelancer, she writes for the *New Yorker, Esquire*, the *Village Voice* and the *Sunday Times* of London, among other publications. Her current work-in-progress is a nonfiction account of the infanticide trial of the Rochester nun that inspired *Unholy Child.*

WILLIAM BRISICK lives in California. He has a novel in progress.

DULCY BRAINARD, a contributing editor of *Publishers Weekly,* is Forecasts's Mysteries editor.

MICHAEL COFFEY is working on a novel about John Brown. He lives in New York City.

CHRIS GOODRICH is a contributing editor of *Publishers Weekly* and the author of *Anarchy and Elegance: Confessions of a Journalist at Yale Law School* (Little, Brown).

WILLIAM GOLDSTEIN, now a senior editor at Charles Scribner's Sons, was an editor at *Publishers Weekly* from 1982–1988.

MARK HARRIS writes for *Entertainment Weekly* in New York.

ROSEMARY HERBERT is the author of *The Fatal Art of Entertainment: Interviews with Mystery Writers*, forthcoming from G. K. Hall in spring of 1993.

PENNY KAGANOFF is a book review editor of *Publishers Weekly* and a member of the Board of Directors of the National Book Critics Circle.

SALLY LODGE is a freelance writer living in Connecticut. She is the author of three books for children, including *Minnie 'N Me: Cooking Together* (Disney/Gallery Books).

HERBERT R. LOTTMAN lives in Paris, where he is international correspondent for *Publishers Weekly*. He is the author of biographies of Albert Camus, Gustave Flaubert and Colette, and of other books.

MOLLY McQUADE is an associate editor of *Publishers Weekly*.

PENELOPE MOFFET is a poet and nonfiction writer who is currently writing a book about the loves of contemporary American poets.

JOHN MUTTER is bookselling editor of *Publishers Weekly*.

DIANE ROBACK is a senior editor of *Publishers Weekly*.

JUDITH ROSEN is a freelance writer living in Cambridge, Mass.

JIM SAGEL is the author of 11 books of bilingual poetry and fiction, and a winner of the Premio Casa de la Américas for his collection of short stories, *Tunomqs Honey*.

LISA SEE has been *Publishers Weekly*'s West Coast correspondent for nine years. She is currently working on a book titled *On Gold Mountain*, about the history of the Chinese in California seen through the eyes of one family.

BEV SLOPEN is *Publishers Weekly*'s Canadian correspondent. A literary agent based in Toronto, she writes a weekly column on the book industry for the *Toronto Star*.

AMANDA SMITH is a Manhattan-based freelance writer who writes frequently for *Publishers Weekly*.

WENDY SMITH is the author of *Real Life Drama: The Group Theatre and America, 1991–1940* (Grove). She also writes regularly for *New York Newsday*, the *Chicago Sun-Times*, *Entertainment Weekly*, the *Cleveland Plain Dealer* and the *Philadelphia Inquirer*.

TOM SPAIN is the video columnist for the *Washington Post* and has worked at Simon & Schuster and Bantam.

SAM STAGGS, author of the novel *M.M. II: The Return of Marilyn Monroe* (Donald I. Fine), is completing a novel based on the life of Maria Callas.

SYBIL STEINBERG edits Interviews and Fiction Forecasts for *Publishers Weekly*.

BOB SUMMER is *Publishers Weekly*'s southeastern correspondent and lives in Nashville.

MARCELLE THIÉBAUX is the Manhattan-based author of books, articles and reviews on literary subjects, including *Ellen Glasgow* and *The Writings of Medieval Women*. She is a recipient of The Pen and Brush Club award for her fiction, and her short stories have appeared in *The Cream City Review*, *Karamu* and *Twisted*. She is working on her second novel.

JOSÉ YGLESIAS is a journalist, playwright and novelist whose most recent book was the novel *Tristan and the Hispanics* (Simon & Schuster).

KATHARINE WEBER, a frequent contributor to *Publishers Weekly* and other publications, is working on her first novel.

BIBLIOGRAPHY

(Books currently in print by interviewed authors)

ISABEL ALLENDE

Eva Luna
The House of the Spirits, translated by Magda Bogin
Of Love and Shadows, translated by Margaret S. Peden
The Stories of Eva Luna, translated by Margaret S. Peden

JEAN M. AUEL

The Clan of the Cave Bear
The Mammoth Hunters (Earth's Children Series)
The Clan of the Cave Bear and *The Valley of Horses* (2-volume boxed set)
The Plains of Passage (Earth's Children Series)
The Valley of Horses (Earth's Children Series)

PAUL AUSTER

The Art of Hunger
City of Glass
Disappearances: Selected Poems
Facing the Music
Ghosts
In the Country of Last Things
The Invention of Solitude
Leviathan
The Locked Room
Moon Palace

The Music of Chance
The New York Trilogy: City of Glass, Ghosts, The Locked Room
White Spaces

RUSSELL BANKS

Affliction
The Book of Jamaica
Continental Drift
Family Life
Hamilton Stark
The New World: Stories
The Relation of My Imprisonment
Searching for Survivors
Snow
Success Stories
The Sweet Hereafter
Trailerpark

RICHARD BAUSCH

The Fireman's Wife and Other Stories
The Last Good Time
Mr Field's Daughter
Spirits & Other Stories
Violence

ANN BEATTIE

Alex Katz
The Burning House
Chilly Scenes of Winter
Distortions
Falling in Place
Jacklighting
Love Always
Picturing Will
Secrets & Surprises
What Was Mine & Other Stories
Where You'll Find Me

WILLIAM BOYD

Brazzaville Beach
A Good Man in Africa
The Ice-Cream War: A Tale of the Empire
The New Confessions
On the Yankee Stadium: Stories
Stars and Bars

T. CORAGHESSAN BOYLE

Budding Prospects
Descent of Man & Other Stories
East Is East
Greasy Lake & Other Stories
If the River Was Whiskey
Water Music
World's End

ANITA BROOKNER

The Debut
Family & Friends
A Friend from England
The Genius of the Future: Essays in French Art Criticism
Hotel du Lac
Jacques-Louis David
Latecomers
Lewis Percy
The Misalliance

LARRY BROWN

Big Bad Love
Dirty Work
Facing the Music
Joe

FREDERICK BUSCH

Absent Friends
Closing Arguments

Domestic Particulars: A Family Chronicle
Harry & Catherine
Hawkes: A Guide to His Fictions
Invisible Mending
Manual Labor
Rounds
Sometimes I Live in the Country
Too Late American Boyhood Blues
War Babies

JOSEPH CAMPBELL

Erotic Irony: And Mythic Forms in the Art of Thomas Mann
The Flight of the Wild Gander: Explorations in the Mythological Dimensions of Fairy Tales
The Hero with a Thousand Faces
The Hero's Journey: Joseph Campbell on His Life and Work, edited by Phil Cousineau
The Historical Atlas of World Mythology
In All Her Names: Four Explorations of the Feminine Divinity
The Inner Reaches of Outer Space: Metaphor as Myth and as Religion
The Masks of God
Volume I: Primitive Mythology; Volume II: Oriental Mythology;
Volume III: Occidental Mythology; Volume IV: Creative Mythology
The Mythic Image (with M.J. Abadie)
Myths to Live By
An Open Life
The Power of Myth (with Bill Moyers)
Renewal Myths and Rites of the Primitive Hunters and Planters
Tarot Revelations (with Richard Roberts)
Transformations of Myths through Time
The Way of the Animal Powers, Pt 1: Mythologies of the Primitive Hunters and Gatherers
The Way of the Animal Powers, Pt 2: Mythologies of the Great Hunt
The Way of the Seeded Earth: Mythologies of the Primitive Planters (2 volumes)
Myths, Dreams and Religions (edited by Joseph Campbell
Papers from Eranos Yearbooks (edited by Joseph Campbell)
Vol. I: Spirit and Nature
Vol. II: The Mysteries
Vol. III: Man and Time
Vol. IV: Spiritual Disciplines
Vol. V: Man and Transformation

RAYMOND CARVER

Cathedral
Elephant
Fires: Essays, Poems, Stories
A New Path to the Waterfall: Poems
No Heroics Please: Uncollected Writings
Ultramarine
What We Talk About When We Talk About Love
Where I'm Calling From: New and Selected Stories
Where Water Comes Together with Other Water: Poems
Will You Please Be Quiet, Please?

SANDRA CISNEROS

The House on Mango Street
My Wicked Wicked Ways
Women Hollering Creek & Other Stories

TOM CLANCY

The Cardinal of the Kremlin
Clear and Present Danger
The Hunt for Red October
Patriot Games
Red Storm Rising
The Sum of all Fears

ROBERT COLES

The Call of Stories: Adolescents and Moral Development
Children of Crisis, Vol. I: A Study of Courage and Fear
Children of Crisis, Vol. II: Migrants, Sharecroppers, Mountaineers
Children of Crisis, Vol. III: The South Goes North
Children of Crisis, Vol. IV:
Children of Crisis, Vol. V: Privileged Ones: The Well-Off and Rich in America
Dorothy Day
Erik Erikson: The Growth of His Work
A Festering Sweetness: Poems of American People
Harvard Diary: Reflections on the Sacred and the Secular

*Irony in the Mind's Life: Essays on Novels by James Agee, Elizabeth
     Bowen and George Eliot*
The Moral Life of Children
The Political Life of Children
Robert Coles: An Intimate Biographical Interview
Rumors of Separate Worlds
Simone Weil: A Modern Pilgrimage
The Spiritual Life of Children
That Red Wheelbarrow: Selected Literary Essays
Times of Surrender: Selected Essays
Uprooted Children: The Early Life of Migrant Farm Workers
William Carlos Williams: The Knack of Survival in America
Women of Crisis: Lives of Struggle and Hope
Women of Crisis II: Lives of Work and Dreams

PAT CONROY

The Boo
The Great Santini
The Lords of Discipline
The Prince of Tides
The Water Is Wide

K. C. CONSTANTINE

Always A Body to Trade: A Mario Balzic Mystery
A Fix Like This
Joey's Case: A Mario Balzic Mystery
The Man Who Liked Slow Tomatoes
The Rocksburg Railroad Murders
Sunshine Enemies
Upon Some Midnights Clear

ROBERT COOVER

After Lazarus: A Filmscript
Hair O' The Chine
The Origin of the Brunists
Pinocchio in Venice
Pricksongs and Descant
Spanking the Maid
The Universal Baseball Association, Inc., J. Henry Waugh, Prop.

DON DeLILLO

Americana
The Day Room: A Play
End Zone
Great Jones Street
Libra
Mao II
The Names
Players
Ratner's Star
Running Dog
White Noise

PETE DEXTER

Brotherly Love
Deadwood
God's Pocket
Paris Trout

JAMES DICKEY

Alnilam
Bronwen, the Traw, and the Shape-Shifter
Buckdancer's Choice: Poems
The Central Motion: Poems 1968–1979
Deliverance
The Eagle's Mile
The Early Motion: Drowning with Others and Helmets
Falling, May Day Sermon, and Other Poems
For a Time and Place
Night Hurding
Of Prisons and Ideas
Poems: 1957–1967
Self-Interviews
Sorties
Starry Place Between the Antlers: Why I Live in South Carolina
Summons
The Water-Bug's Mittens
Wayfarer
The Zodiac

ANNIE DILLARD

An American Childhood
*The Annie Dillard Library: Living by Fiction, An American Childhood,
   Holy the Firm, Pilgrim at Tinker Creek, Teaching a Stone to Talk*
Encounters with Chinese Writers
Holy the Firm
Living by Fiction
Pilgrim at Tinker Creek
Teaching a Stone to Talk
*Three by Annie Dillard: Pilgrim at Tinker Creek, An American Child-
   hood, and The Writing Life*
Tickets for a Prayer Wheel
The Writing Life
The Best American Essays, 1988 (ed. Annie Dillard and Robert Atwan)
The Joy of Songbirds (by Annie Dillard et al.)

MARGARET DRABBLE

The Garrick Year
The Ice Age
Jerusalem the Golden
Middle Ground
The Millstone
A Natural Curiosity
The Needle's Eye
The Radiant Way
The Realms of Gold
Summer Bird-Cage
The Waterfall
A Writer's Britain: Landscape in Literature
The Oxford Companion to English Literature, 5th edition (edited by
   Margaret Drabble)
The Concise Oxford Companion to English Literature (edited by
   Margaret Drabble and Jenny Stringer)

UMBERTO ECO

The Aesthetics of Chaosmos: The Middle Ages of James Joyce, translated
   by Ellen Esrock
The Aesthetics of Thomas Aquinas, translated by Hugh Bredin
Art and Beauty in the Middle Ages

The Bomb and the General, translated by William Weaver
Foucault's Pendulum, translated by William Weaver
Leonardo Cremonini: Paintings and Watercolors 1976–1978
The Limits of Interpretation
The Name of the Rose, translated by William Weaver
The Open Work, translated by Anna Cancogni
The Role of the Reader: Explorations in the Semiotics of Texts
Semiotics and the Philosophy of Language
A Theory of Semiotics
The Three Astronauts
Travels in Hyperreality: Essays, translated by William Weaver
On the Medieval Theory of Signs (edited by Umberto Eco and Costantino Marmo)
The Sign of Three: Dupin, Holmes, Peirce (edited by Umberto Eco and Thomas A. Sebeok)
Meaning and Mental Representations (edited by Umberto Eco et al.)

STANLEY ELKIN

Criers and Kibitzers, Kibitzers and Criers
Early Elkin
The Franchiser
George Mills
The MacGuffin
The Magic Kingdom
Pieces of Soap
Searches and Seizures: Three Novellas
The Six-Year-Old Man

LOUISE ERDRICH

Baptism of Desire: Poems
The Beet Queen
Jacklight: Poems
Love Medicine
Tracks
The Crown of Columbus (with Michael Dorris)

HOWARD FAST

April Morning
Being Red: A Memoir

The Call of the Fife and Drum: Three Novels of the American Revolution
Citizen Tom Paine
Citizen Tom Paine: A Play in Two Acts
The Confession of Joe Cullen
The Crossing
The Dinner Party
The Establishment
The Glorious Brothers
The Immigrants
The Immigrant's Daughter
The Jews: Story of a People
The Legacy
Max
The Outsider
The Pledge
The Proud and the Free
The Second Generation
Spartacus
Time and the Riddle
The Picture Book History of the Jews (with Bette Fast)

LESLIE FIEDLER

Being Busted
Collected Essays of Leslie Fiedler (2 volumes)
Cross the Border–Close the Gap
End to Innocence
*English Literature: Opening up the Canon—Selected Papers from the
    English Institute* (edited by Leslie Fiedler)
Fiedler on the Roof: Apostle to the Gentiles
A Fiedler Reader
Love and Death in the American Novel
Nude Croquet
Return of the Vanishing American
Waiting for the End

KEN FOLLETT

The Bear Raid
The Big Needle
Eye of the Needle
The Key to Rebecca

Lie Down with Lions
The Man from St. Petersburg
The Modigliani Scandal
The Mystery Hideout
Night Over Water
On Wings of Eagles
Paper Money
Pillars of the Earth
The Power Twins
The Shakeout
Triple
Under the Streets of Nice: The Bank Heist of the Century (with Rene L. Maurice)

RICHARD FORD

A Piece of My Heart
Rock Springs
The Sportswriter
The Ultimate Good Luck
Wildlife

EDUARDO GALEANO

The Book of Embraces
Century of the Wind: Memory of Fire, Vol. III, translated by Cedric Belfrage
Days and Nights of Love and War, translated by Judith Brister
Faces and Masks: Memory of Fire, Vol. II, translated by Cedric Belfrage
Genesis: Memory of Fire, Vol. 1 translated by Cedric Belfrage
Open Veins of Latin America: Five Centuries of the Pillage of a Continent, translated by Cedric Belfrage
We Say No: Chronicles 1963–1991, translated by Mark Fried and others

GEORGE GARRETT

Death of the Fox
Entered from the Sun
Poison Pen
Understanding Mary Lee Settle

NADINE GORDIMER

Burger's Daughter
The Conservationist
Crimes of Conscience
The Essential Gesture: Writing, Politics and Places
A Guest of Honour
July's People
Jump and Other Stories
Late Bourgeois World
Lifetimes: Under Apartheid
My Son's Story
Selected Stories
Six Feet of Country
Something Out There
A Sport of Nature
A World of Strangers

DORIS GRUMBACH

Chamber Music
Coming into the End Zone: A Memoir
The Ladies

ALLAN GURGANUS

Blessed Assurance: A Moral Tale
Oldest Living Confederate Widow Tells All
White People

JIM HARRISON

Dalva
Farmer
A Good Day to Die
Just Before Dark: Collected Fiction
Legends of the Fall
Selected and New Poems
Sundog
Sunset Limited
The Theory and Practice of Rivers and New Poems
Warlock

Wolfe: A False Memoir
The Woman Lit by Fireflies

SHIRLEY HAZZARD

The Bay of Noon
Cliffs of Fall
Countenance of Truth: The United Nations and the Waldheim Case
The Evening of the Holiday
People in Glass Houses
Transit of Venus

MARK HELPRIN

Dove of the East and Other Stories
Ellis Island and Other Stories
Refiner's Fire
A Soldier of the Great War
The Winter's Tale
Swan Lake (as told by Mark Helprin)

JOHN HERSEY

Antonietta
A Bell for Adano
Blues
The Call
The Child Buyer
Fling and Other Stories
Hiroshima
Into the Valley: A Skirmish of the Marines
Life Sketches
Of Men and War
A Single Pebble
The Wall
White Lotus

OSCAR HIJUELOS

The Mambo Kings Play Songs of Love
Our House in the Last World

TONY HILLERMAN

The Blessing Way
The Boy Who Made Dragonfly: A Zuni Myth
Coyote Waits
Dance Hall of the Dead
The Dark Wind
The Fly on the Wall
The Ghostway
The Great Taos Bank Robbery and Other Indian Country Affairs
Hillerman Country: A Journey through Navajo Country
*The Jim Chee Mysteries: Three Classic Hillerman Mysteries Featuring
    Officer Jim Chee: The Dark Wind, People of Darkness and The
    Ghostway*
*The Joe Leaphorn Mysteries: Three Classic Hillerman Mysteries Featur-
    ing Lt. Joe Leaphorn: The Blessing Way, Dance Hall of the Dead,
    Listening Woman*
Listening Women
People of Darkness
Skinwalkers
Talking God
A Thief of Time

LAURA Z. HOBSON

Gentleman's Agreement
Laura Z—A Life: Years of Fulfillment, Vol. II
Laura Z—The Early Years & Years of Fulfillment (two volumes in one)

WILLIAM HUMPHREY

The Collected Stories of William Humphrey
Home from the Hill
The Last Husband and Other Stories (facsimile edition)
No Resting Place
Open Season
The Ordways

JOSEPHINE HUMPHREYS

Dreams of Sleep
The Fireman's Fair
Rich in Love

JOYCE JOHNSON

In the Night Café
Minor Characters
What Lisa Knew

WARD JUST

The Congressman Who Loved Flaubert and Other Stories
In the City of Fear
Jack Gance
Stringer
The Translator
Twenty-One Selected Stories

TRACY KIDDER

Among Schoolchildren
House
The Soul of a New Machine

BARBARA KINGSOLVER

Animal Dreams
Another America
The Bean Trees
Holding the Line: Women in the Great Arizona Mine Strike of 1983
Homeland and Other Stories

DAVID LEAVITT

Equal Affections
Family Dancing
The Lost Language of Cranes
A Place I've Never Been: Stories

PENELOPE LIVELY

According to Mark
City of the Mind: A Novel
Dragon Trouble

The Ghost of Thomas Kempe
A House Inside Out
Judgment Day
Moon Tiger
Pack of Cards: Stories
Passing On
The Road to Litchfield
Stitch in Time
Uninvited Ghosts
The Whispering Knights
The Wild Hunt of the Ghost Hounds

MARIO VARGAS LLOSA

Aunt Julia and the Scriptwriter
Captain Pantoja and Special Services
Conversation in the Cathedral
The Cubs and Other Stories
In Praise of the Stepmother
The Perpetual Orgy
The Real Life of Alejando Mayta
The Story-teller
Three Plays
The Time of the Hero
The War of the End of the World
Who Killed Palomino Molero?
A Writer's Reality

COLLEEN McCULLOUGH

A Creed for the Third Millennium
The First Man in Rome
The Grass Crown
An Indecent Obsession
The Ladies of Missalonghi
The Thorn Birds
Tim

TOM McGUANE

The Bushwacked Piano
In the Crazies: Book & Portfolio

Cutting Horse
Keep the Change
Ninety-Two in the Shade
Nobody's Angel
Nothing but Blue Skies
An Outside Chance: Classic & New Essays on Sport
Panama
Something to Be Desired
The Sporting Club
To Skin a Cat

PAULE MARSHALL

Brown Girl, Brownstones
The Chosen Place, the Timeless People
Daughters
Praisesong for the Widow
Reena & Other Stories
Soul Clap Hands & Sing

BOBBIE ANN MASON

In Country
Love Life: Stories
Shiloh & Other Stories
Spence + Lila

PETER MATTHIESSEN

African Silences
At Play in the Fields of the Lord
The Cloud Forest: A Chronicle of the South American Wilderness
Far Tortuga
In the Spirit of Crazy Horse
Indian Country
Killing Mr. Watson
Men's Lives: The Surfmen & Baymen of the South Fork
Midnight Turning Gray
Nine-Headed Dragon River: Zen Journal
On the River Styx & Other Stories
Partisans
Race Rock

Raditzer
The Snow Leopard
The Tree Where Man Was Born
Under the Mountain Wall

SUE MILLER

Family Pictures
The Good Mother
Inventing the Abbotts and Other Stories

TONI MORRISON

Beloved
The Bluest Eye
Jazz
Playing In the Dark: Whiteness and the Literary Imagination
Song of Solomon
Sula
Tar Baby

BHARATI MUKHERJEE

Jasmine
The Middleman and Other Stories
Days and Nights in Calcutta (with Clark Blaise)

ALICE MUNRO

The Beggar Maid
Dance of the Happy Shades and Other Stories
Friend of My Youth
Lives of Girls and Women
The Moons of Jupiter
The Progress of Love
Something I've Been Meaning to Tell You

TIM O'BRIEN

Going After Cacciato
If I Die in a Combat Zone

The Nuclear Age
Tennessee: Off the Beaten Path
The Things They Carried

TILLIE OLSEN

Silences
Tell Me A Riddle
Yonnondio

CYNTHIA OZICK

The Cannibal Galaxy
The Messiah of Stockholm
Metaphor and Memory
The Pagan Rabbi: and Other Stories
The Shawl

GRACE PALEY

Enormous Changes at the Last Minute
Later the Same Day
The Little Disturbances of Man
Long Walks and Intimate Talks
New and Collected Poems

JAY PARINI

An Invitation to Poetry
The Last Station: A Novel of Tolstoy's Last Year
The Love Run
The Patch Boys
Theodore Roethke: An American Romantic
Town Life: Poems
A Vermont Christmas

ROBERT B. PARKER

A Catskill Eagle
Ceremony
Crimson Joy
Early Autumn

The Early Spenser: Three Complete Novels: The Godwulf Manuscript,
  God Save the Child, Mortal Stakes
God Save the Child
The Godwulf Manuscript
The Judas Goat
Looking for Rachel Wallace
Love and Glory
Mortal Stakes
Pale Kings and Princes
Pastime
Perchance to Dream
Playmates
Promised Land
A Savage Place
Stardust
Taming a Sea-Horse
Valediction
The Widening Gyre
Wilderness

RICHARD POWERS

The Gold Bug Variations
Prisoner's Dilemma
Three Farmers on Their Way to a Dance

ANNE RICE

Belinda
Cry to Heaven
The Feast of All Saints
Interview with the Vampire
The Mummy, or Ramses the Damned
The Queen of the Damned
Vampire Chronicles
The Vampire Lestat
The Witching Hour

HENRY ROTH

Call It Sleep
Shifting Landscape

PHILIP ROTH

The Anatomy Lesson
The Breast
The Counterlife
Deceptions
The Facts: A Novelist's Autobiography
The Ghost Writer
Goodbye, Columbus
Goodbye, Columbus and Five Short Stories
The Great American Novel
Letting Go
My Life as a Man
Patrimony: A True Story
A Philip Roth Reader
Portnoy's Complaint
The Professor of Desire
Reading Myself and Others
When She Was Good
Zuckerman Bound: A Trilogy and Epilogue
Zuckerman Unbound

SUSAN FROMBERG SCHAEFFER

Anya
Buffalo Afternoon
Falling
The Injured Party
The Madness of a Seduced Woman

LYNNE SHARON SCHWARTZ

The Accounting
Acquainted with the Night and Other Stories
Balancing Acts
Disturbances in the Field
The Four Questions
Leaving Brooklyn
The Melting Pot: And Other Subversive Stories
Rough Strife

CAROLYN SEE

The Best Is Done with Mirrors
Golden Days
Making History
Mothers, Daughters
Rhine Maidens

GAIL SHEEHY

Character: America's Search for Leadership
The Man Who Changed the World: The Lives of Mikhail S. Gorbachev
Passages
Pathfinders
The Silent Passage: Menopause
Spirit of Survival

KATE SIMON

Etchings in an Hourglass
Italy: The Places in Between
Mexico: Places and Pleasures
A Renaissance Tapestry: The Gonzaga of Mantua
A Wider World: Portraits in an Adolescence
Bronx Primitive: Portraits in a Childhood

ISAAC BASHEVIS SINGER

Alone in the Wild Forest
The Collected Stories of Isaac Bashevis Singer

JANE SMILEY

Ordinary Love and Good Will
A Thousand Acres

ELIZABETH SPENCER

Jack of Diamonds: and Other Stories
The Light in the Piazza
Marilee
The Night Travelers
On the Gulf
The Salt Line
The Stories of Elizabeth Spencer

WALLACE STEGNER

All the Little Live Things
American Places
The American West as Living Space
Angle of Repose
Beyond the Hundredth Meridian: John Wesley Powell and the Second Opening of the West
The Big Rock Candy Mountain
The Collected Stories of Wallace Stegner
Crossing to Safety
Joe Hill
Mormon Country
Recapitulation
Second Growth
The Sound of Mountain Water
The Spectator Bird
The Uneasy Chair: A Biography of Charles DeVoto
Wolf Willow
The Women on the Wall

ROBERT STONE

Children of Light
Dog Soldiers
A Flag for Sunrise
A Hall of Mirrors
Outerbridge Reach

PETER TAYLOR

The Collected Stories of Peter Taylor
Families at War: Voices from the Trouble
Happy Families Are All Alike
In the Miro District
Miss Lenora When Last Seen and Fifteen Other Stories
The Old Forest and Other Stories
A Stand in the Mountains
A Summons to Memphis
A Woman of Means

WILLIAM TREVOR

Family Sins: and Other Stories
Fools of Fortune
Mrs. Eckdorf in O'Neill's Hotel
The News from Ireland
Nights at the Alexandria
Other People's Worlds
The Silence in the Garden
The Stories of William Trevor
Two Lives: Reading Turgenev; My House in Umbria

BARBARA TUCHMAN

Bible and Sword: England and Palestine from the Bronze Age to Balfour
A Distant Mirror: The Calamitous Fourteenth Century
The First Salute: A View of the American Revolution
The Guns of August
The March of Folly: From Troy to Vietnam
Notes from China
Practicing History: Selected Essays
Proud Tower
Stilwell and the American Experience in China
The Zimmerman Telegram

SCOTT TUROW

The Burden of Proof
One L
Presumed Innocent

GORE VIDAL

At Home: Essays, 1982–1988
The Best Man: A Screen Adaptation of the Original Play
Burr
The City and the Pillar
Creation
Dangerous Voyage
Dark Green, Bright Red
Duluth
1876
Empire
Hollywood: A Novel of America in the 1920s
Homage to Daniel Shays: Collected Essays, 1952–1972
The Judgement of Paris
Julian
Kalki
Lincoln
Matters of Fact and Fiction: Essays 1973–1976
Messiah
Myra Breckinridge and Myron
Myron
A Search for the King
The Second American Revolution: And Other Essays
A Thirsty Evil: Seven Short Stories
Two Sisters
Washington, D.C.
Who Owns the U.S.?
Williwaw

KURT VONNEGUT

Between Time and Timbuktu: or, Prometheus-5, a Space Fantasy
Bluebeard
Breakfast of Champions
Cat's Cradle
Deadeye Dick
Fates Worse Than Death: An Autobiographical Collage of the 1980s
Galapagos
God Bless You, Mr. Rosewater
Happy Birthday, Wanda June
Hocus Pocus

Jailbird
Mother Night
Palm Sunday
Player Piano
The Sirens of Titan
Slapstick; or, Lonesome No More
Slaughterhouse Five
Wampeters, Foma and Granfalloons
Welcome to the Monkey House
Who Am I This Time? For Romeos and Juliets

DAN WAKEFIELD

Going All the Way
Island in the City: The World of Spanish Harlem
New York in the Fifties
Returning: A Spiritual Journey
The Story of Your Life: Writing a Spiritual Autobiography

JAMES WELCH

The Death of Jim Loney
Fools Crow
Indian Lawyer
Riding the Earthboy Forty
Winter in the Blood

FAY WELDON

The Cloning of Joanna May
Darcy's Utopia
Down Among the Women
The Fat Woman's Joke
Female Friends
The Heart of the Country
The Hearts and Lives of Men
Leader of the Band
Letters to Alice: On First Reading Jane Austen
The Life and Loves of a She-Devil
Life Force
Polaris and Other Stories
Praxis

Puffball
Remember Me
Sacred Cows: A Portrait of Britain, Post-Rushdie, Pre-Utopia
The Shrapnel Academy
The Wife's Revenge and Other Stories

JOHN EDGAR WIDEMAN

Brothers and Keepers
Damballah
Fever: Twelve Stories
*The Homewood Books: Damballah, Hiding Place, and Sent
   for You Yesterday*
A Glance Away
Philadelphia Fire
Sent for You Yesterday
The Stories of John Edgar Wideman